ID335009

Llyfrgell Ceredigion
Ceredigion Library

LLYFRGELL CEREDIGION LIBRARY

3802196450218 2

BATTLE Royal

Hugh Bicheno was awarded a first class degree in History at Cambridge. He later joined SIS (MI6) and later still spent many years working as a kidnap and ransom negotiator, mainly in Latin America. His previous books include *Crescent and Cross: The Battle of Lepanto, 1571* (2003), *Razor's Edge: The Unofficial History of the Falklands War* (2006) and *Elizabeth's Sea Dogs* (2012).

Also by Hugh Bicheno:

Gettysburg
Midway
Crescent and Cross: The Battle of Lepanto, 1571
Rebels and Redcoats: The American Revolutionary War
Razor's Edge: The Unofficial History of the Falklands War
Vendetta: High Art and Low Cunning at the Birth of the Renaissance
Elizabeth's Sea Dogs: How the English Became the Scourge of the Seas

BATTLE Royal

THE WARS OF LANCASTER AND YORK, 1440-1462

HUGH BICHENO

HEAD
of ZEUS

First published in 2015 by Head of Zeus Ltd
Copyright © Hugh Bicheno 2015

The moral right of Hugh Bicheno to be identified as the author of this work has
been asserted in accordance with the Copyright, Designs and Patents Act of 1988.

All rights reserved. No part of this publication may be reproduced, stored
in a retrieval system, or transmitted in any form or by any means, electronic,
mechanical, photocopying, recording, or otherwise, without the prior permission
of both the copyright owner and the above publisher of this book.

1 3 5 7 9 8 6 4 2

A catalogue record for this book is available from the British Library.

ISBN (HB) 9781781859650
ISBN (E) 9781781859681

Designed and typeset by Broadbase

Printed and bound in Germany by GGP Media GmbH, Pössneck

Head of Zeus Ltd
Clerkenwell House
45–47 Clerkenwell Green
London EC1R 0HT

www.headofzeus.com

FOR KATTY

Grace under pressure

CONTENTS

MAPS

TABLES

FAMILY TREES

PROTAGONISTS AND MARRIAGES

With few exceptions, mainly titles held by elderly or ill men, single women or minors, the entire peerage was drawn into the first phase of the conflict.

PRECURSORS

Beauchamp, Richard (1382–1439), 13th Earl of Warwick. Dominant lord in south Wales and west Midlands. Married (1st) Elizabeth Berkeley and (both 2nd) Isabel Despenser.

Beauchamp, Richard (d.1422), 1st Earl of Worcester and 2nd Baron Bergavenny. Welsh Marcher lord. First husband of Isabel Despenser. Sole heir married Edward Neville (see Yorkists).

Beaufort, Henry (d.1447), Cardinal Archbishop of Winchester.

Beaufort, Joan (d.1440). Her marriage to Ralph Neville created much of the tinder for the Wars of the Roses.

Beaufort, John (1404–44), 1st Duke of Somerset. Married Margaret Beauchamp of Bletsoe.

Bedford, John (1389–1435), Duke of. Brother of Henry V. Heirless.

Gloucester, Humphrey (1390–1447), Duke of. Brother of Henry V. Heirless.

Montacute, Thomas (1388–1428), 4th Earl of Salisbury. Sole heir Alice married Richard Neville (see Yorkists).

Mowbray, John (1415–61), 3rd Duke of Norfolk, also Earl of Nottingham and Surrey. Nationwide landowner, main holdings in East Anglia diluted by the dower of his mother Katherine née Neville. Married Eleanor, sister of Henry, John, Thomas and William Bourchier.

Neville, Ralph (1364–1425), 1st Earl of Westmorland. His second marriage to Joan Beaufort created much of the tinder for the Wars of the Roses.

Pole, William de la (1396–1450), 1st Duke of Suffolk. East Anglian and, through marriage to Alice Chaucer, Oxfordshire lord. Chief minister of Henry VI until 1450.

Valois, Catherine de (1401–37), dowager queen. Henry VI's mother. Lover of Owen Tudor.

LANCASTRIANS

Henry VI, King of England (1421–71) (r. 1422–61; 1470–71).

Marguerite d'Anjou (1430–82), Henry VI's queen.

Edward of Westminster (1453–71), Prince of Wales.

· ❧ ·

Audley – see Tuchet, James.

Beauchamp, Alice – see Yorkists.

Beauchamp, Eleanor (1408–67). Daughter of Richard and Elizabeth Berkeley. Dowager Baroness Roos, mother of Thomas, 9th Baron Roos. Married (2nd) Edmund Beaufort. See Appendix D.

Beauchamp, Elizabeth (1415–48), 3rd Baroness Bergavenny by right. Sole heir of Richard and Isabel Despenser. Married Edward Neville. See Appendix D.

Beauchamp, Elizabeth (1417–80). Daughter of Richard and Elizabeth Berkeley. Married George, dubious Baron Latimer, son of Ralph Neville and Joan Beaufort. See Appendix D.

Beauchamp, Margaret (1404–67). Daughter of Richard and Elizabeth Berkeley. Married John Talbot, 1st Earl of Shrewsbury. See Appendix D.

Beauchamp of Bletsoe, Margaret (1405–82). Wealthy Bedfordshire, Wiltshire and Dorset landowner. Married (2nd) John Beaufort, by whom Margaret Beaufort, and (3rd) Lionel, 6th Baron Welles.

Beaufort, Edmund (1406–55), 2nd Duke of Somerset. Lieutenant of Normandy. Younger brother and heir of John. Added estates in Gloucestershire, Denbigh and Isle of Wight. Married Eleanor Beauchamp.

Beaufort, Henry (1436–64), 3rd Duke of Somerset. Eldest son of Edmund and Eleanor Beauchamp.

Beaufort, Margaret (1443–1509). Daughter of John. Married (1st) Edmund Tudor, by whom the future Henry VII, and (2nd) Henry Stafford, younger son of the Duke of Buckingham.

Beaumont, John (1410–60), 1st Viscount. East Midlands and East Anglian lord. Lifelong friend of Henry VI. Married (2nd) Katherine Neville, dowager Duchess of Norfolk.

Beaumont, William (1438–1507), 2nd Viscount. Son of John's first marriage.

Boteler/Butler, Ralph (1394–1473), 1st Baron Sudeley. Lord Treasurer 1443–6. Gloucestershire lord. Member of William de la Pole's affinity. His only son Thomas, who predeceased him, was married to Eleanor, daughter of John Talbot, 1st Earl of Shrewsbury, who was later betrothed to Edward IV.

Bromflete, Henry (1412–69), 1st Baron Vescy. Father-in-law of Thomas, 8th Baron Clifford.

Buckingham – see Stafford, Humphrey.

Butler, James (1420–61), 1st Earl of Wiltshire, later 5th Earl of Ormonde. Estates in the West Country, Gloucestershire, Staffordshire, Oxfordshire and Cambridgeshire. Close friend of Henry VI. Married Eleanor, daughter of Edmund Beaufort and Eleanor Beauchamp.

Chaucer, Alice (1404–75), dowager Duchess of Salisbury. East Anglian and Oxfordshire landowner. Married William de la Pole. Their son first betrothed to John Beaufort's daughter Margaret, later married Elizabeth, Richard of York's second daughter.

Clifford, Thomas (1414–55), 8th Baron. Northern lord. Married Joan, daughter of 6th Baron Dacre.

Clifford, John (1435–61), 9th Baron. Married Margaret, sole heir of Lord Vescy.

Courtenay, Thomas (1432–61), 14th Earl of Devon. West Country magnate. See entry for his namesake father under Yorkists. Married Marie of Anjou, illegitimate daughter of Charles, Count of Maine, Queen Marguerite's uncle.

Dacre of the North, Randolph (1412–1461), 1st Baron. Scots Marcher lord. Son of 6th Baron Dacre. Henry VI created new title for him after the barony went with his niece to Yorkist Richard Fiennes.

Devon – see Courtenay, Thomas.

Dudley – see Sutton, John.

Exeter – see Holland, Henry.

Fiennes, James (1390–1450), 1st Baron Saye and Sele. Kent lord. Close friend of Henry VI. Murdered 1450 during Cade's Rebellion. His son became a Yorkist.

Grey of Codnor (1435–96), Henry, 7th Baron. Midlands lord.

Grey of Groby, John (1432–61). Son of Elizabeth, 6th Baroness Ferrers of Groby by right, and Edward Grey. First husband of Elizabeth Woodville, later Edward IV's queen.

Holland, Henry (1430–75), 3rd Duke of Exeter and Earl of Huntington. Hereditary Admiral of England, minor landowner. Married Anne, Richard of York's eldest daughter.

Hungerford, Robert (1431–64), 2nd Baron, also Lord Moleyns by marriage. Mainly West Country lord.

Kemp, John, (1380–1454), Cardinal Archbishop of Canterbury.

Lisle – see Talbot, John.

Lovell, John (d.1465), 8th Baron, plus several other titles. Wealthy Midlands lord. Married Joan, daughter of John, 1st Viscount Beaumont.

Luxembourg, Jacquetta (1416–72), dowager Duchess of Bedford. Lands in Normandy and Richmondshire. Married (2nd) Richard Woodville.

Moleyns – see Hungerford, Robert.

Neville, John (d.1461), 1st Baron. Northern lord. Brother of Ralph, 2nd Earl of Westmorland, acted as his guardian after he became demented.

Northumberland – see Percy.

Ormonde – see Butler, James.

Oxford – see Vere, John.

Percy, Henry (1394–1455), 2nd Earl of Northumberland (attainted title restored 1416). Dominant lord in Northumberland, major landowner in Cumberland and Yorkshire. Married Eleanor, second daughter of Ralph Neville and Joan Beaufort.

Percy, Henry (1421–61), 3rd Earl of Northumberland. Through marriage to Eleanor, Baroness Poynings, acquired lands in Sussex and Kent.

Rivers – see Woodville, Richard.

Roos, Thomas (1427–64), 9th Baron. East Midlands and Yorkshire lord. Son of Eleanor Beauchamp by her first marriage, half-brother to her sons by Edmund Beaufort. Married Philippa Tiptoft, sister of Yorkist John, 1st Earl of Worcester.

Rougemont Grey, Thomas (d.1461), 1st Baron. Minor West Country lord. Brother of the Yorkist Edmund, Lord Grey of Ruthyn. Married Margaret, daughter of 5th Baron Ferrers of Groby.

Saye and Sele – see Fiennes, James.

Scales, Thomas (d.1460), 7th Baron. Mainly Norfolk lord. Leading commander in Normandy. Godfather of Edward, Richard of York's eldest son. Sole heir Elizabeth married (2nd) Anthony Woodville.

Shrewsbury – see Talbot, John.

Stafford, Humphrey (1402–60), 1st Duke of Buckingham. Nationwide landowner. Lieutenant of Calais. Married Anne, daughter of Ralph Neville and Joan Beaufort.

Stafford, Humphrey (1424–58), courtesy earldom of Stafford. Eldest son of the Duke of Buckingham whom he predeceased. Married Margaret, daughter of Edmund Beaufort and Eleanor Beauchamp.

Stafford, Henry (1455–83). Younger son of the Duke of Buckingham. Second husband of Margaret, daughter of John Beaufort and Margaret Beauchamp of Bletsoe.

Stourton, John (1454–85), 3rd Baron. West Country lord.

Sudeley – see Boteler/Butler, Ralph.

Sutton, John (1400–87), 1st Baron Dudley. Cheshire lord. Close associate of William de la Pole, changed sides after being severely wounded while fighting for Lancaster.

Talbot, John (1384–1453), 1st Earl of Shrewsbury. Welsh Marcher lord. Outstanding commander in Normandy. Married (1st) Maud Nevill (*sic*), Baroness Furnivall, and (2nd) Margaret Beauchamp.

Talbot, John (1413–60), 2nd Earl of Shrewsbury. Eldest son of 1st Earl and Maud Nevill. Married Elizabeth, daughter of James Butler.

Talbot, John (d.1453), 1st Viscount Lisle. Gloucestershire lord. Son of 1st Earl of Shrewsbury and Margaret Beauchamp.

Talbot, Thomas (d.1470), 2nd Viscount Lisle. See Appendix D.

Trollope, Andrew (d.1461). Talbot and later Somerset retainer. Immensely experienced Normandy veteran.

Tuchet, James (1398–1459), 5th Baron Audley. East Midlands lord. Married (1st) Margaret, daughter of 6th Baron Roos, and (2nd) Eleanor, daughter of Edmund Holland, 4th Earl of Kent, and Constance of York.

Tudor, Edmund (d.1456), 1st Earl of Richmond. Eldest son of Owen and Catherine de Valois. Married Margaret, daughter of John Beaufort and Margaret Beauchamp of Bletsoe.

Tudor, Jasper (1431–95), 1st Earl of Pembroke. Second son of Owen and Catherine de Valois.

Tudor, Owen (1400–61), Lover of dowager Queen Catherine de Valois.

Vere, John (1408–62), 12th Earl of Oxford. Mainly Essex lord.

Vescy – see Bromflete, Henry.

Welles, Lionel (1406–61), 6th Baron. Lincolnshire lord. Married (2nd) Margaret Beauchamp of Bletsoe.

Welles, Richard (1428–70), 7th Baron Willoughby by marriage. Also a Lincolnshire lord. Heir to Lionel.

Willoughby – see Welles, Richard.

Wiltshire – see Butler, James.

Woodville, Richard (1405–69), 1st Baron Rivers. Minor Kent lord. Married Jacquetta of Luxembourg. Eldest child Elizabeth married (1st) John Grey of Groby and (2nd) Edward IV.

YORKISTS

York, Richard (1411–60), 3rd Duke. Nationwide estates, main concentrations in the Welsh Marches and East Anglia. Lieutenant of Normandy and of Ireland. Married Cecily Neville.

Neville, Cecily (1415–95), known as 'Proud Cis'. Youngest daughter of Ralph Neville and Joan Beaufort, sister to Richard, Earl of Salisbury and aunt to Richard, Earl of Warwick.

March, Edward (1442–83), Earl of. Richard of York's eldest son. Later King Edward IV.

Rutland, Edmund (1443–60) Earl of. Richard of York's second son.

· ಏ ·

Arundel – see FitzAlan, William.

Audley – see Tuchet, John.

Beauchamp, Anne (1426–92), 16th Countess of Warwick by right. Married Richard Neville. See Appendix D.

Bergavenny – see Neville, Edward.

Berners – see Bourchier, John.

Bonville, William (1392–1461), 1st Baron. West Country magnate. Married (1st) Margaret, sister of Edmund, Lord Grey of Ruthyn, and (2nd) Elizabeth Courtenay, daughter of the 3rd Earl of Devon. Initially Lancastrian, he became Yorkist through alliance with the Nevilles.

Bonville, William (d.1460), Eldest son of 1st Baron Bonville and Margaret Grey. Married Elizabeth, heir to the barony of Harington in Dorset.

Bonville, William (1442–60), 6th Baron Harington. Son of William Bonville and Elizabeth Harington. Married Katherine, daughter of Richard Neville and Alice Montacute.

Bourchier, Henry (1406–83), 1st Viscount. Dominant lord in Essex and Middlesex. Eldest of the Bourchier brothers. Married Isabel, Richard of York's only sister.

Bourchier, John (1415–74), 1st Baron Berners. Younger brother of Henry and William, older brother of Thomas and of Eleanor, Duchess of Norfolk.

Bourchier, Thomas (1413–86), Cardinal Archbishop of Canterbury. Youngest of the Bourchier brothers.

Bourchier, William (1412–71), 9th Baron FitzWarin by marriage. Devon lord.

Brooke, Edward (d.1464), 6th Baron Cobham. Kent lord. Married Elizabeth, daughter of James Tuchet.

Cobham – see Brooke, Edward.

Clinton, John (1410–64), 5th Baron. Northamptonshire and Staffordshire lord. Married Joan, daughter of 5th Baron Ferrers of Chartley.

Courtenay, Thomas (1414–58), 13th Earl of Devon. West Country magnate. Married Margaret, sister of John and Edmund Beaufort. Initially strongly Yorkist he became Lancastrian when York allied with the Nevilles, allies of his deadly rival William Bonville.

Cromwell, Ralph (d.1456), 3rd Baron. Rapacious east Midlands lord.

Dacre – see Fiennes, Richard.

Devereux, Walter (1432–85), 7th Baron Ferrers of Chartley by marriage. Lands around Weobley, Herefordshire, and in Staffordshire, Leicestershire and Lincolnshire. York retainer.

Devon – see Courtenay, Thomas.

Dudley – see Sutton, John.

Fauconberg – see Neville, William

Ferrers of Chartley – see Devereux, Walter and Clinton, John.

Fiennes, Richard (d.1483), 7th Baron Dacre by marriage to Joan, granddaughter of the 6th Baron, initiating a feud with her Lancastrian uncle Humphrey Dacre.

Fiennes, William (d.1471), 2nd Baron Saye and Sele. Kent lord. Became Yorkist after his father was abandoned by Henry VI and murdered in 1450.

FitzAlan, William (1417–87), 16th Earl of Arundel. Prominent lord in south-east England. Married Joan, eldest daughter of Richard Neville and Alice Montacute.

FitzHugh, Henry (d.1472), 5th Baron. Yorkshire lord. Neville retainer. Married Alice, daughter of Richard Neville and Alice Montacute.

FitzWarin – see Bourchier, William.

Grey of Ruthyn, Edmund (1416–90), 4th Baron. Welsh Marcher and Bedfordshire lord. Married Katherine, daughter of Henry Percy, 1st Earl of Northumberland, and Eleanor Neville.

Grey of Wilton, Reginald (d.1494), 7th Baron. Herefordshire lord. Married (1st) Tacinda, daughter of Owen Tudor and dowager Queen Catherine de Valois, and (2nd) Thomasine, illegitimate daughter of John Beaufort, Duke of Somerset.

Greystoke, Ralph (1414–87), 5th Baron. Yorkshire lord. Neville retainer. Married Elizabeth, sister of 5th Baron FitzHugh.

Herbert of Raglan, William (1423–69), 1st Baron. Monmouth lord. Lifelong Yorkist retainer, also key man in Glamorgan for Richard Neville, Earl of Warwick. Married Anne, sister of Walter Devereux. Half- brother to the Vaughans by his mother's first marriage.

Montacute, Alice (1406–62), 5th Countess of Salisbury by right. Extensive estates in Warwickshire, the South West and around Bisham, Berkshire. Married Richard Neville.

Montagu – see Neville, John.

Mowbray, John (1444–76), 4th Duke of Norfolk. Landownings diluted further by his mother's dower. Married Elizabeth, daughter of John Talbot, 1st Earl of Shrewsbury, and Margaret Beauchamp.

Neville, Edward (1407–76), 3rd Baron Bergavenny by marriage to Elizabeth Beauchamp. Youngest son of Ralph and Joan Beaufort. When his wife died he was dispossessed by his nephew Richard, Earl of Warwick, but remained a loyal Yorkist.

Neville, George (1432–76), Bishop of Exeter. Youngest son of Richard and Alice Montacute.

Neville, John (1431–71), 1st Baron Montagu. Second son of Richard and Alice Montacute.

Neville, Katherine (d.1483), eldest daughter of Ralph and Joan Beaufort. Married (1st) John Mowbray, 3rd Duke of Norfolk, (2nd) Thomas Strangeways, (3rd) John, 1st Viscount Beaumont and (4th) John Woodville, forty-six years her junior.

Neville, Richard (1400–60), 5th Earl of Salisbury by marriage to Alice Montacute, adding her lands to his dominant lordships in Yorkshire and Richmondshire. Eldest son of Ralph and Joan Beaufort.

Neville, Richard (1428–71). Became 16th Earl of Warwick and dominant lord in the east Midlands and south Wales by marriage to Anne Beauchamp. Eldest son of Richard and Alice Montacute.

Neville, Robert (1404–57), Bishop of Durham. Third son of Ralph and Joan Beaufort.

Neville, William (d.1463), 6th Baron Fauconberg by marriage. Second son of Ralph and Joan Beaufort. The most experienced Yorkist commander.

Norfolk – see Mowbray, John.

Ogle, Robert (1406–69), 1st Baron. Northumberland lord. Experienced commander and lifelong Neville retainer.

Oldhall, William (d.1460). Speaker of the Commons 1450–51. Much persecuted Yorkist retainer.

Pole, John de la (1442–92), Earl of Suffolk (father's dukedom forfeited in 1450). Infant betrothal to Margaret, daughter of John Beaufort, annulled. Married Elizabeth, Richard of York's second daughter.

Salisbury – see Montacute, Alice and Neville, Richard.

Saye and Sele – see Fiennes, William.

Scrope of Bolton, John (1437–98), 5th Baron. Yorkshire lord. Neville retainer. Married Joan, sister of 5th Baron FitzHugh.

Scrope of Masham, Thomas (1429–75), 5th Baron. Yorkshire lord. Neville retainer. Married Elizabeth, daughter of 5th Baron Greystoke.

Stafford of Hooke, Humphrey (1439–69). Captured at Calais and defected to become one of Edward of March's closest companions.

Stanley, Thomas (d.1504), 2nd Baron and titular King of Mann. Dominant lord in Lancashire. He betrayed, successively, Henry VI, Edward IV, Henry VI again, Edward V and Richard III. Married Eleanor, daughter of Richard Neville and Alice Montacute.

Stanley, William (d.1495). Younger brother of Thomas. Totally loyal to the Yorkist cause.

Suffolk – see Pole, John de la.

Sutton, John (1400–87), 1st Baron Dudley. Cheshire lord. A close companion of Henry VI, he changed sides after being severely wounded in battle.

Tiptoft, John (1427–70), 1st Earl of Worcester. Welsh Marcher and Cambridgeshire lord. Married Cecily Neville, dowager Duchess of Warwick and daughter of Richard and Alice Montacute. Heartbroken when she died a year later. On pilgrimage to the Holy Land and in Italy 1457–61.

Tuchet, John (1426–90), 6th Baron Audley. Father killed at Blore Heath. John changed sides after being captured at Calais and became one of Edward of March's closest companions.

Vaughan, Roger (d.1471), of Tretower Court and Crickhowell in Radnor. Half-brother of William Herbert. Lifelong Yorkist retainer. Youngest of the Vaughan brothers.

Vaughan, Thomas, (d.1400–69), of Hergest and Kington in Herefordshire. Half-brother of William Herbert. Lifelong Yorkist retainer. Second of the Vaughan brothers.

Vaughan, Thomas (n.d.), son of Walter. Fanatical Yorkist.

Vaughan, Walter/Watkin (d.1456), of Bredwardine in Herefordshire. Lifelong Yorkist retainer. Eldest of the Vaughan brothers.

Warwick – see Beauchamp, Anne and Neville, Richard.

Wenlock, John (d.1471), 1st Baron. Speaker of the Commons. Lancastrian suborned by Warwick.

Worcester – see Tiptoft, John.

OTHER

Anjou, Marie d' (1404–63), aunt of Queen Marguerite. Married Charles VII of France.

Anjou, René (1409–80), Duke of. Father of Queen Marguerite. Married Isabelle of Lorraine.

Aragón, Yolande de (1384–1442), grandmother of Queen Marguerite.

Brézé, Pierre de (d.1465). Fiercely loyal to Yolande de Aragón, her daughter Isabelle and granddaughter Marguerite. Rose to high office in France thanks to the influence of Agnès Sorel.

Burgundy, Philippe (1396–1467), Duke of (r. 1419–67).

Charles VII (1403–61), King of France (r. 1422–61). Married Marie d'Anjou.

Charolais, Charles 'the Bold' (1433–77), Count of. Heir to Philippe III of Burgundy.

Coppini, Francesco (d.1464). Papal Legate.

Dauphin – designation of French heir- apparent.

Louis XI (1423–83), King of France (r. 1461–83).

Guelders, Mary of (1434–63). Queen to James II of Scotland, regent for her son 1460–3.

James I (1394–1437), King of Scotland (r. 1406–37). Married Joan Beaufort, John of Gaunt's daughter.

James II (1430–60), King of Scotland (r. 1437–60). Married Mary of Guelders, cousin of Philippe II of Burgundy.

James III (1451–88), King of Scotland (r. 1460–88).

Lorraine, Isabelle (1400–53), Duchess of. Mother of Queen Marguerite.

Luxembourg, Louis (1418–75), Count of Saint-Pol. Brother of Jacquetta of Luxembourg.

Maine, Charles (1414–72), Count of. Uncle of Queen Marguerite. Married Isabelle of Luxembourg, sister of Jacquetta and Louis.

Richemont, Arthur de (1393–1458). Breton prince. As Charles VII's Constable of France he was the architect of France's first standing army and of the campaign that expelled the English from France. Duke of Brittany for one year in 1457–8.

Sorel, Agnès (1422–50), Charles VII's official mistress.

Pius II (1405–64), Pope (r. 1458–64).

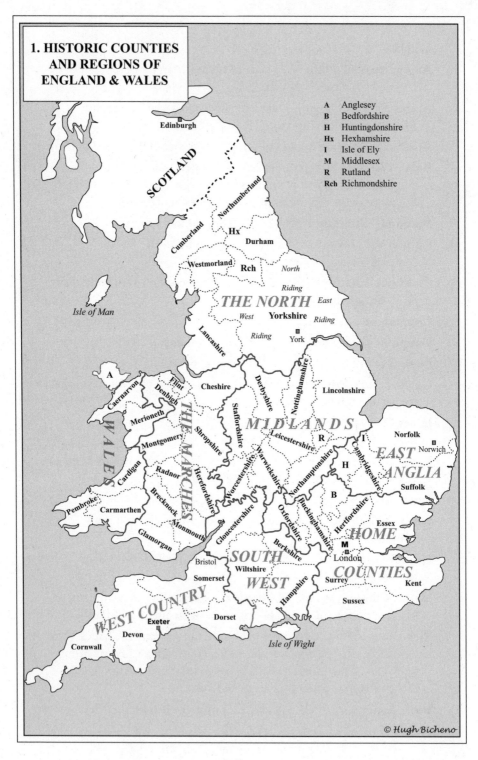

1. HISTORIC COUNTIES AND REGIONS OF ENGLAND & WALES

A   Anglesey
B   Bedfordshire
H   Huntingdonshire
Hx   Hexhamshire
I   Isle of Ely
M   Middlesex
R   Rutland
Rch Richmondshire

© Hugh Bicheno

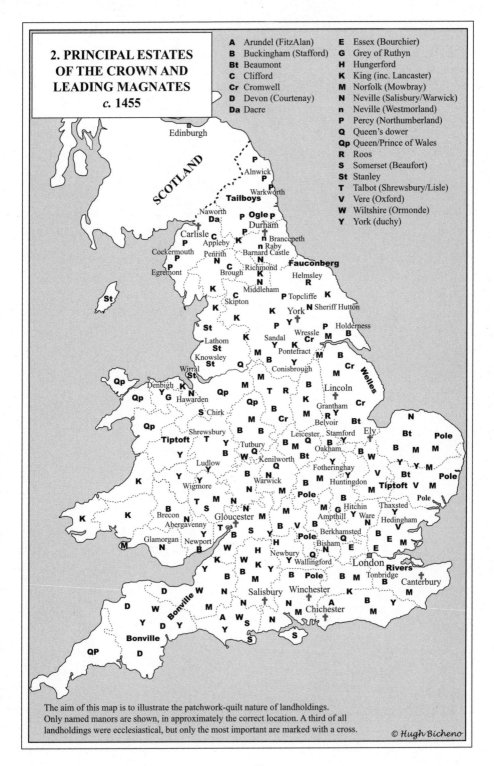

2. PRINCIPAL ESTATES OF THE CROWN AND LEADING MAGNATES *c.* **1455**

A	Arundel (FitzAlan)
B	Buckingham (Stafford)
Bt	Beaumont
C	Clifford
Cr	Cromwell
D	Devon (Courtenay)
Da	Dacre
E	Essex (Bourchier)
G	Grey of Ruthyn
H	Hungerford
K	King (inc. Lancaster)
M	Norfolk (Mowbray)
N	Neville (Salisbury/Warwick)
n	Neville (Westmorland)
P	Percy (Northumberland)
Q	Queen's dower
Qp	Queen/Prince of Wales
R	Roos
S	Somerset (Beaufort)
St	Stanley
T	Talbot (Shrewsbury/Lisle)
V	Vere (Oxford)
W	Wiltshire (Ormonde)
Y	York (duchy)

The aim of this map is to illustrate the patchwork-quilt nature of landholdings. Only named manors are shown, in approximately the correct location. A third of all landholdings were ecclesiastical, but only the most important are marked with a cross.

© Hugh Bicheno

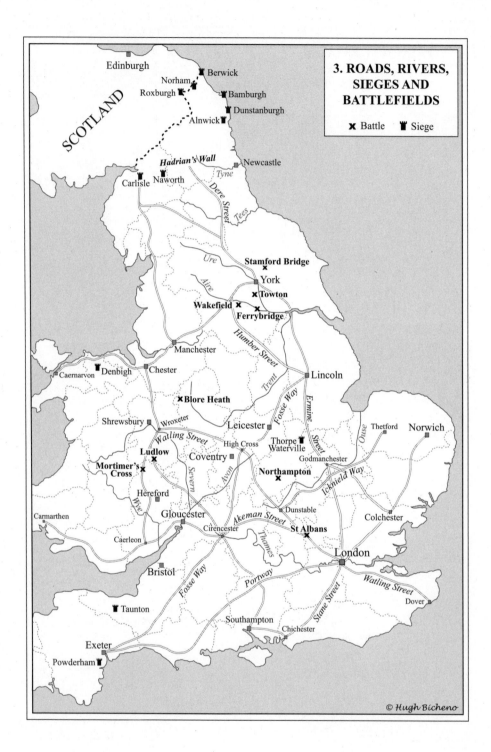

xxiv

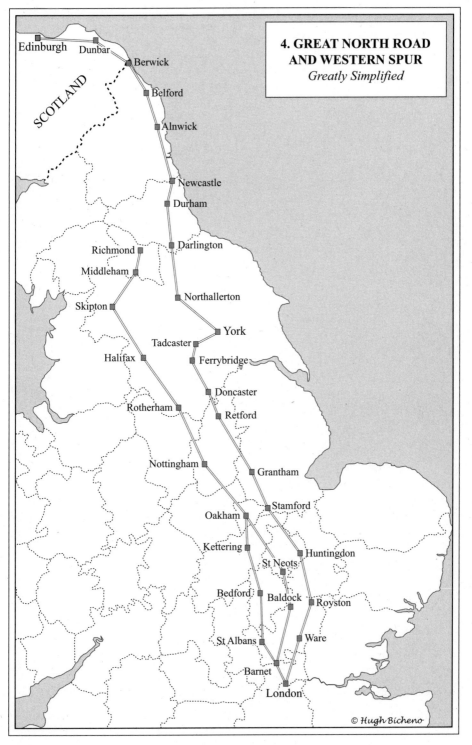

4. GREAT NORTH ROAD AND WESTERN SPUR
Greatly Simplified

Edinburgh
Dunbar
Berwick
SCOTLAND
Belford
Alnwick
Newcastle
Durham
Richmond
Darlington
Middleham
Northallerton
Skipton
York
Tadcaster
Halifax
Ferrybridge
Doncaster
Rotherham
Retford
Nottingham
Grantham
Stamford
Oakham
Kettering
Huntingdon
St Neots
Bedford
Baldock
Royston
St Albans
Ware
Barnet
London

© Hugh Bicheno

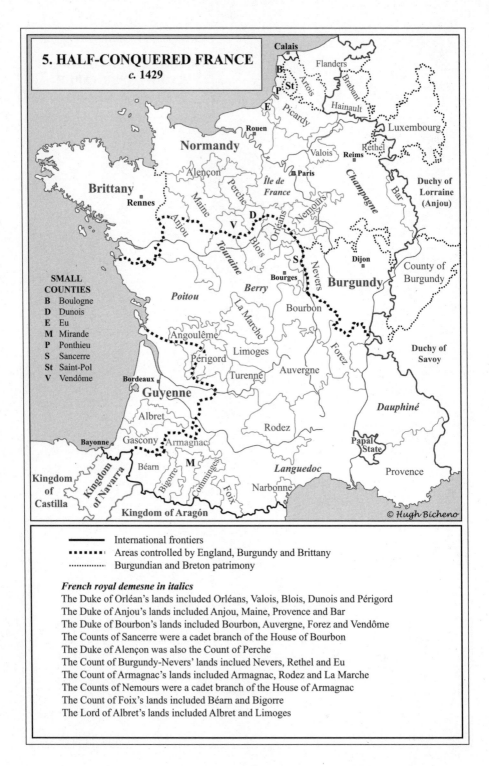

5. HALF-CONQUERED FRANCE
c. 1429

Calais
Flanders
B
St
Artois
Brabant
P
Hainault
E
Picardy
Luxembourg
Rouen
Normandy
Valois
Rethel
Alençon
Reims
Paris
Duchy of
Lorraine
(Anjou)
Brittany
Perche
Île de
France
Champagne
Bar
Rennes
Maine
D
Nemours
Anjou
Orléans
V
Blois
Dijon
County of
Burgundy
Touraine
S
Nevers
Bourges
Burgundy
Poitou
Berry
Bourbon
La Marche
Bourbon
Duchy of
Savoy
Angoulême
Forez
Limoges
Périgord
Auvergne
Turenne
Dauphiné
Bordeaux
Guyenne
Albret
Rodez
Bayonne
Gascony
Armagnac
Papal
State
Provence
Béarn
M
Languedoc
Kingdom
of
Castilla
Bigorre
Comminges
Foix
Narbonne
Kingdom of Aragón

**SMALL
COUNTIES**
B Boulogne
D Dunois
E Eu
M Mirande
P Ponthieu
S Sancerre
St Saint-Pol
V Vendôme

Kingdom of Navarra

© Hugh Bicheno

──────── International frontiers
■■■■■■■ Areas controlled by England, Burgundy and Brittany
·············· Burgundian and Breton patrimony

French royal demesne in italics
The Duke of Orléan's lands included Orléans, Valois, Blois, Dunois and Périgord
The Duke of Anjou's lands included Anjou, Maine, Provence and Bar
The Duke of Bourbon's lands included Bourbon, Auvergne, Forez and Vendôme
The Counts of Sancerre were a cadet branch of the House of Bourbon
The Duke of Alençon was also the Count of Perche
The Count of Burgundy-Nevers' lands included Nevers, Rethel and Eu
The Count of Armagnac's lands included Armagnac, Rodez and La Marche
The Counts of Nemours were a cadet branch of the House of Armagnac
The Count of Foix's lands included Béarn and Bigorre
The Lord of Albret's lands included Albret and Limoges

PRINCES OF THE BLOOD

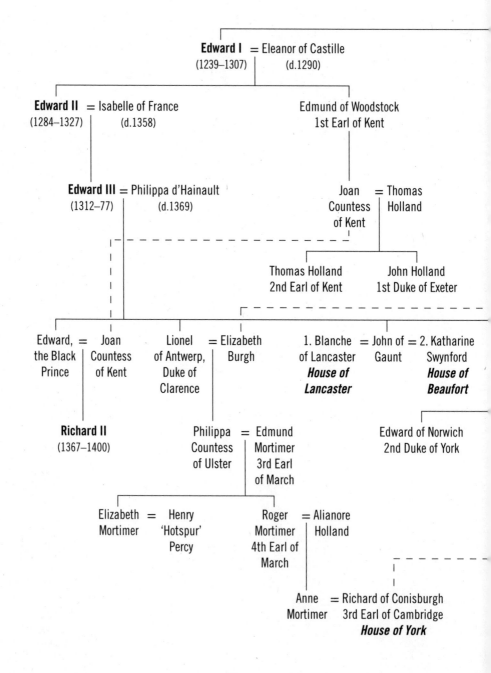

Edward I = Eleanor of Castille
(1239–1307) (d.1290)

Edward II = Isabelle of France
(1284–1327) (d.1358)

Edmund of Woodstock
1st Earl of Kent

Edward III = Philippa d'Hainault
(1312–77) (d.1369)

Joan = Thomas
Countess Holland
of Kent

Thomas Holland
2nd Earl of Kent

John Holland
1st Duke of Exeter

Edward, = Joan
the Black Countess
Prince of Kent

Lionel = Elizabeth
of Antwerp, Burgh
Duke of
Clarence

1. Blanche = John of = 2. Katharine
of Lancaster Gaunt Swynford
House of **House of**
Lancaster **Beaufort**

Richard II
(1367–1400)

Philippa = Edmund
Countess Mortimer
of Ulster 3rd Earl
of March

Edward of Norwich
2nd Duke of York

Elizabeth = Henry
Mortimer 'Hotspur'
Percy

Roger = Alianore
Mortimer Holland
4th Earl of
March

Anne = Richard of Conisburgh
Mortimer 3rd Earl of Cambridge
House of York

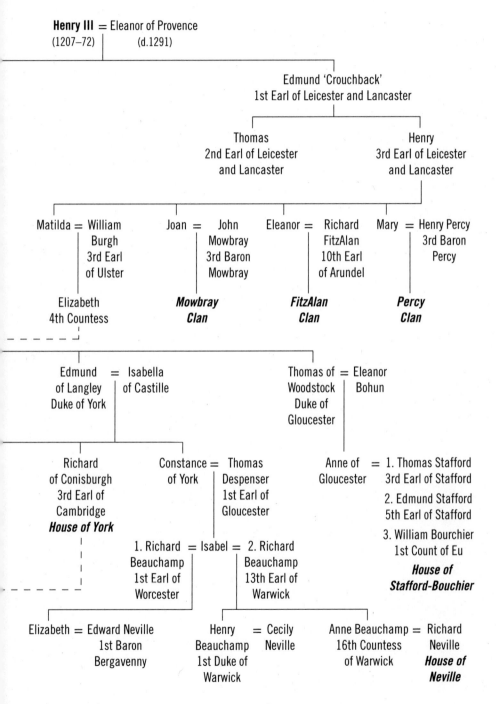

Henry III = Eleanor of Provence
(1207–72)   (d.1291)

Edmund 'Crouchback'
1st Earl of Leicester and Lancaster

Thomas
2nd Earl of Leicester
and Lancaster

Henry
3rd Earl of Leicester
and Lancaster

Matilda = William   Joan = John   Eleanor = Richard   Mary = Henry Percy
           Burgh   Mowbray   FitzAlan   3rd Baron
           3rd Earl   3rd Baron   10th Earl   Percy
           of Ulster   Mowbray   of Arundel

Elizabeth   *Mowbray*   *FitzAlan*   *Percy*
4th Countess   *Clan*   *Clan*   *Clan*

Edmund = Isabella   Thomas of = Eleanor
of Langley   of Castille   Woodstock   Bohun
Duke of York   Duke of
                                     Gloucester

Richard   Constance = Thomas   Anne of = 1. Thomas Stafford
of Conisburgh   of York   Despenser   Gloucester   3rd Earl of Stafford
3rd Earl of   1st Earl of
Cambridge   Gloucester   2. Edmund Stafford
House of York   5th Earl of Stafford

                   1. Richard = Isabel = 2. Richard   3. William Bourchier
                   Beauchamp   Beauchamp   1st Count of Eu
                   1st Earl of   13th Earl of
                   Worcester   Warwick   *House of*
                                                              Stafford-Bouchier

Elizabeth = Edward Neville   Henry   = Cecily   Anne Beauchamp = Richard
            1st Baron   Beauchamp   Neville   16th Countess   Neville
            Bergavenny   1st Duke of   of Warwick   *House of*
                                Warwick   *Neville*

xxix

PREFACE

At an early stage of my research I found it necessary to create two reference lists of the English peers, by seniority (A) and alphabetically (B), and another of the senior clergy (C). Appendix D details the most violently divisive of all the many inheritance disputes.

The Protagonists and Marriages list and the family trees in the appropriate chapters illustrate networks of kinship too burdensome to stress sufficiently in the text. Genealogy defined status and title to property, and also the alliances and disputes that exploded into the Wars of the Roses. It really was a 'Cousins' War'.

The French participle 'de' was still commonly used by the English nobility well into the fifteenth century, but for simplicity's sake I have omitted it while retaining the more distinctive 'de la'. I have anglicised most non-English titles, while retaining the participle for French names only when stated in full (thus Pierre de Brézé).

The pound sterling (£), the mark, and the *livre tournois* were not coins, but units of account. The mark was two-thirds of a pound sterling. The *livre tournois* to pound sterling exchange rate fluctuated from 6.6 = £1 in the 1420s to 11.3 = £1 in 1436–7, and then back down again. The continental gold crown was a coin worth one-fifth of a pound sterling.

To provide the 2012 standard of living equivalence given in [square brackets] after the sums in contemporary units, I averaged the figures from MeasuringWorth.com at ten-yearly intervals to arrive at a rough and ready rate of £1 = £636 for the period 1430–85. Had I used the 'economic status' equivalence instead, it would have been £1 = £18,166.

None of the contemporary or near-contemporary accounts are entirely dependable, and some are deliberately misleading. When even an accurate factual narrative is elusive, character and motive is almost entirely speculative. Modern facial reconstruction techniques can put flesh on skulls, but only imagination and empathy can suggest what went on inside them.

PASSIONATE PRINCESSES

T HE ULTIMATE WINNERS OF THE WARS OF THE ROSES WERE the grandchildren of two enchanting women. The quality was so strong in one of them that she was accused of witchcraft in 1469 and again, *post mortem*, in 1484. The first, potentially lethal accusation was made at the instigation of Richard 'the Kingmaker' Neville, Earl of Warwick, following a *coup d'état* during which he murdered her husband and one of her sons.

The woman thus accused was Jacquetta (christened Jacqueline) de Luxembourg, widow of John, Duke of Bedford, the eldest surviving uncle of King Henry VI of England and at the time of their marriage the next in line for the throne. He was so taken with 17-year-old Jacquetta that in 1433 he married her with indecent haste five months after the death of his first wife Anne, the sister of the Duke Philippe of Burgundy, thereby deeply offending a crucial English ally in the endgame of the Hundred Years War.

After Bedford died two years later, childless Jacquetta was granted permission to enjoy her generous dower lands on condition she not remarry without a royal licence. This she omitted to obtain in 1437, when she secretly married the famously handsome 32-year-old Sir Richard Woodville, by whom she was pregnant. While she risked losing her dower, technically he committed treason by changing the legal status of a member of the royal family without the king's permission.

The couple were fortunate that 15-year-old King Henry VI was mourning the recent death of his mother Catherine, who had blazed a wide trail by cohabiting with her Welsh major-domo Owen Tudor without benefit of clergy. Catherine de Valois was the youngest daughter of King Charles VI of France and Isabeau of Bavaria. When Charles first lapsed into paranoid schizophrenia, Isabeau was forced to play a leading role in the uniformly disastrous subsequent events of her husband's reign.

Between 1407 and 1435 the Valois endured a 'Cousins' War' among the many branches of the French royal family that was far more threatening to the survival of the kingdom than the divisions among the English Plantagenets. Isabeau steered a pragmatically shifting course among the factions and was accused by her enemies of every vice imaginable, sometimes without cause.

Anarchy in France encouraged Henry V to assert his claim to the French throne after he became king of England in 1413. After his crushing victory at Agincourt two years later, he conquered Normandy, lost to the English crown over 200 years earlier. Rouen, the Norman capital, fell to the English in January 1419, and in September, after the Dauphin Charles had his cousin Duke Jean II of Burgundy treacherously assassinated, Jean's heir Philippe joined the assault on his Valois cousins' territories. The Anglo-Burgundian alliance became formal in May 1420, when Charles VI signed the Treaty of Troyes, a near total capitulation to Henry's demands.

The lynchpin of the treaty was Henry's marriage in June to Catherine, but Charles VI also disinherited his 17-year-old name-sake son (whom Isabeau said was not his at all) in favour of Henry. Disaffected French nobles rallied around the disowned dauphin and invoked alliances with Castille and with Scotland, whose uncrowned King James I, a captive in England since 1406, served with the English army in 1420–21. Spanish ships transported a Scots army led by the Earl of Buchan, son of the regent Duke of Albany, to the dauphin's capital at Bourges.

Catherine's eldest sister Isabelle, then 7 years old, had been married to Richard II of England in 1396. After Richard was over-thrown and murdered by his cousin Henry IV (Bolingbroke) three years later, Isabelle bravely refused to marry Henry's namesake heir. Almost from the moment Catherine was born the two Henrys had seen her as a suitable dynastic alternative. When Henry V finally met the 17-year-old in the summer of 1419 he was so captivated by her that he abandoned his demand for a huge dowry in addition to the territorial concessions he and Duke Philippe won at Troyes.

After their marriage at Troyes Cathedral in June 1420 and a honeymoon spent on campaign, Henry and his bride crossed to England, where Catherine was crowned queen at Westminster Abbey in February 1421. The couple embarked on a royal prog-ress through the kingdom, but a month later, at about the time Catherine became pregnant, shocking news from France inter-rupted their journey.

Henry's brother Thomas, Duke of Clarence, lieutenant in France during the king's absence, had been killed at Baugé in Anjou, leading a hot-headed charge by men-at-arms unsupported by archers against the elite Scots component of a larger Franco-Scots army.* Henry returned to France in June to retrieve the situation and never saw his namesake son, who was born on 6 December.

The king regained the initiative with two successful sieges, of Dreux in the late summer of 1421 and Meaux from October until May 1422, when Catherine joined him. It was not to be a happy reunion. Henry had contracted cholera and died at Vincennes, just outside Paris, on 31 August 1422, sixteen days short of his thirty-sixth birthday.

Four miles away and less than two months later his father-in-law Charles VI also died. In 1435, to justify breaking his alliance with England, Duke Philippe of Burgundy was to argue that the line of succession agreed at Troyes became void when Henry predeceased Charles.

---

* Buchan was killed and the Scots army annihilated by Bedford at Verneuil, the 'second Agincourt', in August 1424.

Both 9-month-old Henry VI and 19-year-old Charles VII were proclaimed kings of France. Neither was crowned until the visionary teenager Jeanne d'Arc shamed Charles out of his defeatist lethargy. In July 1429, following Jeanne's tide-turning victory over the English at Orléans in May, he was crowned at newly recovered Reims Cathedral, France's Westminster Abbey.

Henry was not even crowned king of England until four months later. Two years later he was crowned king of France at Nôtre-Dame Cathedral in Paris by his uncle Cardinal Henry Beaufort, Bishop of Winchester. The royal party had spent the previous eighteen months at Rouen, the capital of occupied Normandy. Also at Rouen was Jeanne d'Arc, captured in May 1430 and sold to the English by Jacquetta's uncle Jean, Count of Ligny. Despite having evaded the theological traps set for her, to the lasting shame of the House of Lancaster she was condemned for heresy by a French ecclesiastical court suborned by Bedford, with Cardinal Beaufort presiding. She was burned at the stake in Rouen marketplace on 30 May 1431.

When Henry V died there was no chance that his widow, a 21-year-old woman and sister to the rival claimant to the French throne, would be permitted to play any political role; nor was there any indication she wished to do so. Catherine was a devoted mother and gave no cause for concern until 1427, when she fell in love with the dashing Edmund Beaufort, six years her junior, who had been setting hearts aflutter ever since arriving at court.

Like the ruling House of Lancaster, the Beauforts were descendants of John of Gaunt, Edward III's third son. However, while the royal family were descended from his marriage to Blanche of Lancaster, the Beauforts were the product of his subsequent love affair with Katherine Swynford. Although the Beaufort children were legitimated by papal decree and royal charter after John and Katherine married in 1396, in 1407 Henry IV added the proviso *excepta regali dignitate*, barring his half-siblings and their descendants from inheriting the throne. Whether or not he had the right to alter what was supposed to be a fair copy of the original charter was a moot issue as long as the legitimate Lancastrian succession was assured.

The second generation of Beauforts were an attractive brood. The hostage King James I of Scotland fell in love with Edmund's sister Joan. Dowager Queen Catherine was dame of honour at the wedding. At his long-delayed coronation in 1424 James obliged the surly Scots nobles to swear allegiance to Joan as well as himself.

So, even before falling for Edmund, Catherine de Valois was well acquainted with the Beauforts and would have known that Edmund's older brother John, Earl of Somerset, had been taken prisoner after following his stepfather the Duke of Clarence to defeat at Baugé. Irrespective of Catherine's charms, Edmund must have regarded dalliance with the richest woman in England, who might influence the court to help ransom his brother, as practically a fraternal obligation, while the prospect of marriage was mouth-watering.

The possibility was far from appealing to Henry VI's uncle Humphrey, Duke of Gloucester, the youngest son of Henry IV and the senior member of the Council that governed England during the king's minority. Bedford, Gloucester's one-year-older brother, was regent in France. None of Henry V's brothers had legitimate issue and the survival of their dynasty was vested in the boy Henry VI. The prospect of a royal stepfather from the bastard Beaufort line was intolerable.

Bishop Henry Beaufort, by 1424 the last male survivor of the first generation of Beauforts, was the crown's principal creditor. He had been instrumental in denying Gloucester the regency in England and was his main rival in the Council. Their retainers came close to doing battle at London Bridge in October 1425, when Gloucester blocked what he believed was an attempt to take the infant king into the bishop's custody. At issue were not only influence and power, but also surety for the bishop's loans, on which the crown had defaulted.

Bedford was obliged to return from France to mediate during

1426. There were many strands to the compromise eventually reached, including the appointment of the neutral Richard Beauchamp, Earl of Warwick, to be the young king's governor. The core deal, however, was a partial financial settlement with Bishop Beaufort. In return the bishop resigned from the office of lord chancellor and the ruling Council.

Bedford also required Beaufort to travel back with him to France in March 1427. As regent, Bedford was empowered to grant Beaufort permission to accept promotion to cardinal, which Henry V had refused him when the pope first proposed it in 1419. Beaufort's career in papal service only briefly diverted his attention from English politics, but it gave Gloucester grounds to accuse him of divided loyalties when he resumed his place in the Council.

With the new cardinal out of the way, Gloucester dealt with the threat from Edmund by an Act of Parliament stating that if Catherine remarried without the king's consent, the husband would be stripped of his lands. The Act also specified that permission could only be granted by the king, then 6 years old, once he reached his majority. Finally, the Act also declared that any children of an unsanctioned marriage would still be members of the royal family, a proviso designed to give the royal uncles control over them. With his hopes thus dashed, Edmund departed for France to begin a long military career.

In rebellion, Catherine left the court and moved to Wallingford Castle in Oxfordshire, part of her dower. There she proceeded to raise a family with her servant Owen Tudor, a man with no lands to lose, furthermore without benefit of clergy, thus finessing the letter of Gloucester's act. Henry IV had deprived Welshmen of many civil rights during the last great Welsh revolt led by Owain Glyn Dŵr in 1400–12, but Owen Tudor had earned English rights by military service in France, even though his father was Glyn Dŵr's nephew.

The couple produced a child almost every year from about 1429. The first we can be sure of was named Edmund, which has led some to speculate that Beaufort might have been the true father.

A second son, Jasper, was to be a major player in the Wars of the Roses. Another son and two daughters followed them. It is possible a last daughter died in childbirth along with her 35-year-old mother in January 1437, although by then Catherine had retired to Bermondsey Abbey outside London, and in her will wrote of a 'grievous malady, in the which I have been long, and yet am, troubled and vexed'.

Catherine was buried in Westminster Abbey. Her painted wooden funeral effigy in the abbey museum is one of the oldest surviving life-like depictions of any member of the royal family. We cannot be sure the original of a much-copied portrait profile of Henry V was painted from life (his right profile was disfigured by a near-fatal arrow wound at the 1403 Battle of Shrewsbury), but it fits a contemporary description of an oval face, a long straight nose, straight dark hair and a ruddy complexion.

Apart from the nose his son fits this description barely at all, whereas the similarities between Catherine's effigy and another much-copied portrait of Henry VI when he was 19 years old are striking. Mother and son shared the same hair, complexion, cheekbones, jaw-line, chin, rosebud mouth and arching eyebrows. More remarkably, a portrait of Catherine's Tudor great-grandson Henry VIII at about the same age also shows a strong family likeness.

Did Henry VI inherit his maternal grandfather's schizophrenia? The condition commonly peaks between the ages of 15 and 25, with women experiencing a second peak between 25 and 35, and this may have been Catherine's 'grievous malady'. Even so, the heritability of schizophrenia from a single parent is low. It is much higher when both parents are afflicted, and Henry VI may also have inherited a predisposition to mental illness from his father, who had a messianic delusion that he could unite Christendom under his banner.

Following Catherine's death, Tudor took sanctuary at Westminster Abbey when summoned by Gloucester to appear before the Council. He was assured he could depart in safety, but was then arrested and locked up like a common criminal in Newgate prison. His confis-cated worldly wealth was £137 10s. 4*d*, no small amount [about £87,500 in today's purchasing power], but minuscule in compar-ison with Catherine's dower.

In a manifest charade Tudor 'escaped' early in 1438, was alleg-edly recaptured by John, Baron Beaumont, one of the king's closest friends, taken to Windsor Castle and held there under the protec-tion of none other than Catherine's former suitor Edmund Beaufort. Owen was later pardoned and his property restored, and he became a member of the king's household. Meanwhile his sons were placed in the care of the Abbess of Barking, sister of William de la Pole, Earl of Suffolk, the king's chief minister. Owen never married and many years later, on learning he was to be executed, his last words were 'that head shall lie on the stock that was wont to lie on Queen Catherine's lap'.

· ☙ ·

Upon the death of the king's mother 20-year-old Jacquetta, dow-ager Duchess of Bedford, became the highest ranking lady in the royal family, with precedence over Gloucester's ambitious second wife Eleanor Cobham. Eleanor had previously been Gloucester's mistress when she was a lady-in-waiting to his first wife, Jacqueline d'Hainault, whom he brutally discarded in 1428. Consequently the duke was not in a position to adopt a high moral tone when a pregnant Jacquetta revealed she had married Richard Woodville not long after Catherine's death.

Also, Gloucester was once again struggling for influence with Cardinal Beaufort, who was delighted to see Gloucester's highly eli-gible sister-in-law Jacquetta take herself off the political chessboard. Better still, although Woodville was the son of one of the late Duke of Bedford's closest officials, and knighted by the duke himself, he had subsequently served under Suffolk – who began his service to the king as a protégé of the cardinal. Suffolk was also, by marriage, lord of the Woodville estate at Grafton in Northamptonshire.

We may presume the newly orphaned young king was inclined to leniency towards a young woman whose conduct mirrored his late mother's. It was in his gift to legitimate Jacquetta's marriage, and he did so. However, in contrast to Jacquetta's first visit to England after marrying Bedford, when she was inducted into the Order of the Garter, on this occasion the couple was not received at court and Woodville was fined £1,000 [£636,000].

Cardinal Beaufort put up the money, nominally in exchange for a few of her manors, but clearly to bind the couple to his interest. Their exclusion from court may have been at the suggestion of Gloucester, but it also resolved the problem of protocol posed by the gross imbalance of rank between Jacquetta and Richard Woodville.

If the noble councillors believed Richard had married Jacquetta for her money, they could not have been more wrong. Theirs was a lastingly passionate relationship, and she bore him fourteen children over the next twelve years. Given how dangerous childbirth was, that Jacquetta's dower was for her life only and how politically exposed he would become if she died, Richard would certainly have restrained his enthusiasm if cold calculation played any part in the marriage.

The couple returned to France, he to pursue his military career and she to attempt to secure her income from lands in Normandy that constituted a major part of her Bedford dower. With Burgundy now hostile, the English position in northern France was precarious, which kept Richard busy but would have made Jacquetta's task difficult even if she had not been almost constantly pregnant. She appears to have shuttled across the Channel to give birth at Grafton, leaving the babies in her father-in-law's household while she returned to France to pursue her claims – and get pregnant again.

It is to be expected that two such beautiful people as Jacquetta and Richard would produce stunningly good-looking offspring. Sadly, presumption is all we have, as no likenesses from life survive of either of the parents or any of their fourteen children – save one. Three copies survive of a lost original portrait of Elizabeth, their eldest child, painted after she married Edward IV. The least over-painted is at Queens' College, Cambridge – she and her ill-fated predecessor Marguerite d'Anjou being the founders for whom the college is named. Although crudely executed, the portrait conveys a luminous quality, which helps to explain why Elizabeth Woodville became the first commoner queen regnant of England.

The distinctive course taken by English history under Henry VIII may well have owed something to the mitochondrial DNA of Catherine and Jacquetta. Having acquired financial independence by fulfilling their dynastic duty as daughters, they found fulfilment with men who prized them as women above all. We know Owen Tudor's last thoughts were of long-dead Catherine, and we may safely assume Richard Woodville's were of Jacquetta in the grim hours before he, too, was beheaded.

Sometimes love does conquer all: despite having turned their backs on the game of power, Catherine and Jacquetta became the common ancestors of every English monarch since 1485. Before that could happen, all those with a superior claim to the throne had first to wipe each other out. This they did in what was in essence a decades-long, murderously sordid dispute over an inheritance within a deeply dysfunctional extended family. It became merciless not despite but *because* the combatants had so much in common, and projected their own darkest intentions onto each other.

This was something so humanly fascinating that the greatest author to adorn the English language wrote eight plays about it. Prudent sycophancy towards the dynasty under which he lived gave Shakespeare the unifying theme of his first historical series, three-part *Henry the Sixth* and *Richard the Third*, namely that divinely ordained order was overthrown by the deposition and murder of Richard II by his cousin Henry of Bolingbroke, Duke of Lancaster. Decades of strife ensued before the restoration of divine order under the Tudors.

The theme is absent from his subsequent, more accomplished series from *Richard the Second* through two-part *Henry the Fourth*, leading to the patriotic apotheosis of *Henry the Fifth*. The final chorus laments that after Henry V's early death, 'so many had the managing, that they lost France, and made his England bleed'. The plays have indelibly coloured popular perception of late medieval England, and historians cannot ignore them.

Nor should they: it was an extraordinary period in English history. Four of the six kings crowned between 1399 and 1485 were usurpers who killed their predecessors, undermining the concept of divine right as well as the prestige of the ruling class. A more mature appreciation of history and of human nature led Shakespeare to discount the role of divine judgement when he wrote the second, more psychologically penetrating series.

I

HOUSE OF LANCASTER

In his *Commentaries* Pope Pius II dismissed his contemporary Henry VI of England as 'a man more timorous than a woman, utterly devoid of wit or spirit, who left everything in his wife's hand'. The verdict of history is equally implacable: he was one of the most ineffectual and divisive monarchs with which any nation has ever been cursed. The only open question is how many of the disasters that characterized his reign can be attributed to his wife or his proverbial 'evil councillors', and how many to personal initiatives.

Henry was at the younger end of the age bracket in which schizophrenia commonly declares itself when he assumed the full powers of personal kingship in November 1437. A portrait of him four years later shows the staring, vacant facial expression characteristic of the disease, and he ticked many other diagnostic boxes long before disabling symptoms became apparent. Chief among them were an inability to feel normal joy or pleasure (later portrayed as saintliness), extreme sensitivity to disagreement, inappropriate emotional responses to serious events (such as giggling at bad news), and no facility to weigh the likely consequences of his decisions, from which came a cavalier disregard for abiding by them.

The word 'childlike' was often applied to him, which explains why he commanded (often exasperated) affection from so many. Children, however, are often cruel, and on occasions Henry acted in a way that can only be described as sadistic. One such was his vindictive persecution in 1441 of Eleanor Cobham, wife of his uncle the Duke of Gloucester, for treasonable necromancy. Suffolk was behind the prosecution, but he would not have dared attack a prince of the blood without the king's support. Eleanor was paraded through the streets of London in her shift like a prostitute, and then imprisoned for life. Her alleged accomplices were first tortured to implicate her, and then cruelly executed.

It was not the first time a Lancastrian king employed an accusation of witchcraft against an inconvenient woman. Henry V used it against his stepmother Joan of Navarre, but spared her a trial after legally stealing much of her dower. She was under house arrest first at Pevensey Castle in Kent, where her youngest stepson Gloucester was a frequent visitor. In 1429 Joan gifted her chapel and its furnishings to Gloucester's wife Eleanor Cobham.

Although Gloucester was not implicated in his wife's supposed crimes and divorced her, his status as the king's heir presumptive was irrevocably compromised. He was forced into retirement, leaving the way clear for Suffolk and other members of the king's inner circle, to whom Henry began to grant the reversion of crown lands and offices held by the duke. For these to take effect Gloucester had to die. In 1447 he was arrested on a charge of treason and conveniently died in custody two days later. Suffolk was made a duke the following year.

In July 1447 a court presided over by Suffolk convicted the late duke's illegitimate son and eight others of plotting to kill the king and sentenced them to be drawn, hanged and quartered. Suffolk only appeared with a royal pardon after they had been dragged through the streets, cut down alive after hanging and stripped naked in preparation for ritual disembowelment. A visiting French delegation was disgusted by the charade, and reported that the people of London shared the sentiment.

The episode marked the start of the cult of 'Good Duke Humphrey' among the common people, and a corresponding hatred of Suffolk.

HOUSE OF LANCASTER

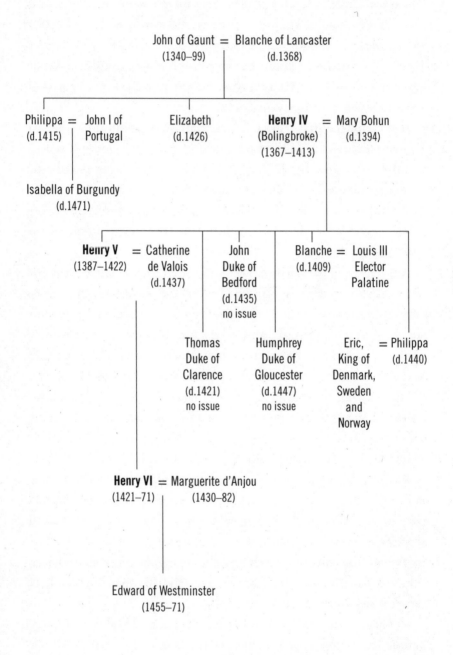

John of Gaunt = Blanche of Lancaster
(1340–99)   (d.1368)

Philippa = John I of   Elizabeth   **Henry IV** = Mary Bohun
(d.1415) Portugal   (d.1426)   (Bolingbroke)   (d.1394)
                                          (1367–1413)

Isabella of Burgundy
(d.1471)

Henry V = Catherine   John   Blanche = Louis III
(1387–1422) de Valois   Duke of   (d.1409)   Elector
             (d.1437)   Bedford   Palatine
                           (d.1435)
                           no issue

              Thomas   Humphrey   Eric, = Philippa
              Duke of   Duke of   King of (d.1440)
              Clarence   Gloucester   Denmark,
              (d.1421)   (d.1447)   Sweden
              no issue   no issue   and
                                           Norway

Henry VI = Marguerite d'Anjou
(1421–71)   (1430–82)

Edward of Westminster
(1455–71)

It is an error to believe that, like many another chief minister before and after him, Suffolk was simply the lightning rod for growing popular discontent with the king. Although many others shared in the ill-gotten spoils from Gloucester's estate, Suffolk's greed was particularly flagrant.

Nonetheless, he undoubtedly did get blamed for the king's failings. The once canonical view of Henry as a well-meaning soul misled by self-seeking courtiers has been comprehensively demolished.* Contemporary French and other non-English sources reveal that the manner in which England lost its French empire, which destabilized Henry's reign, bears the imprint of the king's own dithering personality.

Seen through the lens of current understanding of schizophrenia this is not surprising. Henry was almost unsteerable by his councillors, evil or otherwise. They could, obviously, encourage him to pursue a certain policy, but only if it was in accordance with his inclinations. What they could not do was control its implementation, because his aversion to disagreement made it impossible to discuss the pros and cons of any particular decision.

Anyone who has acted as an adviser to powerful individuals knows how to frame a question so the preferred outcome appears to be the correct answer. Medieval courtiers were masters of the process of subtle manipulation recently dubbed 'nudge theory'. But in the end, and most acutely with regard to Henry VI, they had to be, above all, 'yes' men willing to greet every royal pronouncement as wise and insightful. 'Yes – but' men were compelled to walk a fine line with any monarch; in Henry's case that line simply did not exist.

A further contributing factor to Henry's psychology was growing up in the overpowering shadow of the legendary father he never knew, and being schooled to govern as he had. Yet Henry V had been a terrifyingly focused and above all immensely brave individual,

* Notably by Bertam Wolffe's exhaustively researched biography.

who came to the throne as a fully grown man and commanded respect and devotion not merely as king but also as a victorious leader of men in battle. Objectively his were shoes too big to fill: Henry VI did not even try.

On the plus side his father and grandfather had crushed domestic challenges arising from the 1399 usurpation, and Henry VI's absolute right to rule was fully accepted not only by the nobility but also by the country at large. The minority Council and the king's uncles preserved and extended Henry V's conquests, and sizeable assets reverted to the crown following the deaths of the dowager queens and his uncles. When Henry VI assumed personal kingship he was more politically and financially secure than his father had been, and disposed of considerably more patronage.

Feudalism – the holding of lands in exchange for service or labour – had long ago ceased to provide the basis of political power in England. In its place, the country was a patchwork of 'affinities' – networks of those deriving benefit from noble patronage and influence (known as 'good lordship'). Henry had a liveried retinue of over 300 knights and esquires, and the next largest personal following, a mere thirty-six of similar rank, wore the livery of the wealthy Humphrey Stafford, Duke of Buckingham, who owned manors in twenty-two counties. However, their *affinities* were an order of magnitude greater than their retinues.

In the king's case this was further multiplied by direct patronage. When Henry assumed personal kingship there were only 61 lay peerages, several of them multiple holdings by one peer – 3 dukedoms, 14 earldoms and 43 baronies. By 1450 he had created or recreated 36 more – 6 dukes, 2 Marcher lords, 2 marquesses, 8 earls, 2 viscounts and 16 barons. Even today, largely honorific life peerages are an important element of government patronage; in the fifteenth century, men would do almost anything to be granted the lands and legal privileges of hereditary nobility.

The king also had in his gift over a thousand royal offices. These were additional to those in his private estate, which included the principality of Wales (conjoined with the earldom of Chester), the dukedoms of Cornwall, Lancaster and Hereford, earldoms of Leicester, Lancaster, Derby and Northampton, the barony of Halton in Cheshire, the royal appanage of Richmondshire and the royal peculiar of Hexhamshire. Royal appointments were commonly devolved to the members of the king's household, but he could revoke them all at will.

· ∾ ·

Alongside these many advantages, however, Henry faced challenges in the form of changes to the deep political culture of the nation, which would expose his failings to a higher degree of public scrutiny. His reign saw the ruling house complete the transition from being a French family that governed England to being an English family struggling to retain its holdings in France. English only became the language of government under Henry V, the first monarch since the Norman Conquest to use it in his private correspondence.

The monarchy lost some of its majesty along with the element of mystery when the king's subjects could better understand how they were governed – although the genie of doubt about the natural order of things was already well out of the bottle. In the fourteenth century a diffuse proto-Protestant religious movement known as Lollardy followed the lead of the lay theologian John Wycliffe in rejecting the corruption of the Church. Papal authority had already been severely undermined by the French capture of the papacy from 1305 to 1378, followed by a vituperative schism between rival papacies at Avignon and Rome.

In the midst of all this, starting in 1348, repeated pandemics of bubonic, pneumonic and septicaemic plagues, known collectively as the Black Death, nearly halved the population. Unfortunately the best of the clergy took a deadly hit from the plague, which in its airborne, almost invariably fatal pneumonic form, struck down the most diligent among them as they tended to the dying. Meanwhile the bubonic plague wiped out even cloistered communities, whose grain stores were magnets for infected rats.

Secondary consequences included a sharp decline in rental income as the countryside became depopulated. Many landowners were compelled to enter into agreements with the reduced labour force, under which they assumed the capital costs and most of the risks in return for, typically, half the produce. The Church's relative income, however, increased steadily through donations. The massive transfer of wealth from secular to clerical hands eventually led to the clergy's expropriation and the Protestant Reformation – but long before that, outrage at the venality of the princes of the Church had reached boiling point.

Wycliffe produced the first partial translation of the Bible into English in 1382. In February 1395, 122 years before Martin Luther nailed his Ninety-Five Theses, in Latin, to the door of the castle church in Wittenberg, a group of Lollards nailed their Twelve Conclusions, in the vernacular, to the door of Westminster Hall, the heart of secular government in England.

Although Wycliffe and his followers had enjoyed the protection of John of Gaunt and other nobles who wished to get their hands on Church wealth, this ended after the 1381 Peasants' Revolt, which Wycliffe condemned but one of whose leaders, John Ball, preached Lollardy. Widespread unrest opened noble eyes (in particular Gaunt's, after his Savoy palace was sacked by the London mob) to the threat it posed to their own authority. After he seized power, John of Gaunt's son Henry IV forbade translation and private ownership of the Bible, and authorized the burning of heretics.

The name 'Peasants' Revolt' is, anyway, an historical solecism. It was more like a strike by agricultural workers empowered by their relative scarcity, led by minor officials and smallholders. The old historical consensus of medieval England as a peasant society where people were tied to the land by communal obligations, as in mainland Europe and Scotland, has long since been demolished. There is compelling evidence, as early as the thirteenth century, of a sizeable body of hired labour, and that land was a commodity owned by individuals – of either sex – who could buy, sell and bequeath it at will.*

As they did in their simultaneous conquest of Sicily, the Norman invaders of 1066 simply overlaid their authority on existing laws and customs. Anglo-Saxon property rights were refined by the contractual basis of feudalism, with the concept of binding contracts remaining after the link between land and service eroded. As a result England was a highly litigious society, which demanded at least a pretence of impartiality from state officials.

• ℰℐℴ •

Impartiality was something that Henry VI's administration signally failed to provide. He certainly must have known Richard II's downfall was precipitated by his illegal seizure of entailed Lancastrian lands from his cousin, who overthrew him to become Henry IV. He did not appreciate, however, that the cumulative effect of many small abuses of power by royal household members and their affinities could have a similar effect. Even when not committed in his name, every unpunished arbitrary act by his household diminished his sovereign authority.

Although England had been governed for fifteen years without domestic disturbances by his minority Council, once he was free to do so Henry seldom stayed at the Palace of Westminster, preferring Windsor Castle, Sheen, Eltham, Kennington and, after 1447, Gloucester's opulent palace at Greenwich. He ruled through a small number of trusted ministers, in permanent attendance during his 'progresses' through the country. Apart from a two-year period in 1442–3, when he was fully taken up with a strategy he hoped would lead to peace in France, his tours averaged three months per year between 1437 and 1453.

---

* This evidence was unearthed by Alan Macfarlane in his groundbreaking *The Origins of English Individualism.*

In principle Henry's regular peregrinations should have enabled him to gain the trust of his kingdom. Unfortunately they sowed ill will instead, because his entourage did not pay the roaming court's bills to local suppliers. Also, he mainly stayed at royal palaces, within a growing cocoon of liveried retainers. Chief among those most constantly with him was Suffolk and his own close associate John Sutton, created Baron Dudley in 1440. Two who became part of Henry's inner circle thanks to Cardinal Beaufort's influence were the erudite Adam Moleyns, made Bishop of Chichester in 1445, and Reginald Boulers, made Abbot of Gloucester in 1437 and Bishop of Hereford in 1450.

Three others were Henry's bosom friends. The closest was the royal chaplain William Ayscough, appointed Bishop of Salisbury shortly after Henry assumed personal kingship, and subsequently the king's confessor. James, Baron Beaumont, had been the king's companion since infancy and was created the first ever viscount in the English peerage in 1432. Another royal friend was James Fiennes, created Baron Saye and Sele in 1447, who probably abused Henry's trust more than any other.

The young king's alienation of crown revenues through gifts to his favourites was similar to the behaviour of his ill-fated great-uncle Richard II. Ironically, the principal beneficiary of Richard's fecklessness had been his uncle John of Gaunt, who thereby built up the affinity that made it possible for his own son to seize the throne and found the Lancastrian dynasty. One of the few things Henry VI's grandfather and father agreed on was that none of their subjects should become as over-mighty as the founder of their dynasty had been.

At the same time pressure for territorial expansion and consolidation was growing, because landowners' incomes per acre declined in absolute terms from the middle of the fourteenth century. Land ownership was a zero-sum game and nobles could only expand their holdings through inheritance, marriage or royal gift. Among the most valuable forms of royal patronage were permission to marry and the assignment of wardships – the care and control of wealthy orphans during their minorities. In the case of orphan girls, their estates were generally captured by their guardians through marriage to their own sons.

A startling illustration of this involved the girl co-heirs of the wealthy Humphrey Bohun, Earl of Hereford, Essex and Northampton. After Eleanor, the elder, married Edward III's youngest son Thomas of Woodstock, they pressured Eleanor's sister Mary into becoming a nun, to give them sole possession of the Bohun inheritance. Thomas's older brother John of Gaunt abducted Mary from the convent and, following payment of a large fine to his nephew the king, married her to his own eldest son, the future Henry IV.

Not the least of Henry V's reasons for embarking on a career of conquest was to provide an outlet for the martial energy and the rapacity of his land-hungry nobles. The Norman Conquest of 1066 had established a unitary English state under a monarchy kept strong by ensuring that few nobles were ever permitted to accumulate the large contiguous holdings that enabled the great French lords to defy their king. The exceptions were the lords expected to police the borders (Marches) of Wales and Scotland. Unsurprisingly, they were historically the most troublesome of the king's subjects.

In 1326 Queen Isabella and her lover, the Welsh Marcher lord Roger, Baron Mortimer, overthrew and killed her husband Edward II. Four years later, by then Earl of March, Roger suffered a degrading death at the end of a rope, was attainted (see explanation below) and all his titles and lands declared forfeit by the young Edward III.

The Scots Marcher Henry, Baron Percy, helped overthrow Richard II and was created Earl of Northumberland by a grateful Henry IV. Although Percy's son Harry 'Hotspur' rebelled and was killed at the 1403 Battle of Shrewsbury, the father was spared retribution. He was attainted for another failed rebellion two years later, after which he fled to Scotland. Three years later his head ended up adorning London Bridge.

There was usually a third act to the cycle of treason and exemplary punishment. Attainder, also known as 'corruption of blood', declared the individual a non-person in a legal sense and so terminated rights of both patrilineal and matrilineal inheritance. Thus the attainted noble's forfeiture of hereditary titles and lands also deprived his family. Punishing the innocent sat ill with medieval concepts of kingship, however, and attainder was rarely sustained.

Thus the ancestral Mortimer lands and the earldom of March were restored to Roger's grandson in 1354, while Percy's attainder was revoked and the earldom restored to Hotspur's son in 1416. In part this was because of the strategic importance of the lands in question and the deep local roots of the Mortimer and Percy affinities; but it also illustrated how respectful of property rights even kings had to be.

There was another consideration. A subject permanently deprived of his family lands could only hope for redress by force of arms. He might claim to be rebelling only to recover his patrimony, as Henry Bolingbroke did in 1399, but in practice he could only be secure if the monarch was overthrown. Meanwhile, if the king kept the expropriated lands he was regarded as a thief, and if he awarded them to others he would experience the paradox of patronage succinctly summed up by the infamous Mayor James Curley of Boston: 'Every time you do a favour for a constituent, you make nine enemies and one ingrate'.

In sum, successful kingship was a balancing act requiring a wide range of political skills. The main reason why primogeniture became the sanctified mechanism of succession was to avoid a civil war every time a king died; but another reason to abide with one ruling family was that the heir could be expected to have learned the necessary skills by observing them exercised by his father. Henry VI was denied the opportunity to learn from his father and, bombarded by exhortation to live up to the idealized example of a man with whom he never formed a living bond, must have secretly resented his memory.

In practical terms the most burdensome part of Henry V's legacy was the war in France. His son was the antithesis of a warrior and regarded conquered Normandy as more trouble than it was worth – something his father's generation could never accept. However, in early 1447 the leading figures of the old guard departed the scene when Cardinal Beaufort died sixteen days after Humphrey of Gloucester. Their furious disagreements had caused their influence to decline once Henry VI assumed personal kingship and they had, anyway, fought each other to a standstill by 1440.

Uniquely for the period we have handsome contemporary likenesses of the two men: a crayon copy of an earlier drawing from life of Gloucester as a young man, and Van Eyck's portrait of the plainly dressed cardinal in his late fifties, the earliest naturalistic painting of any Englishman. Apart from the Lancaster nose, it is hard to discern a family likeness; but both project a strength of character sadly lacking in their young nephew and king.

For all their rancour they were princes of the blood devoted to their dynasty. Both shared Henry V's vision of Christendom united under a dual Lancastrian monarchy, and differed only on the means to pursue what was, objectively, an insane ambition. Gloucester could never bring himself to accept that his brother's legacy was unsustainable, but by the end of the 1430s the cardinal had reluctantly concluded that Henry VI was a broken reed.

Unfortunately Beaufort tried to salvage the Lancastrian dynasty's fortunes while simultaneously advancing the interests of his younger relatives. Although this was normal behaviour by senior prelates – the word 'nepotism' comes from the favours showered on their *nipoti* (nephews, often actually sons) by popes and princes of the Church – it was to have tragic consequences for his king, and for England.

II

HOUSE OF
BEAUFORT

THE BEAUFORTS TOOK THEIR FAMILY NAME FROM THEIR birthplace, a castle in the Loire valley owned by their father John of Gaunt, 15 miles east of Angers, the capital of Anjou. The four Beaufort siblings, John, Henry, Thomas and Joan, were born illegitimate during the 1370s, but in 1396 John of Gaunt married their mother, Katherine Swynford. Church law viewed all the children of parents who married as legitimate, no matter when the marriage took place. Further legitimated by papal decree and royal charter, the Beauforts regarded themselves as – and the bordure of their coat of arms proclaimed them to be – the cadet branch of the Lancastrian dynasty.

English civil law was less accommodating with regard to inheritance, something emphasized by their half-brother Henry IV when he barred the Beauforts from the succession. Henry's policy was to keep them closely tied to his own family by curtailing any independent ambition they might entertain. Thus he revoked the senior titles and the lands awarded by Richard II to John, the eldest of the Beauforts. Instead, Henry gave him a revocable annuity of £1,000 [£636,000]. John retained the earldom of Somerset and the lands settled on him by their father, but these yielded only another £1,000.

Likewise, when Bishop Henry Beaufort resigned as Lord Chancellor following his appointment to the wealthy see of Winchester, Henry IV's attitude towards him changed. Even though the bishop performed his office admirably during the Percy rebellion and had undone a simultaneous French threat to Calais through skilled diplomacy, the king now began to view everything he did with suspicion. Perhaps with good reason, as the bishop was a key figure in Prince Henry's attempt to supplant his father's authority.

When, after distinguished military and diplomatic service, John Beaufort died in 1410, within four months his widow Margaret Holland, a wealthy woman in her own right, was betrothed to Thomas, Duke of Clarence, Henry IV's second son. Clarence claimed custody of John's heirs and took possession of the income from John's estate. This went plainly against John's will and was contested – with little success – by Bishop Henry, his brother and executor.

Only 9 miles north of Beaufort lay Baugé, scene of the disastrous battle in which the king's younger brother, the Duke of Clarence, met his death in 1421. The two eldest surviving sons of John Beaufort, who accompanied their stepfather on the Anjou campaign, were captured after the battle. The younger, 15-year-old Thomas, was released in 1427 through a prisoner exchange arranged by Cardinal Beaufort, but died four years later. Seventeen-year-old John Beaufort, Earl of Somerset, remained in French hands until 1438. John's captivity was prolonged because his mother refused to diminish the estates she administered in his name.

The rivalry between the Duke of Gloucester and Cardinal Beaufort also added to the young earl's misfortune, as the French first demanded an exchange for the Duke of Bourbon, captured at Agincourt. After Bourbon died in captivity they proposed an exchange for the Count of Angoulême, held as surety since 1412 for the Duke of Orléans's debt to Clarence, John's late stepfather. Gloucester prevented both exchanges.

After Henry VI assumed personal kingship he lent a sympathetic ear to the petition of Edmund, John's youngest brother, on his sibling's behalf. Agreement was reached for John's ransom to be offset by the payment due from Angoulême, plus the release of the Count

HOUSE OF BEAUFORT

k. = killed in battle   x. = executed

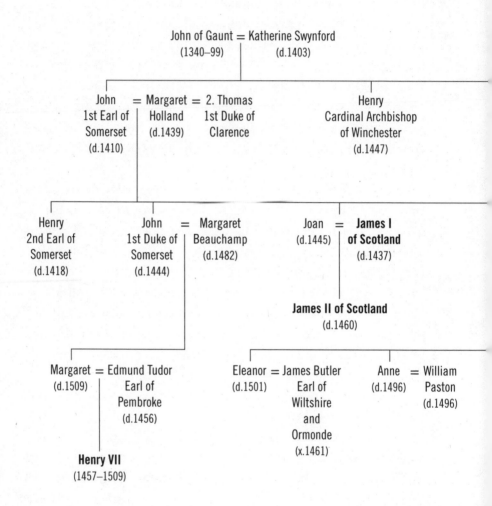

John of Gaunt = Katherine Swynford
(1340–99)   (d.1403)

John = Margaret = 2. Thomas
1st Earl of | Holland | 1st Duke of
Somerset | (d.1439) | Clarence
(d.1410)

Henry
Cardinal Archbishop
of Winchester
(d.1447)

Henry
2nd Earl of
Somerset
(d.1418)

John = Margaret
1st Duke of | Beauchamp
Somerset | (d.1482)
(d.1444)

Joan = **James I**
(d.1445) | **of Scotland**
| (d.1437)

James II of Scotland
(d.1460)

Margaret = Edmund Tudor
(d.1509) | Earl of
Pembroke
(d.1456)

Henry VII
(1457–1509)

Eleanor = James Butler
(d.1501) | Earl of
Wiltshire
and
Ormonde
(x.1461)

Anne = William
(d.1496) | Paston
(d.1496)

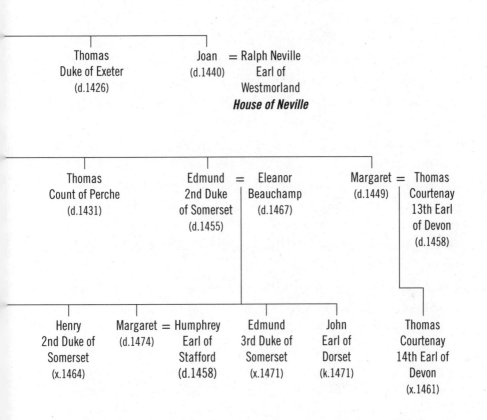

of Eu, captured at Agincourt, whose ransom John purchased from the crown for £24,000 [£15.26 million]. The debt was crippling, as even after inheriting the Holland lands from his mother John's annual income was only £2,250 [£1.43 million].

In his absence Edmund, after his courtship of Queen Catherine was thwarted, was made Count of Mortain, near the border with Maine in western Normandy, and took service under Bedford. He saw some action in 1427 and a great deal in 1429, a year of multiple English defeats following Jeanne d'Arc's relief of Orléans, during which Bedford made him a constable of the army. Edmund formed part of the escort for Henry VI from Rouen to Paris for his coronation as king of France in November 1430, during which he first met Richard, Duke of York, at the time a member of the young king's household.

After returning to England Edmund married Eleanor Beauchamp, dowager Baroness Roos, without obtaining the required royal licence. The dates are uncertain, but it seems Edmund forced the issue by getting her pregnant. Eleanor was the middle of three daughters of the very wealthy Richard Beauchamp, Earl of Warwick, and his also wealthy first wife, Elizabeth Berkeley, heiress of the baronies of Berkeley and Lisle. After Elizabeth died in 1422 Beauchamp married another wealthy heiress, Isabel Despenser, who bore him Henry and Anne.

While he lived, Warwick blocked the royal licence for Edmund's marriage. Determined to deny his unwanted son-in-law any profit from it, he entailed his entire estate to his son Henry, depriving the daughters of his first marriage of what they (and their outraged husbands) regarded as their due inheritance from their mother. The ultimate beneficiary was Richard Neville, betrothed to Anne Beauchamp in 1434 when he was six and she was eight. He was to become Earl of Warwick by marriage and one of the wealthiest men in England after Anne's older brother Henry died in 1446, followed by his only child in 1448.

Though his matrimonial fortune-hunting failed, Edmund benefited greatly from his uncle Henry's wealth. It bought him his first independent command in March 1436, when the cardinal loaned the crown the money to equip a 2,000-man expedition to Normandy, conditional on his nephew being in command. Edmund's role, however, proved to be less autonomous than he had hoped, as the king required him to join the Duke of Gloucester at Calais.

Gloucester, the king's lieutenant in France following the death of his brother Bedford, thirsted to punish Duke Philippe of Burgundy, who at Arras the previous year had reneged on his treaty with England and entered into a military alliance with France. Under Gloucester's command Edmund led damaging raids (known as *chevauchées*) into Picardy, the province ceded to Burgundy by Charles VII at Arras, and performed so well that Gloucester left him in command while he returned to England to gather reinforcements.

Stung by Edmund's raids, Philippe raised a huge army, mainly Flemish militia, and besieged Calais and the frontier fortress at Guînes. Edmund conducted an aggressive defence, and thwarted an attempt to close Calais harbour with rock-filled blockships by sending men to dismantle them. When he learned that Gloucester was returning with 10,000 men, Philippe was compelled to lift both sieges and retreat south. Gloucester then embarked on a massive *chevauchée* into Flanders while ships out of Calais plundered along the coast, prompting a two-year revolt by the Flemish cities against Philippe's policies, which forced him to abandon any further military action against the English.

On his triumphant return to England, Edmund was made a Garter knight and constable of the royal castles of Aberystwyth and Kidwelly in Wales. Subsequently he was made warden of Windsor Castle, where the king charged him with guarding his late mother's lover Owen Tudor after he 'escaped' from Newgate prison.

For a few years Edmund achieved the remarkable feat of being highly esteemed by Gloucester as well as enjoying Cardinal Beaufort's continuing patronage. In 1438 he was appointed governor of the county of Maine, and four years later was awarded the land rights.

Along with his county of Mortain it made him the principal English lord in the area conquered from the Duke of Anjou.

This steep rise of Edmund's fortunes increased John Beaufort's resentment when he returned to England in late 1438. It was bad enough to have had his own career put on hold for seventeen years, but galling to find his youngest brother had flourished so outstandingly during his absence. John's return forced his uncle to switch political and financial influence away from the abler and more charismatic Edmund during the crucial years when the cardinal emerged the winner in his long feud with Gloucester.

In the spring of 1439 the cardinal funded an expedition led by John to join Edmund in Normandy. John was made captain of the fortresses of the Cotentin peninsula in the face of a Franco-Breton offensive that captured Harfleur and Montvilliers, and besieged Avranches. In April, after the death of Edmund's hostile father-in-law the Earl of Warwick, John became the acting overall military commander in France.

In November John returned to England, where his uncle tried to have him formally appointed the king's lieutenant in France in succession to Warwick. Gloucester thwarted him and John was only made senior commander on a temporary basis. In early 1440 he was sent to prove himself with an army of 2,100 men, again financed by his uncle. His subordinate commanders were his brother Edmund and Lord Talbot, each married to one of the late Earl of Warwick's daughters and fellow litigants against the terms of his will.

With Charles VII distracted by a rebellion, Edmund recaptured Harfleur and Montvilliers, stabilizing the situation in western and central Normandy. Meanwhile, on the eastern front, John led a *chevauchée* into Picardy. The aim was to provoke Franco-Burgundian conflict by drawing in the French, but he encountered no opposition. John could not know it, but this marked the beginning of a new strategy by Arthur de Richemont, Constable of France, designed to wear down the English without risking the new standing army he was building.

John's chance of being appointed lieutenant in France was a casualty of Gloucester's last attempt to discredit Cardinal Beaufort, before Gloucester was himself discredited by the prosecution of his wife in 1441. During the 1439–40 parliament Gloucester submitted an indictment of Cardinal Beaufort's entire career, arguing it was characterized by corruption and accusing him of putting the interests of the papacy ahead of his loyalty to the crown. Unsurprisingly, given that at this point the war in France was being maintained by the cardinal's wealth, the indictment did not prosper.

Henry VI was the first English king never to command an army in battle. He was a passionate hunter, by no means a risk-free activity, but took no part in martial tournaments. This may have been because those entrusted with his care as a minor did not dare expose him to the dangers, but the outcome was a man who regarded warfare with distaste. Henry's parliaments increasingly took a similar view, and became less and less inclined to vote for the necessary taxes. Henry could not expect his subjects to make sacrifices for a war to which he was not prepared to commit himself.

Furthermore, after the exhilaration of Henry V's conquest of Normandy had passed, there was scant enthusiasm among the professional fighting men for the grinding war that followed. Without much prospect of winning lands for themselves, commanders and men alike needed to be sure they would be paid, and their physical and military needs supplied, if they were to cross the Channel at all. Bedford, Gloucester and Warwick had deep pockets and could afford to advance money against sporadic royal reimbursement; John Beaufort could not.

One man who seems not to have been considered for the role of lieutenant in France was John Mowbray, Duke of Norfolk and hereditary Earl Marshal of England. He suffered from ill health brought on by debauchery and was afforded little respect by his peers throughout his life. That left only one man with the rank and wealth required to replace Warwick: Richard, Duke of York, who had already served as lieutenant in France in 1436–7. Humphrey,

Earl of Stafford, was appointed Captain of Calais and three years later made Duke of Buckingham.

Denied the prospect of glory and enrichment in Normandy, John and Edmund Beaufort returned to England at the end of 1440. John was made a Garter knight, and not long afterwards married Margaret Beauchamp (only distantly related to Edmund's wife), sole heir of the barony of Bletsoe and a widow with seven children. In May 1443, at the manor at Kingston Lacy, lent by the king and close to John's own lands in Dorset, Margaret bore him a daughter, also named Margaret, who was to become the most influential royal matriarch in English history.*

John preferred to reside at his own Corfe Castle, which broods over the peninsula known as the Isle of Purbeck, 90 miles directly north of Cherbourg in Normandy. From there he supervised the assembly at Portsmouth of the last army he was to lead. Faced with a French offensive against Guyenne, the king agreed to a major counter-attack out of Normandy in 1443. It was the largest expedition since Gloucester's in 1436 and was intended to draw the French away from Guyenne and bring them to battle. It was financed entirely by Cardinal Beaufort to the tune of £22,666 [£14.4 million] on condition it was led by his nephew John.

The Beaufort expedition was a departure from the previous strategy of forcing Charles VII to negotiate by making Normandy too hard a nut to crack. Two years previously York had provided his brilliant field commander Talbot with enough men to blunt a major French offensive into Normandy. Even so, they could not prevent the fall of Pontoise, a key fortress in the strategically vital Oise valley, and the case for persisting with this strategy was decreasingly persuasive. It required more money than Henry VI could obtain from Parliament, or wished to spend, and he wanted a quicker fix.

Cardinal Beaufort's offer to assume the entire cost of a counter-offensive in 1443 was therefore irresistible. Although it meant York's

---

* Margaret would be married to Edmund Tudor in 1455, when she was just 12 years old. Their only child, born in 1457, was the future Henry VII.

siege of Dieppe must be abandoned, he was assured the new expedition would operate in enemy territory, outside his area of authority, and accepted that John Beaufort's raid in force would relieve pressure on the rest of Normandy as well as Guyenne. The hope was that John could also defeat the French army in the field and force them to negotiate.

While Henry VI held Edmund Beaufort in high esteem, only their uncle's money and influence obtained royal favour for his older brother John. Somerset was made Baron of Kendal in Cumberland with an income of £400 [£254,500], but he was not promoted to duke until his delayed arrival at Cherbourg in late August 1443. This was to grant him parity of status with York, a quid pro quo demanded by Cardinal Beaufort.

PEERAGE PARTICIPATION IN SELECTED CAMPAIGNS 1415–53[*]

	Dukes/Earls			Barons	
Date	Commander	Summoned	Response	Summoned	Response
1415	Henry V	15	14	28	18
1430	Bedford	10	8	25	11
1436	Gloucester	10	8	27	17
1441	York	9	York + 1	26	3
1443	Somerset	14	Somerset	29	0
1452–3	Talbot	14	Talbot + 1	40	3

Henry V and his brothers had drawn a vigorous response from the peers summoned by Parliament for military service in France, but their successors could not. This reflected the deteriorating strategic situation, but in addition York and Somerset were not regarded as charismatic leaders. York did not actually recruit the

[*]Table from Adrian Bell et al. (eds.), *The Soldier in Later Medieval England.*

three barons listed for 1441 – Lords Talbot, Scales and Fauconberg – as they were already in Normandy. John Beaufort's 1443 expedition attracted no barons at all and was joined by only one banneret (a knight commanding his own company), Thomas Kyriell, and six other knights.

In sharp contrast to the speed with which Gloucester mobilized his massive 1436 expedition, those led by York and Somerset took a long time to assemble. Delay severely eroded the effectiveness of such ventures, as indentures (contracts) were for a limited time, and soldiers and horses cost much more to maintain in England and occupied France than they did in enemy territory, where they could live off the land.

Mounting a cross-Channel expedition was a major logistical challenge. Even a mounted archer needed at least two horses, esquires three and knights and above four or more. Soldiers' stipends covered their own costs, but if the horses could not graze – for example, while waiting to board ships – they consumed tons of feed at an additional cost to the chief contractor. Shipowners, also contracted for a limited time, needed to be paid whether or not they were used to transport the expedition during the stipulated period.

John's long-delayed expedition was a dismal failure. Forced to spend too much of his uncle's money before setting out, he needed to replenish his war chest as soon as possible. On his way south he crossed the border into neutral Brittany to attack the town of La Guerche, which he believed was owned by the Duke of Alençon, the local French commander. Alençon, however, had sold La Guerche to the Duke of Brittany in 1429. The 20,000 *saluts d'or* [£2.9 million] John demanded to spare the town from being sacked were paid by the enraged duke, who sent a strongly worded protest to Henry VI.

John marched on through Edmund's lands in Maine into Anjou, where he laid siege to Pouancé, one of Alençon's fiefs. A small French relief force was easily defeated, but Alençon himself refused to be drawn. Despite having carted boats from Cherbourg to bridge the Loire, John flinched from crossing the river to bring about the battle that was the strategic purpose of his expedition. Instead he marched east to Rouen, paying off his troops as he went, some of whom took service with the frontier garrisons.

After a frosty reception from York, John received a copy of the Duke of Brittany's protest from Henry VI, who ordered him to make full restitution. Compelled to disgorge whatever he had not spent, in January 1444 he returned to England in disgrace, sick, and once more in straitened circumstances. Barred from court, he spent his remaining months at Corfe and nearby Wimborne, where he died in May 1444, aged 42, probably by his own hand.

Edmund, created a marquess when his brother was made a duke, inherited the earldom and Corfe Castle, but the barony of Kendal and John's French fiefs reverted to the crown. John's entailed estate went to one-year-old baby Margaret, who remained with her mother. However the king broke a solemn undertaking given to John prior to his expedition, that her mother should also have the right to decide whom the child should marry. Instead, he made Margaret Beaufort the ward of his chief minister William de la Pole, at this point still only Earl of Suffolk, who promptly betrothed her to his two-year-old son John.

Edmund, to some extent, shared his brother's disgrace at this time, and may have traded off his niece's future in order to regain favour. On the other hand he must have secretly despised Suffolk for exploiting the situation to his own advantage, and the king for permitting him to do so. Some of Edmund's future behaviour may have been conditioned by this sordid episode.

HOUSE OF
VALOIS-ANJOU

I N THE FIRST ACT OF THE THIRD PART OF HIS *HENRY VI* trilogy Shakespeare dubbed Marguerite d'Anjou the 'she-wolf of France'. Her demonization by Tudor propagandists had its roots in the efforts of Henry VII to have his namesake Lancastrian predecessor declared a saint, which required the transfer to Marguerite of much of the blame for the catastrophes of her husband's reign. Although the Bard did not mean it as a compliment, she-wolves are in fact admirable animals that mate for life and are fiercely protective of their young.

Thus also Marguerite, who was a loyal and supportive consort to Henry VI until it became apparent his weakness was endangering their son's birth right, after which she felt compelled to provide the necessary leadership. Her relentless determination, and the loyalty she commanded from some seriously hard men, leads one to wonder whether her son Edward of Westminster might have made a great king.

Marguerite was born in Lorraine, the duchy inherited by her mother Isabelle in 1431. Her father was René of the House of Valois-Anjou, second son of Louis II, Duke of Anjou, Count of Maine and Count of Provence, and Princess Yolande de Aragón. Louis devoted most of his energies to wider dynastic ambitions and left the government of Anjou almost entirely to Yolande. After he died, Yolande became regent for her young sons and fought the

English invasions of Maine and northern Anjou.

This she continued to do for the rest of her life, while her sons were mainly occupied elsewhere. She was also the surrogate mother of the disinherited Dauphin Charles, who married Yolande's daughter Marie six months before he claimed the kingdom in 1422. Later, Yolande was closely involved in the emergence of Jeanne d'Arc, with whom her son René rode to the 1429 relief of Orléans, the first major French victory over the English.

Yolande recruited and ran a network of courtesans who became the mistresses of high-ranking men in the courts of Brittany, Burgundy and Lorraine, and in the French royal household. In the process of detaching Brittany from its alliance with England, she won the loyalty of Arthur de Richemont, younger brother of Duke Yann VI of Brittany. Richemont became Constable of France in 1425, with Yolande's own subject Pierre de Brézé by his side.

In 1433, at Yolande's instigation, Richemont and Brézé expelled Charles VII's Grand Chamberlain Georges de la Trémoille, who had frittered away the military momentum won by Jeanne d'Arc in pointless negotiations. Richemont and Brézé were the architects of the 1435 Treaty of Arras with Burgundy, which marked the definitive turning-point of the war, and of the policies that earned Charles VII the sobriquets 'Well-Served' and 'Victorious'.

It would be hard to overstate how important Yolande was to the final stages of the Hundred Years War, or the significance for our story of the fact that during the last four to five years of Yolande's life (she died in 1442), her granddaughter Marguerite came to live with her during her transition to adolescence.

Marguerite's mother Isabelle was cast in the same mould as her mother-in-law and placed Agnès Sorel, who became the first officially recognized royal mistress, in Charles VII's household. It was thanks to Agnès's influence that Brézé rose so rapidly in the king's service from 1444 until her death in 1450. In 1435 Isabelle led an army in an unsuccessful effort to rescue her hapless husband from Burgundian captivity. In return for freeing René, the Burgundians

HOUSE OF VALOIS-ANJOU

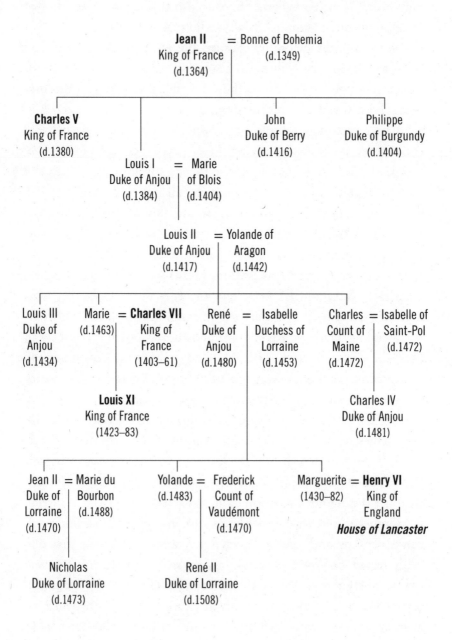

Jean II = Bonne of Bohemia
King of France (d.1349)
(d.1364)

Charles V
King of France
(d.1380)

Louis I = Marie
Duke of Anjou | of Blois
(d.1384) | (d.1404)

John
Duke of Berry
(d.1416)

Philippe
Duke of Burgundy
(d.1404)

Louis II = Yolande of
Duke of Anjou | Aragon
(d.1417) | (d.1442)

Louis III
Duke of
Anjou
(d.1434)

Marie = **Charles VII**
(d.1463) | King of
France
(1403–61)

René = Isabelle
Duke of | Duchess of
Anjou | Lorraine
(d.1480) | (d.1453)

Charles = Isabelle of
Count of | Saint-Pol
Maine | (d.1472)
(d.1472)

Louis XI
King of France
(1423–83)

Charles IV
Duke of Anjou
(d.1481)

Jean II = Marie du
Duke of | Bourbon
Lorraine | (d.1488)
(d.1470)

Yolande = Frederick
(d.1483) | Count of
Vaudémont
(d.1470)

Marguerite = **Henry VI**
(1430–82) | King of
England
House of Lancaster

Nicholas
Duke of Lorraine
(d.1473)

René II
Duke of Lorraine
(d.1508)

not only required a hefty ransom but also took his two sons hostage, one of whom would die in prison. Left impoverished, René and Isabelle sent young Marguerite to live with her grandmother Yolande.

Marguerite's father René became Duke of Anjou and Count of Provence on the death of his elder brother Louis in 1434. Four years earlier he had become (by marriage and adoption) Duke of Bar and Count of Piedmont. He also claimed the kingdom of Naples, but lost it to Alfonso V of Aragón in 1442. René was also titular King of Hungary and Jerusalem, and in 1466 made a futile claim to the throne of Aragón through the right of his mother.

He went through the motions of being a prince, but after his formidable mother and wife died he devoted himself to artistic pursuits. He looks remarkably like a toad in the only portraits we have of him, but they were painted when he was older. The striking portrait of Isabelle of Lorraine in the Uffizi Gallery leaves no doubt about the source of their daughter's looks.

Both genetically and through training by experts, therefore, Marguerite had the potential to be a dynamic queen consort, and grew up witnessing how strong women could make something of weak men. Lamentably for her and for England, while her husband Henry VI was even more ineffectual than her father he was also less pliable, and circumstances completely beyond her control doomed her attempt to emulate her grandmother.

Properly handled, a marriage alliance with the House of Valois-Anjou had much to offer the English crown. Charles VII had no eligible daughter, and his queen's niece was as good a French match as Henry VI could hope for. That said, England's best chance of imposing a negotiated settlement evaporated in 1440, when it failed to exploit the opportunity presented by a rebellion against Richemont's centralizing policies by the Duke of Bourbon and the deposed Grand Chamberlain Trémoille, who enticed the Duke of Brittany and Charles VII's teenaged heir apparent Louis to join them in a rebellion known as the 'Praguerie' (by analogy with a revolt that had recently occurred in Bohemia).

Henry's first choice had been to marry a daughter of Count Jean IV of Armagnac, one of the few remaining French magnates not of royal blood. This would have strengthened England's position in south-west France, off-setting the deep commitment to Charles VII of the Lord of Albret, whose lands lay within and adjacent to English Guyenne. Charles VII put an end to the count's dalliance with the English by invading Armagnac, imprisoning him and installing royal officials to administer La Marche, Rodez and Armagnac-Comminges (see Map 5).

So it was that when Suffolk was sent to treat for the hand of Marguerite in 1444, his negotiating position was weak and he insisted on the explicit backing of the Council and Parliament. At the time it was recognized that his contacts among the magnates of France made him uniquely qualified for the task; later they were viewed in a more sinister light. Suffolk's embassy met Charles VII and Richemont at Tours, the capital of Touraine, with René d'Anjou in attendance. At the end of May a two-year truce was agreed and a betrothal ceremony, with Suffolk as proxy for the king, was performed.

Suffolk also made a number of informal proposals authorized by Henry, including a temporary suspension of the English claim to the French throne in return for an extension of the truce, and the possibility that lands seized by the English in Maine and Anjou might be returned to René. These proposals were, rightly, interpreted by the French as evidence of Henry's lack of the will to prosecute the war, and Richemont used the truce to accelerate the establishment of the first standing army in French history.

Suffolk, by then a marquess, returned to collect the new queen the following November with a large retinue including 28-year-old Jacquetta, newly delivered of her second son, and her husband Richard Woodville. In 1443, Jacquetta's younger sister had married Marguerite's uncle Charles, the dispossessed Count of Maine, so she was able to greet the young queen as a kinswoman. As foreigners married into the English ruling family they had much in common and became good friends.

• ⁊ •

A key member of Suffolk's retinue was his duchess, 40-year-old Alice de la Pole, granddaughter of the poet Geoffrey Chaucer. Marguerite would form a daughterly bond with Alice who, like Jacquetta, would become one of her ladies-in-waiting. The Chaucer connection reveals how Suffolk became part of the Beaufort affinity. Geoffrey Chaucer was married to the sister of John of Gaunt's mistress and later wife Katherine Swynford, mother of the Beaufort clan.* Alice's father Thomas, elected Speaker of the House of Commons five times between 1407 and his death in 1434, was a key intermediary between Henry IV and his son, and as a result was Henry V's most trusted official. After the king's death, Thomas worked closely with Bishop Beaufort to deny Gloucester the regency.

Alice was Thomas's sole heir, having previously inherited a large estate from her short-lived first husband, whom she married when she was 11 years old, and an even larger one from her second, Thomas Montagu, Earl of Salisbury, whom she married when still a teenager. He was killed in 1429 at the siege of Orléans, after which Suffolk, Salisbury's second-in-command, was defeated and captured by Jeanne d'Arc herself. He was released a year later after payment of a £20,000 [£12.7 million] ransom and promising to do all he could to obtain the release of the Count of Angoulême, a hostage since 1412, and his older brother the Duke of Orléans, captured at Agincourt in 1415.

Impoverished Suffolk became betrothed to now very wealthy Alice immediately after his release. Although she sensibly insisted on a 'what's mine is mine and what's yours is mine also' prenuptial

---

* If to Chaucer's robust appreciation of female sexuality we add the evidence of John of Gaunt's infatuation, it is reasonable to assume that the Swynford sisters were also passionate princesses.

settlement, theirs was a genuine love-match, strongly suggesting
there may have been a previous relationship. Suffolk became lord of
the Woodville estate at Grafton as Alice's husband, not in his own
right, so it is reasonable to assume she and Jacquetta knew each
other before they formed part of the young queen's retinue.

• ℰℐ •

The bridal party made a progress through occupied Normandy,
during which Marguerite was greeted as queen of France. At Rouen,
pleading illness but possibly ashamed of the poverty of her wardrobe, she did not take part in a procession and pageant organized
by the Duke of York, the king's lieutenant in France. Although
Jacquetta was of senior rank as dowager duchess of Bedford, she
stood aside to let Alice represent the queen.

The most commonly reproduced likeness of Marguerite is from a
magnificently illustrated book given to her at Rouen by John Talbot,
by now Earl of Shrewsbury and Marshal of France. Although the
depictions of Talbot himself and of his superior Richard of York
(among the spectators) would have been taken from life by the
Rouen miniaturists, the illustration shows Talbot presenting the
book to Marguerite as crowned queen, holding hands with a depiction of Henry VI that bears no resemblance to any other portrait
of him.

Sadly, the charming portrait of Marguerite bears no relation to
her appearance, either. The loose hair represents virginity, and by
convention all English queens were portrayed as fair-haired. She
was described as dark-haired, and as 'handsome' rather than beautiful. The only reliable likeness of Marguerite is her profile on a
medallion made for René d'Anjou by the sculptor Pietro da Milano
in 1464, after she had fled England.

After her arrival at Southampton on 9 April, genuinely ill after
a rough crossing, Marguerite was visited by the king in disguise,
a convention of courtly love she was too distracted to recognize.

Henry ordered she should be bedecked and adorned as befitted a queen, and on 22 April they were married at Titchfield Abbey in Hampshire by his confessor, Bishop William Ayscough of Salisbury. Pageants and tableaux celebrating peace marked her entry into London on 28 May, and she was crowned in Westminster Abbey two days later.

Three days of feasts and tournaments followed. Not only was 15-year-old Marguerite herself rapturously received, but Suffolk was unanimously commended by the Lords, led by the Duke of Gloucester, and by the Commons. He was later to be made the scapegoat for the failure of English policy in France, but in mid-1445 he was applauded for accomplishing the king's commission, and for acting in accordance with the consensus of the political nation.

Tragically for Marguerite and fatally for Suffolk, her marriage was the keystone of a peace policy based on wishful thinking. It was not politically possible for Henry VI to surrender his dynasty's claim to the throne of France (not formally renounced by the British crown until 1801), or to pay homage to Charles VII for Normandy and Guyenne. With the strategic balance tipping more in his favour every year, however, Charles was not going to accept anything less.

If not often active allies of France, Burgundy and Brittany were no longer making common cause with England, and French royal authority was stronger than ever after the 1440 rebellion was crushed. Previously dependent on revenues from the ravaged royal domain and exceptional grants from the Estates General, in 1438 Charles helped himself to the substantial proportion of Church revenues previously paid to Rome.

The following year the Estates General voted to make permanent the *taille*, a previously exceptional tax on land, specifically to pay for a standing army.* Charles's appointment in 1436 of the talented

---

* As John Fortescue observed in his near-contemporary *On the Laws and Governance of England, or the Difference between an Absolute and a Limited Monarchy*, the *taille* and the standing army defined the French monarchy.

merchant Jacques Coeur as Master of the Royal Mint had brought rip-roaring inflation under control, and in 1438 he made him Steward of the Royal Expenditure. Improving fiscal order helped to sustain a boom in production and commerce sparked by the inflation, taxes from which further enhanced the royal exchequer.

The final factor dooming the English empire in France was demographics. Although reduced by pandemics from a peak of 17 million a century earlier, at 10 million France still had a population four times as large as England and Wales in the mid-fifteenth century. However, the estimated 'French' population includes Brittany, Burgundy, English Guyenne and the vast areas occupied by the Anglo-Burgundian alliance in northern and north-eastern France. Until the Burgundians changed sides in 1435 the demographic imbalance was not great, but Duke Philippe's desertion of his former allies tipped the scales decisively in France's favour.

The most fought-over areas, in particular Normandy, Maine, Alençon and the Île-de-France, suffered population declines of 70–75 per cent against an average of 40 per cent for the rest of the country. Unlike stable and prosperous Guyenne, the northern areas conquered after Agincourt became so devastated by marauding armies and endemic banditry that the cost of holding them outstripped the surpluses that could be extracted from them.

For all the certainty of England's impending defeat, the manner in which they were bundled out of Normandy within five years of the royal marriage, followed by the loss of neglected Guyenne, was a national humiliation. Suffolk and Edmund Beaufort were to be made the scapegoats, because to blame the king would have been high treason. In their innermost thoughts, however, all knew that the manner in which England lost its continental empire was primarily attributable to Henry VI's incompetence.

The failure of her marriage to bring peace and the consequent loss of Normandy and Guyenne therefore did not affect Marguerite's popularity, which soared against a backdrop of the collapse both of English rule in France and her husband's fragile morale. Her response was the first occasion on which she would step in to fill the void of authority left by her husband. Thereafter she played an increasingly activist role, as one would expect of a woman born of Duchess Isabelle of Lorraine and prepared for life by Princess Yolande de Aragón.

IV

HOUSE OF YORK

THE ARMS OF RICHARD, THIRD DUKE OF YORK, PROVED predictive of his life. The first and fourth quarters proclaimed him the great-grandson of Edward III, the second quarter was his grandmother's arms of Castille and León, and the third quartered the arms of the Mortimer earls of March and the Burgh earls of Ulster. The most potent element, however, was the central inescutcheon of the arms of England.

As the only son of two direct descendants of Edward III, the burden of ancestry lay heavily on him. His father Richard of Conisbrough, Earl of Cambridge, was the grandson of Edward III's fourth son Edmund, Duke of York. His mother Anne Mortimer, who died bearing him, was the great-granddaughter of Lionel, Duke of Clarence, Edward's second son. As Henry IV's father John of Gaunt was only the third son of Edward III, the Mortimer claim to the throne was stronger than the Lancastrian.

In 1415, when his namesake son was three years old, Cambridge was involved in a plot to put his brother-in-law Edmund Mortimer, 5th Earl of March, on the throne. Alas, he had failed to consult Edmund, who informed Henry V of the plot as soon as he learned of it and was a member of the court that condemned Cambridge to death. Even so, Henry V pointedly pardoned Edmund for his entirely unwitting role in the plot, to leave him in no doubt about the thinness of the ice under his feet.

The complicated backstory to the 1415 conspiracy began with the 1st Earl of March, Roger Mortimer, who was executed and attainted in 1330 after seizing power and murdering Edward II. After the title and Mortimer lands were restored to the 2nd earl in 1354, in 1368 the 3rd Earl of March married Philippa, only child of Lionel, Duke of Clarence, through whom he became Earl of Ulster. As the next in line to the throne after the Black Prince's son, the future Richard II, March was a leader of the nobles opposed to John of Gaunt's influence over Edward III during his final, senile years.

The 4th Earl of March was heir presumptive to Richard II until he was killed in an Irish ambush in 1398. Richard went to Ireland the following year to avenge his death, and on his return found he had lost his kingdom to Henry Bolingbroke, John of Gaunt's eldest son. In 1402, the 4th earl's brother was captured by Owain Glyn Dŵr and, after Henry IV refused to ransom him and looted his estate, joined the Glyn Dŵr-Percy rebellion, proclaiming his nephew Edmund, the 5th earl, to be the true king of England.

To thicken the plot further, Constance of York and Edward, Duke of York, the daughter and eldest son of Edmund of Langley, Edward III's fourth son, were involved in a plot to spring March from custody in Windsor Castle. Henry IV imprisoned York for four months; but he kept Edmund Mortimer in custody for the remaining years of his reign. There were good reasons for distrust of the Mortimers to be practically written into the DNA of the Lancastrian dynasty.

Edward of York was not involved in the later plot that led to the execution of Richard of Conisbrough, his younger brother, and shortly afterwards died heroically at Agincourt. Having saved his neck by denouncing Richard's plot, Edmund Mortimer was released from custody and restored to his inheritance by Henry V, under whose supervision he served in France. Although subsequently a member of the regency Council, he was never fully trusted by the Lancastrians and was sent to Ireland, where he died of the plague in 1425.

HOUSE OF YORK

k. = killed in battle   x. = executed

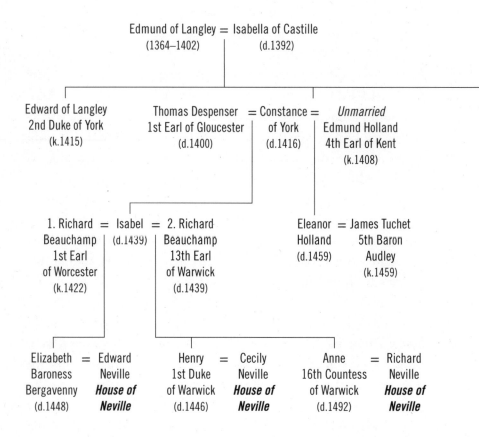

Edmund of Langley = Isabella of Castille
(1364–1402)   (d.1392)

Edward of Langley
2nd Duke of York
(k.1415)

Thomas Despenser   = Constance =   *Unmarried*
1st Earl of Gloucester   of York   Edmund Holland
(d.1400)   (d.1416)   4th Earl of Kent
                              (k.1408)

1. Richard = Isabel = 2. Richard
Beauchamp   (d.1439)   Beauchamp
1st Earl   13th Earl
of Worcester   of Warwick
(k.1422)   (d.1439)

Eleanor = James Tuchet
Holland   5th Baron
(d.1459)   Audley
          (k.1459)

Elizabeth = Edward
Baroness   Neville
Bergavenny   *House of*
(d.1448)   *Neville*

Henry = Cecily
1st Duke   Neville
of Warwick   *House of*
(d.1446)   *Neville*

Anne = Richard
16th Countess   Neville
of Warwick   *House of*
(d.1492)   *Neville*

Anne = Henry Holland
(1439–76)   3rd Duke Exeter
          (k.1477)

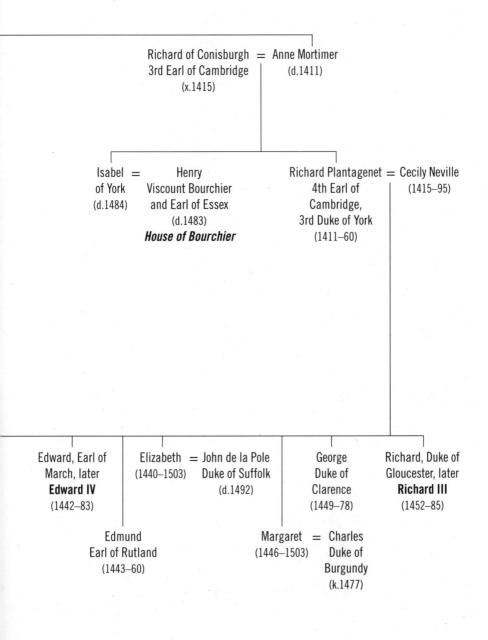

Richard of Conisburgh = Anne Mortimer
3rd Earl of Cambridge   (d.1411)
(x.1415)

Isabel = Henry   Richard Plantagenet = Cecily Neville
of York Viscount Bourchier   4th Earl of   (1415–95)
(d.1484) and Earl of Essex   Cambridge,
          (d.1483)   3rd Duke of York
       House of Bourchier   (1411–60)

Edward, Earl of   Elizabeth = John de la Pole   George   Richard, Duke of
March, later   (1440–1503) Duke of Suffolk   Duke of   Gloucester, later
Edward IV   (d.1492)   Clarence   **Richard III**
(1442–83)   (1449–78)   (1452–85)

Edmund   Margaret = Charles
Earl of Rutland   (1446–1503) Duke of
(1443–60)   Burgundy
                                           (k.1477)

Henry V had not attainted Richard of Conisbrough, so his name-sake son inherited the earldom of Cambridge, although his young stepmother, Maud née Clifford, occupied Conisbrough Castle and several other manors until her death in 1446. When the childless Edward, Duke of York, was killed, however, the king hesitated before granting the boy succession to his uncle's duchy, with entailed holdings in Hertfordshire, Lincolnshire, Northamptonshire, Yorkshire, Wiltshire and Gloucestershire.* Having done so, Henry V kept him in custody for the rest of his reign, ominously guarded by Robert Waterton, one of the men responsible for the murder of Richard II.

In 1423 the minority Council sold Richard of York's wardship for 3,000 marks [£1.27 million] to Ralph Neville, Earl of Westmorland (of whom much more later), who had become the greater of the northern Marcher lords after being instrumental in the defeat of the Percy rebellions. That the Council should have entrusted him with a boy whose very existence called the legitimacy of the Lancastrian dynasty into question was almost certainly because Joan, Ralph's formidable second wife, was Bishop Henry Beaufort's sister.

In 1424 Ralph bestowed the magnificent gift of betrothal to 13-year-old York on the youngest of his sixteen surviving children, 9-year-old Cecily, who was over-indulged all her life and whose imperiousness led to her being known as 'Proud Cis'. Not long afterwards York inherited the earldoms of March and Ulster from his childless maternal uncle Edmund Mortimer, and became the largest landowner in England after the king.

Joan Beaufort inherited York's wardship when Ralph Neville died in October 1425. Until then, York and Cecily grew up together at Raby, one of the finest castles in England. The title, the Durham castles of Raby and Brancepeth, and little else passed to the 19-year-old heir of Ralph's eldest son from his first marriage, who had died in France in 1420. The vastly greater part of Ralph's estate was left to Joan and her children.

She moved with the younger children and Richard of York to

* Richard also inherited York's earldom of Rutland, a landless, courtesy title.

London. York had been presented at court earlier, but from this time he was able to observe at first hand the power struggle between Bishop Beaufort and Gloucester. When Bedford returned to part the warring princes in 1426, he took the time to knight York and other young lords who travelled back to France with him. In 1429 York sailed back to England to take up residence in the royal household and, in May, he and Cecily were married. Later in 1429 they were present at the coronation of 7-year-old Henry VI in Westminster Abbey, and then formed part of the cortege that accompanied him to Rouen and then to Paris, where he was crowned king of France in December 1431.

Twenty-year-old York finally came into his inheritance in May 1432. The 5th Earl of March had left the Mortimer estate heavily encumbered, but the deaths of the dowager Duchess of York in 1431 and of the dowager Countess of March in 1432 gave York the cash flow to settle with his debtors, among them Cardinal Beaufort, who behaved benevolently towards his nephew by marriage. With the Beauforts disqualified, York was next in line to the throne after the king's aging and childless uncles, and the cardinal was keen to win him.

York's estates in England and Wales plus annuities were worth about £4,600 [£2.92 million] per annum. He also had estates in Normandy, and although revenues from them and his Irish earldom of Ulster and the lordships of Connacht and Trim were meagre, his total annual income was well in excess of £5,000. The administrative centre for his holdings in Wales, the Middle March and the West Country was at Ludlow Castle in Shropshire, for Yorkshire at Sandal Castle, and for his eastern holdings at Fotheringhay Castle in Northamptonshire.

To put this in perspective, crown rents from its own lands in England and France, plus church subsidies, feudal and other dues (including payments in lieu of military service), and customs receipts from the export of wool, were about £70,000 [£44.52 million] per annum during 1438–53, the period of Henry VI's personal kingship prior to the loss of English France. The loss of Guyenne, in particular, was a severe blow and reduced annual crown revenues to about £44,000 up to 1461, when the first round of the Wars of the Roses came to a climax.*

York did not, therefore, approach the 'over-mighty subject' standard set by John of Gaunt. There was no reason for Henry VI's entourage to regard him as even a potential threat until, the king being still childless, he became the heir presumptive following the death of Gloucester in 1447. Initially York was treated with deference, and he was described as a 'great prince of our blood' in a royal commission of May 1436, by which he was first appointed the king's Lieutenant of Normandy following the death of Bedford.

The appointment pitched him into a potential disaster. As we saw in Chapter 2, Edmund Beaufort's separate expedition, funded by his uncle Cardinal Beaufort, which might have drawn French forces to the west, was diverted to the Calais theatre, where Gloucester was confronting the treaty-breaking Duke of Burgundy. Meanwhile the French had recaptured Paris and most of the Île-de-France, and had taken the Channel port of Dieppe and its hinterland along the eastern flank of Normandy.

The forces York brought with him permitted Talbot, whom he appointed Marshal of France, to blunt the French offensive. He himself led a campaign to restore English authority in the rebellious Pays de Caux, the large area between the northern Seine valley and the Channel. York's principal contribution, however, was political and administrative. He restored the shaken confidence of the Norman Estates General, and in the process of stripping out reinforcements for Talbot he imposed discipline on predatory English garrisons. He inherited Bedford's military and administrative staff, and continued his custom of hearing grievances in person, assuming the role of viceroy without having been authorized to do so.

Neither in 1436–7 nor during his second lieutenancy in 1441–5 did York command men in battle. His was the leadership of an

---

* From the table in Peter Karsten, *The Military-State-Society Symbiosis*.

able administrator and an even-handed magistrate, who chose good subordinates and made sure they stayed good. Although he did not command the tribal loyalty that exalts the warrior prince, he was widely respected. He had a clear idea of how things should be done, but a high sense of his own worth made him a poor politician. He also regarded greed and corruption with lofty disdain, which made him no friends among his less high-minded peers.

After Talbot went home following the 1436 campaign, York appointed Richard Neville, Earl of Salisbury and his wife Cecily's oldest brother, as his military lieutenant. York had already requested permission to return home, and although his successor Richard Beauchamp, Earl of Warwick, was nominated in May 1437, he did not relieve York until November. Salisbury came at the request of Warwick, with whom he had recently concluded a double matrimonial alliance, but it gave York and his brother-in-law – who was eleven years his senior – an opportunity to get to know each other.

York cited the expiry of the indentures of the men he had brought with him and the inability of the Norman exchequer to cover the cost of renewing them as the reason for wishing to relinquish his post. He was substantially out of pocket, as by the terms of his own indenture he was supposed to be reimbursed from the Norman exchequer, which was now bankrupt.

When Warwick and his wife died in April 1439, Salisbury returned to England to administer their estate and to look after his own children's interest in the succession, which was to keep him busy through the next decade. Asked to resume the lieutenancy, York demanded and was granted a promise of an annual subsidy of £20,000 [£12.72 million] from the English exchequer, plus the viceregal powers previously enjoyed by the Duke of Bedford.

Although York was unable to recruit the nobles summoned by Parliament, a trio of effective field commanders were already in place. William Neville, Baron Fauconberg, another brother-in-law, had come with York in 1436 and was now Lieutenant-General of central Normandy. Thomas, Baron Scales, had spent his entire adult life in Normandy and was marshal and Lieutenant-General of western Normandy. York was to make him godfather to Edward, his eldest son.

However the star, once again, was the newly returned Talbot, 53 years old in 1440. He had fought in Wales and Ireland before first being sent to Normandy in 1420 to separate him from the violent disputes with his peers in which he revelled. York now handed him the troops he had brought with him from England, and also thinned the Norman garrisons to provide him with additional forces. His role was to deal with the eastern sector, facing the main French thrust. Talbot's fast-moving 1441 campaign was a tactical masterpiece that demoralized Charles VII's new army and came close to capturing the king himself.

In early 1442, anticipating the French would renew their offensive, York sent Talbot to England to request urgent reinforcements. This was the only period when the king devoted his full attention to events in France, and he gave Talbot all he asked for. He also created him Earl of Shropshire (although he became known as the Earl of Shrewsbury), and recreated the barony of Lisle for his namesake son. Talbot's expedition did not, however, deliver the hoped-for returns. Royal enthusiasm for the strategy pursued by York and Talbot waned, leading to John Beaufort's ill-fated 1443 expedition.

• ℘ •

On 28 April 1442 Cecily gave birth to the future Edward IV. Given the dynastic significance later attached to the circumstances of his birth, they repay close consideration. The marriage had been barren for ten years when Anne was born in August 1439 in Fotheringhay, York's Northamptonshire castle. After the couple moved to Rouen, baby Henry was born in February 1441, but died unbaptised. Edward was baptized immediately after birth, without ceremony, in a side chapel of Rouen Cathedral. By contrast, after the next boy,

Edmund, was born in May 1443, his baptism was a lavish occasion for public celebration.

Nine months before Edward's birth, York had been dealing with the Pays de Caux rebellion. He could perhaps have made a brief but fruitful visit to Cecily at Rouen in late July 1441, but many years later Edward's youngest brothers (George, born in Dublin in 1449, and Richard, born at Fotheringhay in 1452) were in no doubt that Edward was the product of their mother's adultery. In 1483 the Italian chronicler Dominic Mancini was told that when Cecily learned of Edward's secret marriage to the commoner Elizabeth Woodville in 1464, she 'fell into a frenzy' and threatened to expose him as illegitimate.

One has only to contrast the depiction, from life, of York in the book Talbot presented to Marguerite at Rouen in 1445, with portraits of Edward IV to doubt they could have been father and son. Furthermore, when Edward IV's skeleton was measured in 1789 it was found he was 6ft 4in, much the tallest monarch in English history, and built in proportion. Following the recent discovery of the skeleton of York's namesake youngest, the future Richard III, we know he was slightly built and were it not for severe scoliosis, which reduced his standing height below 5ft, would have been about 5ft 8in. This corresponds closely with a contemporary description of his father as small, dark and 'spare'. Height is almost entirely hereditary, and although there are other cases where short men have had immensely taller sons, there are compelling reasons to doubt that this was one of them.

Cecily, bereft and vulnerable after the death of baby Henry and left alone while York was fire-fighting the 1441 crisis, may well have looked for comfort from someone else. Perhaps the individual was indeed a strapping archer called Blaybourne, named in 1469 by her nephew Richard Neville, Earl of Warwick, without contradiction from her son George, allied with him at the time against Edward. However, the most persuasive indication that Edward was a cuckoo is York's coldness towards him. When they fled England in October

1459 he took Edmund with him to Ireland while Edward, the heir he should have wanted by his side, went with the Nevilles to Calais.

So much of what followed fits the cuckoo hypothesis that to reject it requires the greater leap of faith. Had York denounced Cecily's adultery it would have made him a laughing stock and would have caused a rift with both the Nevilles and the Beauforts. Conversely, by not doing so, he put his haughty wife in his debt. Perhaps working on the principle that if he kept Cecily pregnant she could not cuckold him again, he made sure she bore him Edmund a year later, and Elizabeth the following year.

• ℰℛ •

Following the failure of John Beaufort's expedition the king veered back to York, paying the £20,000 due to him at the end of 1443 unusually promptly. The truce negotiated at Tours in May 1444 greatly reduced York's military expenses and permitted him to exercise a benevolent government that won him the lasting loyalty of the Anglo-Normans. Although he was not paid his dues for 1444, he was granted an appanage (a form of tenure traditionally awarded to younger sons of the French monarchy) of lands around Évreux in south central Normandy, worth £650 [£413,400] a year. In 1445 the king also gave his consent for York to pass his earldoms of March and Cambridge to Edward, and Rutland to Edmund, and even endowed Edmund with lands to go with what was an otherwise hollow title.

York was never a member of a supposed 'war party' led by the Duke of Gloucester – who was anyway, by this time, a spent force. To the contrary, he fully embraced the alternative strategy accomplished by Suffolk at Tours in May 1444 and, as we have seen, organized a lavish reception for Marguerite d'Anjou at Rouen early in 1445. He also sent troops to support a 1444 French invasion of Alsace in 1444, led by the dauphin. Nor did he voice any criticism of the king's decision to appease Charles VII with the cession of

Maine – which was, after all, Edmund Beaufort's fief.

The reason York returned to England in September 1445 was straightforward: he was owed a great deal of money, his indentures were about to expire and he would not renew them unless his own contract was honoured. It was not a case of abandoning a sinking ship: Normandy was at peace, he was enjoying his viceregal role and was willing to resume it. At the suggestion of the king, he had even opened negotiations for a marriage between his son Edward and Princess Madeleine, Charles VII's youngest daughter.

York's claim of £38,666 [£24.6 million] in arrears was a bargaining position. In the end he settled for £26,000 [£16.54 million] plus the borough of Waltham in Essex and the wardship of his 17-year-old son-in-law Henry Holland, who became Duke of Exeter when his father died in 1447. As a descendant of Edward III through both John of Gaunt and Thomas of Woodstock, Holland's claim to being the heir presumptive after Gloucester's death was as good as, and in Holland's opinion better than, York's. The king's consent to the marriage between Holland and York's 8-year-old daughter Anne in 1445 had been a mark of unqualified trust.

Unable to obtain the terms he wanted to return to Normandy, York had no reason to object to the appointment of Edmund Beaufort, and, in the light of subsequent events, must have judged he was well out of it. Nor was he necessarily piqued not to be granted a prominent role in government, as he would have been well aware of Suffolk's magpie-like attitude to power, and of the king's aversion to disagreement. As it was, he attended numerous Council meetings and was a witness to most of the charters issued in 1446–8.

In mid-1446 Bishop Adam Moleyns, Bishop of Chichester, Lord Privy Seal and a key member of the king's inner circle, attempted to attribute the deteriorating situation in Normandy to York's mismanagement. The duke petitioned the king to clear his name and in reply, Moleyns swore he never said such a thing, nor would he of a prince as eminent and highly respected as York. He had merely, he said, reported the opinion of unspecified others. This was, perhaps, a shabby bargaining ploy in the negotiation of the crown's outstanding debt to York – but if so, it was singularly ill-advised.

York was appointed Lord Lieutenant of Ireland in July 1447. It has been argued that this posting was intended to 'get him out of the way', but it manifestly did not. He was permitted to appoint a deputy and did so, not moving to Dublin until two years later. By that time the writing was on the wall for Normandy. Like many of his peers, York wisely sought to put as much distance as possible between himself and the doomed Suffolk administration.

Trying to pacify Ireland was like ploughing the sea, but in the fourteen months York was there he received the submissions of several Irish clan leaders, and showed 'good lordship' to his tenants in Ulster. He also ensured the election of one of Queen Marguerite's chaplains to the archbishopric of Dublin, and sided with James Butler, Earl of Ormonde, in his bitter dispute with Thomas Fitzgerald over the succession to the earldom of Kildare. This was a politically astute display of deference on York's part: Ormonde's namesake son was a member of Henry's inner circle, and was created Earl of Wiltshire the same month that York finally moved to Dublin.

Although hindsight permits us to see some straws in the wind, there is no evidence before 1450 that Richard of York was anything other than a loyal subject, who benefited greatly from the king's 'good lordship', or that the king's councillors believed him to be a threat even after he became the heir presumptive. Ironically, the break came about because, by governing Normandy and Ireland competently in the king's name, he won a reputation around which those who had suffered as a result of the king's fecklessness could rally.

V

FACTION AND FEUD

I T WAS NOT ONLY IN FRANCE THAT HENRY'S DITHERING unwillingness to deal with inconvenient reality created a combustible situation. Failure to impose order on his unruly nobles, and to restrain the rapacity of his household, undermined royal authority at home as well. During the 1440s, fear of legal retribution eroded to the point that nobles and knights increasingly resorted to arms in territorial disputes and competition for local influence.

The most serious breakdown was in the West Country, where a local rivalry was inflamed by Henry's intervention. In 1441, he awarded the prestigious stewardship of the royal duchy of Cornwall to Thomas Courtenay, 13th Earl of Devon, a descendant of Edward I and husband to Margaret Beaufort, Henry VI's aunt. This was the year Eleanor Cobham, the Duke of Gloucester's wife, was convicted of witchcraft and Devon's appointment was just one of several similar awards designed to affirm the Beaufort clan at a national level.

The rather large fly in the ointment was that the office had previously been awarded, for life, to William Bonville, a member of Suffolk's affinity. Bonville was the most prominent of a group of gentry and lesser nobility whose influence in the West Country had grown during Devon's long minority (1422–33), when his mother devoted her best efforts to frustrating her son. She continued to reside at Tiverton, the seat of the earls of Devon, and to control half the revenues from the estate until her death in 1441.

Bonville's second marriage, in 1427, was to Margaret Courtenay, widow of John, Baron Harington, and daughter of the 12th Earl of Devon – hence Thomas Courtenay's aunt. Bonville also married his namesake son from his first marriage to Margaret Courtenay's daughter from hers.* From Devon's point of view, it was bad enough that Bonville had gained so much from marriage with his own family. What made it all the more galling was that the dowager duchess's occupation of Tiverton obliged him to make his residence at Colcombe Castle, 2 miles from Bonville's main residence at Shute, which he had obtained by his marriage to Courtenay's aunt.

The Earl of Devon saw the appointment of Bonville in 1437 as royal steward in Cornwall for life as reflecting the government's belief that his rival was now the pre-eminent political figure in the West Country. Despite the erosion of his family's status, however, Devon's electoral and legal patronage remained more extensive than Bonville's. To prove the point he sent his retainers out to provoke Bonville's, secure in the knowledge he could frustrate any legal recourse by his rival.

Low intensity brawling began in 1439 and continued into 1441 despite a feeble royal attempt at arbitration. This was when the king appointed Devon to the stewardship of Cornwall, without revoking his prior grant to Bonville. Although the new appointment was promptly withdrawn, it was a classic illustration of the king's unerring instinct for getting the worst of both worlds. The consequences could have been more immediately dire had chance not intervened through the death of Devon's mother. Being able at last to take up residence at Tiverton Castle seems to have mollified him. In December 1441 Devon and Bonville were formally reconciled and required to post bonds for future good behaviour.

It is not clear whether Bonville renounced the stewardship of

---

* Their son became Baron Harington in 1458 following the death of his maternal grandfather. When all the male Bonvilles were killed his daughter Cecily became sole heir of both the Harington and Bonville estates.

Cornwall, but Courtenay was definitely re-awarded it in 1444. Bonville, meanwhile, had been appointed seneschal (steward) of Gascony and sailed to Bordeaux in March 1443, not returning to Devon permanently until 1447. Possibly he judged the Cornwall office not worth the aggravation and concentrated instead on strengthening his political connections. He was with Suffolk at the betrothal of Marguerite d'Anjou in May 1444, and married his eldest daughter to William Tailboys, a member of the king's household and Suffolk's most notorious henchman.

• ∾ •

As a living embodiment of the collapse of the rule of law under Henry VI, Tailboys almost merits a chapter in his own right. He was a wealthy man with estates in Lincolnshire and in Northumberland, where he owned the large moorland estate of Redesdale. Yet he chose to become the leader of a gang of thugs that rampaged through southern Lincolnshire during most of the 1440s. He overreached himself in March 1448 when he assaulted a servant of Robert, Baron Willoughby, who had the influence to get writs issued against Tailboys and his followers. Suffolk, however, prevailed on the sheriff of Lincolnshire not to enforce them.

Tailboys also developed a murderous hatred of Ralph, Baron Cromwell, another major Lincolnshire lord and a member of Richard of York's ducal council. In 1443 Tailboys' patron, Suffolk, had forced Cromwell to resign as Lord Treasurer after ten years' service, and Cromwell returned the favour by leading parliamentary attacks on Suffolk. Incensed by this, in November 1449 Tailboys physically assaulted Cromwell as he emerged from Parliament.

There followed the first impeachment by the House of Commons since 1386, in which Tailboys was 'named and famed for a common murderer, manslayer, rioter and continual breaker of [the king's] peace'. He was held in the Tower of London for twelve months while the case against him was prepared. He spent the next five years in prison while a series of judgements were made against him, notably damages awarded to Cromwell in the amount of £2,000 [£1.27 million].

• ❧ •

Bonville's long association with Suffolk paid off in July 1449, at the end of the first Parliament summoned that year, when he was created Baron Bonville of Chewton. In a defiant signal to Thomas Courtenay, Earl of Devon, Bonville chose a coat of arms modelled on the arms of the duchy of Cornwall. The same Parliament saw the royal favourite James Butler, son of the Earl of Ormonde, created Earl of Wiltshire. He and Bonville were to make common cause against Courtenay. These were, however, among the last significant acts of patronage by Suffolk.

The impeachment of Tailboys started the rockslide that swept Suffolk from power, but the build-up of instability had been many years in the making. He was never as powerful as he seemed, evidence of which was his inability to maintain order even in East Anglia, his area of greatest influence. By far the richest contemporary source for our period are the Paston letters, a collection of over a thousand letters and papers to, from and relating to the Paston family of Norfolk between 1422 and 1509. They contain a detailed account of an outrageous breach of the peace committed against the family, which we may take as representative of the lawlessness prevailing in the county.

It involved the manor of Gresham, 4 miles inland from the north Norfolk coast. In 1427 William Paston bought Gresham from Thomas Chaucer, father of Alice, Duchess of Suffolk. After William's death in 1444 his son John enjoyed unchallenged possession of the manor until 1448, when it was forcibly seized by 17-year-old Robert, namesake eldest son of Baron Hungerford and, by right of his wife, Baron Moleyns. Although heir apparent to the wealthy barony of Hungerford, with the expectation of inheriting an even larger estate from his mother, sole heir of William, Baron Botreaux, he chafed at the relatively minor extent of his Moleyns estate.

Moleyns' teenaged hormones and aristocratic arrogance made him a willing listener to the malicious advice of John Heydon of Baconsthorpe, a lawyer who, in association with the Keeper of the King's Wardrobe Thomas Tuddenham – both members in good standing of Suffolk's affinity – exercised a predatory ascendancy at the expense of the local gentry. Heydon, no doubt seeking to promote lucrative litigation, persuaded Moleyns that John Paston's title to the manor of Gresham could be challenged. Instead of suing, however, Moleyns simply took possession of the manor by force in February 1448.

It being pointless to bring a legal action in a jurisdiction run by Heydon and Tuddenham, John Paston obtained the intercession of William Wainflete, Henry Beaufort's successor as Bishop of Winchester and the king's right-hand man in the projects dearest to him, the building of colleges at Eton and Cambridge. Moleyns' solicitors made no serious attempt to defend the spurious title Heydon had created for their principal at a conference sponsored by Wainflete, and urged Paston to put his case to Moleyns directly. Paston tried to obtain an audience with him at several places, but was never received.

Accordingly, in early October 1449 he simply reoccupied his property, which the absentee Moleyns had failed to guard adequately. Paston did not make the same mistake and remained in possession with armed retainers. It took time for news of his coup to reach Moleyns in Wiltshire, and for him to plan his response, but in late January 1450 upwards of a thousand armed men hired by Moleyns launched a full-scale assault while John Paston was in London on business.

Margaret Paston held out with twelve servants, who put up stout resistance but were soon forced to surrender. Margaret was carried bodily from the mansion, which was then thoroughly ransacked and left in ruins. Paston estimated the damages at £200 [£127,200].

Before they left, Moleyns' rent-a-mob told Margaret that if they had found John or his solicitor, they would have killed them.

Paston sent a petition for redress to Parliament, and another to Wainflete, but 1450 was to be a year of unending crises for the regime and neither petition prospered. In subsequent years, Paston's insistence on obtaining redress was thwarted by Moleyns' seven-year captivity in France and the influence at court of the Duke of Norfolk, who made common aristocratic cause against Paston. In the end, all Paston could obtain was Moleyns' tacit abandonment of a claim he should never have made. His spiteful vandalism remained unpunished.

The swaggering behaviour of the knightly class has a flavour of the American Wild West about it. Then as later, men trained at arms and very little else, many with what today we coyly call anger management issues, were a very present danger. Still, we should beware of believing that anything like a complete breakdown of legal authority occurred. Trouble was concentrated in counties where there was no locally dominant lord, or where he was not normally resident. The biggest offender in this respect was Suffolk, permanently in attendance on the king, who perforce delegated the management of his local interests and affinities to crooks like Tuddenham and Heydon.

· ↄ ·

The Harcourt–Stafford feud can be taken as representative of many local disputes that flourished in the absence of a dominant magnate or any realistic legal deterrent. Robert Harcourt of Stanton Harcourt in Oxfordshire enjoyed the 'good lordship' of Suffolk, while Humphrey Stafford of Grafton in Worcestershire was a distant kinsman of the Duke of Buckingham. In May 1448, the two knights, each with an entourage of armed retainers, encountered each other in Coventry. An exchange of insults between Harcourt and Stafford's eldest son Richard led to a brawl in which Richard and two of Harcourt's men were killed. Stafford himself was unhorsed and only narrowly escaped death.

The next day Harcourt, who had initiated the violence by striking Richard with his sword, was charged with murder by the city coroner and detained. Suffolk abused the Privy Seal to order the local sheriff not to proceed against Harcourt, who was released. After Suffolk was impeached, Stafford with 200 men made an overnight march on Stanton Harcourt. Harcourt took refuge in the tower of the parish church and withstood a six-hour siege during which the tower was peppered with arrows, killing one of his men. After a failed attempt to burn him out, Stafford withdrew.

In 1450, faced with the popular uprising known as Jack Cade's Rebellion, the king quickly pardoned all involved in the Harcourt–Stafford affray. Less than two months later Humphrey Stafford and his brother were killed after leading a column of the king's forces into an ambush set by Cade. Retribution for the killing of Richard Stafford was delayed until 1470, when Humphrey's illegitimate son murdered Robert Harcourt.

Cade's Rebellion itself drew its strength from the chronic abuse of power by agents of James Fiennes, Lord Saye and Sele since 1447, the king's bosom friend, Lord Treasurer and household chamberlain. Saye was represented in Kent by his son-in-law William Cromer, whose underlings duplicated the nefarious activities of Tuddenham and Heydon in Norfolk. Although there were no outrageous assaults comparable to Moleyns' attack on the manor at Gresham, rapacious lawlessness prevailed across Kent and East Sussex.

The king's regular progresses through East Anglia and the southeast were not replicated in the West Country, the Welsh Marches and the North, which were a law unto themselves. However, even when he did visit a region he was not accompanied by judges to hold assizes (properly 'commissions of oyer and terminer'), nor did he receive complaints or dispense justice himself. Henry's neglect of his duty as first magistrate was to prove particularly damaging in areas like Kent, where his household members were most dominant.

• ℰℐ •

We should also consider the Ampthill dispute, out of historical sequence but a classic illustration of the continuing undercurrent of aristocratic lawlessness. According to a petition later presented to Parliament, in June 1452 Henry Holland, Duke of Exeter, with 300 men seized a Bedfordshire estate, including the manor and castle of Ampthill, owned by Lord Cromwell. During his years as Lord Treasurer Cromwell had built up holdings that gave him an income only exceeded by the greater magnates. By contrast Exeter's landed patrimony produced an income well below the amount expected of a duke, and he did not even inherit the whole of it until the death of his stepmother in 1457. He was consumed with envy.

Exeter's claim was entirely spurious, concocted with the suborned help of three servants of the previous owner of Ampthill, now dead, and by one of his executors. Possessed to an even greater degree of the aristocratic arrogance that motivated Moleyns' seizure of Gresham, Exeter calculated he could spin out legal wrangling over Ampthill until the elderly and heirless Cromwell died, after which possession would be the proverbial nine-tenths of the law. Exeter was not clever enough to have conceived the scheme, and it was probably Tailboys who suggested manufacturing the claim as part of his feud with Cromwell.

The supposition hardens into certainty when we consider the second prong of Exeter's assault, which was to make a charge of treason against Cromwell, his allies the Bedfordshire and Marcher Lord Edmund Grey of Ruthyn, and John Fastolf, an East Anglian knight. The accusation was made by Robert Collinson, parson of Chelsfield in Kent, who swore that the leader of a post-Cade revolt in Kent, condemned for treason, had confessed, on the hurdle drawing him to be hanged and quartered, that Cromwell and the other two were traitors. Deathbed confessions carried a great deal of legal weight, as it was assumed nobody would wish to go into the afterlife with a lie on their lips.

Cromwell was ordered to appear in the Lord Chancellor's office and was suspended from the Council. However, in February 1453 Cromwell submitted a dossier that damned Collinson as a liar, a trickster and an epic whoremonger. Collinson's charges were dismissed, but Exeter's purpose had been achieved: a high-level panel of arbiters appointed by the king to decide the Ampthill dispute had been unable to proceed while a charge of treason was pending, and now events pushed it to the bottom of a pile of more urgent business.

Exeter countered Cromwell's suits with counter-suits and intimidated the sheriff of Bedfordshire, while juries could not be empanelled to hear the suits for fear of what Exeter might do to them. This moved the king to make one of his sporadic and typically ineffectual efforts to bring his nobles under control by briefly detaining Exeter at Windsor Castle, Cromwell at Wallingford Castle and Grey at Pevensey Castle.

Cromwell, who died in 1456, is a deeply unsympathetic figure, only somewhat redeemed by the fact that Exeter was even more loathsome. He did, however, leave us an excellent summary of the legal anarchy that increasingly characterized the reign of King Henry VI:

> Where any of so great estate puts any man out of his lands and tenements and wrongs him of his goods, the aggrieved party suing for his remedy in that behalf by special assize or otherwise there will be no judge, learned counsel nor jury [that will] take upon them to sit, come or appear, nor sheriff to make any restitution or mediate or do anything appertaining to his office in such case at any special or general assize or other place where remedy by course of law should be had.

VI

DEFEAT AND HUMILIATION

LTHOUGH APPOINTED TO THE LIEUTENANCY OF Normandy for three years in December 1446, Edmund Beaufort did not move there until early 1448. His own men took over from York's Anglo-Normans during 1447, but the province was essentially leaderless during a period of great uncertainty about the peace policy launched in 1444. Charles VII had agreed to extend the two-year truce agreed at Tours, but Henry failed to follow through with a journey to meet him in France in 1446. The main reason was financial – he had exhausted his credit to pay for Suffolk's two embassies and could not afford the magnificence the occasion demanded.

A greatly aggravating factor was Edmund's insistence that he be compensated for the loss of his holdings in Maine before he would consent to handing over the county, as privately agreed by Henry in a letter to his 'dear uncle of France' dated 22 December 1445. The letter stressed entreaties by his 'most dear and well-beloved companion the queen', who had been assured by her father and Charles himself that the cession of Maine would lead to a lasting peace.

Finally Edmund obtained a settlement of 10,000 *livres tournois* [nearly £1 million], to be paid annually by the already hard-pressed Norman exchequer. Only then did he move to Rouen, perhaps to ensure he received the agreed compensation. Although he was supposed to share it with the Anglo-Normans who would also be dispossessed, he did not. Consequently a deputation of English knights and squires obstructed the negotiations for the handover, to the point that in February–March 1448 they were besieged at Le Mans and even bombarded by a French army commanded by Pierre de Brézé. The knights handed over the town on 15 March after Charles VII agreed to compensate them himself, but of course they never saw a penny.

Henry was so greatly relieved that on 31 March he recreated the dukedom of Somerset for Edmund. This was further salt in the wounds of the dispossessed Anglo-Normans, particularly those of Richard of York's affinity, some of whom trickled back to England seeking his 'good lordship'. The trickle became a flood in 1449–50, and was the reason York became such a determined enemy of Somerset; which, since Somerset enjoyed the unconditional support of the king, brought York into ultimately mortal conflict with the house of Lancaster.

Somerset's performance of his duties as Lieutenant of Normandy was abject. When all the arguments about the inevitability of the outcome are weighed, the outstanding fact is that he made no serious preparation to resist French aggression. He appears to have shared Henry's wishful thinking, in the teeth of abundant evidence that Richemont's military organization was well advanced and could only have one purpose. Even if there might have been some doubt previously, there can have been none after the siege of Le Mans.

Possibly he thought the French would continue to nibble at the edges of Normandy through a process of armed negotiation. This would have granted him time to accumulate as much money as he could before returning to England, leaving his successor to deal with the consequences. The French did not oblige, and Somerset's ruin would have been complete were it not for the king's dogged loyalty to him, which may have been born in part of guilty knowledge that he should never have appointed Somerset to an office which required great personal wealth.

Another, stronger reason was that the collapse of the truce was

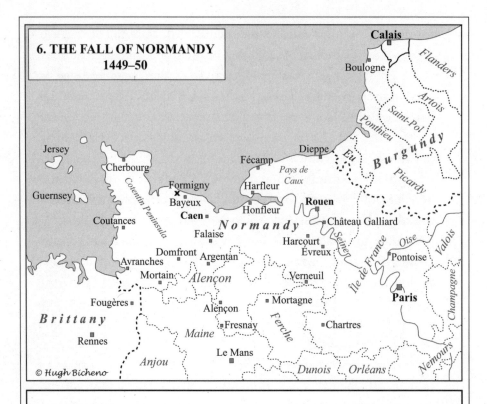

6. THE FALL OF NORMANDY 1449–50

Calais
Boulogne
Flanders
Artois
Saint-Pol
Ponthieu
Burgundy
Picardy
Eu
Jersey
Cherbourg
Dieppe
Fécamp
Pays de Caux
Harfleur
Formigny
Bayeux
Honfleur
Rouen
Château Galliard
Guernsey
Coutances
Cotentin Peninsula
Caen
Normandy
Seine
Oise
Valois
Falaise
Harcourt
Évreux
Île de France
Pontoise
Domfront
Argentan
Avranches
Verneuil
Mortain
Alençon
Paris
Champagne
Fougères
Mortagne
Brittany
Alençon
Ferche
Chartres
Maine
Fresnay
Rennes
Le Mans
Anjou
Dunois
Orléans
Nemours

© Hugh Bicheno

SEQUENCE OF EVENTS

	1449		**1450**
24 Mar.	Surienne takes Fougères	1 Jan.	Fall of Harfleur
19 Jul.	Brézé invests Verneuil	17–18 Jan.	Fall of Honfleur
30 Jul.	Declaration of war	15 Mar.	Kyriell lands Cherbourg
24 Aug.	Fall of Verneuil	22 Mar.	Fall of Fresnay
25 Aug.	Fall of Mortain	15 Apr.	Battle of Formigny
End Aug.	Fall of Évreux	12 May	Fall of Avranches
	Fall of Harcourt	16 May	Fall of Bayeux
Early Sep.	Fall of Fécamp	5–25 Jun.	Siege of Caen
	Start Avranches siege	6 Jul.	Start Falaise siege
	Fall of Coutances		Start Cherbourg siege
Sep.	Alençon reconquers his duchy	21 Jul.	Fall of Falaise
	Fresnay holds out	23 Jul.	Start Domfront siege
Late Sep.	Fall of Argentan	2 Aug.	Fall of Domfront
	Start Château Galliard siege	12 Aug.	Fall of Cherbourg
16–22 Oct.	Siege of Rouen		
23 Nov.	Fall of Château Galliard		
	Fall of Fougères		
8 Dec.	Start Harfleur siege		

precipitated by a personal decision made by Henry. During the night of 23/24 March 1449, the Aragonese captain known as François de Surienne, a Garter knight for his services to the English crown, took the Breton border fortress of Fougères in a daring escalade. The purpose was to force the Duke of Brittany to release Gilles of Brittany, Henry VI's childhood friend, imprisoned since June 1446. Henry knew Gilles had been arrested in the first instance by French soldiers acting on the orders of Charles VII. He regarded it as a breach of the truce, and the seizure of Fougères as therefore justified.

Charles, however, saw it as the opportunity he had been waiting for to conclude an explicitly anti-English alliance with Brittany, denounce the truce, and to declare war on 31 July. A year and a fortnight later, to the exhilarated satisfaction – and no small surprise – of the French commanders (among them Marguerite's father, René d'Anjou), the last of Henry V's and the Duke of Bedford's conquests were in French hands.

Hardly any of the smaller fortified towns put up a fight. In most, the inhabitants opened their gates and welcomed the French armies or, as at Verneuil, helped them scale the walls. Most of the English garrisons that prevented this were persuaded to capitulate on generous terms. One such was Regnéville, a port on the coast of the Cotentin peninsula near Coutances, where the king's stepfather Owen Tudor surrendered to the Bretons after six days. He was permitted to take ship to England with his men, their dependants and possessions.

Obdurate garrisons were bypassed, to fall like ripe fruit in due course. The outstanding example was Fresnay-sur-Sarthe, a small town on the border of Maine. Fresnay held out from September 1449, when the Duke of Alençon recovered his long-lost county in a whirlwind campaign, until March 1450, when the last hope of relief was extinguished. Somerset must have expected many more such hold-outs to buy him time, but Fresnay was held by Anglo-Normans dispossessed in Maine, who judged they had nothing more to lose. Somerset's own fief of Mortain welcomed the French invaders with open arms, as did Évreux, the chief town of Richard of York's appanage.

The English were vastly outnumbered. Not counting the Bretons, the four French armies numbered over 30,000 against 6,000–8,000 English in scattered garrisons. But the crowning humiliation was that they were defeated by equal numbers in the only pitched battle of the campaign. On 15 April 1450, about 4,500 men sent from England under Thomas Kyriell (the only knight banneret to respond to John Beaufort's summons in 1443), joined by 1,500 drawn from the Cotentin peninsula garrisons, were routed at Formigny by two French armies totalling about 5,000. The French commanders were Richemont himself and the Duke of Bourbon, leader of the 1440 revolt against Charles VII.

There is a common belief that Formigny was the first battle won by field artillery, but its role was only indirect. It was an encounter battle in which neither side had been well served by scouts. Taken by surprise and outnumbered, Bourbon did employ a couple of light cannon: but his aim was to keep the enemy out of longbow range. After the English archers rushed the guns he was in serious trouble and was on the verge of defeat when Richemont, marching towards the sound of the guns, appeared on Kyriell's flank. So, although the guns brought about the timely convergence of the French armies, it was tactical agility, supposedly the decisive advantage enjoyed by the English, which won the day.

The new French guns did, however, bring about the rapid capitulation of major fortresses that in former times had confidently withstood prolonged sieges. In 1414–15 the port of Harfleur held out against Henry V's primitive bombards for over a year. It fell in three weeks in 1450. Massive Château Gaillard, built on an immensely strong position overlooking the Seine, resisted Henry V for a year in 1419. In 1449 it was battered into submission in less than two months, and was never rebuilt.

Accordingly, when in 1452 York accused Somerset of treachery for capitulating at Rouen after a siege lasting barely a week, and seven months later at Caen after twenty days, he could not argue that further resistance would have affected the final outcome. By convention a fortress commander would hold out while there was hope his own side might send an army to lift the siege, and there was no dishonour in seeking terms when there was no such prospect. It was Somerset's haste and the terms he negotiated that York judged contemptible.

Somerset had thoroughly alienated the people of Rouen, probably because he needed to wring every penny out of his lieutenancy. Even though the Norman capital had much the largest garrison, commanded by none other than Somerset's fearsome brother-in-law John Talbot, Earl of Shrewsbury, in October 1449 they abandoned the city to a popular uprising and pulled back to the enormous castle. The main French armies were elsewhere and their heavy guns were at Château Gaillard, so even the minimum precondition of an effective siege had not been met when Somerset capitulated.

Along with the castle, he surrendered the fortified towns of the Pays de Caux and the port of Honfleur on the southern bank of the Seine estuary, which would have isolated Harfleur, on the north bank. In addition, he agreed to pay a ransom of 50,000 Norman *saluts d'or* [£7,314,000] for himself and his family to travel to Caen. As a guarantee he left Talbot and four other officers as hostages.

Intriguingly, Talbot bore Somerset no ill will; indeed he and his sons were to support him against York in the following years. A hypothesis to fit these facts is that by becoming a hostage for Somerset's debt Talbot avoided being held to ransom in his own right. What is generally judged to have been an exceptionally shameful act turns out, on closer examination, to have been probably an act of clever collusion between the two peers.

The captain of Honfleur refused to obey Somerset's order and held out until after Harfleur surrendered, capitulating on 18 January 1450. Talbot remained a hostage until July, when Andrew Trollope, one of his retainers and captain of Falaise, one of the last Norman towns still in English hands, made his release a condition of capitulation. Talbot swore never to bear arms against France again, and was to abide by the letter of his oath. He was unarmed when killed three years later during the last battle of the Hundred Years War.

The Earl of Oxford's son Robert Vere, commanding the Caen garrison, was able to prevent a revolt by the inhabitants. Besieged during June 1450 by an army led by Charles VII himself, he conducted an active defence of the city that may have included a bribe to Scots members of Charles's bodyguard to kill him. This, at least, was the charge levelled against them in 1453. One of the illustrations in the 1487 *Vigiles du roi Charles VII* shows an English sortie against the French bombards (the modern guns had not yet arrived), which finally put a stone shot through the window of the room where Somerset's duchess and children were sheltered.

Somerset immediately agreed terms of capitulation including an astronomical ransom of 300,000 écus *d'or* [£43,884,000], with 18 hostages as surety, to permit Somerset, his family and the garrison to evacuate by sea. The ransom was totally unrealistic – it would have wiped out both the Norman and English exchequers – and the hostages were later released for the derisory sums they raised themselves. Understandably uncertain of the loyalty of his troops or of the reception awaiting him in England, Somerset sailed separately to Calais.

With the Normandy debacle well under way, the Parliament summoned to vote emergency funds in November 1449 was in a vengeful mood. Driven by Lord Cromwell, the Tailboys impeachment segued into a full-scale parliamentary attack on Suffolk. The first notable rat to desert the sinking ship was Adam Moleyns, Bishop of Chichester, who in early December resigned the office of Lord Privy Seal, pleading ill health and a belated desire to attend to his neglected diocese, which he had visited only to be invested in 1446.

A month later, he was in Portsmouth delivering wages to the troops assembling for Kyriell's expedition when a group of Normandy veterans seized him and announced he must die for his role in handing over Maine. He tried to save himself by accusing Suffolk of embezzling the money intended for the defence of Normandy, but was slaughtered regardless. The murder of a bishop was a deeply shocking act in itself; but for the royal household the more worrying aspect was that the killers were men who had served under York, who may have been avenging Moleyns' attempt to blame him for the parlous state of Normandy's defences.

Suffolk issued a statement denying Moleyns' accusation at the opening of the new session of Parliament on 23 January 1450, but it backfired. The Commons cited his own words as proof 'there was an heavy noise of infamy upon him', which required he should be brought to trial. Suffolk's response was worded in a way to imply that the murdered bishop was indeed to blame for the surrender of Maine. This was demeaning: everybody knew the king was personally responsible, but it was treasonable to say so. The feeling was that Suffolk, having profited so greatly from being the king's chief minister, should now manfully accept his role as chief scapegoat.

On 7 February, the Speaker read out a very long indictment accusing Suffolk of a fantastical plot with the French king to depose Henry VI and to replace him with Suffolk's son John, whom he had betrothed to his ward Margaret Beaufort to give him a claim to the throne. This and other wild accusations about dealings with the French were simply embellishments to the core charges, which concerned the alienation of crown lands and rights to himself and his affinity. The result, said the indictment, was that there was not enough left to support the king's government, requiring the Commons to make good the deficit with taxation.

Suffolk was consigned to the Tower to await trial. When he was brought out on 9 March, he did the only thing he could and cast himself on the king's mercy. On 17 March the king summoned the lords to his inner chamber. In their presence, Suffolk knelt before him to assert his innocence, and once again threw himself on his mercy. Henry made no judgement on the charges against him, but banished him for five years from 1 May. The intention, clearly, was to recall him when the heat had died down.

Suffolk departed for his home in Ipswich, heavily guarded against a London mob intent on lynching him in revenge for what they believed was his murder of 'Good Duke Humphrey' in February 1447. When he got home he put his affairs in order and wrote a loving valedictory letter to his young son. The second paragraph, couched as advice, gives us an insight into how Suffolk himself had won the unreserved confidence of the king (my italics):

> Next [to God], above all earthly things, be a true liegeman in heart, in will, in thought, in deed, unto the King, our elder, most high, and dread Sovereign Lord, to whom both ye and I be so much bound; charging you, as father can and may, rather to die than to be the contrary, or to know anything that were against the welfare and prosperity of his most royal person, but that so far as your body and life may stretch, ye live and die to defend it *and to let His Highness have knowledge thereof,* in all the haste ye can.

Suffolk sailed from Ipswich on 30 April, bound for Calais. His two ships were intercepted by a flotilla led by the 'great ship' *Nicholas of the Tower*, flying the royal colours, which summoned him. He had himself rowed across without hesitation, perhaps believing the king had changed his mind, only to be seized, 'tried' for treason by the crew and his head hacked off with a cutlass. His torso was cast ashore at Dover.

Although Henry and Marguerite were devastated by the news, the circumstances of Suffolk's death were not investigated. It was clearly not an act of piracy – there must have been collusion with the master of Suffolk's ship for the interception to take place at all, and no pirate operated a 'great ship'. One is inescapably drawn to the conclusion that the murder was the work of young Henry Holland, Duke of Exeter. As Lord Admiral, Exeter's father had enjoyed a unique naval affinity, which made him, in practice, pirate-in-chief. The shamelessly corrupt Court of Admiralty was an extremely lucrative operation that provided his principal source of income, and continued to do so for his successors well into the seventeenth century.

When the older Exeter died, Suffolk added the Court of Admiralty to his own bag of offices. As we saw in Chapter 5, without the income from the court the younger Exeter was decidedly poor. Not only did this give him reason to hate Suffolk, but he would also still have had contacts within the seafaring community made while his father was alive. The remaining members of the royal household would not have dared suggest to the king that a prince of his blood would be capable of such a thing, and the office of Lord Admiral now reverted to the psychopathic young man.*

The household's suspicion that Exeter had assassinated Suffolk would have been subsumed into a growing panic about what they believed was a greater threat. Their fear, which soon infected the king himself, was that the murders of Moleyns and Suffolk were the product of a conspiracy with Richard of York at its heart. Suffolk's downfall had been initiated by Lord Cromwell, one of York's councillors, and Exeter was York's son-in-law. To their fearful minds it looked a lot like two plus two adding up to a deeply ominous four.

After the leader of the London riot against the release of Suffolk suffered the gruesome fate reserved for traitors, his quarters were sent to Coventry and Winchester, where there had been disturbances of the peace, and to Newbury and Stamford, where there had not. They were, however, boroughs owned by York. Further panicked by a lightning strike that severely damaged his favourite palace at Eltham, and by an outbreak of the plague, the king fled to Leicester. On his way there, another man earned a traitor's death by lashing the ground in front of Henry's horse, calling for York to do the same to the king's government.

---

* As Constable of the Tower he took such pleasure in torturing people that the rack became known as 'the Duke of Exeter's daughter'.

There is not the slightest evidence that York had anything to do with any of the shocks suffered by the court at this time. Barring the lightning strike, they were the result of a long period of misgovernment. This was not, however, an explanation the king and his household were prepared to contemplate. Much better to blame an external agency of infinite cunning and resource – the essential ingredient of every conspiracy theory throughout history.

VII

HENRY AND RICHARD

Suffolk's assassination on 2 May 1450 was the catalyst for a cascade of events that ripped apart the cocoon around the king. William Cromer, sheriff of Kent and Sussex and son-in-law of Lord Saye and Sele, took custody of Suffolk's body and threatened retaliation against the people of Kent. Summoned by commissioners of array on their own authority, and led by their local constables, in June several thousand minor Kentish gentry, yeomen and labourers assembled at Ashford and marched on London, joined by a smaller contingent from east Sussex.

The host, at this point without a conspicuous leader, camped at Blackheath, where the main roads from Kent converged south of the Thames. When ordered to disperse by the king's heralds on 15 June, they said they were not rebels but petitioners, and would remain until their grievances were heard. However, the spokesman they elected was a bold ex-soldier, possibly of Irish origin, called Jack Cade – who had chosen to call himself Mortimer 'for to have the more favour of the people'.

The name was a red alert. By blood, the Mortimer claim to the throne was better than the ruling dynasty's, and Richard of York was the heir to the claim. Lest there should be any doubt why Cade chose the name, the first item in the 'The Complaint of the Poor Commons of Kent' denounced those said to be spreading rumours that York wished to seize the throne. Their purpose, the petition declared, was to make the king 'hate and destroy his real friends and to cherish the false traitors that call themselves his friends'.

This appears to be an accurate appreciation. The king's household were now a leaderless rabble, and rather than accept their responsibility for the widespread unrest it suited them to blame York, now out of the way in Ireland and unable to defend himself. The Kentish petition went on to denounce the abuses committed by the agents of the absentee lords of Kent, with particular venom directed at Lord Saye. It demanded that the king banish Suffolk's 'false progeny and affinity' and replace them with York, the Dukes of Buckingham and Norfolk, and 'all true earls and barons of this land'.

It is not for this but for the immortal dialogue with Dick, a confederate, put in their mouths by Shakespeare, that the spirit of Jack Cade lives on among the English-speaking peoples:

> Dick: The first thing we do, let's kill all the lawyers.
> Cade: Nay, that I mean to do.

While still at Leicester the king summoned Buckingham, who had been awarded Gloucester's palace at Penshurst, near Tonbridge in Kent, and Jacquetta's husband Richard Woodville, created Baron Rivers in 1448, with lands around Maidstone on the road from Ashford to London. They were commissioned to raise troops from their estates and meet the king in London, where he returned on 8 June. Joined by troops from royalist Cheshire under Lord Stanley, and the personal retinues of Henry Percy, Earl of Northumberland, the Neville Earls of Salisbury and Warwick, and the veteran Thomas, Baron Scales, the king rejected the petition and led his army across the river to confront the Blackheath encampment.

The massed petitioners melted away that night – and then Henry overplayed his hand. He sent punitive columns into Kent under Percy, Woodville, Scales and Buckingham's kinsmen, the brothers Humphrey (he of the recent attack on Stanton Harcourt) and William Stafford. The Staffords' column was ambushed by Cade and the two brothers killed in woods near Sevenoaks. Henry then compounded his error by ordering Buckingham's and Woodville's Kentish men to avenge the defeat. Instead they mutinied and declared solidarity with Cade.

From browbeating arrogance to abject panic was for Henry but a short step, and he fled to Westminster via Marguerite's (previously Gloucester's) palace at Greenwich. All would have contrasted his behaviour with the regal courage of young Richard II in 1381, when he rode out of London with only an escort to face down the so-called Peasants' Revolt. Henry also ordered Lord Saye and William Cromer detained in the Tower, and issued a proclamation echoing the petition's denunciation of unspecified traitors.

Once given into, fear is uncontrollable and this was the moment when Marguerite first stepped up to provide the courage her husband lacked. Despite the entreaties of the mayor and aldermen of London, Henry could not be persuaded to stay and she guided his further flight to the comforting security of her castles at Berkhamsted in south Hertfordshire and Kenilworth outside Coventry, the latter at the heart of her substantial Midlands dower. She, however, heroically remained at Greenwich, no more than a mile from Blackheath.

Henry tried to save Saye, but Exeter, the Constable of the Tower, refused to release him because the king had earlier ordered a formal trial for his friend. Cade returned to Blackheath on 23 June wearing the armour of one of the slain Staffords. Now that the fear of reprisals seemed to have been confirmed, his following – stripped of the respectable element – was far more radical. Another large gathering of petitioners emerged from Essex and on 2 July the two groups converged on the city. Cade occupied Southwark, next to London Bridge, whose ropes he cut so it could not be drawn against him, while the Essex men advanced north of the river to Mile End, opposite Aldgate.

Named by the rebels as one of the 'false traitors', Bishop William Ayscough of Salisbury, who had officiated at the king's wedding and was his revered confessor, fled London in mid-June for his castle at

Sherborne in Dorset, with a caravan bearing his personal wealth. He got only as far as the monastery at Edington, in Wiltshire. On 29 June a mob dragged him out of the church where he was celebrating Mass, stripped him of his finery and hacked him to death. They then looted his caravan of goods and cash worth about £4,000 [£2.5 million] and sacked the monastery, while others despoiled his palace at Salisbury.

Other senior churchmen found themselves under attack around this time. Only their armed retainers saved the Bishops of Bath and Wells, Coventry and Norwich, and the Abbots of Gloucester and Hyde, from sharing Ayscough's fate. Intriguingly, the king's close friends Reginald Boulers, Abbot of Gloucester and soon to be Bishop of Hereford, and John Sutton, Baron Dudley, fled for sanctuary to Richard of York's castle at Ludlow.

It is telling that – with the exception of Hyde (today in Greater Manchester) – all these attacks took place in areas where Lollardy remained strong. Lollardy was also strong in Sussex and Essex, but not so in Kent or Surrey, the counties that provided the majority of Cade's followers. Their anger was triggered less by the wealth and corruption of the church than by the thuggish behaviour of royal officials and their agents, and was exacerbated by the influx into these counties of destitute soldiers evacuated from Normandy.

The events we have been reviewing merely caused the cup of unrest to overflow – it had been filled by an economic contraction that began in the late 1430s and ran on until the 1480s. The north and Wales were hit by several harvest failures and the decimation of livestock, which sharply reduced income from rents. The south was adversely affected by a slow collapse of trade across northern Europe, mainly as a result of war. English cloth exports fell by over a third at the end of the 1440s, with the West Country particularly hard hit. The incomes of those who murdered Ayscough and looted Church property in Wiltshire had quite recently fallen precipitously, escalating chronic resentment of ecclesiastical tithes and excessive wealth to a peak of murderous hatred.

Cade's men crossed the river into London and Exeter ordered Lord Scales, the Keeper of the Tower, to hand over Saye and Cromer for a formal trial at the Guildhall. Cade now lost control of his men, who dragged the two men out of the Guildhall for summary execution. Saye was beheaded at Southwark and Cromer at Mile End, perhaps seeking to tie the Essex contingent to the Kentish men in common guilt. Instead the Essex group, which had not gone through the same process of radicalization, went home. Cade's men then began behaving like a conquering army and on 8–9 July, after a day of looting and indiscriminate violence, Scales led out the Tower garrison to win back control of London Bridge in a savage battle.

The next day – very bravely, given that it seemed to be open season on bishops – Cardinal Archbishop John Kemp of York (who had replaced John Stafford, Archbishop of Canterbury, as Lord Chancellor after the fall of Suffolk) and Bishop William Wainflete of Winchester crossed the bridge and persuaded Cade and his men to sign up for a royal pardon. Although Kemp proposed it and prepared the documents, he did so at the instigation of Marguerite.

The leader of the rebellion signed the pardon as Mortimer, but would be killed as Cade five days later. He fled when a 'Writ and Proclamation by the King for the Taking of Cade' was issued shortly after the rebellion, placing a price on his head, and was fatally wounded when resisting arrest on 12 July. His body was brought back to London and underwent a mock trial before being beheaded and quartered. The head was displayed on the bridge he had once crossed in triumph, and his body parts were sent to Blackheath and to Norwich, Salisbury and Gloucester, three cities whose senior clergy had been attacked.

This was the sole reprisal for the rebellion – the pardons were respected for everyone else who did not rebel again. Kemp emerged from the crisis with his prestige greatly enhanced, and with the deepest respect for Marguerite. It was one of her many great misfortunes that he was to die in the midst of the next great crisis to envelop the Lancastrian regime.

As reports of these events filtered across the Irish Sea, York became increasingly worried. The fate of his Mortimer ancestors and his father's death on the block for conspiring to put Edmund Mortimer on the throne were burned into his psyche. Although only 3 years old when his father was executed, York himself had spent the next eight years in the custody of the regicide Robert Waterton. He had every reason to be alarmed that his name was on so many seditious lips, and was enraged to learn that members of the king's household were seeking to deflect their culpability onto him.

York also felt that the collective honour of English chivalry had been defiled by the manner in which Somerset surrendered Normandy, the details of which lost nothing in the telling by destitute members of his old Anglo-Norman affinity who came to him in Ireland. They, supported by his chamberlain William Oldhall, fixed in York's mind the erroneous belief that the uprisings in England were caused by discontent over the loss of Normandy.

The only real link between Normandy and the disturbances was a widespread belief that the increases in taxation to maintain the province had been misappropriated by the king's rapacious household. Apart from the displaced Anglo-Normans, few in England felt the humiliation of defeat as strongly as York. For most, including his peers, the Normandy crisis had been like a festering boil, brought to a head by the failure of the king's misguided peace policy, and lanced by the deposition and murder of Suffolk.

The Commons still had scores to settle with the king's government, but these were over money. The parliaments of 1449–51 made the king's resumption of alienated crown lands and revenues a condition of voting further taxation. Henry fought a rearguard action to protect his household, until he lost his nerve across the board in the face of Cade's revolt. The murders of Suffolk and Saye did the crown a backhanded favour, as they had indulged the king's whims so that his household could continue to enjoy its privileges and extortion rackets. With them dead, it was easier for Henry to distance himself from his own previous behaviour.

One can only keep reality at bay for so long, and the dam broke in 1449–50, taking with it the painfully maintained illusion of the king's majesty. He was revealed as a rather pitiable figure, not hated but certainly not revered. The loss of crown income from the French provinces was the ultimate reality check, although this was offset to a certain extent by a drastic decrease in military expenditure. The appointment as Lord Treasurer of wealthy John, Baron Beauchamp of Powick, announced an intention to restore order to the royal finances.

York was one of the magnates most affected, in absolute terms, by the loss of Normandy and the Acts of Resumption, but it was a small proportion of his overall wealth. In relative terms the biggest loser was Somerset, who lost a great deal more than York in Normandy, and who needed those lands to maintain the income required of a duke. Although he lacked the means to develop an affinity, common interest gave him a ready-made following among the minor nobles – particularly those created during the 1440s – who also stood to lose much of their wealth if resumption was pursued too vigorously.

Once Marguerite recovered from the shock of bereavement following the murder of her father figure Suffolk, she must have looked with very cold eyes indeed on the household men whose failures had exposed her husband's frailties so cruelly. Henry remained away from London from July to the end of September 1450. At some point the queen joined him at Kenilworth, and brought him back to Westminster in the first week of October.

She then accompanied him to the palace of William Wainflete at Bishop's Waltham in Hampshire. She probably suggested the visit to lift Henry's spirits, as Wainflete was the inspiration and executor for the king's beloved Eton College project. The royal couple returned to London at the end of October and spent most of the next three months in Westminster, at last attending to business.

The timings are important, because hindsight permits us to see that the first substantial domino in the descent to civil war fell during this period. Somerset had returned to England in early August with no expectation of further royal favour, but his prospects were transformed when the king learned that York intended to make an unauthorized return from Ireland. Henry must have gone into panic mode again: nothing else can explain why he sent orders to his officers in north Wales and Cheshire to prevent York landing, and to arrest him if he did so.

Finding other ports closed to him, York landed at his lordship of Denbigh in north-east Wales on 7 September 1450 and proceeded south to Shrewsbury, in Shropshire. There, on the 12th, he met John Talbot, Earl of Shrewsbury, his namesake son Baron Lisle, and Lord Lionel Welles, a Lincolnshire baron who had married John Beaufort's widow. We do not know why they were there and what was said, but after the meeting York sent a letter to the king, explaining his reason for returning: 'I have been informed that diverse language has been said of me to your most excellent estate which should sound to my dishonour and reproach, and charge of my person.'

After asserting his unqualified loyalty, he humbly requested the king to permit him to confront his detractors and clear his name. The letter came too late. On 11 September Henry appointed Somerset as Constable of England, a post previously held by the totally loyal and militarily unsullied Duke of Buckingham. Possibly Buckingham had tried to reason the king out of his panic, and had resisted the move towards confrontation. The appointment also offended John Mowbray, Duke of Norfolk and hereditary Earl Marshal, who was outraged to be made subordinate to a man he despised.

York learned of this and more when he reached the capital of his Marcher lordships at Ludlow, and his second letter to the king was considerably less conciliatory. In it he demanded an explanation why orders had been given to arrest him and for a jury to be empanelled to indict him for treason. He also alleged that orders had been issued to imprison his stewards Walter Devereux and Edmund

Mulso, and to execute his chamberlain, William Oldhall.

All these allegations appear to be true, and confirm that the king and his entourage had convinced themselves that York was bent on seizing the throne. The murder of William Tresham, Speaker of the 1449–50 Parliament, while travelling to meet York wearing the king's livery chain, further fed their paranoia. In fact Tresham's killing was carried out by retainers of Lord Edmund Grey of Ruthyn (whom last we saw involved in the Ampthill dispute) over yet another Bedfordshire property dispute. Henry fled to Kenilworth again.

By the time York reached London in late September, the die was cast. He was received graciously when the king returned (pausing at St Albans to learn if it was safe to do so), but the presence of Somerset was a red rag. York issued a widely circulated 'bill', in effect a manifesto, which echoed the terms of the Kentish petition and requested full authority to salvage the regime from enemies internal and external.

Although York's bill was a blunt assertion of the king's incompetence to choose his own ministers, Henry did not reject it outright. As usual flinching from face-to-face confrontation, he had said nothing during their meeting, but replied in writing that the duke's request would be put to the Chancellor, and promised a greater role in government for a 'sad [solemn] and substantial council in which we have appointed you to be one'.

Marguerite had a good relationship with Duchess Cecily, dating back to their first meeting at Rouen in 1444, and must have suspected the arrest orders of August–September were a tactical error on Henry's part. However, now that he was overcompensating for his earlier weakness, she would have prudently kept her views to herself. After learning that York's primary purpose had been to clear his name, and that his demands had only hardened in response to the king's appointment of Somerset as Constable of England, she may have regretted not being more forthcoming with her husband.

Sadly, there was now no going back. York had thrown down the gauntlet and it remained to be seen what support he commanded from his peers and the Commons. It may be that Marguerite proposed the visit to Bishop's Waltham not only to get her brittle husband away from the febrile atmosphere at Westminster, but also to show confidence in Somerset by giving him a free hand to rally a household unmanned by mortal terror.

VIII

HOUSE OF NEVILLE

Among the strongest supporters of Henry VI's prerogative to choose his own ministers were the father and son Earls of Salisbury and Warwick. They were to play a decisive role in the Wars of the Roses, and Warwick has gone down in history as 'the Kingmaker'. They were the junior branch of the great northern Neville clan, and owed their rise to national prominence to a combination of relentless dynastic ambition and astoundingly good fortune.

The Nevilles also owed much to Henry VI's favour, and the large retinues they brought to London in June 1450 played an important part in quelling disorder and securing the capital. Salisbury and Warwick remained in London for the rest of 1450, seeking to ensure that the lands they held by favour of the king were exempted by him from the Acts of Resumption passed by Parliament. This brought them into collision with York after he demanded wholesale resumption as a first step to restoring good governance.

Consequently they supported Somerset as a less-bad alternative to the 'sad and substantial council' promised by the king, in which York's influence might have predominated, as it already did in the Commons. York's chamberlain William Oldhall – whom the king had ordered hanged earlier in 1450 – had been elected Speaker in replacement of the murdered Tresham. Although nobody could have predicted it at the time, Oldhall's election marked the high tide of York's campaign to be formally recognized as the heir presumptive, and to make himself the king's chief minister. It would ebb quickly.

The Duke of Norfolk, who had struggled against the Suffolk affinity in East Anglia and the South East, and wanted the king's household purged of its remaining members, supported York. However, ranged against them were lords outraged by York's solidarity with the Kentish petition. These included the Duke of Buckingham, whose palace at Penshurst had been attacked, and Lord Scales, who had battled Cade on London Bridge. The defection of Scales, long one of York's councillors and godfather to Edward, his eldest son, was painful.

In addition, York's determination to ruin Somerset through acts of resumption earned him the opposition of all the other lords who stood to lose from them. Among the minor peers ranged against York, one who stood out both as a Kentish lord and as one who owed everything to royal favour was Richard Woodville, recently created Lord Rivers thanks mainly to the fact that his wife, Jacquetta, had been Queen Marguerite's lady-in-waiting since 1444.

On 1 December 1450 Yorkist supporters (presumably Anglo-Normans) attempted to kill Somerset at his lodgings at the Dominican monastery of Blackfriars, which the mob looted on finding him gone. The next day York rode in with a large force of retainers to restore order. He arrested one of the ringleaders and handed him over to the king, who passed him on to Salisbury for execution. York also lodged Somerset in the Tower, and then had him spirited away by river on a barge belonging to the Earl of Devon. Despite York's prompt action the damage was done and his standing as the champion of good order was tarnished.

It all went downhill for him very quickly in the new year. As a first step to undermine York's influence the king – no doubt at the urging of Somerset – nominated York to a commission charged with conducting assizes in order to quell continuing unrest in Kent. If he obeyed the king's summons he would lose popular support, so York did nothing. Then, at the end of January, another Kentish rebellion was sparked by a man who had been a member of York's household in Ireland, who revived the fears of royal retribution that had sparked Cade's rebellion, and once again portrayed York as the man to restore good governance.

The king at last acted decisively, riding into Kent with Somerset, Exeter, Shrewsbury, Lisle, Roos and Cromwell, the last now anxious to disassociate himself from York. According to William Gregory, Mayor of London in 1451, they conducted assizes at Canterbury that concentrated on punishing those of Cade's men who had rebelled again after taking the king's pardon, and for:

> Having more favour towards the Duke of York than to the king, and the condemned men were drawn hanged and quartered. Nine men were beheaded, at the same time, at Rochester, their heads sent to London at the king's command, and all set upon London Bridge; and at another time twelve heads were similarly brought to London at the king's command. Men in Kent call it the harvest of heads.

On return to London, the king dispensed with all talk of a 'sad and substantial council' and York found himself increasingly marginalized. In part this was because the French had embarked on the conquest of Guyenne and Gascony, and to continue to remonstrate with the king about the loss of Normandy would have seemed unpatriotic. Somerset was appointed Captain of Calais and Lord Rivers was commissioned to assemble reinforcements to send to Guyenne in Devon.

When Parliament was summoned in early May to vote money for Rivers' expedition, Thomas Young, one of York's MPs, tried to link the funds to a declaration that his master was the heir presumptive. This led to Young's arrest, the suspension of Parliament, and a series of measures making it abundantly clear that the king not only rejected York's pretension to become his first minister, but also

THE HOUSE OF NEVILLE

Descendants of Ralph Neville and Margaret Stafford

k. = killed in battle   x. = executed

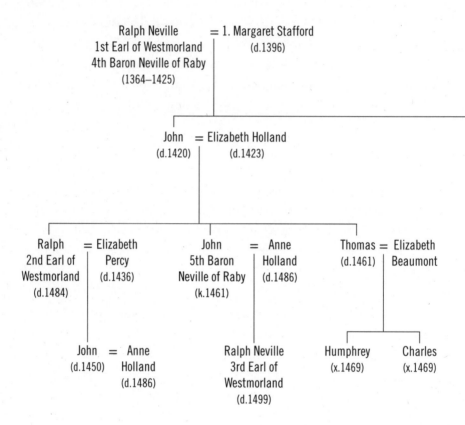

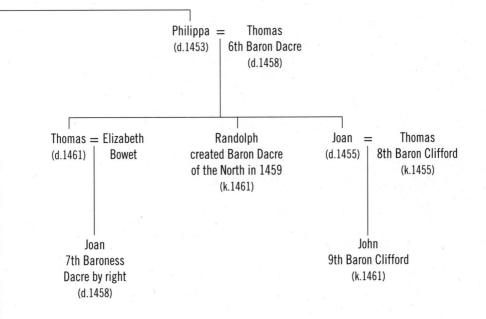

Philippa = Thomas
(d.1453) 6th Baron Dacre
(d.1458)

Thomas = Elizabeth   Randolph   Joan = Thomas
(d.1461) Bowet   created Baron Dacre   (d.1455) 8th Baron Clifford
                    of the North in 1459   (k.1455)
                         (k.1461)

Joan   John
7th Baroness   9th Baron Clifford
Dacre by right   (k.1461)
(d.1458)

THE HOUSE OF NEVILLE

Descendants of Ralph Neville and Joan Beaufort

k. = killed in battle   x. = executed

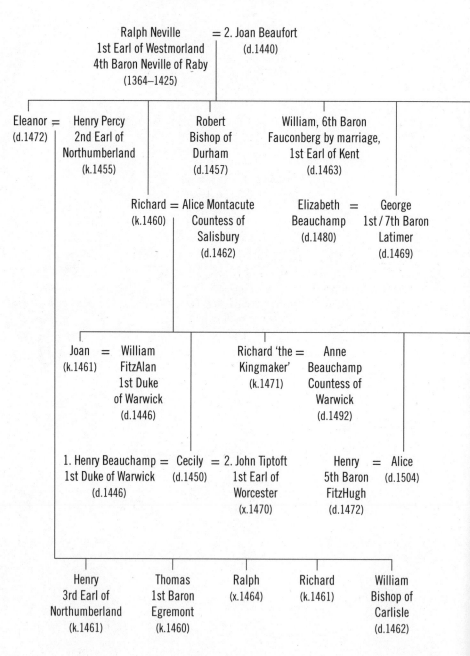

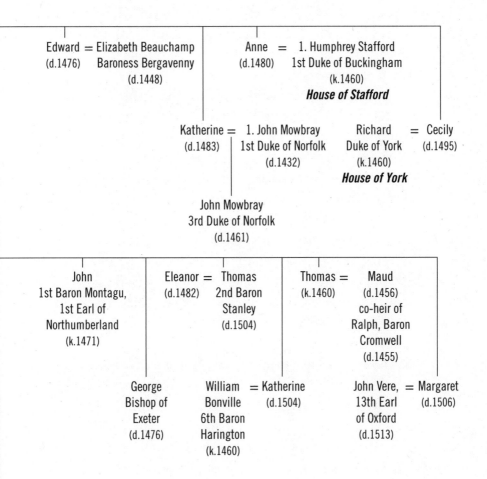

Edward = Elizabeth Beauchamp
(d.1476)　Baroness Bergavenny
　　　　　(d.1448)

Anne　=　1. Humphrey Stafford
(d.1480)　1st Duke of Buckingham
　　　　　　(k.1460)
House of Stafford

Katherine = 1. John Mowbray
(d.1483)　1st Duke of Norfolk
　　　　　　(d.1432)

Richard　= Cecily
Duke of York　(d.1495)
(k.1460)
House of York

John Mowbray
3rd Duke of Norfolk
(d.1461)

John
1st Baron Montagu,
1st Earl of
Northumberland
(k.1471)

Eleanor = Thomas
(d.1482)　2nd Baron
　　　　　Stanley
　　　　　(d.1504)

Thomas = Maud
(k.1460)　(d.1456)
　　　　　co-heir of
　　　　　Ralph, Baron
　　　　　Cromwell
　　　　　(d.1455)

George
Bishop of
Exeter
(d.1476)

William = Katherine
Bonville　(d.1504)
6th Baron
Harington
(k.1460)

John Vere, = Margaret
13th Earl　(d.1506)
of Oxford
(d.1513)

intended to exclude him from any role in his government whatso-
ever. The worm had turned with a vengeance.

• ℰℐ •

A high proportion of all the peers and peers' offspring killed in battle
or executed during the Wars of the Roses were first- or second-
generation descendants of Ralph Neville, 1st Earl of Westmorland.
Furthermore, it is improbable that tensions would have escalated
to full-blown civil war if Henry VI had retained the loyalty of the
main branch of the Nevilles.

There was a Beaufort ingredient in this mix, as well. Within
months of the death of his first wife in 1396, Ralph married 18-year-
old Joan Beaufort, sister of the future cardinal and a recent widow
with two daughters of her own. Joan captivated her 32-year-old
second husband, bore him fourteen children, and had him wrapped
around her little finger.

Three years after their marriage, Joan's half-brother Henry IV
seized the throne. Although Ralph owed his title to Richard II, he
supported Henry's usurpation and held the North for him against
the rebellious Percy clan in 1403, 1405 and 1408. Finally, in 1415,
while Henry V was away on the Agincourt campaign, Ralph defeated
an invading Scots army much larger than his own at Yeavering in
Northumberland.

Ralph's family by his first marriage did not stand a chance against
Joan. John, Ralph's eldest son from his first marriage and heir to the
earldom of Westmorland, agreed a settlement sometime before his
death in 1420, whereby he would inherit only the ancestral Neville
castles and manors of Raby and Brancepeth in Durham.

Richard, Joan's eldest son by Ralph, got almost everything else –
which by 1425, when his father died, was a great deal. He became
the largest secular lord in Yorkshire with his seat at Sheriff Hutton,
and the largest in the county of Richmondshire with his seat at
Middleham. He also inherited the wardenship of the West March

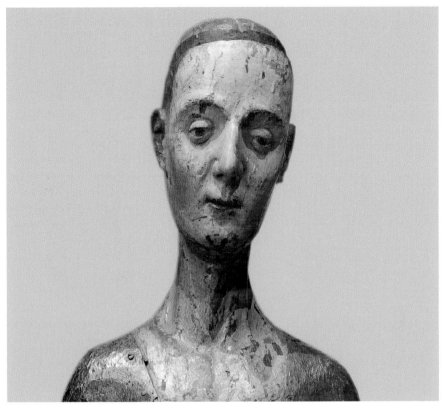

Funerary effigy of Catherine de Valois.

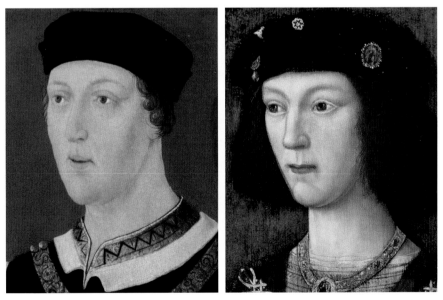

Henry VI, *left*, and a young Henry VIII, *right*, share certain facial features with, respectively, their mother and great-grandmother.

A contemporary Flemish sketch of the young Humphrey, Duke of Gloucester.

A portrait by Jan van Eyck, *c.* 1431, believed by some to portray an Italian cardinal named Niccolò Albergati and by others to depict Cardinal Henry Beaufort.

Marguerite d'Anjou's mother, Isabelle, Duchess of Lorraine by right and of Anjou by marriage.

Marguerite d'Anjou's father, René, Duke of Anjou and Bar, Count of Provence and unsuccessful claimant to the kingdoms of Sicily, of Jerusalem and of Aragon.

Detail of a miniature from the Shrewsbury Book, with John Talbot, 1st Earl of Shrewsbury, presenting the book to Marguerite d'Anjou. Richard, Duke of York, is the figure wearing a coronet on the far left, behind Henry VI.

A medallion of Marguerite d'Anjou by Pietro da Milano, 1464.

Duke Philippe 'the Good' wearing the Order of the Golden Fleece. Ruler of Burgundy from 1419 until 1467, Philippe's desertion of his English allies in 1435 tipped the balance of the Hundred Years War decisively in favour of France.

Charles VII 'the Victorious', king of France from 1422 to 1461. During his long reign Charles would expel the English from all of the territories they occupied in France, with the exception of Calais.

Isabella of Portugal, Duchess of Burgundy and granddaughter of John of Gaunt, wearing a headdress typical of the court clothing of the day.

The French and English courts followed the Burgundian fashion of extravagantly impractical clothing and headdresses.

Funerary monument of Richard Beauchamp, Earl of Warwick, in the Collegiate Church of St Mary, Warwick. His daughter Anne's marriage to Richard Neville would bring the future 'Kingmaker' huge wealth, a prestigious earldom – and immense political influence.

Mourners around Richard Beauchamp's tomb: Richard Neville, Earl of Salisbury, and his namesake son, Richard Neville, Earl of Warwick.

with his seat at Penrith in Cumberland, and the stewardship of most of the northern duchy of Lancaster estates.

Ralph added to his second family's prosperity by means of matrimonial larceny. He married William, his third son by Joan, to the feeble-minded heiress of the barony of Fauconberg. After the death of his brother, Baron Latimer by marriage, he claimed the title and took effective possession of the lands of the barony, both assigned to George, his fourth son. He married his fifth son, Edward, to Elizabeth Beauchamp, Baroness Bergavenny by right. He also used his influence to accelerate the ecclesiastical career of his second son, Robert, who became Bishop of Salisbury at the age of 23 in 1427, two years after Ralph's death.

Ralph and Joan also arranged brilliant marriages for their daughters: Katherine to the Duke of Buckingham, Anne to the Duke of Norfolk and, as we have seen, Cecily to the Duke of York. Eleanor, the eldest of their children, was married to Hotspur's son Henry. Joan designed the marriage as a means to reconcile the Percys with Henry V, who in 1416 restored Henry Percy to his grandfather's attainted title, to the wardenship of the East March and to those of the Percy estates not previously awarded to others, principally to Ralph Neville himself.

Of all these unions, the prize was the marriage in 1420 of Richard, the eldest, to Alice, heiress of Thomas Montacute, 4th Earl of Salisbury, Alice Chaucer's second husband. Richard became a regional magnate when he inherited his father's lands and offices; but when Montacute was killed at the siege of Orléans in late 1428, he became one of the richest peers in England. The Salisbury inheritance included the huge manor of Bisham in eastern Berkshire and a broad spread of estates from Somerset through Wiltshire and Dorset to Hampshire.

We know very little about the man who became, by marriage, 5th Earl of Salisbury. The only surviving likeness is a figurine of him as one of the 'mourners' around the magnificent tomb of Richard Beauchamp, Earl of Warwick, in the Church of St Mary, Warwick.

It makes him look like a benevolent priest, which is hard to square with his harsh reputation. On the other hand, although he was 20 when he married Alice Montacute, seven years his junior, he had the decency to wait a few years before consummating the union. Between 1423 and 1444 she bore him many children, ten of whom survived infancy.

Other than that we really only know he was supremely blessed by good fortune and much favoured by the king's Council. This naturally bred envious resentment, not least among Ralph's first family. The new Earl of Westmorland tried to obtain a modification of the lop-sided settlement agreed by his father, but could not prevail in the face of Salisbury's power. Many years later the dispossessed Nevilles were to eat the dish of revenge very cold indeed.

Contrary to what most histories allege the feud that developed between Salisbury and the Percys took a long time to gestate. Despite the Nevilles having grown so greatly at his family's expense, until 1453 the Earl of Northumberland combined with Salisbury against Scots incursions, and the two frequently worked together on royal commissions and in other regional legal capacities. There was, however, no doubt which of the two was the dominant partner.

Northumberland itself remained a solidly Percy fief, but in every other northern county the 'good lordship' of Salisbury predominated, and most of the lesser local peers were drawn into his gravitational field. Two who looked instead to Percy for leadership were the intermarried families of Lord Clifford and Ralph Dacre of Naworth, in Cumberland. Among the reasons why they resisted Salisbury's hegemony must have been Dacre's marriage with one of the daughters of Ralph Neville's first marriage.*

The cascade of royal favour for the Earl of Salisbury continued after Henry VI assumed personal kingship, with the promise of the

* Ralph Dacre was not in the direct line of succession to the Dacre barony, which in 1458 went by marriage to Richard Fiennes of Herstmonceux Castle in Sussex. To avoid confusion Ralph was known as Dacre of the North after he was made a baron in his own right in 1459.

lands (but not the title) of the earldom of Richmond in heredity, and the lifetime grant of the West March wardenship for himself and his eldest son, as well as the remaining stewardships of the duchy of Lancaster in Yorkshire.

Suffolk, the king's chief minister, did not view Salisbury's growing power with equanimity. Towards the end of the 1440s he directed royal favour towards the long-neglected Percys in an effort to balance the Nevilles. In November 1447, Northumberland's second son, Thomas Percy, was granted the recreated title and the meagre lands of the barony of Egremont, to part of which Salisbury had laid claim. Suffolk also put the payments due to Northumberland as warden of the East March on a par with those due to Salisbury for the West March.

By this time Northumberland had become a more assiduous courtier. He really did not have the means to maintain a suitably grand presence in London, but had learned he must try to do so. He also spent a much higher proportion of his relatively modest income on maintaining his remaining influence in Cumberland and Yorkshire, as otherwise he could not hope to recover the assets lost by his family following the 1405 attainder.

It was, therefore, a crushing blow to Northumberland's hopes – as well as those of quite a few others – when in 1448 the Nevilles won the matrimonial lottery yet again. It began in 1435, when Salisbury and the Welsh Marcher magnate Richard Beauchamp, Earl of Warwick, agreed a double matrimonial alliance, with Salisbury's daughter Cecily (aged 10) betrothed to Warwick's heir Henry (9), and his eldest son Richard (6) to Warwick's daughter Anne (8).

When both Beauchamp and his wife died in 1439, Salisbury became the lead administrator of his estates on behalf of Henry and Anne, until Henry was granted his majority in 1444. Because his father had been the tutor chosen by Henry V for his infant son, Henry Beauchamp had been Henry VI's closest friend since childhood. In 1445, the king made him Duke of Warwick and also declared him King of the Isle of Wight, in order to put him on a more equal standing. It was a terrible blow to him when Henry died, aged only 21, the following year.

Not long before his death Henry and Cecily had a baby daughter, named Anne after her aunt, Henry's sister and the younger Richard Neville's wife. When Henry died the baby became Countess of Warwick by right, but three years later, in 1449, she also died. Salisbury was perfectly placed to ensure that Anne, his daughter-in-law and the sole full blood heir, secured as much as possible of an enormous inheritance.

At the age of 21 the younger Richard Neville became Earl of Warwick by marriage and inherited, through Anne, lands that rivalled his father's in acreage, although poorer. Apart from Barnard Castle in Durham and one or two other scattered holdings, the Beauchamp estate was concentrated in Wales and the South March, in Gloucestershire, and in Warwickshire itself.* The new Earl of Warwick's aunt Cecily did him one last favour by dying in 1450, with the reversion of her dower lands to the estate.

Another timely death – for Warwick – was that of his wife's half-sister in 1448, which in 1450 enabled him to gain control of the lands of the barony of Bergavenny on behalf of her minor son, supplanting her widower, his uncle Edward. Salisbury also ceded to him the guardianship of George, Baron Latimer, another uncle, who had been declared mentally incompetent in 1447, which gave him control of the lands of the youngest of the daughters from Richard Beauchamp's first marriage.

He was also outstandingly fortunate in the timing of the Beauchamp succession. The claims of the eldest daughters of Richard Beauchamp's first marriage were swept aside more easily because their husbands, the Duke of Somerset and Earl of Shrewsbury, who would have violently resisted Warwick's takeover, were so deeply involved in the Normandy debacle.

Another key factor in Warwick's rise and rise was the fall of

* For a fuller appreciation of this hotly contested succession, see Appendix D: The Beauchamp Inheritance.

Suffolk, who viewed the union of the Salisbury and Warwick earldoms as highly undesirable and might have restrained Henry VI, who regarded the new earl as a close friend. Warwick had been in attendance at court alongside Henry Beauchamp, and some of the glow of his double brother-in-law's lifelong friendship with the king rubbed off on him. Overwhelmed by the crisis of 1449–50 and by his growing fear that York was plotting to overthrow him, the king gave Warwick's succession his unreserved blessing.

What sort of a man was the new Earl of Warwick, this sudden meteor in the English political firmament? Like Salisbury, his father, the only likeness we have of him is one of the figurines around the funerary monument of Richard Beauchamp, his father-in-law. Since he oversaw the construction of the tomb, we must assume he thought it portrayed him to best advantage. If so, he must have been strikingly ugly in real life – although we should not, perhaps, read too much into the strange face, which makes him look like a discontented cat.

As with all medieval biography, we must pick and choose among hagiographic and hostile commentaries. Two characteristics are common to both: even by the standard of his age, Warwick was extremely ruthless, and he was also highly charismatic. The Greek root of the word charisma means 'gift of grace', and it is not much of a leap of imagination to assume he saw the hand of fate in the improbable sequence of events that thrust greatness upon him at such an early age. His history bears the mark of a man convinced he was destiny's child, with no need to compromise with those who opposed him.

MARGUERITE

I N *The Treasure of the City of Ladies*, written in about 1405, the Venetian-French writer Christine de Pisan sought to buttress what she saw as an erosion of respect for the role of women as mediators and peacemakers between their husbands and the rest of the world. Their supportive role, she wrote, was to advocate chastity, charity, patience and humility, to which end rhetorical skill (her own forte) was an indispensable attribute. However, she also argued that a noble lady must play an active role during her husband's absences, not only employing her well-honed administrative skills but also, if necessary, as a military leader.

Marguerite of Anjou was a queen straight out of *The Treasure of the City of Ladies* until circumstances obliged her to take hold of the reins falling from her husband's hands. It was his failure that forced her to 'act like a man'. Although she was just 20 years old in 1450, Marguerite handled the moral collapse of her 28-year-old husband with remarkable maturity and aplomb. She had received a thorough education on how to rule through weak men from her mother and grandmother, and that training now paid off.

Henry VI had grown up crushed by knowledge that he could not possibly live up to the idealized example of his father, the alpha male of a warrior aristocracy in which natural selection had distilled an abundance of testosterone. Deficient in that respect, he had willingly surrendered his institutional power to Suffolk, twenty-five years older and a distinguished veteran of the Normandy conquest. Now, with Suffolk and Ayscough brutally murdered, his carefree cocoon ripped away and his entourage behaving like the proverbial headless chicken, he desperately needed someone to supply parental guidance. Who better than his wife, who had acted so bravely and decisively to defuse Cade's Rebellion?

The evidence points to Somerset being the queen's choice to replace Buckingham as Constable of England and as the new chief minister. Marguerite was probably not immune to his charm – few women were – but his principal attraction to her was that he owed everything to the crown. Without royal protection he would be hounded to death by York and the vengeful Anglo-Normans, and following his losses in Normandy and the Acts of Resumption, without royal favour he could not sustain the standard required of a duke.*

The collapse of the peace policy she symbolized made it all the more important for Marguerite to adopt a low profile, for which she needed a front man. Although she had been as much wrapped in Suffolk's cocoon as Henry, she would have been better informed about the true state of his realm through ladies-in-waiting such as Jacquetta and Alice Chaucer, and the other noblewomen who attended her court. They would have functioned as an intelligence service at a time when Henry's retinue was feeding him panic-inducing rumours.

We may also infer there was considerable scope for women to play a major, if informal, role in government if they could persuade their men to keep their testosterone under control. While we should not presume aristocratic women were any less ruthlessly ambitious than their male kin, their instincts would oppose a drift towards combat. The marital alliances in the list of 'Protagonists and Marriages' and the family trees do not, unfortunately, give us any indication of how effective they were, of who were the strong women and who

---

* Starting early in 1451, the queen began to pay him an annuity of £100 [£63,600] from her own exchequer.

the weak. What they do show, however, is that in less fraught times Marguerite might have made herself the hub of a powerful sorority working for compromise.

The immediate task was to see off the threat from York, and he was firmly put back in his box during 1451–2. We have seen how little the support of the Commons mattered once the Lords realized their interest was best served by opposing the cause of reform espoused by York. Somerset required no encouragement from Marguerite to go after the man who wanted to destroy him and, not surprisingly for a man far more accustomed to warfare than to government, he chose to run the political equivalent of a *chevauchée* against him.

York was far too eminent for someone like Somerset, admired by few and lacking the means to buy followers, to attack directly. Instead, he set out to erode York's prestige and popularity by showing he could not protect his own people. In June 1451, following the vehement rejection of his petition to recognize York as heir pre-sumptive, Thomas Young and other Yorkist councillors were sent to the Tower. In July, Somerset turned his guns on William Oldhall, York's chamberlain and Speaker of the Commons. The arrest for sedition of the vicar and others of Standon, a Hertfordshire manor held by Oldhall from York, was the first shot. In November Oldhall took sanctuary in St Martins-le-Grand in London.

Even though there was credible evidence Oldhall had conspired against him, the king was outraged when, in January 1452, Somerset had him dragged out, and ordered him returned to sanctuary. It was an unheeded warning that Somerset's impatience could bring royal authority into further disrepute. The king was right to over-rule him, not only because the violation of sanctuary was impious, but also because it was unnecessary. Oldhall no longer posed a threat. Even so he was impeached, and on 22 June found guilty of treason, outlawed and attainted. He remained in sanctuary under close supervision until 1455.

Adding to the sense of crisis, in September 1451 the dormant feud between the Earl of Devon and the recently created Baron Bonville erupted into open warfare. It is not entirely clear why it did so, but there must be a strong assumption the main culprit was Bonville, if only because he was now allied with the restless James Butler, Earl of Wiltshire. Devon was now supported by the hot-headed Lord Moleyns, whose arbitrary actions against the Paston family we reviewed in Chapter 5, and by Edward Brooke, Baron Cobham. After failing to capture Wiltshire at Bristol, they ran Bonville to earth at Taunton Castle in Somerset.

A short while previously the Berkeley–Lisle feud* had also burst into flames when John Talbot, Lord Lisle, seized Berkeley Castle and kidnapped Berkeley's wife. York intervened against Lisle, and then took 2,000 men south to separate the combatants at Taunton. Devon had been one of his few aristocratic supporters, while Bonville and Wiltshire were strongly associated with the court party. By taking Bonville into custody he saved Devon from being tainted by murder, and by submitting the dispute to royal arbitration he demonstrated that he could keep the king's peace where Somerset could not.

Fed false reports that York's people were responsible for outbreaks of unrest in East Anglia, the king reacted angrily to the actions taken in his name by York in the West Country. Marguerite's imperfect understanding of how England was governed may have led her to see a parallel with her cousin Charles VII's humbling of his overmighty nobles in France. For whatever reasons, the royal couple accepted uncritically Somerset's interpretation of York's actions as a usurpation of the king's prerogative, when most would have seen it as the justified exercise of regional lordship to restore law and order.

Although Lisle had plainly been in the wrong at Berkeley Castle, he was created a viscount. York was also insultingly cast as a party to the Courtenay–Bonville feud when the king summoned all involved to court. Moleyns, Cobham, Bonville and Wiltshire obeyed and were briefly detained, separately, in the queen's castles at

---

* See Appendix D: The Beauchamp Inheritance.

Berkhamsted and Wallingford. Devon and York ignored the summons, and it was probably because the king refused to pursue the matter any further that Somerset vented his frustration on Oldhall.

By January 1452 York was sufficiently alarmed by reports of the king's anger towards him to send a grovelling declaration of loyalty, and took the further step of publicly swearing to it in the presence of the Bishop of Hereford and the Earl of Shrewsbury. Then came Somerset's violation of sanctuary, after which York became convinced his enemy would stop at nothing to destroy him. Accordingly, he summoned his tenantry from all over England to join him in a march on London. A manifesto dated 3 February recited the now tired accusation against Somerset for the loss of Normandy, and continued:

> After my coming out of Ireland, as the king's true liegeman and servant (as I ever shall be to my life's end), I brought to his royal majesty's attention certain articles concerning the well-being and safeguard both of his most royal person and the tranquillity and conservation of all this his realm. These terms of advice... were laid aside, to have no effect, through the envy, malice and untruth of the Duke of Somerset [who]... labours continually about the king's highness for my undoing, and to corrupt my blood, and to disinherit me and my heirs and such persons as are about me.

Since Somerset 'ever prevails and rules about the king's person', York announced his intention to proceed 'in all haste against him', and called on his kinsmen and friends to join him. For all the protestations of loyalty to the king this was a call to armed rebellion, and seen as such even by peers such as Norfolk, who had hitherto supported York against Somerset. Such an extraordinary misjudgement must have been the product of obsession, nurtured by York's isolation at Ludlow with men who could see their own fate in Oldhall's.

After London shut its gates to him at the king's command, York took his force, which included artillery, south of the river and established a fortified camp at Dartford in Kent. He may have expected the Kentish men to rally to his standard, but if so he was disappointed. Only Devon and Cobham were with him. Ranged against them were the Dukes of Buckingham, Norfolk, Exeter and Somerset, the Earls of Salisbury, Warwick and Shrewsbury, the viscounts Bourchier and Lisle, the Bishops of Winchester and Ely, and a dozen barons including the veteran Scales and the new creations Bonville and Stourton.

The ensuing negotiations were designed to grant York and his confederates a face-saving formula to escape a charge of treason. They were permitted to submit their accusations against Somerset – which were dismissed by an arbitration panel packed with the king's men – a royal pardon for their followers was agreed, and then York had to kneel before the king in St Paul's cathedral on 10 March and swear a humiliating oath of allegiance (my italics):

> I, Richard Duke of York confess and acknowledge that I am *and ought to be* a humble subject and liegeman to you, my sovereign lord, King Henry VI, and *ought* therefore to bear you faith and truth as my sovereign lord... [and when summoned] *to come in humble and obeisant manner.* I shall never hereafter make any assembly of your people without your command or licence, or in my lawful defence. In the interpretation and declaration of my lawful defence, I shall report at all times to your highness...

York undertook to confine himself to his own estates and departed for Ludlow on the 24th. He was compelled to depart for Fotheringhay when the king came to Ludlow to conduct assizes after a judicial progress through Devon, accompanied by Bonville and Moleyns, to punish the Earl of Devon's followers. At Ludlow tenants who had followed York were indicted and found guilty of treason before being told of the pardon negotiated at Dartford. It was a demeaning trick to play on men who had no choice but to obey their lord's summons, and done to demonstrate York's powerlessness.

York had to move again when Henry, accompanied by a retinue of lords including York's erstwhile ally Norfolk, made a judicial progress through Hertfordshire, Cambridgeshire, Huntingdonshire, Northamptonshire and Lincolnshire. These areas had provided the bulk of York's army at Dartford and the assizes at his boroughs of Grantham, Newbury and Stamford were harsher than at Ludlow. At least one man suffered a traitor's death and his quarters were displayed in Yorkist towns.

Sadly for Marguerite, her husband's new-found self-confidence did not lead to a fresh start, but instead to a stubborn repetition of the mistakes of the past. He had learned nothing from the debacle in 1450 and the survivors of Suffolk's regime were permitted to resume the old pattern of abuses. Objectively, Somerset had fulfilled his function and should have been let go after Dartford. Unfortunately Henry was unwilling, perhaps indeed psychologically unable, to deal with the stress of being a hands-on king and, once again, fell into the damaging error of over-investing in his chief minister. By delegating too much of his power to Somerset, Henry risked confirming to the world the correctness of York's opinion of him.

The king awarded Somerset several benefits York had lost to resumption, including the lease of the Isle of Wight. York also lost offices he previously held, with the lieutenancy of Ireland going to his enemy Wiltshire, who had become Earl of Ormonde on the death of his father in August 1452. York's office of Justice of the Forests south of the Trent went to Somerset in July 1453, the grant gloatingly stating it was for good service 'on both sides of the sea' to rub in the king's opinion that he had done no wrong in Normandy.

At the same time the government did address some of the grievances that had shaken the country in 1450. An executive council was set up to manage the royal finances and to handle routine matters of administration, and the Commons became more amenable once the king was seen to be putting his house in order. They may also have been abashed that, after they refused to vote the money for Rivers' expedition, Guyenne and Gascony had fallen easily to the armies of Charles VII in mid-1451.

The people of the conquered province had been governed by distant English kings for 300 years and resented their new overlords, who did not even speak the same language.* They sent emissaries to London and, with Parliament now willing to vote the necessary funds, an expeditionary force of 3,000 men was rapidly assembled by inspiring 66-year-old John Talbot, Earl of Shrewsbury, and sailed for Guyenne in October 1452.

Timing his assault to coincide with a rebellion by the citizens of Bordeaux, Talbot quickly seized the city, after which other towns and castles along the Garonne and Dordogne valleys fell like dominoes. Further funding was voted for 3,000 reinforcements led by his son Viscount Lisle, accompanied by Lord Moleyns, to face the inevitable French counter-offensive in 1453.

Given her husband's over-investment in Somerset, it was probably Marguerite's initiative to dilute the new favourite's status by promoting two more princes of the blood. In late 1452 the king's bastard half-brothers, previously commoners, were vaulted to earldoms. The elder, 21-year-old Edmund Tudor, was created Earl of Richmond, and his one-year-younger brother Jasper was created Earl of Pembroke. An Act of Parliament lifted the stigma of illegitimacy from them the following year.

Pembroke was no great prize, but the honour of Richmond was a wealthy endowment where the benefit of the king's many manors had been granted for decades – with the promise of hereditary right – to Salisbury. Once again Henry was guilty of awarding the same patronage twice, with the added aggravation that Edmund Tudor was also declared the premier earl over the head of Warwick, to whom the king had awarded the status only a year earlier.

For a family as dependent on royal favour as the Nevilles, who must have been expecting reward for their robust support of the

* The Occitan languages of southern France have completely different roots from metropolitan French.

king against York, the promotion of the obscure – and Welsh – Tudors at their expense was a very unpleasant surprise. In conjunction with royal support for Somerset's machinations with regard to the Beauchamp inheritance, however, it took on a far more sinister complexion.

Once confirmed in office Somerset wasted no time in attacking the rulings made in the Beauchamp inheritance case while he and Shrewsbury had been extricating themselves from Normandy. In typical Henrician fashion, two royal grants made to Warwick in 1450 were reversed in favour of Somerset in 1451. The first was the wardship of the minor George Neville, heir to the barony of Bergavenny; both awards were disgraceful, as they usurped the natural right of the boy's father. The second was the office of Chamberlain of the Exchequer, awarded to Warwick before Christmas and given to Somerset a few months later.

Somerset and Shrewsbury also obtained a grotesque ruling on behalf of their wives that they were entitled to equal shares with their half-sister Anne, Warwick's wife, of the dower lands of her – not their – mother. If Somerset thought he could simply take possession of over half the dower lands as well as the whole of the Bergavenny estate, he was mistaken. Warwick, in possession of both, let him know the only way he could get any of it was by force. Ordered to submit and surrender Cardiff and Cowbridge castles to the king's friend Lord Dudley, Warwick refused him entry and increased their garrisons.

Taken together, the estates of Warwick and Salisbury put them on a par with the Dukes of York, Norfolk and Buckingham. Having made an embittered enemy of York it was breathtakingly foolish of Henry to alienate the Nevilles as well. One would be inclined to believe it was a case of the Somerset tail wagging the royal dog, were it not for the promotion from nowhere of the Tudor brothers, which was clearly not in Somerset's interest. Marguerite simply did not appreciate that it would be perceived by the Nevilles as further evidence of a concerted royal plot to undermine them.

X

MITRE AND CROWN

THE ELEMENTS OF STATESMANSHIP THAT LEAVENED THE febrile squabble between the houses of Lancaster and York were largely the work of Cardinal Archbishop John Kemp, who became Lord Chancellor in 1450 and was promoted from York to Canterbury in 1452. John Stafford, his predecessor in both offices, had been Chancellor since 1432, but had been excessively accommodating to the Suffolk regime, even granting Lord Saye and the infamous William Cromer stewardship of all the estates of the Canterbury archbishopric.

Kemp was unsullied by association with the fallen regime and was also a notably able administrator. The pope had made him a cardinal-priest as early as 1439, and he had previously been Lord Chancellor in 1426–32. He was the obvious candidate to deal with the crisis of 1450, as he also was to succeed Stafford at Canterbury two years later, when Rome made him a cardinal-bishop. His only price was the appointment in 1450 to the bishopric of London of his (genuine) nephew Thomas, which had been opposed by Suffolk.

As we have seen, it was Kemp in combination with Marguerite who defused Cade's Rebellion, and it was certainly he and not Somerset who introduced fiscal restraint and more rational administration through the new executive council, and won back the support of the Commons. It was Kemp who devised the face-saving formula that averted bloodshed at Dartford, and he was also instrumental in obtaining the taxes from the Commons and the clerical subsidy which had made possible Talbot's initially successful expedition to Guyenne.

In sum, it was practically entirely thanks to Kemp that the regime won back a considerable degree of popular acceptance. When Parliament assembled at Reading in March 1453 it voted the king, for life, customs dues, increased wool subsidies and a poll tax on aliens (later revoked), along with the customary tax on the value of moveable goods (a fifteenth for rural and a tenth for urban areas). The last time the Commons had shown this much honour to their monarch was to Henry V after Agincourt. They even voted an additional three fifteenths and tenths to raise a force of 20,000 archers, an invitation for Henry to lead an army for the reconquest of the lost empire in France.

• ℰↄ •

The emergence of Kemp as the regime's saviour is perhaps the most unreported aspect of the crisis, and the reason is not hard to identify. Even today journalists report the easy stuff – the public doings of politicians – and hardly ever mention the senior permanent officials without whom the inadequacy of their political 'masters' would become apparent. Although historians may eventually be able to draw on the minutes of today's confidential discussions, there were no such records in earlier times.

The Church's moral and social power was in decline, but churchmen were valued as civil servants for a number of interrelated reasons. As the clergy were, in theory, celibate, there was less chance they would advance their families' interests at the expense of the state. The priesthood was also a career open to talent, and provided a pool of literate and numerate individuals from which the monarchy and the aristocracy preferentially drew their clerks and accountants. They were the 'technocrats' of the Middle Ages.

Senior churchmen also represented a powerful constituency and

7. ARCHDIOCESES AND DIOCESES OF ENGLAND & WALES

See also Appendix C
Archbishops and Bishops
1440–62

SCOTLAND

✝ Carlisle

Durham ✝

YORK
✝

✝ Bangor

✝
St Asaph

✝ Chester

✝ Lincoln

Lichfield
✝

Hereford
✝

✝ Coventry

✝
Ely

Norwich ✝

St David's
✝

✝
Worcester

Llandaff
✝

✝ Dorchester

London
✝

Bath ✝

Salisbury
✝

✝
Rochester ✝

CANTERBURY

Wells ✝

Winchester
✝

Chichester
✝

Exeter
✝

© Hugh Bicheno

were no less self-serving than today's permanent officials. Since the
1430s the archdioceses of Canterbury and York, under constant pressure to finance secular government, had merged their convocations
(assemblies). While most frequently summoned in response to royal
requests for subsidies, ecclesiastical matters had also become subject
to the approval of the convocation. The Archbishop of Canterbury,
whose own see was relatively poor, was in a position vis-à-vis his
bishops and lesser clergy somewhat akin to the king and his Lords
and Commons.

Bishops played an active part in secular political life through
membership of the House of Lords, and traditionally occupied two
of the three most senior non-ceremonial offices of state. The first
was the Lord Chancellor, Keeper of the Great Seal and Chief Royal
Chaplain. He was not only the king's senior adviser in matters spiritual but also the senior legal officer, without whom the business
of government could not be conducted. The second was the Lord
Keeper of the Privy Seal, the king's personal signet, which travelled
with him while the Great Seal remained in Chancery, the Lord
Chancellor's London office. Almost all non-judicial documents
requiring the Great Seal were first warranted by the Privy Seal.

Beyond these office-holders we know little of the role of the clergy
in government. Some questions are easier to answer than others.
The relatively tiny diocese of Ely was prized out of proportion to
its size in part because, like Durham, the Isle of Ely was a county
palatine – one ruled by a magnate with special authority elsewhere
possessed only by the sovereign. Its principal attraction, however,
was that although it was only the fifth most richly endowed see, it
had much the lowest outgoings. The handsome surplus could be
spent to buy influence.*

Bishops also enjoyed the rights by which a later age defined constitutional monarchy: to be consulted, to encourage, and to warn.
Perhaps above all, the Church provided institutional memory and

---

* In 1454 Pope Nicholas V took advantage of the paralysis of English government to
appoint William Grey, one of his own officials.

continuity. If to these attributes we add that about a third of the land in England was held by the Church, whose members were immune from civil or even criminal prosecution by the secular authorities, the wonder is not that a figure like Kemp should emerge in a crisis, but rather that it was not a more common occurrence.

Although most people compartmentalized religion apart from their worldly pursuits, everyone took it seriously. This had practical consequences. Throughout the Middle Ages, rebellion against the monarch was justified as an action taken against 'evil councillors' because the rebels had sworn allegiance to the king himself. When York finally articulated his claim to the throne he stressed the prior Lancastrian violation of divine order in a bid to absolve himself of the sacramental oaths he had sworn to Henry VI. Nobody was convinced.

• ℰℓ •

Kemp would have disapproved of the king's provocative assizes in the Yorkist heartlands and his support for Somerset's perversion of legal process in his attack on the Beauchamp settlement. They indicate that after Dartford Henry was no longer paying as much attention as previously to his Chancellor's political advice. Kemp did not tell the king what he wanted to hear, and could not prevail against a household of sycophants led by Somerset, a man even more rapacious and considerably less politically astute than Suffolk had been.

Then came a totally unforeseeable event, which threw everything into the melting pot and brought Kemp to the forefront again. On or about 7 August 1453, at his hunting lodge at Clarendon, east of Salisbury in Wiltshire, Henry VI went into a frenzy, followed by a deeply catatonic state from which he could not be aroused. The breakdown is commonly ascribed to his learning that Talbot and his son Lisle had been killed and their army destroyed at the Battle of Castillon on 13 July. Six weeks earlier, the news of the fall of Constantinople to Ottoman Sultan Mehmed II must also have been a terrible shock.

Henry may have been building up to a psychotic episode for some time. It would be in keeping with a diagnosis of schizophrenia that the harbinger of his catatonic withdrawal from reality was his acute sense of persecution in 1450, followed by his surrender of personal autonomy. Possibly Marguerite, alarmed by the purposeless agitation that characterizes the disease, suggested Henry should unwind at Clarendon, far from London, as he had in 1450 when she whisked him off to Bishop's Waltham.

Henry's collapse brought Kemp back into play. Although genuinely concerned to protect the dynasty, he had his own agenda. The king was effectively the supreme governor of the Church in England long before Henry VIII expropriated the monasteries and, like all European princes, regarded it as a dependable cash cow. After being ruthlessly milked by Henry V, the bishops had become accustomed to far greater indulgence under Henry VI. Consequently the bishops were even more anxious than most lay lords that cold-eyed York should not become the king's chief minister, still less replace the king himself.

Over the coming months Kemp did all he could to buy time for Henry to recover. Although of supreme dynastic significance, the birth on 13 October 1453 of baby Edward, the long-awaited heir apparent, did not address the immediate problem of governance. Marguerite chose Kemp and Somerset as the baby's godfathers (his godmother was Anne, Duchess of Buckingham and older sister of Cecily, Duchess of York), but Kemp could not put himself forward as Protector, and Somerset lacked the prestige to do so.

Despite the fact that her uncle had just extinguished English hopes of recovering their empire in France, motherhood exalted Marguerite's status and popularity – already high following her heroism in 1450 – to an extraordinary degree. Cecily, Duchess of York, captured the public mood in her letter of congratulations when she learned the queen was pregnant. It was, she wrote, 'the most precious, most joyful, and most comforting earthly treasure that might come into this land and to the people thereof'.

Politically, however, there was to be a serious downside to the queen's confinement (from which men were strictly excluded). For a month before the birth and for forty days after it Marguerite was out of the loop at a crucial time, when the severity of her husband's incapacity could no longer be concealed and Parliament was becoming alarmed about the power vacuum it created.

What Marguerite and Kemp needed, and did not get, was domestic tranquillity. The Lord Chancellor could not provide executive leadership. Somerset could only act with the authority of the king's warrant and could not forge one because the Privy Seal was under the control of Thomas Lisieux, Dean of St Paul's and a Kemp protégé. The accepted role for the queen, as for any noble lady, was to intercede with her husband to prevent or repair injustice, and to reward faithful service rather than to punish transgressions. Unfortunately, even before Henry's catatonia, transgressions were what had to be dealt with.

First, there was the continuing defiance of royal authority by Warwick's refusal to surrender Cardiff and Cowbridge. The issue was taken off the boil because, in the face of Kemp's disapproval and without the king's warrant, Somerset could not push his spurious claims any further. His ambition to undo the Beauchamp settlement had, anyway, been dealt a severe blow by the deaths of Shrewsbury and Lisle at Castillon. Had they returned in triumph from Guyenne they would undoubtedly have supported him against Warwick, in arms if necessary, with every possibility of success.

Secondly, and potentially more threatening to royal authority, the tinder of conflict in the North between the houses of Percy and Neville began to smoulder. It was a generational thing. Sixty-year-old Henry Percy, restored to the earldom of Northumberland in 1416 through the good offices of Joan née Beaufort, Countess of Westmorland, and married to her eldest daughter, had to accept that he must play second fiddle to 53-year-old Salisbury, his much wealthier and better connected brother-in-law.

His sons, however, yearned for the days when the Percys were 'Kings of the North', and chafed at Neville supremacy. The spark to the tinder was the marriage in August 1453 between Thomas Neville, Salisbury's youngest son, and Maud Stanhope, niece and joint heir of Lord Cromwell. Cromwell's many estates included Burwell in Lincolnshire and Wressle in south-east Yorkshire, both

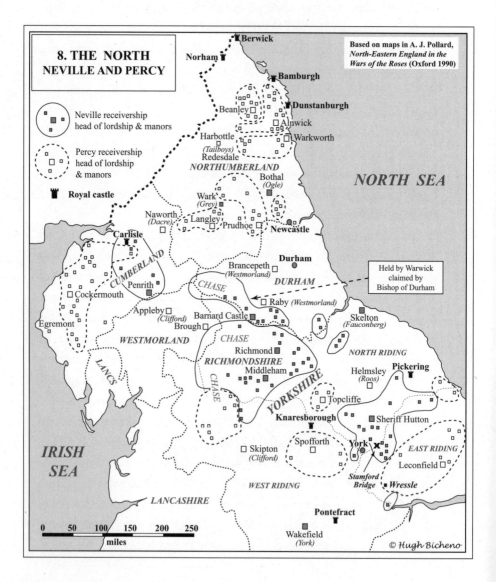

previously owned by Thomas Percy, Earl of Worcester, who had been beheaded and attainted in 1403 after the failure of his nephew Hotspur's rebellion.

Wressle, where Worcester had built a splendid castle-mansion, was among the properties the Percys most wanted to recover, and Northumberland's second son (also Thomas Percy) believed the Stanhope–Neville marriage would lead to the permanent loss of the castle and manor. Bearing in mind how Thomas Percy had been created Baron Egremont over the objections of Salisbury in the last flourish of Suffolk's ascendancy, and that the title brought with it very little land, it is possible some assurance about Wressle had been given to Thomas. He certainly reacted as though he had been robbed after the king gave consent to the Neville–Stanhope marriage.

Egremont issued his livery to a gang of hard cases recruited in York and, joined by his younger brother Richard, began to maraud Neville lands, ignoring orders from the king to desist and to take his men to Guyenne. Salisbury's second son, John Neville, retaliated by riding through the Percy manor of Topcliffe with a column of armed retainers.

Egremont's anger over Wressle is usually seen as the culmination of growing tension between the two families, but he had a genuine and specific grievance. Apart from Ampthill, which we reviewed in Chapter 5, Lord Cromwell was a party to a number of other disputes, and when he died in 1456, his executors returned lands worth £5,500 [£3.5 million] to illegally dispossessed owners. Probably he and the Nevilles were indeed planning some chicanery over Wressle, although it was a royal manor only granted to him for life. Common hostility towards Cromwell later brought together the younger Percys and the 23-year-old Duke of Exeter, making them enemies of York as well.

On 24 August Egremont and Richard Percy, joined by John Clifford, the eldest son of Thomas, Baron Clifford, waylaid the Neville–Stanhope wedding party, which included Salisbury himself, at Heworth, outside York. Although there was much shouting and jostling, no blood was spilt – but the affront to Salisbury brought the fathers openly into the dispute. They called out their retainers, and on 20 October the two armies came into dangerous proximity 4 miles north of Topcliffe. The younger men may have been champing at the bit, but Salisbury and Northumberland sought the mediation of Archbishop William Booth of York, and disbanded their forces for the winter.

Even though blood did not flow, the salient political fact was that both parties had ignored repeated injunctions and indictments issued under the Great Seal, just when Marguerite played the top dynastic trump card by giving birth to a healthy baby boy. Ironically, by taking the issue of York's possible succession off the table, it made him more acceptable as the champion of good governance he had always claimed to be. An orderly realm might be governed by a council – as it had been during Henry's minority. However, one where great lords were circling each other with fur bristling required a firmer hand than even a council guided by Kemp could provide.

XI

RICHARD

I N NOVEMBER 1454 YORK RODE INTO LONDON ACCOMP-
nied by the king's Tudor half-brothers, the Earls of Richmond
and Pembroke. What makes this doubly significant is that
no other peers wished to be publicly identified with the duke.
Furthermore, although Somerset had tried to prevent it, York had
come because members of the royal household and bishops closely
associated with the regime had voted to include him in a summons
to a Great Council, which was to decide on governance during the
king's incapacity.

It is possible, indeed probable, that the queen had in mind the
creation of a royal 'centre', above faction, a project which remained
viable until the king emerged from catatonia around Christmas
1454. Discarding Somerset was the price she had to pay to bring
York on board, and there is no reason to believe she hesitated to pay
it. Somerset had become a political liability, and a distraction from
the serious business of deciding how to cope with the constitutional
conundrum of a living king who was unable to rule.

York had almost ruined himself pursuing the Anglo-Norman vendetta against Somerset, and would not have wanted to expend any
of his diminished political capital in reopening old wounds. It was
Norfolk, with his own axe to grind, who formally accused Somerset
of treason. Although York took advantage of Norfolk's accusation
to argue that Oldhall's conviction for treason should be set aside, he

did not pursue the matter after Kemp ruled the Council lacked the legal authority to do so. The Chancellor did, however, agree that York's councillors had been unlawfully purged from the Commons.

Somerset was sent to the Tower to await the preparation of the terms of impeachment, which Norfolk insisted should be by English law only for abuses of power as the king's chief minister. His alleged treasonous dealings with the King of France were to be judged by Norman law, which would have put his fate in the hands of nobles who had lost their French estates. We cannot know whether this was a genuine effort to see him punished for the loss of Normandy, or a ploy to drag out the proceedings indefinitely. Somerset's retainers took up residence around the Tower, and there he remained for the next fourteen months. York may have had few lords on his side, but Somerset had even fewer. He was neutralized.

By the end of November 1453 some forty-six lords had obeyed the summons to the Great Council. They all solemnly swore to abstain from and to suppress lawlessness, but evaded discussion of the constitutional crisis. On 5 December a mere fourteen peers put their names to a minimal agreement that the Council should act when required to maintain 'politic rule and governance'. The first such action, supported by York and voted the next day, was to make provision for the on-going functioning of the king's household.

York would not have subscribed to this if he believed the household was hostile to him. He and his wife certainly must have paid their respects to Marguerite and her baby after she emerged from confinement, so either face-to-face at that time or indirectly later he may have received the queen's assurance that she wanted to work with him. This would explain a number of things, not least why he did not pursue the impeachment of Somerset during 1454.

More intriguing is that York made no attempt to bring forward discussion of constitutional matters, the very reason why the Great Council had been summoned. The reason for his reticence was to avoid a clash with Kemp, who was determined to delay any such discussion for as long as possible. To make sure the Council did not try to grant itself royal prerogatives, Kemp kept Privy Seal, his man Lisieux, away from Westminster, thus maintaining a veto for the Great Seal.

The only move to fill the political void was an astonishing proposal circulated in mid-January that has Kemp's fingerprints all over it. Evidence of it is limited to a single report from one of Norfolk's informants in London, but it is plausible:

> The Queen hath made a bill of five articles, desiring those articles be granted; whereof the first is that she desireth the whole rule of this land; the second is that she may make the Chancellor, the Treasurer, the Privy Seal, and all other officers of this land, with sheriffs and all other officers that the King should make; the third is that she may give all the bishoprics of this land, and all the other benefices belonging to the King's gift; the fourth is that she may have sufficient livelihood assigned her for the King, and the Prince and herself. But as for the fifth article, I cannot yet know what it is.*

Marguerite and Kemp must have known that a Council reluctant to address substantive matters of governance would be hostile to the constitutional novelty they were proposing. They were setting out a strong negotiating position, designed to pre-empt any discussion of a regency unless it were hers. Some of the lords will have understood this, but it would have added to their resentment of a chancellor who was exceeding his traditional authority, and an emerging consensus in favour of York.

On 13 February, the day before Parliament convened, Kemp moved that the Council should decide 'to whom the king's power should be committed', with the Council retaining the right to prorogue and dissolve Parliament. The councillors overrode him and included the right 'to dissolve the said parliament and to do all

---

* The fifth item probably concerned her custody of the prince and matters to do with his upbringing.

things that shall be necessary thereto or to any of the premises' when they nominated York. Undeterred, Kemp altered the wording back to what he had originally proposed before affixing the Great Seal.

At about the same time York made a shrewd legal thrust to ensure the neutrality of the Commons. One of the charges brought against Oldhall to depose him as Speaker had been that he stole property worth about £2,000 [£1.27 million] from Somerset. York now obtained a judgement against Somerset's man Thorpe, who had replaced Oldhall, for stealing property to the same value from him, and had him consigned to the Fleet prison. When Parliament convened, the Commons sent a delegation to the Lords to protest, but accepted York's argument (which Kemp might perhaps have ruled invalid, but did not) that since Thorpe's arrest had taken place during the recess, it did not infringe on parliamentary privilege.

The new Speaker, one of the royal household MPs, made no advocacy for Thorpe or Somerset. York also obtained the acquittal of the Earl of Devon of the charge of high treason pending since Dartford. In a quid pro quo, he then led the lords in reciting an oath of allegiance as 'true and faithful Liegemen to the King our Sovereign Lord', and the next day subscribed to the Act by which 5-month-old Edward was created Prince of Wales.

Simultaneously with these developments, on 19 March 1454 the Commons refused a request from the Chancellor for a grant of £40,000 [£24.44 million]. They argued that they had been generous already and had not received in return the 'sad and substantial council' promised several times since the king first agreed to it in 1450. It is quite possible Kemp had made the request to provoke an excuse to dissolve a Parliament now unresponsive to his will, and to return power to a Council he could override; but whatever he intended to do became moot when he dropped dead on the 22nd.

The next day the Lords sent a deputation led by Buckingham to visit the king at Windsor, and, after they reported that he remained catatonic, the political log-jam constructed by Kemp was washed away. On the 27th, the Lords elected York Protector of the Realm and Chief Councillor. He obtained an Act of Parliament to confirm the appointment, which cited the example of the arrangements made after the death of Henry V in 1422. That is, he was to receive all lawful and reasonable assistance in the service of the public good, but the Council reserved the right to define the public good. His only specifically defined duty was to defend the realm against foreign or domestic enemies.

The true novelty was the election on 28 March of Richard Neville, Earl of Salisbury, as the first secular Lord Chancellor since 1412, when Henry IV appointed his half-brother Thomas Beaufort as a shot across the bow of a politically activist episcopate. The same consideration applied in 1454: the election of Salisbury was retaliation by the secular lords for Kemp's frustration of the Great Council. Salisbury was, however, a most inappropriate choice for the senior legal officer of the kingdom. He had very recently defied royal authority in his family's squabble with the Percys, and he was also a party to other on-going disputes in the Midlands, and through his son in south Wales.

We can only speculate how this appointment, which led to the fateful alignment of the Nevilles with York, came about. It was certainly not due to York's influence, as he had barely managed to achieve a highly circumscribed authority for himself. It was most likely the result of wholesale bribery by Salisbury and Warwick, who wanted to ensure that those seeking to challenge their supremacy should have no legal recourse and would resort to arms, for which they could be condemned for rebellion.

Even though they were brothers-in-law, Salisbury had not previously shown any indication of sympathy with York, and it is not beyond the bounds of possibility that the queen could have instructed her party to vote for him, to balance York. Likewise the promotion from Ely to Canterbury of Bishop Thomas Bourchier, the Duke of Buckingham's maternal half-brother, may have been a move towards the creation of a 'centre' in which the country's greatest magnates were in equilibrium.

If so, it constitutes evidence of a political project too sophisticated to have been the product of the rather dull minds of the household sycophants. It may have been a policy legacy from the wily Kemp, but its continuation must have been driven by Marguerite, advised by Laurence Booth, her own chancellor and holder of the sinecure archdeaconry of Richmond. Further evidence of a carefully planned project is that Booth's brother William, Archbishop of York, did not to seek his own promotion to Canterbury, the more normal progression.

York's most immediate challenge was the captaincy of Calais, held by Somerset since 1451. With the support of the garrison, which had not even received payment on account since July 1453, Somerset's deputy, Lord Rivers, and his subordinate captains Lords Welles and Stourton, refused to admit York as the new captain. We shall discuss this in greater detail in a later chapter. For now let it suffice to say that York delegated negotiations to his brother-in-law Henry, Viscount Bourchier, who was acquainted with the problems from his own service as governor-general of Picardy during York's lieutenancy of Normandy.

York treated the king's appointment of Wiltshire to replace him as lieutenant in Ireland as though it had never been made. Although the Council refused to rule between the two claimants, York asserted his right under the unrevoked terms of his own 1448 patent, appointed his own officials and collected the salary. Wiltshire was infuriated by the affront, which must have involved the complicity of John Tiptoft, the new Lord Treasurer. Previously a king's man and as such created Earl of Gloucester in 1449, Tiptoft had become a member of the Neville affinity through his love-match in 1450 to Salisbury's daughter Cecily, the dowager Duchess of Warwick, tragically cut short by her early death.

In the North, Egremont obliged the Nevilles by embarking on a new round of depredations, in which the Duke of Exeter joined him. That the two men found themselves in such perfect harmony suggests Egremont's hold on sanity was also not too firm. Their cunning plan was for Exeter to assert his superior right by blood to challenge York's protectorship, and to claim the duchy of Lancaster. When Richard of York came north with a light escort in mid-May 1454, he had to retreat from York itself after learning of a plot to assassinate him. He gathered forces from his own estates and returned in mid-June to hold assizes, which condemned the two rebels and their supporters as traitors.

Consistent with his opinion of his own importance, Exeter had meanwhile obeyed a summons to appear before the Great Council. Finding the councillors did not share his opinion, he sought sanctuary in Westminster Abbey. When York returned to London on 8 July, he had his son-in-law snatched from the abbey and sent him north for imprisonment at Pontefract, a royal castle administered by Salisbury. To have put Exeter in the Tower with Somerset would have been folly, but the choice of Pontefract, where the deposed Richard II was starved to death, may have been intended as a reminder that royal blood did not confer immunity.

Reality caught up with Egremont and his brother Richard Percy when they ventured once too often into the concentration of Neville manors north-east of York. On 31 October, their small band of raiders was surrounded at Stamford Bridge by Neville retainers led by Thomas and John Neville, and after a brief struggle they were captured. Held first at Middleham in Richmondshire, they were sent to London to face trial for criminal trespass. Found guilty and unable to pay impossibly large fines, they were imprisoned as common debtors in Newgate.

The reason why no action was taken on their earlier conviction as traitors seems to have been a deal made among Salisbury, Northumberland, Clifford and York. Clifford was brought on board by appointing him to investigate and punish Egremont's accomplices, in the certain knowledge that he was one of them, while York promised to support Percy's petitions to recover estates held by the crown since the 1405 attainder. Meanwhile York obtained payment, equal to the amount he received as Protector, for each of the two Wardens of the Marches and promised to pay the arrears due to Percy. Salisbury also obtained recognition of his claim to Hawarden Castle in Flint, but overall York's even-handedness took the heat out of the Percy–Neville conflict.

York showed the same diplomatic skill in handling the void in command of naval matters created by Exeter's escapade. He did not seek to replace him as Lord Admiral, which would have required a vote by the Council. Instead, under his authority as Protector, on 3 April 1454 he appointed six keepers of the sea for three years, for which he obtained the necessary funds from the Commons. The eastern approaches, including Calais, were assigned to Warwick, the Channel to Lord Treasurer Gloucester, and the Irish Sea to John Talbot's namesake son, now Earl of Shrewsbury, also Earl of Waterford and hereditary Lord High Steward of Ireland.

Bringing Talbot into government was cunning. Although he was a party to the Beauchamp inheritance imbroglio he was a rival to Somerset in the matter of the barony of Bergavenny. Also, although he was brother-in-law to Wiltshire/Ormonde, whom York had just brushed aside as Lieutenant of Ireland, Talbot's marriage to Ormonde's sister had been an attempt to heal the feud between their respective fathers. It was very much in York's interest to revive it by giving Talbot, who had inherited his father's fierce temperament, an Irish bone to chew on.

What York did not do was enrich himself, or show favour to his affinity. Unfortunately his allies Norfolk and Devon completely misread him, and took his appointment as a green light to settle scores with those who had encroached on their local supremacies under Suffolk and Somerset. These were very tricky issues and York appears to have handled them informally, presumably by appealing to Mowbray and Courtenay not to make his job more difficult.

He was probably not too exercised by Courtenay's renewed attack on Bonville, because the latter, as seneschal of lost Gascony, was waging a naval war against French shipping, which included seizing French cargoes carried by neutral ships. His actions were denounced as piracy by the Duke of Burgundy, who retaliated by putting an embargo on the Calais wool trade through his surrounding counties of Artois and Flanders.

Burgundy's embargo actually gave York some much-needed leverage in the Calais impasse, as it dawned on Rivers and Welles that their continued rejection of the Protector's authority could get them included in the accusation levelled against Somerset, their patron, of a treasonous intent to sell Calais to Burgundy. The loss of Calais would have been devastating to York's protectorship, but even if Somerset considered it a price worth paying, Rivers and Welles knew it would cost them their heads.

One problem York did not have to deal with was hostility from the royal household. In recognition of the reduction of the king's needs to doctors and carers, the money voted for his household was drastically reduced – but the reduction was matched by a corresponding increase in the votes for the households of the queen and the Prince of Wales. Marguerite, of course, controlled both, and was also the beneficiary of substantial transfers of assets, cleared of encumbrances by resumption, from the duchy of Lancaster to her son's endowment. She could not be regent for the king, but nobody questioned her right to be regent for their son. While Henry remained catatonic it made her a major player in her own right.

Perhaps most notably, York did not make any effort to proceed to the impeachment of Somerset, although he successfully resisted efforts to release him on bail. It is reasonable to assume he could have obtained the necessary articles from a Commons in which Somerset's erstwhile supporters were anxious not to draw attention to themselves, so why did he not? One reason would have been to avoid being seen as vindictive, but another may have been because the queen asked him to let sleeping dogs lie.

One of the most valuable primary sources for this period is contained in the commonplace book written in Latin by the priest John Benet. The duke, he wrote, 'governed the entire kingdom of England well and honourably for a whole year [actually nine months], and miraculously pacified all rebels and malefactors, in accordance with his oath and without great severity'. Allowing for Benet's Yorkist bias, this is still a fair summary. York had achieved as much as he could have realistically hoped, not least the mutually respectful modus vivendi he worked out with the queen.

XII

HENRY

ENRY VI EMERGED FROM CATATONIA AT CHRISTMAS 1454 and within weeks destroyed the neutral royal centre painstakingly constructed by Marguerite and York. He had no memory of anything that had happened in the interim and so, disastrously, resumed personal kingship as though he had never relinquished it. Worse, he overcompensated for once more having abandoned his duties as a king and a man, and tried to act as he imagined his father would have done. On finding the queen had coped very well without him, he foolishly spurned what she had achieved and tried to turn back the clock.

We may feel some residual sympathy for the wretched man because of his mental condition, but there can be none at all for the fecklessness of his conduct in the following months. He acted as though he were still riding high after humbling York, the bogeyman created by his panicked entourage in 1450, and was deceived by the rejoicing at his recovery into believing it reflected widespread dissatisfaction at the way the country had been governed in his absence. Perhaps so, but there was no less widespread awareness that York had been honest and even-handed, qualities the king's personal kingship had always conspicuously lacked.

Rescued from political eclipse by his recovery, Henry's inner circle nurtured his delusion and urged him to make his priority the release of Somerset, their leader. He was duly freed on 26 January

1455 by the king's warrant. In truth, he had been detained for too long without formal charges, and when the Great Council reassembled on 5 February it declared his continued detention violated the clause against arbitrary imprisonment in the Magna Carta. The bishops had been vocally uneasy about this for some time, and the Council might well have insisted he be formally impeached or released even if York had still been Protector.

As soon as Somerset was back at Henry's side his priority was to ensure his survival should the king lapse back into catatonia. A second York protectorate would finish him, so he had to destroy his rival as soon as possible. As a first step, on 4 March Somerset persuaded Henry to dismiss all criminal accusations against him, recasting the remainder as civil suits to be decided by an arbitration panel. The panel included the now rabidly anti-Yorkist Wiltshire/ Ormonde, but its findings would be irrelevant because the king stated he believed the matters left pending were vexatious suits, without merit.

On the same day York, who had resigned the protectorship as soon as the king's recovery was confirmed, was dismissed as Captain of Calais and Somerset restored to the office. Three days later, on being ordered to release Exeter from Pontefract, Salisbury refused to do so and resigned as Lord Chancellor. Without seeking licence to do so, York and Salisbury withdrew to their estates in Yorkshire. Warwick, who resigned from the Council on 5 February, had already gone north, probably to Middleham. When he joined his father later, it was with a contingent led by Robert Ogle, whose family held several castles in Northumberland and had a history of bitter rivalry with the Percys.

On 13 March, Henry ordered his new Chancellor, Archbishop Bourchier, to release Exeter from Pontefract, ludicrously stating that he had only been imprisoned because of 'sinister information made upon him by certain persons not well disposed'. Two days later he dismissed Tiptoft as Lord Treasurer and appointed Wiltshire/ Ormonde in his place. Egremont and his brother had defied the king before his catatonia, and so remained in Newgate, but this was scant consolation to the Nevilles. The king could not have made his ill will towards York and anyone associated with him any clearer.

· ❧ ·

If Henry had appreciated the need for conciliation he would have given Somerset a blanket pardon and a golden handshake, and made Humphrey Stafford, Duke of Buckingham, his chief minister. It is worth examining why he did not. Fifty-three years old in 1455, Stafford was descended from Edward III's youngest son, was married to Anne, one of Salisbury's sisters, and was half-brother to the Bourchiers. With estates in twenty-two counties producing an annual income of about £5,000 [£3.18 million], roughly the same as York's, he had a large affinity and could have played a much more prominent role in affairs of state than he did.

Stafford had served with Henry V and was knighted by him in 1421. Despite marrying one of Cardinal Beaufort's nieces, as a member of Henry's minority Council from 1425 he was not a partisan in the cardinal's rivalry with the Duke of Gloucester. Made a Garter knight in 1429, in 1431 he returned to France with the king and was involved in several military operations as governor of Paris, Constable of France and Lieutenant-General of Normandy. He was also made Count of Perche, worth 800 marks [£340,000] a year.

It must have been galling to Stafford when York, nine years his junior and with negligible military experience, was appointed Lieutenant of Normandy in 1436. However, the appointment was made not only because York was a prince of the blood, but because he also had possession of his estates and could afford it, whereas Stafford's mother controlled all except £1,250 [£795,000] of his landed income until her death in 1438. After Stafford came into the whole of his inheritance he was made Captain of Calais in 1441, and in 1444 he was made Duke of Buckingham.

As we saw in Chapter 4, York had been stung in 1436–7, and he

HOUSES OF
STAFFORD AND BOURCHIER

k. = killed in battle   x. = executed

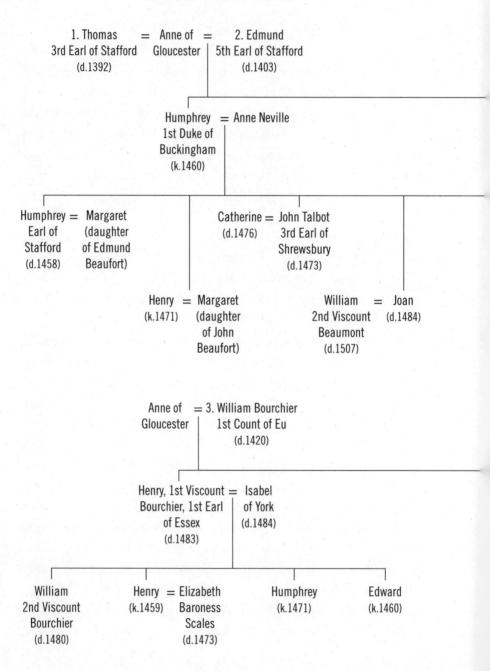

1. Thomas = Anne of = 2. Edmund
3rd Earl of Stafford   Gloucester   5th Earl of Stafford
(d.1392)   (d.1403)

Humphrey = Anne Neville
1st Duke of
Buckingham
(k.1460)

Humphrey = Margaret
Earl of   (daughter
Stafford   of Edmund
(d.1458)   Beaufort)

Catherine = John Talbot
(d.1476)   3rd Earl of
            Shrewsbury
            (d.1473)

Henry = Margaret
(k.1471) (daughter
          of John
          Beaufort)

William = Joan
2nd Viscount (d.1484)
Beaumont
(d.1507)

Anne of = 3. William Bourchier
Gloucester   1st Count of Eu
             (d.1420)

Henry, 1st Viscount = Isabel
Bourchier, 1st Earl   of York
of Essex   (d.1484)
(d.1483)

William
2nd Viscount
Bourchier
(d.1480)

Henry = Elizabeth
(k.1459) Baroness
          Scales
          (d.1473)

Humphrey
(k.1471)

Edward
(k.1460)

Children of Anne of Gloucester (1383–1438)

Eldest daughter of Thomas of Woodstock, Edward III's youngest son. Her mother was Eleanor, Bohun co-heiress. Mary, Eleanor's younger sister and co-heiress, was snatched from a nunnery, where Thomas had placed her, by his brother John of Gaunt to marry his eldest son, Henry of Bolingbroke, later Henry IV. Anne was thus Henry V's aunt.

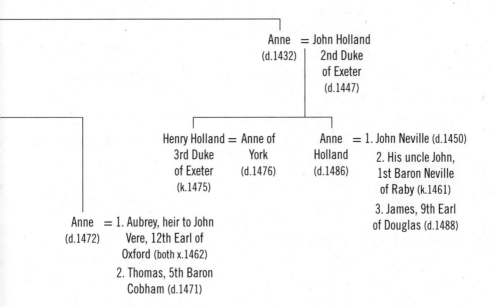

Anne = John Holland
(d.1432) 2nd Duke
of Exeter
(d.1447)

Henry Holland = Anne of
3rd Duke York
of Exeter (d.1476)
(k.1475)

Anne = 1. John Neville (d.1450)
Holland 2. His uncle John,
(d.1486) 1st Baron Neville
of Raby (k.1461)
3. James, 9th Earl
of Douglas (d.1488)

Anne = 1. Aubrey, heir to John
(d.1472) Vere, 12th Earl of
Oxford (both x.1462)
2. Thomas, 5th Baron
Cobham (d.1471)

Eleanor = John
(d.1474) Mowbray
3rd Duke
of Norfolk
(d.1461)

William = Thomasine
(d.1470) Hankeford
Baroness
Fitzwarine
(d.1453)

John = Margery
1st Baron Berners
Berners
(d.1474)

Thomas
Archbishop of
Canterbury
(d.1486)

John Mowbray
4th Duke of
Norfolk
(d.1476)

Humphrey = Joan (d.1490)
(k.1471) co-heir of Ralph,
Baron Cromwell
(d.1455)

negotiated financial conditions permitting him to relinquish the lieutenancy when the money stopped coming. Although Stafford, too, had previously experienced difficulty in getting the money he was due from the exchequer, he did not take the same precaution. He loyally completed his ten-year Calais appointment, even though for the last few years he had to pay the garrison out of his own pocket. Having in the meantime lost the income from Perche, he was owed over £20,000 [£12.72 million] in 1451, and had managed to collect less than half of it by 1455.

Not, one would have thought, an experience likely to make Stafford's heart grow fonder of the feckless king. Yet he remained devoted to him, and his loyalty was rewarded. We have seen how, having connived as Constable of England in the disgraceful downfall of Gloucester, he received the duke's magnificent palace of Penshurst in Kent. He was also made Constable of Dover and Warden of the Cinque Ports, which, together with his captaincy of Calais, should have made him the dominant lord in Kent. Cade's revolt had revealed this was not the case, and may explain why he did not enjoy the king's confidence.

Stafford was loaded with offices but continued to have difficulty collecting the salaries supposed to accompany them. His eldest son married one of Somerset's daughters, but the dowry was never paid, and it did little to increase his influence at court. His wife was made godmother to Prince Edward, but he seems to have held aloof from Marguerite's attempt to construct a non-partisan centre. In sum, if we look for a reason why Henry did not even consider Buckingham as a compromise chief minister, it is that the duke was taken for granted but not taken seriously. The clever ones in his family were his Bourchier half-brothers.

• ᶜ⌀ •

Following the absolution of Exeter in March 1455, events moved rapidly to a bloody climax and other magnates took sides. John

Mowbray, Duke of Norfolk, inherited 150 properties across twenty-five counties, but outside East Anglia none formed a sufficient concentration for him to develop a significant local affinity. He also suffered from chronic bad health, the given reason why he did not attend the Council after Henry's recovery. Forty years old in 1455, he was the son of Katherine, Salisbury's eldest sister, and was married to Eleanor, full sister to Viscount Bourchier and the new Archbishop of Canterbury.

Norfolk inclined to York because the king's party included 46-year-old Viscount Beaumont, who held large estates of his own in Lincolnshire, Leicestershire, Norfolk and Suffolk, and had married Norfolk's widowed mother. It galled the duke that, as a result of the marriage, Beaumont enjoyed the fruits of more than a third of Norfolk's patrimony. Beaumont had been one of York's councillors before 1450 and was not closely associated with Somerset, but he was a lifelong friend of the king, and head of his much-reduced household during 1454.

The motives of 38-year-old William FitzAlan, Earl of Arundel, and 47-year-old John Vere, Earl of Oxford, are more obscure. Arundel was married to Salisbury's eldest daughter, which inclined him to support his father-in-law, but he was a cautious player who went with whatever tide was flowing during the whole period of the Wars of the Roses. Oxford had been an ally of Norfolk against Suffolk and disliked Somerset, and in the early stages of the conflict followed the example of the prudent Arundel. Later, for reasons of his own, he made some fatally bad choices.

Among the barons, in addition to Lord Cromwell, whose landed income was as great as an earl's, two of the most powerful were Thomas, Baron Clifford, and Thomas, Baron Roos. Clifford's lordships were adjacent to Neville strongholds in Cumberland, Westmorland and Yorkshire, and he had backed Egremont's attacks on Neville manors in the north-west. Roos, with the oldest continuous title of nobility in England, held Helmsley in Yorkshire, Belvoir in Lincolnshire and other estates in Leicestershire. Eleanor née Beauchamp, his widowed mother, had married Somerset, and consequently Roos was involved in the Beauchamp inheritance imbroglio. Roos had supported the rebellion by Egremont and Exeter, and became one of the most tenacious enemies of the York–Neville alliance.

The event that did most to crack the body politic irreparably was Salisbury's and Warwick's gamble that the king's incapacity would be permanent. When this proved not to be the case a wiser king would have offered them a way back. Instead, by unconditionally embracing Somerset and all he stood for, Henry doomed him. Somerset continued to believe York was his principal enemy, but it was the Nevilles, whose power and fortune depended on royal favour, who most needed him dead.

In mid-April the king summoned a Council to which York, Norfolk, Salisbury and Warwick were not invited. The small gathering voted to convoke an exceptional Council at the queen's borough of Leicester on Whitsun (25 May), with the stated purpose of providing for the king's safety. Messengers were sent far and wide to pack the Leicester Council with regime loyalists, something York and the Nevilles would have known about before they received their own summons.

They could not construe it as anything other than an attempt by Somerset to repeat the charade engineered by Suffolk to bring down the Duke of Gloucester. Assuming, with some justification, that the deliberations of the exceptional Council were likely to place them in mortal danger, York and Warwick gathered their retinues and prepared to march south – to prevent Henry from reaching Leicester.

The king, however, seems to have believed they would tamely submit. We can take this either as evidence of simple-mindedness, or else as a manifestation of the assertive, over-confident state of mind with which he had emerged from catatonia. Right up to the moment war arrows began to hammer into his entourage, Henry was convinced York and the Nevilles would not dare use violence against their 'king anointed'. Somerset seems to have concurred, and as a result grossly overplayed his hand. The stage was now set for the first military encounter of the Wars of the Roses.

We are better informed about the run-up to the first Battle of St Albans than for any other battle of the Wars of the Roses.* The evidence is partial and often contradictory, but the details are insignificant beside the astounding fact that the king's entourage was unprepared for combat, even after the king raised his banner. To unfurl the royal standard was to declare that those against whom it was displayed were rebels and traitors. It was an action demanding immediate and unconditional submission – or war.

How could such a dislocation of cause and probable effect have come about? Even if Henry, who knew nothing of war, did not fully appreciate its significance, the experienced warrior nobles around him would have fully understood what raising the standard meant. The only possible reason why most of them were not in full harness when the attack came was their shared belief that an outright assault on the king's person was unthinkable.

It was only the last of a series of miscalculations by Henry and his retine. The first, the decision to relocate the exceptional – and handpicked – Council to the Lancastrian Midlands, arose because of concerns about Somerset's unpopularity in London and a concomitant uncertainty that he could control the outcome of a normal election. The second was their assumption that the retainers summoned by York and the Nevilles were intended merely for a show of strength at Leicester. Only on the eve of departure from London, when the king received a letter from York at Royston in Hertfordshire, did they awake to the possibility the royal party might be intercepted before reaching Leicester.

The Roman roads radiating out of London were still the main highways of the realm at this time, as was the pre-Roman Icknield Way, which linked Ermine and Watling Streets laterally. The high road from London to Leicester necessarily passed through St Albans,

---

* Thanks to Charles Armstrong's brilliant 'Politics and the Battle of St Albans, 1455' in the *Bulletin of the Institute of Historical Research*.

where the king wished to spend the night and to pray at the shrine of the martyr, towards whom he had a particular reverence. He may also have wished to pray for the soul of the Duke of Gloucester, victimized in his name, whose tomb was next to the shrine.

Somerset had earlier summoned loyalists to come to Leicester with armed retinues, but now he sent messengers urgently requiring them in the king's name 'to be with us wheresoever we be in all haste possible'. The departure from London could not be delayed if the royal party was to arrive at Leicester by Whitsun, but the choice of the Watford over the more travelled Barnet road was probably made to get further away from the Great North Road, down which York and the Nevilles were presumed to be marching. A second letter from York and the Nevilles, sent from the Neville manor of Ware on 21 May, seemed to confirm it.

It was a deception – by the time the letter arrived at Watford in the early morning of 22 May, York and the Nevilles were marching

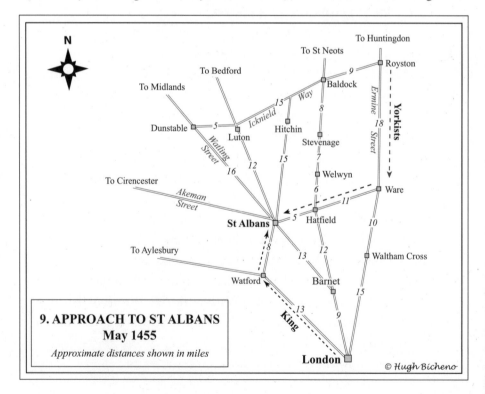

**9. APPROACH TO ST ALBANS
May 1455**

Approximate distances shown in miles

© Hugh Bicheno

west through Hatfield towards St Albans. Somerset must have presumed as much, for he now argued strongly that the king should remain at Watford until reinforcements arrived. A large contingent led by the Earl of Shrewsbury was two days' march away, while the Earl of Oxford, Lord Cromwell and Lord Stanley had also indicated they would join the king shortly. On the other side, the Duke of Norfolk was also closing in on St Albans in support of York. None of them arrived in time, and Shrewsbury was probably the only one who really tried.

The king's retinue included the Dukes of Somerset and Buckingham, and their heirs with the courtesy earldoms of Dorset (Henry Beaufort) and Stafford (Humphrey Stafford). The substantive earls were Pembroke, Northumberland, Wiltshire and Devon. There were also six barons: the king's old friends Lords Dudley and Sudeley, plus Roos, Clifford, Salisbury's brother William, Lord Fauconberg, and Buckingham's half-brother John Bourchier, newly created Lord Berners. The party included only one bishop, William Percy of Carlisle, who was Northumberland's brother. The best estimate for the sum of their retinues, of which the king's would have been the largest, is 2,000 men.

Closing on St Albans from the east were York, his 13-year-old heir Edward, Earl of March, Salisbury and Warwick. They had been joined by Buckingham's eldest half-brother Henry, Viscount Bourchier, and his son Humphrey, plus the Northamptonshire lord John, Baron Clinton, and Edward Brooke, Baron Cobham. They had at least 3,000 men, of whom York perhaps raised half in his progression from Yorkshire, past his manors in Lincolnshire and Hertfordshire. Most of the rest were Neville retainers with experience of the border wars.

With Salisbury's brother Fauconberg and the younger Bourchier in the king's party, it is reasonable to assume that York, the Nevilles and the older Bourchier were well informed about its numbers and composition. Since Somerset did not even know they had come south until York's Royston letter arrived, it is also reasonable to suppose the king's men were as much in the dark about their opponents' numbers as they were about their intentions.

After receipt of the Ware letter, the king took Buckingham's advice not to show fear by proceeding as planned to St Albans. At this point he replaced Somerset with Buckingham as Constable of England. There is much room to speculate about why Henry did this. At the simplest level, if there were to be negotiations, Somerset could not be a party to them, as he was completely unacceptable to York and the Nevilles. At another level, it may have been intended as a signal that the king was not wedded to Somerset. As we know he was, it follows Buckingham's appointment was a stratagem, to buy time until reinforcements arrived.

If this was the purpose of the Buckingham appointment, however, Somerset should have kept keep his head down. Instead, he sent insulting messages to York and Salisbury through an emissary he knew would be obnoxious to them. To understand the provocation, it is necessary to understand the function of heralds in medieval warfare. Their task was to communicate terms before a battle and to issue challenges if terms were not agreed. The herald had four junior officials under him known as poursuivants. They all wore surcoats, called tabards, which displayed the coat of arms of their master.

It was common for the principals in any imminent trial of arms to parley using their political allies' heralds – at St Albans, York used the Duke of Norfolk's – because their own heralds could not pose as neutral intermediaries. Quite the opposite intention can be firmly deduced from Somerset sending one of Exeter's poursuivants. This was a red rag to his opponents' bull, and the use of a junior official may have been insulting as well. The message he brought was blunt: submit or face attainder.

There are three possible interpretations of Somerset's actions. The first is that Somerset had agreed to the venerable negotiating tactic of playing bad cop to Buckingham's good cop. Given what we know about the chilly relations between them, this seems unlikely.

The second is that Somerset, knowing the only issue was his political future, wanted to prevent meaningful negotiations. This would imply he was afraid the king might fold under the pressure and act as he had with Suffolk in 1450, sending him away with a promise of reinstatement when tempers had cooled down. Suffolk's fate would have loomed large in Somerset's mind, and he may have been trying to pre-empt a repeat performance.

Related to the second, the third and most probable alternative is that Somerset was running a bluff, based on an underestimation of his enemies' resolve. He had been a gambler all his life, so why play it safe now, when he was riding a winning streak? Accordingly, the last message York and the Nevilles claimed to have received from the king may have been an invention they produced to justify their actions.* But it could also have been a further bluff by Somerset, taking the king's name in vain, or a last display of the false hair on the chest Henry had been flaunting since he emerged from catatonia:

> I, King Henry, charge and command that no manner of person, of what degree or state or condition that ever he be, abide not but void the field and not be so hardy to make any resistance against me in mine own realm for I shall know what traitor dare be so bold to raise a people in mine own land, wherethrough I am in great dis-ease and heaviness. And by the faith that I owe to St Edward and to the Crown of England I shall destroy them every mother's son and they be hanged and drawn, and quartered that may be taken afterward of them to have example to all such traitors to beware to make any such rising of people within my land, and so traitorly to defy their King and governor. And for a conclusion rather than they shall have this day any Lord here with me at this time I shall this day for their sake and in this quarrel myself live or die.

* The source is the strongly Yorkist *Stowe Relation*. Perversely, textual details like 'every mother's son' are so contrary to what one would expect from Henry that a forgery would have omitted them.

XIII

COUP D' ÉTAT

MEMBERS OF THE KNIGHTLY CLASS WERE REARED FOR war from childhood – it was what had won them their lands and titles, and the justification for their place in society. At St Albans on 22 May 1455 there were men on both sides who also had considerable experience of command in war, in France and along the Scottish border. We should, therefore, expect to find evidence of intelligent calculation in the way the battle was fought.

On the king's side, Buckingham was not only the senior duke but also the most experienced senior commander on either side. He chose to advance to St Albans partly because he believed the king should not be seen to flinch in the face of a challenge to his authority, but also because he knew the town was highly defensible. It was surrounded by a trench and embankment known as the Townman or Tonman ditch, and where roads crossed it there were structures into which heavy beams could be inserted to bar access to the town. He also knew from his experience in France that fighting in a built-up area gave the advantage to the defenders.

York and the Nevilles – for convenience the 'Yorkists' – either arrived after the royal party, or else chose not to enter St Albans to avoid the strong possibility that the two sides' troops might clash spontaneously. They turned left off the Hatfield road and formed up in an area known as Keyfield, halfway to the Barnet road and about 250 yards from the ditch. York was nearest the Hatfield road,

Salisbury nearest the Barnet road, with Warwick in between.

They had achieved strategic surprise by advising their affinities along the way to be ready to join them but not to alert the authorities by gathering beforehand, and operational surprise by intercepting the king before he reached Leicester. They knew the king could not possibly accede to their minimum demand, which was to abdicate his authority and hand Somerset over to them. Therefore, they arrived at St Albans intending to fight, and the only remaining questions were how to disguise their intent, and how to avoid a knock-down, drag-out battle with heavy casualties. That required tactical surprise.

If not before, then soon after arriving they would have known the ditch and the barred roads ruled out the use of cavalry. They would have seen the banners of Northumberland and Clifford at the barriers, and knew they were held by tough northerners who would make them pay dearly should they launch a frontal assault. A breakthrough at Sopwell Street, or a right hook through Cock Lane, would have involved a further advance along streets where they could be sure the royalists would have posted archers in the houses on either side – because that was what they would have done. The weaker of the two barriers was on Butts Lane, flanked by market gardens, but it was consequently more heavily manned.

Keyfield was in full view of the defenders at the barriers and along the embankment, and from the bell tower overlooking the market-place, where the king and his retinue were located. We have no way of knowing where the retinues of the other lords might have been, but some may have been posted along the embankment between the two barriers. It was a clear day and the royalists must have been confident it would be impossible for the Yorkists to achieve tactical surprise. Both sides knew the obvious tactic would be a strong feint at one of the barriers to draw in the reserves, followed by the main thrust at the other.

And that, following an hour or two of heralds pointlessly trotting back and forth, was exactly what the defenders saw coming

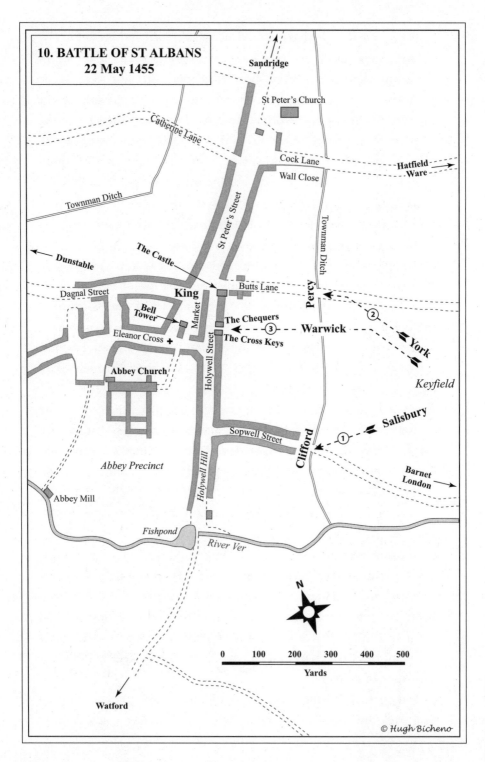

**10. BATTLE OF ST ALBANS
22 May 1455**

Sandridge

St Peter's Church

Catherine Lane

Cock Lane

Hatfield
Ware

Wall Close

Townman Ditch

St Peter's Street

Townman Ditch

Dunstable

The Castle

Dagnal Street

Butts Lane

Percy

King

Bell
Tower

Market

The Chequers

②

Eleanor Cross

Holywell Street

The Cross Keys

Warwick

York

Abbey Church

③

Keyfield

Sopwell Street

Clifford

Salisbury

Abbey Precinct

Holywell Hill

①

Barnet
London

Abbey Mill

Fishpond

River Ver

N

0   100   200   300   400   500
Yards

Watford

© *Hugh Bicheno*

at them. First, a column led by Salisbury, banners displayed and drums beating, attacked the Sopwell Street barrier. A while later, a larger column led by the banners of York and Warwick marched to attack the Butts Lane barrier. So far so predictable – a third of the force to make the feint, two-thirds to make the main attack. The lords and knights with the king in the marketplace still did not hurry to get into harness, so confident were they that Clifford and Northumberland would easily repel the attacks.

Although his banners were at the front of the column with York, Warwick was at the back with Ogle's 600 archers. After the head of the column had been become fully engaged, and the nearby enemy troops along the embankment drawn towards the barrier, he and Ogle peeled off. Without banners or fanfare, they crossed the now lightly defended ditch 100 yards below the barrier, into the market gardens on the other side. If the townscape was indeed as portrayed in Map 10, the manoeuvre was in plain sight of the men at the Butts Lane barrier. They, naturally, would have seen it as an attempt to outflank their position.

The first reaction of whoever was in command in Butts Lane – probably Somerset, who seems to have joined Northumberland once the Yorkist attack began – would have been to reposition archers to cover the flank of the men-at-arms at the barrier. Some of Ogle's men would have loosed a volley or two to maintain the illusion, but Warwick's main force was charging for a gap between two of the many inns along Holywell Street that catered to the pilgrim trade.

With the observers in the tower frantically clanging the curfew bell overhead, Warwick's men burst into the centre of the town, making as much noise as possible to increase shock. In the words of *The Stow Relation*: 'They ferociously broke in by the garden sides between the sign of the Key and the sign of the Chequer in Holywell Street, and immediately they were within the town, suddenly they blew up trumpets and set a cry with a shout and a great voice "A Warwick! A Warwick!"'

The essence of tactical surprise is the dislocation of expectations. An enemy is never so vulnerable as when he believes victory is in his grasp. The men at the Butts Lane barrier believed they had stopped the main Yorkist attack, and thought they had beaten off a flank attack. Nothing, however, can keep troops in line when they hear the noise of battle to their rear. After Warwick's men erupted into Holywell Street, Northumberland's men broke and fled across the market gardens towards the road leading north, back to their homes. A group of men-at-arms, including Somerset and his son, fell back towards the town centre, but were cut off by Warwick's men and took refuge in the Castle Inn.

If there was one thing above all the Yorkists did not want to do, it was to kill the king. It would have put them irretrievably in the wrong and they could expect the moral power of the Church to turn on them. The Scriptures were unequivocal (I Samuel 26): '…who can stretch forth his hand against the Lord's anointed, and be guiltless?… The Lord forbid that I should stretch forth mine hand against the Lord's anointed.'

Yet, possibly because the king's standard-bearer fled and his banner dropped to the floor, Ogle's archers shot indiscriminately into the mass of royalists in the marketplace. Four of the king's bodyguard were killed in his presence, and an arrow grazed Henry's neck before he was hustled to cover in a tanner's cottage. Buckingham and his son, badly wounded, were taken by their men to the abbey church.

Northumberland was probably killed somewhere along Butts Lane, and Clifford in Sopwell Street. The only one whose fate we can be sure of was Somerset. Called upon to surrender, he sortied from the Castle Inn and is said to have killed four men before he was brought down and clubbed to death. His son Henry, badly wounded at his side, survived. Abbot Whethamstede, an appalled eyewitness, wrote, 'here you saw one fall with his brains dashed out, there another with a broken arm, a third with a cut throat, and a fourth with a pierced chest, and the whole street was filled with dead corpses'.

Lord Dudley, who must have been near his friend the king, was hit in the face by an arrow. The other lords – Pembroke, Devon, Sudeley, Roos, Fauconberg and Berners – presumably took cover until it was safe to emerge. Wiltshire fled first to the abbey church and then, disguised as a monk, got clean away. Another notable royalist casualty was John Wenlock, who had served as the queen's chamberlain until 1453. He recovered remarkably rapidly from a disabling wound to become Speaker of the Commons in the Parliament elected seven weeks later. Deeply wounded in his dignity was Bishop Percy of Carlisle, who was stripped of his possessions and driven out of the town on foot and in his underclothes.

We know the names of sixty of those killed, practically all royal-ists and many of them members, some quite humble, of the king's household. Apart from them, the casualty list is top-heavy with knights and esquires who fell with Northumberland, Clifford and Somerset – proof, if any were needed, that it was a decapitation strike as well as a *coup d'état*. Men in harness were not easily killed, and there can be little doubt the York and Neville retainers were set-tling old scores. Another contemporary account states 'all who were on the side of Somerset were killed, wounded or at least despoiled'.

Before Somerset was killed, York had found the king and escorted him to safety in the abbey church. After the fighting ended and his troops turned to stripping the dead and looting, he made his way back to the church and demanded that Buckingham and Wiltshire should come out, or else they would be taken out by force. Buckingham duly emerged but Wiltshire had by now wisely fled. York, Salisbury and Warwick then entered the church and knelt before their king to beg his forgiveness for putting his life at risk. They had, they said, only wished to free him from the clutches of the traitor Somerset.

Showing surprising realism and presence of mind, Henry did not waste time with protests and received their homage, asking only that the fighting should cease. One can discern behind this the entreaties of the abbot that the rampaging Yorkists should be brought under control before they turned their attention to the abbey and its many treasures. Order was restored, and the wounded and dead brought into the abbey precinct for treatment and burial. Somerset, Northumberland and Clifford were buried in the Lady Chapel, and the proper reverence for their memories was to be the cornerstone of the king's last, sadly unsuccessful attempt to stop the slide into all-out war three years later.

York and the Nevilles escorted Henry back to London, where a ceremonial parade was staged with York and Salisbury riding on either side of the king, while Warwick rode in front bearing the royal sword, point uppermost. Henry was lodged at the Bishop of London's palace, and agreed that writs be issued for a Parliament on 9 July. The Whitsun celebrations went ahead as usual, and on Whitsunday (27 May), at the crown-wearing ceremony at St Paul's cathedral, the king insisted it should be Richard of York, not the Archbishop of Canterbury, who placed the crown on his head. It was a subtle move. Archbishop and Chancellor Bourchier might construe it as a snub engineered by York, but it also underlined that York had usurped the authority granted to Henry by God.

Henry's biographers have devoted few pages to the remainder of his reign, and it is true he scarcely features as a leading protagonist in the following years. Yet here we have him, only days after the brutal shock of St Albans, perpetrating a highly symbolic act of passive aggression. Although his brief spasm of active leadership had led to disaster, it is unwise to believe he ceased trying to influence events. Unfortunately for him and for his kingdom, the time for subtle hints and signals was over: the rules of the game had changed irrevocably.

XIV

MARGUERITE'S COUNTER-COUP

MARGUERITE SAW WITH CRYSTAL CLARITY THAT York's action at St Albans must lead, sooner or later, to the usurpation of the crown. A puppet monarch, no matter how benign the puppet master, offended intolerably against the medieval concept of kingship by divine right. Henry and Somerset had blown away her attempt to create a neutral royal centre, and the polarization resulting from Henry's connivance in Somerset's efforts to destroy York now left her with no option but to build up a Lancastrian faction.

Of the dukes, she could count on the unconditional support of the rabid Exeter and the slain Edmund Beaufort's vengeful son Henry, now Duke of Somerset, but both were affinity-light. Buckingham should have been ripe for recruitment after St Albans, but she did not, at this time, try to win him. Possibly she blamed him for persuading Henry to go there in the first place, and his Bourchier half-brothers may also have compromised him in her eyes.

Of the earls, the king's half-brothers Richmond and Pembroke had not had time to develop useful affinities. Only Wiltshire, Shrewsbury and the new Earl of Northumberland could summon numbers to support the Lancastrian regime. The Nevilles of Raby and Brancepeth were led by the ineffectual Westmorland, and Oxford was still a maybe. Marguerite could also count on the unconditional support of Viscount Beaumont and several barons, notably Rivers, Roos, Welles, the veteran warrior Scales and, in particular, John, the new Lord Clifford, who shared Somerset's and Northumberland's passionate desire for revenge.

Marguerite's greater strength lay with the bishops, several of whom owed their promotions to her influence. Firmly on her side were Archbishop William Booth of York, previously her chancellor, and her confessor Walter Lyhert at Norwich. Beckington at Bath and Wells, Percy at Carlisle, Boulers at Lichfield and Coventry, Chedworth at Lincoln and Dorchester, Kemp at London, the king's confessor Stanberry at Hereford, and Wainflete at Winchester were all king's, and by extension queen's men. They controlled vast wealth, and Bishops Booth and Percy were also authorized to maintain armed forces.

The Yorkists could count on only one bishop, Salisbury's brother Robert Neville at Durham, although Salisbury obtained the election of his youngest son, 23-year-old George, to Exeter in November 1455. The Duke of Norfolk, the Earl of Worcester, Viscount Bourchier and Barons Clinton and Cobham supported them, but the rest of the secular peerage was at best lukewarm. The blatant insult to the king's majesty at St Albans was impossible to overlook, and weak national government suited most lords very nicely. Their principal concern – devoutly shared by the bishops – was to avoid the tax increases that any attempt to recover England's empire in France must require.

The Yorkists' first order of business on returning to London was to establish a justification for their actions. Parliament grudgingly accepted a patently false story about the Yorkists' just petitions being kept from the king, with Somerset, his deposed nominee as Commons Speaker Thomas Thorpe and another low-ranking household member made the scapegoats. A popular gloss was applied by the posthumous rehabilitation of the Duke of Gloucester – and the promise to settle his debts, left unpaid after his assets were seized by the crown and distributed by Suffolk.

The second priority was to allocate the offices made vacant by the death of Somerset, with the plums going to Warwick. He was appointed Lieutenant of Calais and was given three castles on the border of Monmouth and Abergavenny, consolidating his south Wales holdings. Viscount Bourchier replaced the fugitive Wiltshire as Lord Treasurer, and his youngest son Edward got Kidwelly Castle in Carmarthen. Lords Fauconberg and Berners, who had been with Henry at St Albans, were made joint Constables of Windsor Castle, where it was expected the king would reside. He chose not to, once again demonstrating that in small matters he could still do as he wished.

Salisbury seized the opportunity to obtain a judgement in his favour over the Oxfordshire estate of the abeyant barony of Camoys, in the wardship of the crown since 1426. Also, the prosecution of the Percys for their attacks on Salisbury's interests in 1453–4 went ahead and they were fined 9,000 marks [£3.8 million], which they could not pay. He also made sure that the payments due to him as Warden of the West March continued to be paid promptly, while the new Earl of Northumberland found it more difficult than ever to collect for the East March.

By contrast with his Neville and Bourchier allies, York once again pointedly refrained from rewarding himself or his affinity. He replaced Somerset as Constable of England and of the largest royal castles in Wales, but these were necessary adjuncts for a protector-ship. The reason for his forbearance is not hard to identify. The new crop of MPs were certain to insist on a radical resumption of crown revenue sources before they would vote new taxes, and York did not want to find himself obliged to seek exemptions for himself or his affinity. With the Lords sceptical of his motives and intentions, he needed the Commons on his side.

This was admirably nuanced politics on York's part; but it was incomprehensible to his peers and to his loyal followers. What was power for, if not to enrich yourself and your friends? To the despair of those who wish human nature were other than it is, people may respect but never love an austere ruler. It is the reason why politicians who make promises they know cannot be kept routinely defeat those who attempt to tell the truth about the allocation of limited resources. York's lofty integrity was his Achilles heel – and Marguerite knew it.

She was determined he should not be made Protector again, since to do so would acknowledge the king was incompetent even when not catatonic. Unfortunately for her, a tacit consensus was forming that Henry was 'unworldly'. How else could he be absolved of personal responsibility for humiliating defeats abroad and borderline anarchy at home? Sovereignty could not, at this time, be detached from the person of the sovereign himself, and an unfit monarch posed a constitutional conundrum not finally resolved until Parliament judged Charles I guilty of treason and detached him from his head two centuries later.

With the king not free to act, and York unable to act with the king's authority, there was a power vacuum during the six months between St Albans and the appointment of York as Protector on 17 November 1455. Disorder surged, notably in the West Country, but it requires a deep faith in conspiracy theories to believe, as the queen and her party did, that any of it was engineered by York to bring about his appointment. That was indeed the outcome, but correlation was not causation in 1455 any more than it had been in 1450.

Although he had been with the king at St Albans, York's long-time supporter Devon judged the moment opportune to re-open the Courtenay–Bonville feud, to the point of open warfare. However, although this was the immediate cause of York's appointment, Devon was a chronic loose cannon and had reasons of his own. Backing York in 1452 had cost him dearly, and over the following years Bonville had replaced him as the leading magnate in the West Country. Devon's attempt to regain royal favour explains why he was on the losing side at St Albans. Now he had less than ever. The final straw came when Devon's cousin, Philip Courtenay of Powderham Castle, married his son to Bonville's daughter.

In late October 1455, retainers led by Devon's son murdered Nicholas Radford, Bonville's senior councillor, and in
early November Devon himself, at the head of 1,000 men, threw
Bonville's men out of the royal castle at Exeter. The castle had been
traditionally held by the earls as hereditary sheriffs of Devon, but
the king had appointed Bonville to punish Devon for backing York
in 1452. Devon now marched south to besiege Powderham, while
Bonville gathered forces at Shute, his stronghold. Devon marched
back through Exeter to confront him, and on 15 December smashed
Bonville's army at Clyst Heath. He then vengefully sacked Shute,
lost to Bonville by his marriage to Devon's aunt.

York himself owned land in Devon but, mindful of how he had
been humiliated after resolving the last outbreak of Courtenay–
Bonville violence, he would do nothing unless specifically
empowered to do so by Parliament and the king. The first protectorship did not provide a precedent, as it lapsed automatically when the
king recovered his faculties. The king suffered some kind of relapse
in late 1455, but York resisted appointment on the same terms as
before. On 10 November, a Great Council of Lords appointed him
the king's lieutenant, but the Commons refused to conduct any
other business until a Protector was formally appointed to resolve
the situation in Devon. The only candidate was York.

He was duly appointed on 17 November, having obtained the
terms he wanted. These were that a Council should be nominated
'to whose advice, council and assent I will obey and apply myself',
and that his appointment should last until Prince Edward came of
age, or earlier if revoked by the king 'with the assent of the lords
spiritual and temporal in Parliament'. Of the eight lords elected
to form the protectorate Council, the Archbishop of York and
the Bishop of Norwich were out-and-out queen's men, and the
Bishops of Rochester and Ely were neutral. The others were the royalists Buckingham and Lord Stourton, balanced by Warwick and
Viscount Bourchier. If York believed this would reassure the queen
he did not mean to act against her interests, his hope was misplaced.

One of York's first actions as Protector was to quell the private war raging in the West Country. A letter signed by the king was sent ordering all involved to 'obey [York] and keep his command-ments as you would and ought to obey us as if we were there in our own person'. Bonville immediately appealed in person to the king, who told him to submit to York. Devon continued his siege of Powderham but was eventually arrested and brought to London, where he spent some time with York before being brought before the protectorate Council. Devon and Bonville were imprisoned, not by the king or York, but by the Council, a constitutional nov-elty that in better times might have prospered.

In a reversal of the situation during Henry's period of catatonia, the queen now rejected compromise. York had backed the Commons' demand for a radical resumption and, once the immediate issue for which he had been elected was resolved, she used the issue to rally the lords against him. The first – and much quoted – reference to Marguerite's newly prominent political role was made with refer-ence to her actions at this time. One of the *Paston Letters*, dated 8 February 1456, describes her as 'a great and hard-working woman who spares no pains to pursue her interests with the purpose of increasing her power'.*

The Lords brought the king to Parliament to repudiate resump-tion and to receive York's resignation as Lord Protector on 25 February 1456. York immediately left London, and we can readily imagine his thoughts. Resumption was unquestionably necessary to restore solvency to the royal finances, and there had never been any suggestion it might impinge on the endowments of either the queen or the Prince of Wales. The queen's actions, therefore, must have been dictated by personal animosity, without regard for the national interest.

York then got into man-think. Whence came Marguerite's fury? It must be because Somerset had been her lover, and she was irrational

---

* The actual words are 'a grete and strong labourid woman spareth noo peyne to sue hire things to an intent and a conclusion to hir power'.

with grief. It would not have occurred to him that a nubile young woman might have made a cold political calculation to forgo a short-term gain for a longer-term objective. The next, short hop of reasoning was perhaps coloured by York's own matrimonial experience: his people begin to circulate rumours casting doubt on the paternity of the Prince of Wales.

Taking away York's formal title did not diminish the need for his services, because St Albans had cured Henry of any illusion that he could be a strong leader. In a decision we may be sure infuriated his wife, the king retained York as his chief councillor and sent him north to deal with a new threat from Scotland. The Battle of St Albans had persuaded King James II the time was ripe to renew the 'auld alliance' with France, and he wrote to Charles VII proposing concerted action to seize, respectively, Berwick and Calais. To muddy the waters, James also announced that York was the rightful king of England, before declaring war and sending raiding parties across the border. Marguerite would have believed York engineered the whole episode – but Henry did not.

In the absence of support by Charles VII, James scuttled back across the border after York moved to his stronghold at Sandal Castle in Yorkshire and issued two stern warnings, the first in Henry's name and the second in his own. Meanwhile the queen took the prince with her to Tutbury in Staffordshire, the westernmost of the triangle of castles at the heart of her Midlands dower, leaving Henry behind. It was an intimate power play and in late August, Henry left London to join her at Kenilworth Castle, outside Coventry, impregnable within its man-made lake, but which Marguerite ostentatiously equipped with additional artillery. A further twenty-six long guns (serpentines) would be brought from the Tower in 1457.

Since York, Salisbury and Warwick were all busy about the king's business at the time, it is worth pondering the motives behind Marguerite's retreat to the Midlands. It is hard to escape the conclusion that she was dramatizing a non-existent threat – although she may have convinced herself it was real – to pressure Henry into taking a harder line with York. Her message could not have been clearer: only *she* could take care of her husband, and he should trust no one else.

The inevitable result of the semi-permanent removal of the court to the queen's Midlands was to indicate distrust of London, which, however deserved, in the end turned out to be a gross strategic error. That, perhaps, is more apparent in hindsight than it was at the time. Marguerite would have had in mind her uncle Charles VII's ability, as dauphin, to rally support at Bourges after his father lost Paris. Unfortunately it was a false analogy. London was more central to the life of England than Paris was to France. It was by far the largest city, not only the political but also the commercial capital, and the hub of all the Roman roads that still provided the country's principal highways.

Marguerite completed her counter-coup at a Great Council summoned to Coventry on 16 October 1456. In the presence of York and Salisbury, the Bourchier Lords Chancellor and Treasurer were sacked and replaced by Bishop William Wainflete and John Talbot, Earl of Shrewsbury. The late Archbishop Kemp's man Lisieux was dying, and he had previously been replaced as Lord Privy Seal by Laurence Booth, the queen's chancellor and younger brother of the Archbishop of York.

Having control of the Privy Seal permitted Marguerite to appoint the officers of her son's estate. John Morton, a previously obscure doctor of civil law, became the prince's chancellor, while the ultra-loyalist Viscount Beaumont became his chief steward, as he already was the queen's. Other offices were filled by members of Marguerite's household.

On 28 January 1457, a formal minority council was set up for Prince Edward, which a month later was given control of his patrimony: the principality of Wales, the duchy of Cornwall, the county palatinate of Chester and select parts of the duchy of Lancaster. Chester and the northern duchy estates were complementary to the queen's Midlands dower, a factor that will help to explain some of her subsequent initiatives.

The ecclesiastical members of the council were the queen's former chancellor Archbishop Booth of York, the new Lord Chancellor Bishop Wainflete, the king's confessor Bishop Stanberry of Hereford, Bishop Boulers of Coventry and Lichfield, and her chancellor Laurence Booth, the new Lord Privy Seal, who was made Bishop of Durham when Salisbury's brother Robert died later in 1457. Three of the six lay members were the king's new Lord Treasurer Shrewsbury, Beaumont again, and Lord Dudley who, like Boulers, had been a member of the king's inner circle since he first assumed personal kingship.

The other three were the Lancashire magnate Lord Thomas Stanley, Humphrey, Earl of Stafford, and, as Treasurer, James Butler, Earl of Wiltshire, whom the Yorkists would have killed at St Albans if they had managed to lay their hands on him. Stanley's lordships and royal stewardships were also complementary to the prince's Cheshire estates. The appointment of Stafford, Buckingham's heir, was clearly intended as a gesture to smooth the duke's feathers, ruffled by the dismissal of his Bourchier half-brothers, without bringing in the reluctant duke himself. Wiltshire's appointment was equally clearly a defiantly rude gesture towards the Duke of York and, at this early stage, surprisingly provocative.

Thus, less than two years after St Albans, Marguerite had totally outmanoeuvred York to set up a parallel government responsive to her will. Nobody questioned her right to act as regent for her son, which she turned into a de facto regency for the kingdom. She controlled the greater part of the unencumbered royal revenues, and all of Henry's senior officials were now hers as well. The bureaucracy in London, as well as the unruly London mob, had been disempowered, and she was free to develop a compact affinity in areas where loyalty to the crown, and to her person, ran deep.

What she lacked, and to her sorrow always would lack, was someone to fill the office much better described in the *Game of*

Thrones saga by George R. R. Martin's invented 'Hand of the King' than by 'lieutenant' or 'constable'. Of the dukes, Buckingham was insufficiently partisan, Exeter too wild and the 20-year-old Somerset too young to be her champion. The Earls of Shrewsbury, Northumberland and Wiltshire were old enough at 39, 35 and 34 respectively, but they would have pursued their personal vendettas against York and the Nevilles without sufficient regard for the queen's overall strategy.

For all the mystique of divine right, the Yorkists had demonstrated at St Albans that power ultimately depended on brute force, intelligently applied. For all her political skill, Marguerite was disqualified by her sex from overtly leading the royalist faction because, until very recently, combat has always been an exclusively masculine activity. She needed a loyal man of rank with brains as well as brawn – and she never found him.

XV

LORD OF CALAIS

S T ALBANS WAS THE MOMENT WHEN THE YOUNGER Richard Neville, known to history as Warwick 'the Kingmaker', first took centre stage. He was to remain there for the next sixteen years. His rise is bound up with Calais, the English outpost across the Channel surrounded by the Duke of Burgundy's domains. While the military significance of the enclave is apparent, unless we fully appreciate its economic, strategic and diplomatic importance we cannot understand why Warwick once said he would give up all his lands in England if he could keep Calais.

The Calais garrison was the English crown's only standing army, and the outpost itself was virtually impregnable. It was protected to the east by the undrained marshes of the Aa River. The marshes to the south and west were drained, but where the drainage canals emptied into the sea, the Newenham bridge, guarded by Nieulay fort, provided the only road into the town.* Under the bridge were sluice gates that could be used to flood the approaches. The canals were a barrier to an attack through the counties of Ponthieu and Boulogne to the west, while a fort at Hammes and a castle at Guînes guarded the wooded hills to the south.

The sea entrance was guarded by a large fort at Rysbank, while

---

* When Calais was finally lost on 1 January 1558 it fell to a night attack that began with the capture of the sluice gates – by that time strongly fortified – while the garrison was drunkenly celebrating the New Year.

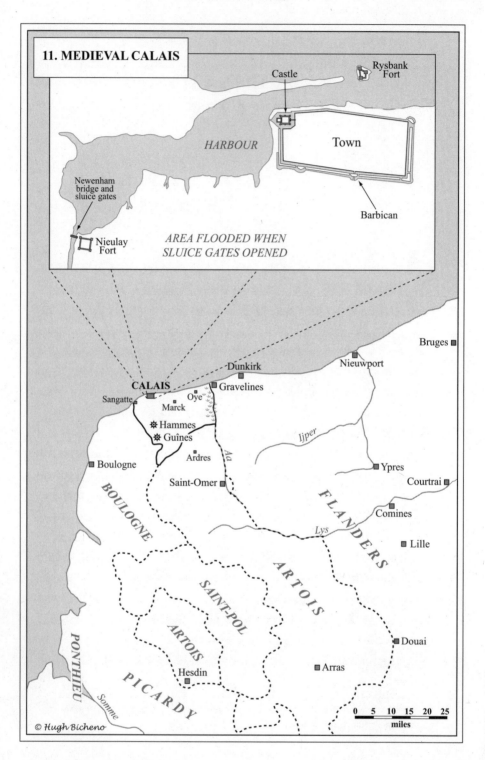

11. MEDIEVAL CALAIS

Castle

Rysbank Fort

HARBOUR

Town

Newenham bridge and sluice gates

Nieulay Fort

Barbican

AREA FLOODED WHEN SLUICE GATES OPENED

Bruges

Dunkirk

Nieuwport

CALAIS

Gravelines

Sangatte

Oye

Marck

Hammes

Guînes

Ardres

Ijper

Boulogne

Saint-Omer

Ypres

Courtrai

Aa

FLANDERS

Comines

Lys

Lille

BOULOGNE

ARTOIS

SAINT-POL

ARTOIS

Douai

PONTHIEU

Hesdin

Arras

PICARDY

Somme

0 5 10 15 20 25
miles

© Hugh Bicheno

the harbour was dominated by powerful Calais Castle. The walled town itself was surrounded on the landward side by a double wet ditch, with outworks between the two channels. The port could not be starved into submission, as distant naval blockade was not possible with the sailing ships of the era, and shifting sandbanks made a close blockade too perilous to contemplate.

Rowing galleys and other shallow draft vessels that could have operated close to shore required a nearby base of operations, but Gravelines and Dunkirk were not available for as long as the prosperity of neighbouring Flanders depended on the English wool trade. This was Calais' strategic defence in depth, as seen after the failed siege of 1436, when a revolt of his Flemish cities forced Duke Philippe to abandon his military alliance with France.

The siege of 1436 had illustrated a further aspect of Calais' military/diplomatic significance, as a potential base for offensive operations. The reason the garrison was so expensive was that it contained a high proportion of men-at-arms and mounted archers, who could launch raids against Burgundian or even French territory at short notice. If reinforced from England they could spearhead devastating *chevauchées*, something Duke Philippe and King Charles VII were not likely to forget.

This aspect of Calais' strategic importance only came to the fore after Duke Philippe ended the Anglo-Burgundian alliance in 1435. Somerset seems to have been the first to realize the outpost could become an independent power base, perhaps when he sailed there after surrendering Caen in 1450. When he returned to England he left behind his bodyguard, later joined by others of his Norman affinity including Andrew Trollope, the Captain of Falaise who had made the release of John Talbot a condition of surrendering the town.

In September 1451, when Somerset became constable at the end of Buckingham's ten-year tenure, he replaced the entire garrison with his own men. In December, he sent Richard Woodville, Lord Rivers, with sixty men-at-arms, to act as his deputy. Subordinate captains at Guînes (Thomas Findern), Calais Castle (Lord Welles),

Hammes (John Marney) and Rysbank (Osbert Mountfort) indented for themselves and for, respectively, 100, 50, 41 and 18 men. Trollope commanded the barbican at the sole gate into the town.

By the end of 1452 Somerset had increased the numbers he could indent for by 160 men-at-arms and 511 mounted archers. This alone was an additional daily cost of £25 per day, £9,125 [£5.8 million] per annum, an increase of about 75 per cent above the peacetime establishment. In addition, the crown already owed Buckingham £20,000 [£12.72 million] for the last years of his captaincy, making Calais much the largest single charge to the exchequer at a time of desperately straightened royal finances.

Somerset almost certainly chose Rivers as his deputy because his wife Jacquetta was the sister of Louis of Luxembourg, Count of Saint-Pol 25 miles south of Calais. Louis inherited Saint-Pol and Brienne in 1433, and continued his family's policy of supporting the English after Duke Philippe renounced his alliance with England in 1435 in return for Picardy, which left Saint-Pol buried deep within Burgundian territory. Louis was also the heir to his uncle, Count of Ligny and Guise, but when he died in 1441 Charles VII seized the counties and only let Louis have Ligny after he swore fealty and ceased helping the English. He was also required to join in the reconquest of Normandy.

Rivers' dealings with Saint-Pol were probably the reason Richard of York believed Somerset intended treason with regard to Calais. Marguerite, also, may have had doubts about his motives. Her father owed fealty to the rulers of France, Burgundy and the Empire for his scattered domains, and she would have had a greater understanding of how the game was played at the borders of rival kingdoms than any other member of the English court.

So, what was Somerset's game? First, Calais was a cash cow, although getting the milk was problematic. In 1457, two years after Somerset's death at St Albans, the crown recognized a debt to his estate of £23,000 [£14.6 million], separate from the arrears separately paid to the garrison. This was a staggering amount for a mere four years' service, and vastly greater than his landed income. The king's aim had been to put him on a financial par with the great magnates, but Somerset exploited his benevolence further by indenting for more soldiers than were actually serving in Calais.

Somerset must have known the cost to the crown was unsustainable, and it is hard to dismiss the suspicion that he had a fall-back position in case he lost the king's favour and was obliged to flee England. It could well have been to enrich himself and those who chose to remain with him by handing over the enclave to the highest bidder, perhaps with Louis of Luxembourg acting as broker, and to remain as Count of Calais.

Whatever plans he had were aborted by his imprisonment during York's first protectorate. Denied emergency taxation by the Commons, the exchequer could no longer pay Somerset's men in Calais. This provoked a mutiny, which, had he been free to attend to it in person, might have served as a step towards whatever outcome he had in mind. Instead, it became a means of undermining his rival's authority, a tricky hand for Somerset's deputies to play when York was the legally appointed authority for the defence of the realm.

The key to resolving the impasse was the Company of the Staple, set up in Calais in 1399 to handle the export of all English wool to northern Europe. Like any monopoly, it depressed producer income and inflated the price paid by consumers, in this case the great textile manufacturing towns of the Low Countries, which paid in gold and silver. After several other expedients had failed, the Staple was set up to provide the crown with a single point of tax revenue from the wool trade, and practically its only source of bullion, without which the English could not have waged the last half of the Hundred Years War.

So great was the difference between the purchase and sale prices that Cardinal Beaufort's great wealth had come largely from the sale of wool to southern Europe, less than a fifth of all wool exports, through his port of Southampton. The Calais Staple could do nothing about that; what infuriated the Staplers were the exemptions from their northern European monopoly, granted by the crown to pay debts to favoured individuals. York, for example, was granted one such exemption to recover some of what he was owed for his Normandy lieutenancy.

Consequently, when in May 1454 the garrison seized the entire stock of wool warehoused in Calais as a guarantee of its unpaid wages, the Staplers were not in a mood to compromise. As we have seen, York had pressing calls on his time in England, and he delegated negotiations to Viscount Bourchier. Bourchier set about driving a wedge between the troops, whose grievances were financial, and their politically motivated commanders. This tactic appears to have been on the brink of success when the king recovered from his catatonia and restored Somerset to all his offices.

One of the reasons Somerset did not pay enough attention to the gathering Yorkist storm may have been because his eyes were fixed on affirming his hold on Calais as a bolt-hole should Henry relapse. Not long after the king dismissed the charges against him, he sent Lord Roos and his two most trusted household officers to arrange for his return. The arrears continued to mount and the Staple was no more interested in backing him than it had been to commit to York. For this reason, on 14 May 1455 Somerset appointed shire commissioners throughout the land to raise a loan to pay the garrison.

This would have encountered considerable resistance, but the issue became moot after Somerset was killed at St Albans eight days later. Anxious not to repeat his previous error of trying to do too much himself, one of York's first acts was to get the king to appoint Warwick as Captain of Calais. With Somerset gone, political resistance from the Calais commanders was limited to a non-negotiable demand for immunity for previous actions, including the theft of the wool. York no longer had cause to find evidence of Somerset's frauds, beside which any his subordinates might have committed were minor. So it came down to money.

With all claims to be honoured at face value, the amount in

question was enormous. The arrears due to the captains and soldiers, net of £17,366 deducted for the stolen wool, were calculated on 20 April 1456 to be £48,080 [£30.6 million]. A cash settlement was provided by the Staple, which accepted £23,000 in crown IOUs ('tallies') held by the treasurer of Calais in part payment. Exemptions from the Staple's monopoly were to cease and, once Buckingham's debt was cleared, the Staple's advance was to be paid down by the customs receipts of Sandwich, Calais' main corresponding port in England. The Staple was also promised the customs receipts from Southampton, although it never collected a penny.

A pardon was issued by the Council on 1 May, and shortly afterwards Warwick entered Calais with his own retinue of 300 men, paid for by a further crown-guaranteed loan from the Staple. He adopted a light-handed approach, and apart from terminating the employment of Rivers, Welles and Mountfort, there was no purge of the remaining Somerset loyalists. Warwick was confident he could win them over – and they were content for him to believe he had. He was to find his confidence misplaced in 1459–60, when Trollope and his men deserted him at a crucial moment, and Findern and Marney handed over Guînes and Hammes to Somerset's heir, Henry Beaufort.

Previous Captains of Calais had been absentees, governing through deputies, and at first it seemed Warwick might follow the same path. After his ceremonial taking of possession he returned to England to consolidate his gains in Wales and to attend Council meetings. As control slipped progressively from York's hands, however, Warwick saw Calais was a good place to sit things out. It would take him away from the danger of assassination by the heirs of the men killed at St Albans, and permit him to continue his pose as the king's loyal servant by distancing himself from active factionalism.

Warwick was a supremely lucky man in an age that believed Lady Luck (the pagan *Fortuna*) ruled over all. How much of his luck was the product of careful planning is hard to say, but in the peculiar circumstances prevailing after Marguerite's counter-coup he strengthened his hand by creating tension with Burgundy. The mechanism was raids from Calais across the border into Artois, falsely reported as a response to Burgundian aggression. After a preliminary meeting between representatives of the two sides at Ardres in late 1456 and early 1457, in April the king commissioned Warwick to negotiate in his name with Duke Philippe.

By this time Warwick had made the momentous decision to move his household to Calais, which made him the idol of the townspeople. He was a big spender, which of course pleased the local merchants, but by establishing a glittering court in what had always been a rather drab garrison town, he and Countess Anne also greatly enhanced the social life of the local aristocracy, the very wealthy members of the Company of the Staple and their wives. This marked him as among the first English nobles to appreciate the political advantages of princely magnificence, a feature of the contemporary Italian Renaissance but late in coming to northern Europe.

In July 1457 Duke Philippe's personal envoy came to meet Warwick between Oye and Marck, inside the pale of Calais. This was Philippe's eldest illegitimate son Anthony, known as 'the Grand Bastard of Burgundy' to differentiate him from his younger brother Corneille, who was merely 'the Bastard of Burgundy'. Anthony was brought up with Philippe's legitimate heir Charles, Count of Charolais, and the two were close. More remarkably they were both loyal sons, a rare occurrence among the Valois. Warwick hosted a splendid banquet, and obtained compensation for the border incidents he had provoked.

In August Lady Luck dealt him the ace of trumps in the shape of a large-scale amphibious raid on Calais' supply port Sandwich led by Pierre de Brézé, Grand Seneschal of Normandy since the reconquest. Although Brézé had lost influence at court since the death of Agnès Sorel, the king's mistress and his patron, he was still the Charles VII's go-to man in military matters. The raid underlined Exeter's complete failure to maintain a fleet to justify his title of Lord Admiral, and Warwick successfully argued for the extension of his power to include Calais' maritime communications.

He was strongly supported by the inhabitants of Sandwich and many other ports, whose trade was suffering from a great increase in French piracy since the fall of Normandy. Although Brézé claimed his raid was retaliation for English piracy, to Henry VI it confirmed he had a naval war on his hands. Exeter kept his title, but in early October 1457 the king and Council made Warwick Keeper of the Seas, de facto Lord Admiral, 'for the resistance of [the king's] enemies and repressing their malice' and 'the comfort and relief of his subjects, friends and allies', with an initial advance of £3,000 [£1.9 million].

Subsequent patents richly gilded the lily. He was authorized to do the king's enemies 'all hurt and annoyance' by sea and, remarkably, by land as well, to issue (for which read sell) safe conducts on his own authority, and to keep a third of any spoils for himself, with another third for his crews, and a wishful thinking third for the crown. He was required to recruit 3,000–5,000 men and to lease or build ships at will, for which he was not only assigned the customs receipts of every port except Sandwich and Southampton (already committed to the Staple), but also to appoint his own customs agents to collect them.

There were an almost infinite number of ways to make money from this astonishingly broad remit. For example, Warwick was already a ship-owner as a result of his lordship (through his wife) of the Channel Islands, and we may be certain the first ships he leased for the crown, no doubt on extremely generous terms, would have been his own. He was not required to render accounts, and we can be sure he would also have received kick-backs from every individual involved in the building, equipping and maintenance of the ships. Not least, the right to issue safe conducts and to collect customs – or not – gave him the option to develop a nationwide coastal and naval affinity.

The powers vested in Warwick, at a time when Marguerite's star was in the ascendant, were enormous. He was made virtually sovereign of Calais, where he controlled the principal source of bullion for England and even had his own mint. He was empowered to negotiate with other sovereigns in the name of the king, with only remote oversight. He had the only standing army in English territory, as well as a navy he could use to make war, commit piracy, or to trade on his own account. All of this in principle paid for by the crown.

Why, after her assumption of leadership of the Lancastrian faction, did Marguerite not seek to clip the wings of the man responsible for the lethal attack on the king's retinue at St Albans and the butchery of Somerset, Northumberland and Clifford? I believe the answer is that he was really the only candidate for a 'Hand of the King', with no claim by blood to the throne, who was capable of facing down York on behalf of the Lancastrian dynasty. Warwick had been a most assiduous courtier before the king's illness – why not try to win him back?

Unlike Suffolk and Somerset, Warwick was not a man who could be won by an accumulation of offices, wardships and other small privileges. He had shown no desire for a role in the administration or the other mundane occupations of indirect power. He fancied himself as a prince, so why not encourage him to seek glory, riches and renown – outside England? Just because we know it backfired does not mean Marguerite was wrong to gamble on building Warwick up in the hope of splitting the Nevilles from York. She was looking for a way to win without incurring the risks of a war in which her gender would preclude her from playing a leading role, and really had no other option.

Her hopes were in vain, as Warwick remained in close communication not only with his father, but also with York. Edmund Mulso, previously York's Midlands steward, came to Calais with Warwick in 1456 and was his marshal until he died in 1458. He was replaced by Walter Blount, another Yorkist councillor whose family home was sacked in 1454 by anti-Yorkists, and who went on to become the treasurer of Calais in 1460.

Even if there had been exploitable differences among Warwick, his father and York, the crown's finances were in such a parlous state that payments for Calais could not be sustained, and soon ceased. The king's government also broke its agreement with the Staple and continued to issue exemptions, persuading the Staplers their future lay with the Yorkists. Warwick was to use his fleet not only to generate income for the garrison by piracy, but also to seize ships carrying non-Staple wool, and to fence the stolen property through Calais.

Warwick won an even wider following by acting as the champion of English merchants against foreign competition. A particularly shrewd blow was the seizure of three exempt Genoese ships with cargoes worth £4,000 [£2.5 million] at Tilbury, down-river from London, cheered by local merchants deeply resentful that their own government was favouring foreign inroads into their trade. At another level he appealed to bruised patriotism by demanding foreign ships should dip their flags to England's, and attacking them if they did not.

Warwick was a phenomenon quite outside the normal run of English history. He was indeed a prince, and a quick-witted warlord who would have been quite at home in Renaissance Italy. Most of the English sources for his life are hagiographic, but reports by Burgundian, French and Milanese agents to their masters support the view that he was not only popular, but also a man of exceptional intelligence, personal charm and steely determination. That he was also a serial killer was, if anything, considered a mark in his favour.

He remained devoted to his wife even though they never had the son for whom he yearned, and she is one of the unexplored aspects of his story. She was, after all, the source of his wealth and a considerable peeress in her own right. He did not appoint a formal deputy to govern Calais during his absences in the crucial early years of his captaincy, which strongly suggests Countess Anne must have played an active political role, as well as being the hub around which his court revolved. They were a formidable partnership.

Warwick's withdrawal to Calais left Wales, the source of his original contention with what was now the Lancastrian party, very much up in the air. It was to play a crucial role, but it is a mistake to see it as simply one more stage on which the evolving rivalry between the English magnates was played out. There was more to it than that.

XVI

HERE BE DRAGONS

WALES MIGHT WELL HAVE BEEN MARKED 'HERE BE dragons' on the Anglo-Norman mental map. Barring rims of settlement along the north and south coasts, it was a mountainous, wooded territory, thinly inhabited by miserably poor and deeply resentful peasants. It preserved its own legal system, with feudalism still the dominant form of land tenure, and of course its own language, thanks to which a separate Welsh identity survives to this day. It is only through translations of the oral history contained in bardic poems that English speakers can even glimpse what was going on in the hearts and minds of the conquered people.

The border marked on Map 12 was not legally defined until the mid-1500s, by the same series of acts that made Wales part of England, granting it representation in Parliament for the first time, but abolishing its legal system and banning the Welsh language from any official role or status. 'The March' occupied most of what we now call Wales. During the prolonged Norman conquest from 1067 to 1283 it was dotted with a profusion of motte and bailey timber castles. These were gradually replaced by a smaller but still large number of masonry castles and walled towns, with the heaviest concentration in the south.

Monmouth and Glamorgan corresponded approximately to the old kingdoms of Gwent and Morgannwg. The royal counties of

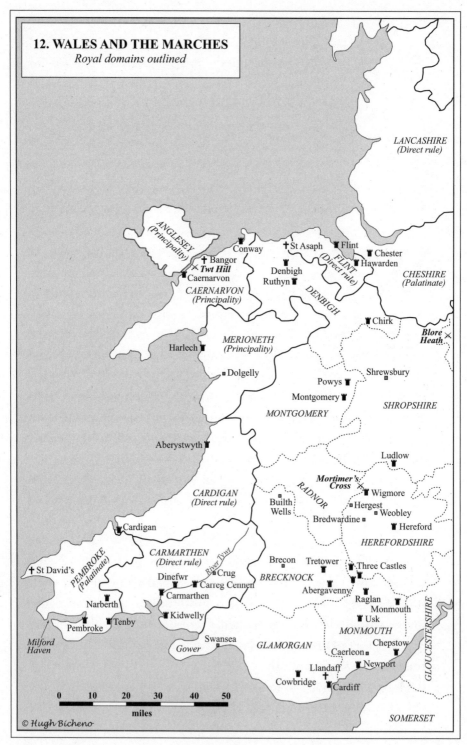

12. WALES AND THE MARCHES
Royal domains outlined

LANCASHIRE
(Direct rule)

*ANGLESEY
(Principality)*

Conway

✝ St Asaph

Flint

Chester

Hawarden

CHESHIRE
(Palatinate)

✝ Bangor
✗ *Twt Hill*
Caernarvon

*FLINT
(Direct rule)*

Denbigh
Ruthyn

*CAERNARVON
(Principality)*

DENBIGH

Chirk

*Blore
Heath* ✗

*MERIONETH
(Principality)*

Harlech

Dolgelly

Powys

Shrewsbury

Montgomery

SHROPSHIRE

MONTGOMERY

Aberystwyth

Ludlow

*Mortimer's
Cross* ✗

RADNOR

Wigmore

Builth
Wells

Hergest

Weobley

Bredwardine

Hereford

*CARDIGAN
(Direct rule)*

HEREFORDSHIRE

Cardigan

Brecon

Tretower

Three Castles

*PEMBROKE
(Palatinate)*

*CARMARTHEN
(Direct rule)*

River Tywi

Crug

BRECKNOCK

✝ St David's

Dinefwr

Carreg Cennen

Abergavenny

Raglan

Carmarthen

Monmouth

Narberth

Kidwelly

Usk

MONMOUTH

Pembroke

Tenby

Chepstow

*Milford
Haven*

Swansea

Caerleon

Newport

Gower

GLAMORGAN

Llandaff

Cowbridge

Cardiff

GLOUCESTERSHIRE

0 10 20 30 40 50

miles

© *Hugh Bicheno*

SOMERSET

Cardigan, Pembroke and Carmarthen had once been the kingdom of Deheubarth, while the borders of the Principality (Anglesey, Caernarvon and Merioneth), along with Denbigh and royal Flint, were those of Gwynedd, the last independent Welsh kingdom. Cheshire, Shropshire, Herefordshire and Gloucestershire were English, but Welsh gentry predominated along the borders. Many adopted English surnames only during our period, under the pressure of penal laws enacted by Henry IV.

The most famous Anglicization was by Owen, son of Maredudd ap Tudur, hence properly Owain ap Mareddud (Meredith), Catherine of Valois' consort. His was not a Marcher family – the Tudors were from north-west Wales. When given Englishman's rights for service in Normandy, Owen chose to use his grandfather's name as his English surname. This was probably in tribute to the role of the three ap Tudur brothers in the last great Welsh revolt, led by their first cousin, Owain Glyn Dŵr, after whom he was named.

The peculiar circumstances of the Wars of the Roses gave Wales a role in English history it had never played before – or has since – thanks to which a Welsh dragon was one of the shield supporters of the royal coat of arms from 1485 to 1604. The Tudor dynasty descended from Edmund, the first-born son of Catherine of Valois and Owen Tudor, but he did not even live to see the future Henry VII born. It was his brother Jasper who piloted the boy to the throne, through vicissitudes that would have broken the spirit of a lesser man.

As Pembroke was so poor and much of it was owned by the Bishop of St David's, the English nobles appointed to senior posts within Wales never performed in person the duties for which they were paid, delegating them to local officials instead. The most outstanding of these was Gruffudd ap Nicholas of Crug, in the Tywy valley, who made himself so useful to successive absentee lords and bishops that by the late 1440s he and his sons Thomas and Owain dominated Carmarthen, Pembroke and much of Cardigan.

Although some of Gruffudd's lands were granted in theory to

Jasper Tudor in 1452, he did not set foot in the county until 1456. Gruffudd resided at Carmarthen Castle and acted in all respects as the lord of south-west Wales until Somerset was killed at St Albans, after which Gruffudd and his sons were replaced by new Yorkist stewards, constables and justiciars throughout the area. York himself became constable of Aberystwyth, Carmarthen and Carreg Cennen. Kidwelly and Dinefwr, held by Gruffudd since the 1430s, went to Edward Bourchier and to the Yorkist retainer William Herbert of Raglan in Monmouth.

Herbert was the son of William ap Thomas, who fought at Agincourt and was made a knight banneret, but never anglicized his name. The older William had been Chief Steward of Usk and Caerleon, York's largest Welsh estates, and High Sheriff of Glamorgan. When he died in 1445 his namesake son, who adopted the surname Herbert and was also knighted for service in Normandy, inherited his offices along with the manor of Raglan, which his father had begun to fortify. Herbert, who made a fortune from the Gascony wine trade, was to make it the last of the great Welsh castles, as a proud display of wealth and power.

Although Gruffudd and his sons were summoned on pain of treason to appear before the Council in London, he had seen it all before and ignored York's authority and appointments, confident that, as always, his isolated corner of the kingdom would be very low on the squabbling English lords' lists of priorities. Thus it came as a nasty surprise when Edmund Tudor, Earl of Richmond, was sent in late 1455 to restore royal authority in south-west Wales.

Jasper was the more obvious choice, but unlike Richmond he had formed part of the king's retinue at St Albans and York did not trust him. In the confrontation with Somerset, who despised them as upstart bastards (what a difference a generation makes!), the Tudors had been, if anything, Yorkist in their sympathies. In early 1453, to Somerset's fury, the king gave them the lucrative joint wardship of the estates of Margaret, sole heir of John Beaufort, Edmund's older brother and predecessor as duke of Somerset. The wardship had previously been awarded to Suffolk, and after his death was exercised by Marguerite, so this concurs with the hypothesis that she built up the Tudors to counterbalance Somerset.

The death of Somerset at St Albans removed any impediment to Richmond marrying his 12-year-old ward, and to the Tudors becoming wholeheartedly associated with the queen's faction. Either York did not fully appreciate this, or else he thought to win Richmond to his own side by entrusting him with gaining control of the castles defiantly held by Gruffudd. Richmond did not do so, however, moving first to the bishop's palace at Lamphey, near his brother's castle at Pembroke. There, so great was his anxiety to guarantee his life interest in his wife's estate that he got her pregnant despite her age and slight build.

Edmund must have been anxious indeed: convention dictated that men of refinement waited until their child brides were in their late teens before consummating their marriages. Such forbearance was practical as well as ethical. Although twelve was the legal age of consent, simply because a girl had reached puberty did not mean her body was fully developed. An early pregnancy risked the girl's life or, as proved to be the case with Margaret Beaufort, could wreck her ability to bear more children.

When Richmond finally took possession of Carmarthen Castle in August 1456, it was by agreement with Gruffudd ap Nicholas. By then York had lost patience with him and sent 2,000 men under William Herbert to do the job properly. With him went Walter Devereux of Weobley, Herbert's father-in-law and constable of York's castle at Wigmore, and the Vaughan brothers of Bredwardine, Hergest and Tretower, who had been brought up with the Herbert brothers after their widowed mother married William ap Thomas. Carmarthen and the other castles were not prepared for defence and quickly surrendered. Richmond was briefly imprisoned, but he was at liberty when he died of the plague in Carmarthen on 1 November.

Jasper Tudor moved to Pembroke Castle in late 1456 and there, on 28 January 1457, his brother's posthumous son was born. It was a difficult birth yet within two months, escorted by Jasper, Margaret travelled to meet the Duke of Buckingham at his manor of Greenfield in Newport in Monmouth. She negotiated her betrothal to his younger son, Henry Stafford, and they were married on 3 January 1458. Confusingly, Buckingham's heir Humphrey had earlier married Margaret's namesake first cousin, the daughter of Eleanor Beauchamp who had been the cause of her 'shot-gun marriage' to Edmund Beaufort.

In the face of the Yorkist onslaught Gruffudd made submission to the queen, and after her counter-coup of October 1456 the king issued a pardon to him and his sons. Jasper Tudor took back the lands pertaining to his earldom, but when he replaced York as the constable of Aberystwyth, Carmarthen and Carreg Cennen in April 1457, things continued as before with Gruffudd's family operating as his agents. The last record of Gruffudd is in late February 1460, when he made a will bequeathing the castle and lordship of Narberth to his son Owain. Along with Jasper Tudor, Gruffudd's family were to be the most tenacious of Lancastrians throughout the Wars of the Roses.

All politics is local and, as was the case throughout the kingdom, it was clan rivalries rather than any overarching commitment to York or Lancaster that tended to define what side noble and gentry families took. The most inveterate opponents of Gruffudd were the Dwnns of Kidwelly, Carmarthen, and they perforce became beleaguered but fanatical Yorkists. The Kynastons and Eytons of Shropshire were rivals of the Talbots of Shrewsbury, and so became York's main supporters in the North March. The Skydmores of Herefordshire had chronic disputes with York and Herbert, and the Pulestons of Denbigh with York's unpleasant ally Lord Grey of Ruthyn, and so became firm Lancastrians.

An exception to the general rule was the Principality of Wales. More than was the case with the royal counties of Wales, there was genuine popular commitment to the Prince of Wales as the successor to Llewellyn the Great in Anglesey, Caernarvon and Merioneth. Unfortunately for his cause they had been wretchedly governed during his father's reign: 'Lawlessness was everywhere rampant, and Merioneth subsisted on cattle stealing, private feuds, burning of houses and murders. Market day at Dolgelly and Conway was a festival of looting and plunder.'*

Thanks to Jasper Tudor, south-west Wales proved a greater asset. He quickly appreciated the strategic importance of the Pembroke peninsula and the great harbour of Milford Haven. Even before it became apparent that war was inevitable, he entered into an agreement with the citizens of Tenby, on the southern side of the peninsula, to build up the fortifications of the port. He also governed fairly. Winning the loyalty of the people of Pembroke proved to be the wisest long-term investment made by any of the participants in the wars.

The Middle and South Marches were the heartland of York's power and, as we have seen, after the failure of his demonstration at Dartford, Henry and Somerset had held assizes in Ludlow to humiliate his tenants. They never turned out in force for York again. From 1457, Marguerite resumed the attack, singling out York's supporters in the South March. In April, at Hereford, William Herbert and Walter Devereux were arraigned before the king, with Marguerite at his side, not for their actions on behalf of York in south-west Wales, but for an arbitrary act committed on their own initiative a year earlier.

Following the murder of Walter Vaughan, Herbert and Devereux had intimidated the coroner's court at Bredwardine and seized Hereford, imprisoning the mayor and pressuring the king's justices to convict the men they said were responsible, whom they promptly hanged. The members of the commission that tried Herbert and Devereux at Hereford were the leading lights of the royalist faction: Buckingham, Shrewsbury, Wiltshire, Beaumont and James Tuchet,

* Quote from Howell Evans' indispensable *Wales and the Wars of the Roses.*

Baron Audley, joined by William FitzAlan, Earl of Arundel, trimming his sails to the prevailing wind in the manner that was to serve him well in the future.

Herbert and Devereux were found guilty of treason, but their subsequent treatment was markedly different. Devereux, who had already been condemned and pardoned for his part in York's armed protest in 1452, was imprisoned and his goods declared forfeit. Herbert, the principal instigator, was granted his life and restored to his property in return for swearing allegiance to the king. The purpose was plainly to divide the two men and to weaken Herbert's allegiance to York.

Herbert was the steward of York's castle at Usk and manor of Caerleon, which together with Herbert's own large estate of Raglan occupied the strategic centre among Buckingham's large holdings in Brecknock and southern Monmouth, and the lands held by Somerset, Wiltshire and the junior Talbots in Gloucestershire. If the Vaughans followed Herbert's lead, a wedge would also have been driven between York's strongholds in the Middle March and Warwick's lordships of Abergavenny and Glamorgan. Herbert was also Warwick's High Sheriff for Glamorgan, and if he could have been won to active support of the king, it would have been a spectacular coup.

• ❧ •

There is little doubt that Marguerite's policy of chipping away at York's support without confronting him directly, and carefully refraining from taking any similar action against Salisbury and Warwick, offered the best chance of achieving her objective. Time was not on her side, however. Keeping the court away from the Westminster bureaucracy was unsustainable, as although Shrewsbury and Wiltshire were able to collect taxes directly from the Midlands, the mobile court lacked the staff to conduct national administration. The struggle against York might be won, but only at the cost of accelerating the fragmentation of a kingdom that could only function as a unitary state.

With the court living hand-to-mouth, Marguerite could not use royal patronage to win followers or to buy conformity to her designs. She became a coalition manager, hostage to the interests of its component parts. While those of her son's Council broadly corresponded to her own, any hope of breaking up the alliance between York and the Nevilles was dashed by the actions of the heirs of the nobles killed at St Albans and their allies, who at this stage must be seen as constituting a third party, and a damagingly loose cannon on Marguerite's deck. She would need them if push came to shove, but they made sure it came to shove.

The heirs were Henry Beaufort, 3rd Duke of Somerset, 21 years old in 1457, Henry Percy, 3rd Earl of Northumberland (36), and John, 9th Baron Clifford (22). Driving them on were the trio who had caused so much trouble in the earlier 1450s: Henry Holland, 3rd Duke of Exeter (27), Henry Percy's brother Thomas, 1st Baron Egremont (35) and Thomas, 9th Baron Roos (30). The Percys and Cliffords had intermarried several times, and Roos was the son of the first marriage of Eleanor Beauchamp. Hence he was the maternal half-brother of Henry Beaufort, and shared his hatred of Warwick for the disinheritance of their mother.*

Politics was not only local, but also highly personal. Although Clifford's and Roos's main grievances were with the Nevilles, they had their own reasons to hate York. Both had been born in York's own birthplace, Conisbrough Castle, when it was part of the dower of his stepmother Maud, Countess of Cambridge. She was the daughter of the 6th Baron Clifford and Elizabeth, daughter of the 5th Baron Roos, and along with her extended family lived there sumptuously while running up debts using the castle as collateral. When she died in 1446, York reclaimed his heavily encumbered property with icy contempt for Maud's heirs.

---

* For the Beaufort-Roos connection see Appendix D: The Beauchamp Inheritance.

The product of all these and other resentments and provocations too numerous to list was a critical mass of unappeasable hatred that demanded bloodshed. Exeter and Egremont had tried to assassinate York during his first protectorate, and they were probably the authors of a sinister threat in September 1456, after Egremont escaped from Newgate. Five dogs' heads were impaled on the railings of the London home of Richard Beauchamp, Bishop of Salisbury, where York was staying. The verses in the dogs' jaws said that although York, the son of a traitor, deserved to die, others had paid the price for his treason:

> What planet compelled me, or what sign
> To serve that man that all men hate?
> I would his head were here for mine
> For he hath caused all the debate.

This was a killer jibe, because it was true. So far, York had paid no material price for seeking to impose himself on the king – but the persecution of his followers after Dartford had seriously eroded their collective loyalty. At the same time, nobody seeking a legal judgement in his favour or public office would now seek York's 'good lordship', and consequently he had to spend more of his own money to maintain influence. The quest for power was a further large drain on his resources, and he was compelled to mortgage more and more of his estates to sustain the regal style his ambition demanded. Added to which, after St Albans he had pressing reasons to retain a considerable number of bodyguards on a permanent basis.

In October 1456, at the Coventry Council where Marguerite staged her counter-coup, Somerset had to be restrained from assaulting York in person, and on 1 December, still at Coventry, his retainers attacked York's party, and were themselves attacked by citizens outraged by their behaviour. Before then, an attempt was made on 5 November to ambush Warwick, returning to London from

Calais, by retainers of Somerset, Exeter and Shrewsbury. It was this episode that persuaded Warwick to appoint deputies to administer his interests in England, and to move to Calais.

There were several other such attacks over the next two years, forcing York and Salisbury to travel with large armed retinues and to reside only in their own castles or fortified manors. If the purpose had been assassination, there were many better ways of accomplishing it than through the very public clash of retainers. There were few if any casualties and one does wonder whether the supposed ambushes were not just threatening displays, akin to the behaviour of male animals in the wild.

To pursue the analogy, the aim of intimidation is to achieve dominance without fighting. If, however, neither party backs down, then the issue has to be settled by force. There may have been an element of bravado in the young lions' challenges to the Alpha males, but at some point the urge to find out who was the stronger would become irresistible. To avoid this, Henry VI made a last effort to dissuade his nobles from tearing his kingdom apart.

XVII

MARGUERITE AND HENRY

Henry VI's situation in 1457 mirrored York's, on a larger scale. Decades of fiscal irresponsibility had shrivelled his possibilities of exercising patronage, although he remained the fount of the judicial powers that might be exercised to buttress the 'good lordship' of his loyalists. However, if York's inability to protect his own followers had diminished his authority, it paled beside the towering fact that the murder of the king's most eminent supporters at St Albans remained unpunished. Few had respect for Henry as a man, or any faith he would keep his word, or honour the tallies littering the country.

Henry's struggle to employ his inadequate resources and negligible personal authority to palliate the confrontational determination of his queen is, I believe, the reason why, in the words of York's biographer, 'the tone of English political life in 1457 is... peculiarly elusive'.* Henry believed, beyond reason, that it was still possible to negotiate a peaceful settlement of the blood feuds born at St Albans. Consequently York was not entirely excluded from favour, with financial compensation promised for the loss of the Welsh castles, and the award of one or two profitable privileges that cost the crown nothing.

In March, York's appointment as Lieutenant of Ireland was

---

* From P. A. Johnson, *Duke Richard of York 1411–1460*.

renewed, six months before it was strictly necessary, along with a payment on account of £446 [£283,656]. This must have been in the form of a tally, as by this time the court was subsisting almost entirely on credit. There may have been an element of wishful thinking involved, with Henry entertaining the hope that York could be persuaded to exercise his kingly pretensions in Ireland, as Warwick's restless ambition was now focused on Calais. Ireland, however, offered no comparable attractions.

The truth, squarely faced by Marguerite but intolerable to her husband, was that nothing he did could fill the void of authority created by his compound personal deficiencies. For a man so profoundly convinced that God's will was paramount, he must have believed his troubles were akin to the biblical trials of Job by Satan. Deprived of everything he previously enjoyed, Job utters one of the most famous biblical aphorisms: 'The Lord gave, and the Lord hath taken away; blessed be the name of the Lord'. Thus also Henry, desperately hoping that if he, too, steadfastly maintained his faith in the face of adversity, he would be rewarded.

During 1457–8, therefore, the king resisted pressure from Marguerite to take a harder line with York. Henry spent most of 1457 in the queen's Midlands domain, yet he was clearly not under her control, even though this was widely perceived to be the case. No doubt there were tense scenes in the royal apartments at Kenilworth, but Marguerite knew better than anyone that once her husband was set on a course of action, the peculiar workings of his mind were impervious to argument. She would also have been haunted by the ever-present fear that, if pushed too hard, he might withdraw once more into catatonia.

The emergence of the royalist faction during this period was characterized by the fundamental contradiction between a quietist king and an activist queen. It was precisely analogous to driving with the brakes and accelerator applied simultaneously. The only question was whether the brakes would burn out before the motor exploded – but neither outcome could avoid a wreck.

To take the brakes first, the product of Henry's prayers and consultation with his confessor, the Carmelite monk John Stanberry, Bishop of Hereford, was the 'Loveday' of 24 March 1458. The good faith of Stanberry, whose diocese covered much of the ancestral Mortimer lands that were York's Marcher stronghold, was at this time still respected on both sides of the factional divide, and probably no one else could have brought the rival nobles together. York and the Nevilles would not have trusted Henry's unsupported word that they were not simply being lured into an ambush.

Henry summoned a Great Council of the entire peerage to meet in Westminster on 27 January, to discuss a wide range of governance issues, leading up to a settlement of the vendettas born at St Albans. York and Salisbury arrived separately to stay at their London palaces, but as they rode out together to the opening session of the Council, surrounded by over 1,000 guards, they encountered a hostile demonstration by a larger number of retainers wearing the livery of Somerset, Exeter, Clifford and Egremont. The two groups were kept apart by a special force of 5,000 armed men that the king had prudently commissioned the Lord Mayor to recruit and equip.

Other nobles, including Warwick (who arrived from Calais with 600 men), were late in coming and Henry withdrew to Chertsey, 25 miles south-west of Westminster, for a week. After Warwick arrived, the king returned to Westminster to declare the main purpose of the Council was 'to set apart such variances as been betwixt divers lords of this our realm'. Discussion of the core issue, St Albans, was again postponed until the arrival of Northumberland. On 26 February the king withdrew even further, to the queen's castle at Berkhamsted. There, he granted an audience to the aggrieved lords, and another to Northumberland when he arrived.

The details of the deal eventually agreed are revealing. York was to pay Somerset 5,000 marks [£2.12 million], Salisbury was to forgo the fines of 9,000 marks awarded to him against the Percys for their breaches of the peace and Warwick was to pay Clifford 1,000 marks. The only reciprocal undertaking was that Egremont's conviction and his escape from Newgate were set aside in return for posting a 4,000 mark bond to keep the peace. The payment York agreed was far from onerous – it was made with royal tallies owed for his lieutenancy, and he was granted a licence to export wool on his own account to a customs value of 10,000 marks, of which about half would be profit.

No doubt similar arrangements were made with regard to the Nevilles' indemnities. Simply put, they were bribed to accept a semblance of culpability for the St Albans killings. Contrition was to be shown with an annuity of £45 [£28,620] to pay for a permanent chantry for the souls of those killed at St Albans, in the abbey church where they were buried. A single payment of £45 was made before these arrangements were overtaken by events.

The terms were published on 24 March, the day the proceedings were crowned by a procession from Westminster to St Paul's in which Warwick walked hand in hand with Exeter (presumably in representation of the Percys and Clifford), Salisbury with Somerset, and York with the queen. In an age that attached great importance to symbolism, the king had arranged a pageant unequivocally reserving the role of arbiter to himself alone, casting the queen, who should have walked by his side, in the role of one of the plaintiffs.

During the remaining months of 1458 Henry resumed his peregrinations. Immediately after the 'Loveday' he spent three weeks at St Albans abbey, to which he returned for a month in September–October, and again for ten days in March 1459. There can be little doubt he went there to pray that the spirits of his uncle of Gloucester, dishonoured by his authority, and of the men who died for his mistakes in May 1455, should rest in peace and cease troubling his realm. Shakespeare was no historian, but his three-part *Henry the Sixth* portrays the tragic fate of a man born to a role no amount of prayer could make him competent to play:

> O God! methinks it were a happy life,
> To be no better than a homely swain.

The 'Loveday' did not, indeed could not, answer what Humpty Dumpty rightly posited as the only question of importance: 'which is to be master – that's all'. One gets tired reading the ceaseless invocations of God to witness their loyalty to the king from men who were evidently disloyal, and constrained from seizing power only because they were deeply distrusted by almost all their peers. Most histories have portrayed the following eighteen months as a period in which the queen forced the issue, yet the issue – and the force – were entirely of the Yorkists' making. With regard to Marguerite, the French saying 'this animal is very wicked: if you attack it, it defends itself' springs to mind.

There was a limited amount Marguerite could do when shackled to a supine king, but she had proved adept at shaping the political environment to strengthen her husband's hands, should they cease to be clasped in prayer. Amid a sea of uncertain loyalties, the seldom savoury but usually sound maxim 'my enemy's enemy is my friend' compelled her to work with men hated by York, among them the egregious Wiltshire and the infamous Thomas Tuddenham and William Tailboys. They used the same techniques to raise money for the cash-strapped court they had employed during Suffolk's ascendancy.

The giving of royal consent to noble marriages and the granting of wardships were areas in which the queen's influence was undisputed, and she made full use of it. In September 1456, she arranged the marriage between the namesake heir of Thomas Courtenay, Earl of Devon, and Marie of Anjou, illegitimate but dearly loved daughter of her brother Charles, Count of Maine. Devon, whose alliance with York had brought him little but grief, was ripe for plucking because the Nevilles favoured Bonville, his mortal enemy. He died on his way to the 'Loveday' Council, and his son became one of the queen's unconditional supporters.

Although Margaret Beaufort, Edmund Tudor's teenaged widow, negotiated her own marriage to Buckingham's younger son Henry, it required royal approval and the price was the queen's wardship of the infant Henry Tudor, Earl of Richmond. Margaret was a considerable heiress in her own right, but the Richmond estates were a strategic royal asset and needed stronger wardship than Henry Stafford could provide. Marguerite entrusted it jointly to Henry's uncle Jasper, Earl of Pembroke, and to John Talbot, Earl of Shrewsbury, Lord Treasurer and the senior lay member of the Prince of Wales's council.

The desire to drive a wedge between York and the Nevilles, which had led to Warwick becoming the virtual lord of Calais and Lord High Admiral in all but name, seems to have lain behind Marguerite's consent to the marriage in April 1457 of her 15-year-old ward Isabel Ingoldisthorpe to John Neville, Salisbury's second son. Isabel had eight manors in East Anglia from her recently deceased father, and was also co-heir of her childless uncle by marriage John Tiptoft, Earl of Worcester, previously and briefly married to Cecily Neville, dowager Countess of Warwick. The expected benefit to John Neville from this marriage can be measured by his agreement to pay the queen £1,000 [£636,000] in ten instalments.

One of the more intriguing matrimonial alliances made at this time was arranged between York and Alice de la Pole née Chaucer, widow of the murdered Duke of Suffolk. She remained, as she had been before she married Suffolk, an acquisitive landowner in her own right, with estates in twenty-two counties. Although the dukedom had been revoked, her only son John was still an earl, and Alice remained a member of the Order of the Garter, a lady-in-waiting to Marguerite, and castellan of her castle at Wallingford. Fifteen year-old John de la Pole was the most eligible bachelor in the kingdom, and his marriage in early 1458 to York's 13-year-old daughter Elizabeth was a highly significant political event.*

The most noteworthy matrimonial initiative of this time came in late 1458, with a proposal for multiple marriages with the French

---

* John de la Pole had previously been married to 7-year-old Margaret Beaufort in 1450. Henry VI declared the marriage annulled in 1453 when he bestowed her wardship on Edmund Tudor, who married her himself.

and Burgundian royal houses for the Prince of Wales, York's eldest son Edward, and Somerset. It did not proceed beyond a preliminary embassy by John Wenlock, lately Speaker of the House of Commons. Although he had extensive diplomatic experience, he was not of sufficient stature to lead such a high-level mission and King Charles VII sent his own herald to London to assess the seriousness of the proposal.

His findings were startling: after meeting with Warwick in Calais, Wenlock had totally subverted the peace-making purpose of the mission by stirring up trouble between Burgundy and France, and by falsely reporting to his own government that a French attack was imminent. Application of the 'who benefits?' test suggests Warwick saw that the embassy, if successful, would undermine his own status as the indispensable man in the confrontation with France. Wenlock's emergence as a committed Yorkist in 1459 strongly suggests Warwick bribed him to make sure the embassy failed.

The Wenlock mission marked the abandonment of the queen's gamble that Warwick might be tempted to break with York, to pursue power and glory on his own account. Marguerite was now faced with a monster of her own creation, and the possibility cannot be dismissed that she authorized an attempt on Warwick's life in November 1458. The attack took place at Westminster after Warwick responded to a personal summons from the king under the Privy Seal. Along with his father and York, Warwick had ignored a previous, more general summons to a Council in which, among other matters, his predation of neutral shipping in the Channel and the failure of Wenlock's mission were to be discussed.

The details of the episode were, of course, disputed. According to the court, Warwick got caught up in a fracas between his retainers and the Westminster kitchen staff. He agreed that the incident took place in the kitchen, but said it was a carefully prepared ambush in which the would-be assassin, posing as a cook, lunged at him with a roasting spit. There are two good reasons to believe Warwick's version was correct. The first is that several of his retainers were killed and he only got away thanks to the intervention of other lords. The second and conclusive reason is the presence at the scene of the royalist thug Thomas Tuddenham, who was later rewarded by promotion to treasurer of the household.

Warwick escaped by boat down the Thames, and never returned in peace. The Lancastrian version of what followed is that he, Salisbury and York had *previously* agreed a plan whereby Warwick would make a sudden advance from Calais to capture Kenilworth, to support a charge of conspiracy to kill the royal family and to seize the throne. The conspiracy had to have been hatched *before* the attempt on Warwick's life, because if not the fuse for war was lit in the Westminster kitchens.

Further dominoes fell steadily in 1459. As the household had done in 1450, so now the queen orchestrated a campaign of disinformation designed to convince Henry that York and his allies intended his downfall. There is no evidence of any such conspiracies, the least believable of which implicated Alice, Countess of Salisbury. Possibly aware of how he had been manipulated nine years earlier, Henry refused to be panicked into precipitate action.

The queen, meanwhile, put the young lions on standby and prepared to recruit her own army in the name of her son in Cheshire, by issuing the knights and squires of the shire the swan livery badge of Henry V's Bohun mother. He had adopted it when he was Prince of Wales, and it was talismanic to English chivalry.

Finally, even appeaser-in-chief Buckingham was convinced. He accused York, the Nevilles, the Bourchiers, the Bishops of Ely and Exeter and several others of conspiracy at a Great Council summoned to Coventry in June 1459. Two Acts, unfortunately lost, were passed, but the king refused to sanction the recommended punishments. In a staged melodrama, Buckingham and the loyalist lords knelt before him and begged:

> Seeing the great jeopardy for your most noble person, and also
> [seeing] the Lords so often charged, and disturbing so often the

great part of your Realm, that it should not please you to show grace hereafter to the said Duke of York, nor none other, if they attempt to do the contrary to your Royal estate, or disturbing your Realm and the Lords thereof, but to be punished as they deserve, and have deserved, for the good of You, Sovereign Lord, and for the good of all your Lords and people.

Henry indicated his assent, and with it all the offences supposedly wiped clean by the 'Loveday' were back on the table. Salisbury and York began to gather forces respectively at Middleham and Ludlow, and Warwick prepared an expedition. The Yorkists issued repeated professions of loyalty, and assurances that they were acting in self-defence. For Henry, this must have been all-too reminiscent of the events leading up to St Albans, and the king could only conclude that another *coup d'état* was in preparation.

Were the Yorkists, as they declared, simply acting in order to pre-empt further false accusations leading to their condemnation and attainder? The assumption that such measures were likely to be taken was an entirely reasonable one. By this stage the only thing that could restore the political standing and financial credit of the Lancastrian dynasty was a massive acquisition of lands and wealth. The lands of the duchy of York and the earldoms of Salisbury and Warwick would have fitted the bill nicely.

Faced with a similar situation, Richard II doomed himself by dispossessing Henry VI's grandfather Henry Bolingbroke, but the precedent was ignored. One of the constants of history is how effortlessly people persuade themselves that, however disastrous a particular course of action was when first attempted, they will achieve a favourable outcome by doing exactly the same thing again.

The Nevilles agreed to join York at Ludlow for two reasons. The first was that York was a royal duke, and still a figure around whom those discontented with the king's government could be expected to rally. The second, however, was that his standing in the Welsh Marches had been successfully undermined by the 1452 and 1457 assizes, and his Marcher affinity was understandably reluctant to sign up for what might prove another Dartford. The arrival of strong contingents from the North and from Calais would provide concrete evidence that, this time, York was not isolated.

This time, however, what we may now regard as the Lancastrian faction was alert and prepared, and Henry gave evidence of an unwonted purposefulness. Whatever methods of persuasion Marguerite used to urge her husband to take decisive action – on past form some encouragement in the bedchamber would have been involved – he now dressed for war, and for a month led his army in the field, not merely as a show of force but with the clear determination to bring his enemies to battle.

THE ENGLISH
WAY OF WAR

OUR STORY NOW MOVES FROM A MAINLY POLITICAL TO a preponderantly military sphere, and a brief digression now will save much explanation later. It is relatively easy for the modern reader to relate to the dynamics of ambition, pride and the bonds of kinship and affinity we have been reviewing. Medieval warfare is another matter.

English military superiority and democratic institutions both owed much to the longbow. Used en masse, its rapid shooting rate (as many as eight aimed arrows per minute) made it an awesomely effective battlefield weapon, while knowledge that common men could puncture their hauberks (mail coats) may have done much to convince the Norman-French ruling class they should not push the English-speaking majority too far. It was the latent power of the independent yeoman class, the distinguishing glory of English social history.

Many other societies had similar weapons, but nowhere else were they as powerful as in the hands of the English. The technique of using the whole body, not just the arms, to draw the bow was first developed in Wales, where Edward I had found it necessary to clear the forests 100 yards on either side of roads to prevent deadly sniping by the Welsh. From there, the technique spread throughout England.

Boys in fourteenth- and fifteenth-century England grew up training with bows of increasing power to accustom their bodies to their demands, and forensic anthropologists have no difficulty identifying medieval archers from their skeletal remains. Constant practice also made them deadly accurate, and their tremendous upper body strength served them well in hand-to-hand combat, when they commonly used the lead-headed mauls also used to drive in the stakes with which they protected their shooting positions.

Properly deployed, massed longbowmen removed cavalry as well as skirmishing by light troops from the battlefield equation. Plate armour evolved to protect those who could afford it, and fully armoured knights could march into an arrow storm with a reasonable expectation of coming to hand strokes, although they had to lean into it, heads down to hide their eye-slits. However, even if the rain of arrows did not find the proverbial chink in their armour, their punishing impacts sapped the strength of the men enduring it.

Longbowmen also greatly diminished enemy command and control. A commander who lifted his visor to look around or to shout orders risked an arrow in the face, as happened to both Harry 'Hotspur' Percy and to the future Henry V at Shrewsbury in 1403. The most effective use of the longbow was direct fire with heavy arrows at 50 yards or less, comparable to the crossbow but with an overwhelmingly faster shooting rate.*

Armour ('harness') was worn over and attached to padded garments ('arming jacks') with fabric or leather laces at the appropriate places. The wealthy wore bespoke harness made in England, which would have been brightly polished hardened steel, with an outer garment (tabard) bearing the heraldic device of the wearer (hence 'coat of arms'). 'Off the peg' hardened steel armour generally came from Italy, while those of more limited means might wear cheaper armour, painted to combat corrosion.

Steel armour of any kind was valuable and common soldiers often wore partial harness looted from enemy casualties. These

* For a full assessment see Mike Loades' splendid *The Longbow*.

trophies aside, foot soldiers and archers wore thickly padded fabric jacks with detachable sleeves, some with strips of armour incorporated, or a canvas garment reinforced with rivets called a brigandine. Either could be worn over a hauberk, although multiple layers of fabric alone are surprisingly effective.

Although some preferred the two-handed sword, the man-at-arm's premier weapon for close-quarter battle was the poleaxe, a reinforced wooden shaft 4–5 feet in length, with a steel head comprising a spike, an axe and a war hammer. Either weapon could be used to lunge, or like a quarterstaff to defend and attack the upper body, but with the poleaxe you could hook an opponent's feet from under him. He could then be dispatched with a jab between plates by the spike on the butt of the shaft, or with a swing of the war hammer.

Billmen used longer-shafted weapons topped with a wide range of variations on the basic agricultural billhook. Most combined a spike, a blade and some kind of hook to drag men off their feet. The principal role of the billmen was area denial, to prevent opponents getting around the men-at-arms from different directions. To finish off the fallen, all would have had daggers in their belts, with pommels to permit a two-handed punch through mail.

Hand-to-hand fighting was exhausting, and battle lines would ebb and flow as combatants backed off from each other to take a breather. As far as we know, there was no formal procedure for men in the rear ranks to relieve those at the front when they grew tired, but it certainly took place continuously during a battle, causing a rippling effect. Fighting in full harness was also hot and thirsty work, and several cases are known of knights killed with arrows through the throat when they removed their bevors (armour worn to cover the lower face and neck under a half-helmet called a sallet) to take a drink.

Although the era of decisive heavy cavalry charges was over, a significant proportion of an army was still mounted. The knights and men-at-arms all rode, as did mounted archers and hobilars (mounted spearmen who rode and fought with the archers). Light cavalry performed essential functions. Lancers (prickers) scouted ahead of an army, as did foragers and harbingers, whose job was to source supplies and to identify places for the army battalions (the contemporary term was 'battles') to bivouac.

These men would be concentrated in the leading battalion (Vanward/Vanguard) on the march, but would revert to their parent battalions, the Main (often, confusingly, called 'the Battle') and the Rearward/Rearguard, when the time came to fight. As in every war, the vast majority of casualties were inflicted on a broken army as it ran away, when the winning side's men-at-arms, hobilars and mounted archers would regain their horses to harry the fleeing men. Pursuit would end at the enemy baggage train, because looting trumped everything.

In England, the bulk of the rank-and-file came from levies raised under commissions of array, a royal order sent to county sheriffs, usually through a local magnate, to summon all adult males for a period of military service. They had an obligation of thirty days' annual service, paid for by their communities, and were expected to muster with the weapons appropriate to their station. This was a fairly well oiled system, as the levies were often summoned for inspection and basic training.

The obligation was for service at home only. Overseas service was voluntary and involved contracts known as indentures. This was ruinously expensive, and lack of money was the main reason the English were so easily bundled out of France. However, even though the wage bill for a campaign at home was reduced, a commander still had to pay surgeons, armourers, bowyers, fletchers, farriers, wheelwrights, blacksmiths, saddlers, masons and carpenters.

Added to which would be the cost of several hundred wagons to carry tens of thousands of arrows, supplementary feed for horses, several days' hard rations for the troops, anvils, tools and tents. If required, siege guns, their specialist crews and ammunition were an additional expense and increased the number of wagons required;

but their greater cost was that they slowed the army's progress, adding further to the per diems.

Two means of reducing the cost of warfare were denied to commanders during the Wars of the Roses. One was the *chevauchée*, which was expected to be profitable as well as self-supporting through plunder once it entered enemy territory. During the Wars of the Roses neither side could afford to plunder the people whose best interests both claimed to represent. The other was ransoms paid by captives, but civil wars are notoriously savage, and chivalrous conventions died at St Albans.

While not entirely dictated by financial considerations, the English way of war diverged from the continental norm by its willingness to stake all on a climactic battle. The exemplar for all the commanders during the Wars of the Roses was fierce old John Talbot. His death and the destruction of his army, attacking artillery-equipped fieldworks at Castillon, cast doubt on the continuing validity of the paradigm and was taken to heart by, in particular, the Duke of Buckingham. But overall the emphasis remained on seeking a decision as quickly as possible.

XVIII

MARGUERITE'S ARMY

STARTING FROM MIDDLEHAM, SALISBURY HAD TO PASS through the royalist heartland to join York at Ludlow in the Middle March. He had to move fast, and would have marched around the Clifford stronghold of Skipton (Craven) to regain what I have called the Western Spur of the Great North Road (Map 4) before it reached Halifax. If he then chose to continue east of the section of the Pennines we now call the Peak District, he would necessarily have had to turn west at Derby or Nottingham and march through the Lancastrian Midlands.

However inappropriate as a location from which to rule the country, the Midlands were ideal in military-strategic terms. In the light of the highly fragmented and dispersed distribution of the main estates of the king, the queen, the Prince of Wales and the principal magnates, generalizations about areas of influence need to be made with caution (see Map 2). Still, the queen's fortress triangle of Tutbury, Kenilworth and Leicester gave her the interior lines beloved of strategists, and in 1459 they worked as the textbooks say they should.

Believing that Salisbury did intend to march through the Midlands, on 20 September the king marched from Coventry through Market Harborough to Nottingham. He had earlier made a circuit from Coventry to Nuneaton, Burton upon Trent, Lichfield and Coleshill to rally supporters. This was the main royalist army,

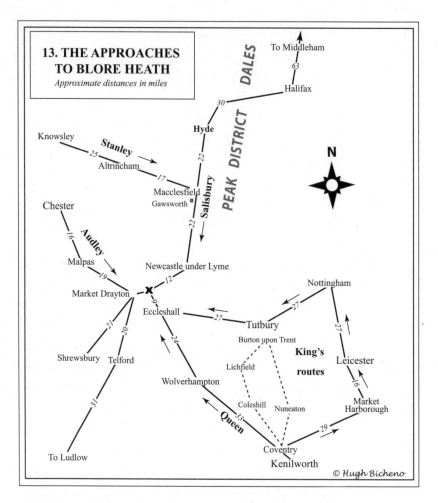

13. THE APPROACHES TO BLORE HEATH

Approximate distances in miles

To Middleham
63
Halifax
DALES
30
Hyde
PEAK DISTRICT
Knowsley
Stanley
25
Altrincham
17
Macclesfield
Gawsworth
22
Salisbury
22
Chester
Audley
16
Malpas
19
Newcastle under Lyme
12
Market Drayton
X
9
Eccleshall
27
Tutbury
Nottingham
27
27
Burton upon Trent
King's routes
Lichfield
Leicester
21
20
Shrewsbury   Telford
24
Wolverhampton
16
Coleshill   Nuneaton
Market Harborough
31
Queen
33
29
To Ludlow
Coventry
Kenilworth

© Hugh Bicheno

and he would have been accompanied by the peers most identified with his cause, with the exception of Somerset and Devon in the West Country, and Shrewsbury in the Welsh Marches.

Salisbury had knights from Lancashire, Cheshire and Shropshire in his entourage, but none from Nottinghamshire or Derbyshire. Accordingly there is no reason to believe he ever contemplated marching east of the Pennines. Instead, he marched west from Halifax and then turned south to skirt the western side of the Peak District, with royalist Lancashire on his right flank. Given that Thomas, Baron Stanley, the local commander of the king's forces, was married to Salisbury's daughter Eleanor, and that his younger brother William rode with Salisbury along with the Cheshire knights Robert Bold and Henry Radford, probably as guides, it is fair to assume a laissez-passer had been arranged in advance.

Stanley's treachery is another illustration of the adverse *fortuna* that dogged Marguerite. His namesake father, handpicked by the queen for her son's Council, had died in February, aged only 54. There are no grounds for doubting the elder Stanley's loyalty to the crown. If he had lived, the outcome of the Blore Heath campaign would have been very different.

Armies commonly bivouacked outside towns for the night, and Hyde, Macclesfield and Newcastle under Lyme are plausible candidates for stopping-points for Salisbury's army. At Newcastle under Lyme, at latest, his scouts would have informed him that he was in the middle of a closing ring of royalist armies. Following him at a prudent distance were Stanley's Lancashire men, while the king was marching west from Nottingham, the queen and her Midlands retainers were approaching from the south, and barring his way were Lords Audley and Dudley with the 'Queen's Gallants' of Cheshire.

Fifty-nine-year-old John Sutton, 1st Baron Dudley, has cropped up at regular intervals in preceding chapters. Originally one of the courtiers who became part of the king's inner circle as a member of Suffolk's affinity, he remained close to the king after his mentor's fall and was wounded by his side at St Albans. A member of the prince's council, he had limited military experience dating back to the 1420s. Sixty-one-year-old James Tuchet, 5th Baron Audley, had considerably more experience, but had last commanded troops in 1431. The queen trusted him, but he also owed his appointment to the retainers he could draw from his estates in Cheshire, Shropshire, Staffordshire and Derbyshire.

The list of ninety-nine known or probable royalist casualties compiled by Blore Heath guru Mark Hinsley is revealing. One would have assumed the Cheshire army came mainly from the queen's and the Prince of Wales's lands, with some drawn from Audley's and Dudley's estates, in particular Dudley's manor of Malpas,

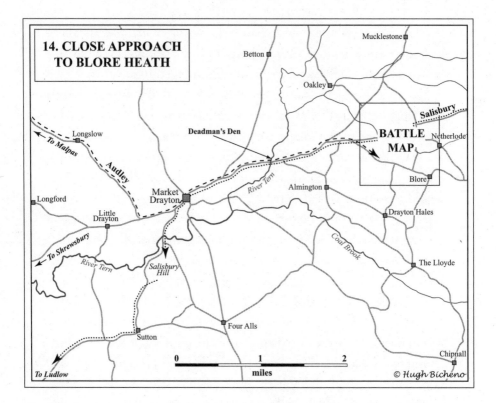

14. CLOSE APPROACH TO BLORE HEATH

Mucklestone · Betton · Oakley · To Malpas · Longslow · Audley · Deadman's Den · Salisbury · BATTLE MAP · Netherlode · Longford · Market Drayton · Little Drayton · River Tern · Almington · Blore · Drayton Hales · To Shrewsbury · River Tern · Salisbury Hill · Coal Brook · The Lloyde · Four Alls · Sutton · Chipnall · To Ludlow · miles · © Hugh Bicheno

0   1   2

through which the army marched on its way from Chester to Market Drayton. Yet thirty-six of the named casualties came from the manor of Gawsworth outside Macclesfield, held by the Fitton family since 1316, among them Thomas Fitton and eight of his kin. He must have marched to join Audley before it was known that Salisbury had crossed the Pennines.

Estimates of the numbers on either side vary too widely to be useful, but something like 8,000 versus Salisbury's 5,000 seems likely. As to quality, although Robert Ogle and his tough Northumbrians remained in the north, experienced Marcher soldiers once again formed the core of Salisbury's force. They were trumped on the Lancastrian side by thousands of Cheshire archers, famed for their deadliness during the Hundred Years War, formed up along a hedgerow running down from Blore village – much of which still exists.

A battle has at least four identities. The closest to reality is the mosaic of participants' perceptions, soon subsumed into the second, which is a body of accepted facts to which memories retrospectively conform. The third is the canonical version, coloured by the propaganda use to which it is put at the time and later. The fourth seeks to rediscover the first, but is shaped by the intellectual climate of the time in which it is written. There are few accounts from either of the first two categories of the battles of the Wars of the Roses, and the third category source for Blore Heath is the *The Attainder of Richard Duke of York and others*, from the rolls of the Parliament that met in Coventry two months after the battle.

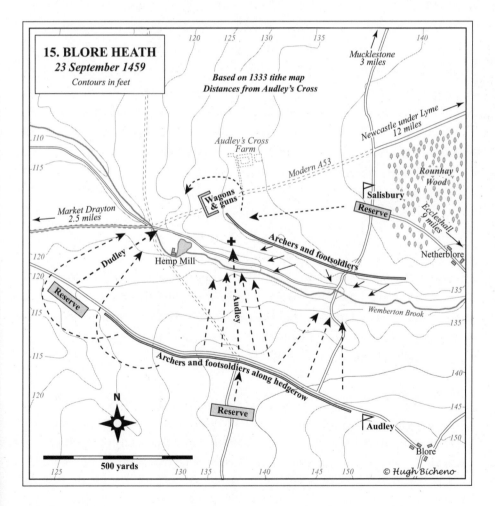

15. BLORE HEATH
23 September 1459
Contours in feet

Based on 1333 tithe map
Distances from Audley's Cross

Mucklestone
3 miles

Newcastle under Lyme
12 miles

Audley's Cross
Farm

Modern A53

Rounhay
Wood

Market Drayton
2.5 miles

Wagons
& guns

Salisbury
Reserve

Eccleshall
miles

Dudley

Hemp Mill

Archers and footsoldiers

Netherblore

Reserve

Audley

Wemberton Brook

Archers and footsoldiers along hedgerow

N

Reserve

500 yards

Audley

Blore

© Hugh Bicheno

The Burgundian Jehan de Wavrin wrote the closest fourth category account in about 1470. It is wildly inaccurate in many respects, yet so curiously exact in its description of the battlefield that it is reasonable to assume he had spoken with participants. This does not mean what they told him was accurate with regard to the tactical calculations of the rival commanders. The most influential history has been Edward Hall's *The Union of the Noble and Ilustre Famelies of Lancastre and York*, first published in 1548, republished in 1809 as *Hall's Chronicle*. He drew on oral family history: his grandfather, one of York's councillors, would have heard accounts of the battle from Salisbury's men when they arrived at Ludlow.

Men in combat understandably focus on their immediate surroundings. Even for modern battles, with dozens of 'I was there' memoirs to draw on, the only dependable witness remains the terrain. Although the battlefield of Blore Heath is almost pristine, the standard account of the battle is two-dimensional, and points the finger of blame at Audley for tactical incompetence. He is supposed to have abandoned an impregnable position to make a mounted charge across the brook to utterly predictable destruction, supposedly tricked into doing so by a feigned retreat by Salisbury's right wing. He did not.

The valley of the Wemberton Brook was described as 'not very broad, but somewhat deep'. As it is today, so in 1459 the brook itself would have been lined with bushes and trees. Even after 556 years of erosion, the modern contours answer a number of questions. The road Salisbury wished to follow would have taken him across a steep-sided ford that would have slowed deployment to a crawl, up a long slope overlooked by the royalist right wing commanded by Audley himself, his banners visible on the Blore village plateau.

This was also the logical place for his guns. The ridge and the hedgerow not only concealed Audley's numbers, but at the western end also permitted troops to move behind the lines without being seen by Salisbury, who would have been with his reserves on the high ground at the edge of Rounhay Wood, between the Newcastle under Lyme and Eccleshall roads.

Salisbury's situation could hardly have been more unfavourable. He knew the queen and her retainers were at Eccleshall, 9 miles to the south-east, with the king and the main royalist army not far behind. He also knew the complicity of his Stanley son-in-law would not extend to permitting him to fall back through Newcastle under Lyme, and that he would come off the fence against him if a Lancastrian victory seemed assured.

He was trapped, yet any assault across the brook would certainly be annihilated. Worse, Audley's left wing extended beyond the Hemp Mill pond to another crossing where the contour lines open up and the brook bed becomes less of an obstacle. This is the point where modern roads cross the brook, and is certainly the *passage* described by Wavrin, where an outflanking move by mounted men was practicable.

Even if he could not see them, Salisbury would have assumed, correctly, that the Lancastrians would have a strong force concentrated on their left wing. Thus the most likely sequence is that he paused at the top of the hill while he brought up the wagons and guns, and then sent them together with the Van towards the lower crossing. At the same time the Main and Rear advanced down the hill to form a line within bowshot of the brook and the track along its northern bank. The wagons and guns went to form an artillery fort beyond the mill pond, to cover the crossing and to anchor his right flank. His left flank was reasonably secure behind the steeper slopes to the east of the upper ford, and he would have had an outpost at Netherblore, covering the approach from Eccleshall.

Why did the Lancastrians not interfere with this deployment? Probably because their plan was to stop Salisbury while reinforcements closed in on him. In the usual preliminary parleys they would have called on Salisbury to capitulate on terms. With these rejected and Stanley dawdling at Newcastle under Lyme, Audley and Dudley would have been in a quandary. The queen had given them explicit instructions to bring her Salisbury, dead or alive. If he slipped away during the night they were sure to be branded as cowards for not seeking battle with the odds so greatly in their favour.

The defensive strength of their position worked against offensive action. Bearing in mind the terrain and the fact that all contemporary armies were organized in three 'battles', an interpretation that does not assume Audley was a blunderer would run as follows. The Van on the right wing would advance downhill towards the upper ford to fix Salisbury's left. Audley would then charge with the Main at a diagonal to cross the brook east of the mill pond, the first wave being mounted men-at-arms who would have ridden rapidly down to the brook, hoping to gain tactical surprise. Nobody had ridden into an arrow storm since the early years of the Hundred Years War, and nobody (bar the Heavy Brigade at Balaclava) ever launched a cavalry charge uphill. Therefore, they dismounted and the advance to contact was made on foot, angling towards Salisbury's right flank.

Meanwhile the Rear would have redeployed behind the ridge to join the reserves commanded by Dudley on the royalist left wing. Once Audley's attack had engaged the attention of Salisbury's right wing, Dudley was to advance across the brook and take the fort by frontal assault. The principal drawback to the plan was that it slighted the Lancastrian advantage in archery, but it is hard to see how they could have used their numerical advantage to better effect. It was a good plan and should have worked – but nothing in battle is certain.

Audley's attack was repulsed and he was killed in hand-to-hand combat by a man thirty-five years his junior, 26-year-old Roger Kynaston of Hordley in Shropshire, who thereafter quartered the Tuchet arms with his own. As noted previously, the Kynastons and Eytons were York's confederates in Shropshire, and Roger was the constable of his castle at Denbigh. He and Roger Eyton had probably joined Salisbury only recently, to guide him along the back roads around Shrewsbury, the Talbot clan's stronghold in the Welsh Marches.

The ancient cross marking where Audley fell is well within 50 yards of where I believe Salisbury deployed his archers, so the charge was first slowed by an arrow storm and then driven back by Kynaston and other knights and men-at-arms. This would have created a shambles in the brook bed, as the Main struggled to advance through a hail of arrows from the archers who advanced with the men-at-arms, and from the unengaged centre of Salisbury's line, which would have swung forward like a door to hit them in the flank.

The overthrow of Audley's attack happened so swiftly that Dudley's advance, which was supposed to be a coordinated, knockout punch, went in too late. He could not be seen to hold back while the Main was slaughtered, but with the attention of the men and guns in the wagon fort no longer engaged by Audley, Dudley's chances of success were greatly diminished. Also, the success of his attack required Salisbury to have committed his reserves already. If he did, they were not required to defeat the first attack, and so were free to ride around the fort to hit the second in the flank.

Dudley's men would already have been unsettled by artillery fire, a novelty to most of them, which began to hit them well outside archery range. They would also have seen their comrades of the Main thrown back. Finally, the Lancastrians again suffered the misfortune of losing their commander early. Once Dudley fell, badly wounded, the Cheshire knights and esquires fled, leaving their foot soldiers to be harried mercilessly back towards Market Drayton. The field next to today's bridge over the Tern, against which they were trapped, was once known as 'Deadman's Den'.

The first battle in a war generally sets the tone for what follows: you do not get a second chance to make a first impression. By any abstract calculation of numbers, strategic planning and operational advantage, the Lancastrians should have annihilated Salisbury's army at Blore Heath on 23 September 1459, and snuffed out the Yorkist revolt. Instead, the flower of the queen's army was shattered, and with it her hopes of being able to control events.

Casualty figures for medieval battles are notoriously unreliable, even when the victorious army took the time to bury the dead. In this case Salisbury had no time to devote to such niceties, and even abandoned his own wounded and his guns. Perhaps 1,000 of Salisbury's men, a fifth of his army, would have fallen, consistent with a battle fought at point-blank range by many skilled archers on both sides, followed by a brutal hand-to-hand struggle. The Lancastrians would have lost more than twice as many, the imbalance coming, as always, from the massacre of fleeing men.

There is a believable anecdote that Salisbury left a 'stay behind' party, possibly including the Augustinian friar mentioned in *Gregory's Chronicle*, to fire the captured royalist guns on the far side of Blore Hill at intervals during the night, in order to discourage an advance by the Lancastrians from Eccleshall. Pausing only long enough to loot the royalist baggage train in Market Drayton, he marched the remnant of his army, severely depleted by casualties and desertion, across the Tern bridge to camp at a place still called Salisbury's Hill.

Among the wounded Salisbury left behind were his sons John and Thomas, and the Lancashire knight Thomas Harrington. They were captured 25 miles north of Market Drayton, presumably on their way to the Harrington manor of Brierley in western Yorkshire. Their captor was the 17-year-old namesake son of John Done of the nearby manor of Utkinton in Cheshire, who had been killed along with his eldest son Richard at Blore Heath.

The three men were held at Chester Castle but released not long afterwards, allegedly in the face of a threat of force by local sympathizers, but almost certainly by order of Stanley. When they were captured they were carrying a note from him to Salisbury, congratulating the earl on his victory and offering further assistance. It would have been difficult to sweep the matter under the carpet if the captives had been brought before magistrates and interrogated.

Although it was an astonishing feat of arms, Blore Heath was a pyrrhic victory. Salisbury had to abandon his equipment and brought relatively few men to Ludlow; but in addition the Yorkist line that they were only in rebellion against the 'evil councillors' around the king lost all credibility once they had destroyed the queen's personal army. The offence was judged so heinous that the terms subsequently offered to the Yorkists specifically excluded Salisbury and his subordinate commanders at Blore Heath from all possibility of grace.

As things turned out, however, the greater effect of the battle was that the talismanic swan livery was discredited and the county palatinate of Cheshire never again responded in such numbers when summoned in the name of the prince. Had Audley won, Marguerite would have ensured he became one of the king's principal military councillors, offsetting and perhaps supplanting the temporizing Buckingham. That weapon had now been dashed from her hand, and her ability to influence military decisions greatly diminished.

XIX

LANCASTER RESURGENT

THE LANCASTRIAN NARRATIVE, SET OUT IN THE PRE-
amble to the Acts of Attainder that followed, was that the
Yorkists had plotted to march on Kenilworth to capture or
kill the king. In fact York remained at Ludlow and, as we have seen,
Salisbury's route was designed to skirt the Midlands. Warwick's
line of march from London to Ludlow did, however, pass through
Marguerite's fortress triangle. His force of 300 Calais veterans (half
the number he brought to the 'Loveday'), swelled by Kentish men
who joined them on the march from Dover, had a near miss with
a Lancastrian force led by Somerset at Coleshill, 13 miles north of
Kenilworth.

On the face of it this would seem to support the Lancastrian
accusation – but in fact the fastest route from London to Ludlow
followed Watling Street (Map 3), which arches through northern
Warwickshire, well to the north of Kenilworth. However, to continue on Watling Street much beyond High Cross would have
lengthened his journey considerably, as well as bringing him dangerously close to Lancastrian Shrewsbury. Assuming he cut the corner,
his line of march would indeed have passed through Coleshill. That
said, Warwick knew it was a highly provocative route, and took it to
distract the Lancastrian armies from closing in on his father.

Somerset may have been leading troops from the South West
to join the queen, making the near encounter accidental. Another

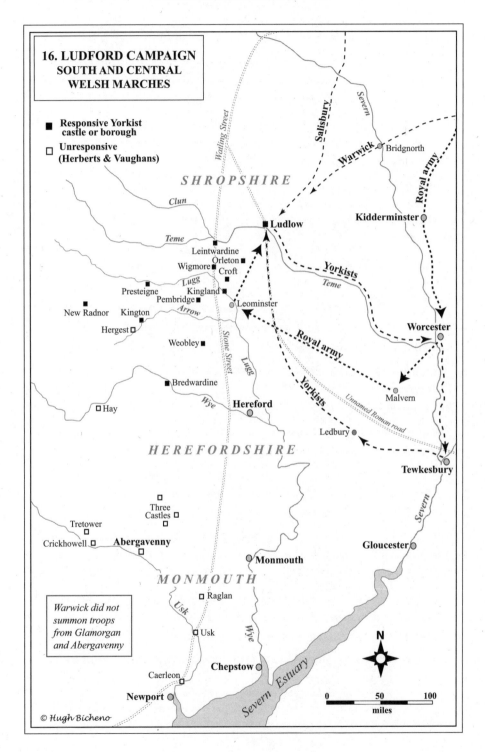

16. LUDFORD CAMPAIGN
SOUTH AND CENTRAL
WELSH MARCHES

■ Responsive Yorkist
castle or borough

□ Unresponsive
(Herberts & Vaughans)

SHROPSHIRE

Clun

Watling Street

Salisbury

Severn

Warwick Bridgnorth

Teme

■ Ludlow

Kidderminster ◉

Leintwardine
Wigmore ■ Orleton ■
■ Croft
Lugg Kingland ■
Presteigne ■
Pembridge ■
Leominster ◉

Yorkists

Teme

New Radnor ■ Kington ■

Arrow

Hergest □

Weobley ■

Royal army

Worcester ◉

Stone Street

Lugg

Bredwardine ■

Wye

Yorkists

Malvern ◉

□ Hay

Hereford ◉

Unnamed Roman road

HEREFORDSHIRE

Ledbury ◉

Tewkesbury ◉

Three
Castles □
□

Tretower
□

Crickhowell □

Abergavenny
□

□

MONMOUTH

Gloucester ◉

◉ **Monmouth**

*Warwick did not
summon troops
from Glamorgan
and Abergavenny*

Usk

□ Raglan

□ Usk

Wye

N

Chepstow ◉

Caerleon ◉

Newport ◉

Severn Estuary

© Hugh Bicheno

0   50   100
miles

possibility is that he had already joined Marguerite and, when they learned of Warwick's movements, Somerset led a column south to keep him under observation. A perceived threat from the south might also explain why the army at Eccleshall did not advance to join the attack on Salisbury at Blore Heath. Such a stratagem would have required a military sophistication Warwick did not possess, and its author would probably have been the veteran Andrew Trollope, commander of the Calais contingent.

On arrival at Ludlow, Warwick found that with the exception of the younger Thomas Vaughan of Bredwardine, already accused of treason in the alleged conspiracy involving Countess Alice, the Herberts and Vaughans had not answered York's summons. Despite the queen's efforts to divide and rule, this was not an act of disloyalty to York. They had valid reasons to stay at home in the face of the threat from Jasper Tudor in Pembroke, and from Buckingham's retainers in Brecon and Newport. The same consideration kept Warwick from summoning his own retainers from Glamorgan and Abergavenny.

Viscount Bourchier was absent, but his brother John, Baron Berners, and his son Edward were there. They were joined by the ever-faithful John, Baron Clinton, and the younger Walter Devereux, *de jure* Baron Ferrers of Chartley; also by Edmund, Baron Grey of Ruthyn, and Henry, *de jure* Baron Grey of Powys, who was married to the late Lord Audley's daughter.* Grey had joint possession of Powys Castle with his cousin John Tiptoft, Earl of Worcester, who went on pilgrimage to the Holy Land early in 1458 and did not return until late 1461. Also present were two previous Speakers of the Commons: John Wenlock, who may have come with Warwick, and York's much-persecuted chamberlain William Oldhall.

With the king were the Dukes of Buckingham, Somerset and Exeter, the Earls of Shrewsbury, Wiltshire, Northumberland, Devon,

---

* *De jure* means that they had not yet been summoned to Parliament by the titles they had inherited, in Devereux's case by marriage. Tiptoft had received the summons that might otherwise have gone to Grey.

Oxford and Arundel, Viscount Beaumont and the northern Barons Clifford, Dacre of the North, Egremont, Greystoke and FitzHugh (another Salisbury son-in-law), plus Grey of Ruthyn's brother Grey of Rougemont, Rivers, Roos, Scales, Sudeley and John Tuchet, the new Lord Audley. Greystoke and FitzHugh were supposedly defectors from the Neville affinity, but with the exception of Arundel the rest were committed Lancastrians and the Yorkists should have expected them to turn out against them.

Clearly they did not, or else grossly underestimated the numbers their enemies would bring to the field. Vastly outnumbered, the Yorkists had brought about the conditions for their own defeat and attainder, the very situation they had mobilized to pre-empt. Any chance of another *coup d'état* was gone, and if they fought, they could expect no mercy from the heirs of the men they had killed at St Albans. It is not clear why they did not immediately disband their followers and go into exile, which they must have known was their only realistic option from the moment they came together at Ludlow.

Instead, they embarked on a peculiar peregrination, marching along the River Teme to Worcester, where they met Richard Beauchamp, Bishop of Salisbury, who brought the king's offer of a conditional pardon for all except Salisbury if they disbanded and made submission within six days. The bishop was accompanied by Garter King of Arms, acting as the royal herald, to emphasize that the alternative was war.

York and the Nevilles swore a solemn oath of loyalty to the king in the cathedral, but they rejected his terms. They replied that the reopening of past, pardoned offences at the Coventry Council in June had shown the worth of the king's grace. In addition, the unpunished and excused assassination attempt on Warwick in the Westminster kitchen had demonstrated the will of the king's councillors to destroy and dispossess them. It was all quite plausible, and it was couched in language that presaged its future use as a manifesto.

When the king advanced towards Worcester the Yorkists retreated down the Severn valley to Tewkesbury, presumably hoping the royal coalition would fall apart through lack of leadership and money. Henry was now in warrior mode, however, and his march from Worcester towards Malvern, threatening their line of retreat to Ludlow, left them in no doubt that he was seeking battle. The Yorkists made a forced march to Ledbury, after which they probably followed the line of a Roman road that once ran from Cirencester to Ludlow.

Passing behind the retreating Yorkists, the king marched to Leominster, where he would have lodged at the Benedictine abbey that owned the borough. It was prime campaigning season, with barns and grain stores full from the recent harvest, and religious establishments probably provided the supplies to maintain an exceptionally large army in the field. Once in the Yorkist heartland, however, they would have been released to forage at will, not quite a destructive *chevauchée*, but painful for York's tenants nonetheless.

When the Yorkists reached the bridge over the River Teme at Ludford, about 600 yards from Ludlow Castle, they could retreat no further. The river was in flood and they dug a wet ditch and rampart around the bridgehead, with artillery mounted in wagons around the perimeter. The Yorkists' collapse is traditionally ascribed to the defection of Trollope and the Calais contingent, supposedly induced by Somerset's appeal to their old loyalty to his father, but by this time desertion was the only rational choice. What followed was described with contempt in the preamble to the Act of Attainder:

> [During the night of 12 October] Almighty God smote the hearts of the Duke and Earls from the most presumptuous pride to the most shameful fall of cowardice that could be thought, so that about midnight they stole away out of the field under colour that they would have refreshed them a while in the town of Ludlow [and], leaving their Standards and Banners in their battle directly opposite [the king's] field, fled out of the town unarmed with few persons into Wales.

York also abandoned Duchess Cecily, his younger sons George and Richard, and his youngest daughter Margaret, found standing forlornly at the market cross when the king entered Ludlow. On the face of it a pragmatic decision to spare them the dangers of accompanying (and slowing) York's flight, it was not an action any wife or child was ever likely to forgive. They were placed in the custody of Cecily's older sibling Anne, Duchess of Buckingham, the wife of a man who now detested York, and who could not resist gloating over their father's over-indulged favourite.

According to *Gregory's Chronicle* the royal army sacked Ludlow – if true, probably a breakdown of discipline provoked by lack of pay. Still, it was the traditional reward for soldiers when they captured an enemy town, and the crowning achievement of the queen's long campaign to demonstrate that York's 'good lordship' was worse than valueless:

> The misrule of the king's gallants at Ludlow, when they had drunken enough of wine that was in taverns and other places, they full ungodly smote out the heads of the pipes and hogsheads of wine, that men went wetshod in wine, and then they robbed the town and bare away bedding, cloth and other stuff, and defouled [sic] many women.

There was further evidence of logistical failure and indiscipline when the royal army continued to loot on its way back to Worcester, even though York and the Nevilles had no estates along the Teme valley. This was probably the work of levies discharged at Ludlow, but the result was that the political outcome of the 'rout of Ludford' was more ambiguous than the phrase implies. In the competition for hearts and minds it was a serious error for the king's forces to be seen to have treated any part of his kingdom like conquered enemy territory. It showed him to be either spiteful, or else too weak to control his men.

The pros and cons of what followed are set out in arguably the most illuminating single document to survive from this period. It was discovered bound with other unrelated papers and listed, presumably from a lost title page, as *Somnium Vigilantis* (the reference is to the Latin aphorism *spes est vigilantis somnium* – 'hope is the dream of the vigilant'). Written in Latin, English and French and clearly intended for the eyes of the highest in the land, it is a lawyerly brief, awkwardly crammed into the literary form of a dream about a debate in the presence of the king between advocates of pardon and attainder for the Yorkist lords. At the end a French-speaking arbitrator (a proxy for Marguerite?) calls for exemplary punishment.

The case for the defence is that mercy is a cardinal virtue in a king, and the Yorkists should also be pardoned because the consequences of attainder would be more harmful. They took up arms for the good of the kingdom, and meant no harm to the king. Those who had died were regrettable collateral damage. At a time when foreign enemies threatened, their power should be harnessed to defend the kingdom. Finally, and going to the heart of Henry's dilemma, they commanded support in the country and 'if they be not received into mercy while they are inclined to accept it, it is to be doubted that at another time they will ask for any'.

The rebuttal is comprehensive: mercy shown to notorious and recidivist offenders would undermine the rule of law; the prospect of reconciliation with such wicked men was a chimera; they posed a greater threat than foreign enemies; any support they enjoyed was won by lies; and they were motivated by insatiable ambition, not by any concern for the general welfare. So far so reasonable, but the concluding indictment restated the patently false accusation that had undone whatever chance the 'Loveday' ever had of bringing about a peaceful settlement:

> Furthermore, was it no harm to kill that merciful and most gracious king that now is? And although the blessed grace of God saved him at that time and suffers him as yet to be alive, they nevertheless did their utmost to undo him, and proceeded as far

as they might within the limits of concealing their pernicious intent.

The 'arbitrator' fully supports the case for the prosecution and also sets out the political argument in favour of attainder. It would strike weapons from the hands of the king's enemies and – properly administered – strengthen his own. By handsomely rewarding his supporters from the proceeds of attainder, their interests and lives would become bound to the survival of his regime. To strengthen the bonds further, all who spoke out against the king's supporters should be put to death as though they had impugned the king himself.

The author of *Somnium Vigilantis* was probably Lawrence Booth, Bishop of Durham and Lord Privy Seal, the queen's chancellor and a member of the Prince of Wales's council. To the modern eye, the realpolitik of the 'arbitrator' is simply common sense. Perceptions were radically different in the Middle Ages, however, and more so in the case of Henry VI. He was still haunted by the injustice committed in his name against his uncle Gloucester, and perhaps more aware of how he had been manipulated in 1450 than historians have been willing to consider.

The handpicked Parliament that met in Coventry in November 1459 was primed to attaint the Yorkists and their supporters root and branch – but the king was not. Acts of Attainder were passed against ten peers present at Ludlow plus Salisbury's countess, but Grey of Ruthyn had got his submission in early, swore he had been deceived and dodged the bullet. The king reserved to himself the application of the judgements against Grey of Powys and Ferrers of Chartley (Walter Devereux, whose much-persecuted namesake father had died in April), who had also submitted. Both were pardoned, but while Powys was promptly restored to his lands, Ferrers had to pay a fine and was not pardoned until March 1460.

Also attainted were twelve knights who fought for Salisbury at Blore Heath including William Stanley, although the king rejected the attainder of Lord Stanley. There was, however, an order under

Privy Seal releasing the knights captured after Blore Heath to Stanley's care – which was pointedly ironic as they were long gone, and the court knew it. The administrators of the dukedom and the two earldoms were largely spared, with the exception of those who were at Blore Heath, plus York's treasurer John Clay and Warwick's chamberlain Thomas Colt. Rounding off the list were Wenlock, Oldhall and others who had accompanied York and the Nevilles into exile, a total of thirty individuals.

Thanks to the prior accusation against Countess Alice, and because the only blood had been shed at Blore Heath, the attainders hit the earldom of Salisbury particularly hard, to the benefit of their local rivals. Northumberland was owed £17,000 [£10.8 million] in back pay as Warden of the East March and Constable of Berwick Castle, and the revenues from many of Salisbury's northern manors were assigned to him – but not the titles. Clifford was made Warden of the West March, Beaumont was made steward of Knaresborough Castle and the duchy of Lancaster lands in the West Riding, and Shrewsbury of the castles at Pontefract and Pickering (see Map 8).

Another beneficiary of the crown's recovery of lands previously entrusted to Salisbury was his son-in-law Henry, Lord FitzHugh, who was made steward of Middleham and Richmond. He was among the most lukewarm of the king's supporters, and the appointments only make sense if the aim was to win over others of Salisbury's affinity. To complete the picture, John, made Baron Neville in July 1460 and acting head of the Nevilles of Raby and Brancepeth by the incapacity of his brother, the Earl of Westmorland, was made steward of Sheriff Hutton. Most of the offices vacated by Salisbury's attainder, however, went to royal officials.

Bishop Booth moved to take possession of Warwick's Durham manors, long claimed by his diocese, even before Warwick was attainted, but otherwise the distribution of spoils went ahead at a glacial pace. In Wales, Warwick's retainers refused to give up his castles in Glamorgan and Abergavenny. Elsewhere due legal process was generally respected, which prevented any rapid transfer of property. Even Somerset's and Shrewsbury's mothers were permitted only to reopen their suits with regard to the Beauchamp inheritance, an admission that previous judgements had been flawed but not a reversal in their favour. A number of those attainted had taken the precaution of settling their lands on Lancastrian trustees, and those properties were specifically excluded in the Acts of Attainder.

Practically all of York's manors were heavily mortgaged and the titles would have brought no immediate benefit, so there was little point in redistributing them. Wiltshire was awarded some unencumbered lands in the South West and drew revenues from them, but Beaumont and Exeter, made stewards of Stamford and Fotheringhay respectively, encountered stubborn popular resistance. York's officials found ways to frustrate the new owners, even when it was the king himself. For example, Henry appointed Egremont constable of forfeited Conisbrough Castle, but a year later it was still held against him by York's lifelong retainer Edmund FitzWilliam. In Wales, Denbigh Castle held out against Jasper Tudor until mid-1460.

From the Yorkist point of view the 'Parliament of Devils', responding to the will of the spiteful queen, committed a monstrous injustice against the king's loyal subjects. Marguerite's view would have been that the attainders were a good start to the restoration of order to the kingdom, but the process failed because the policy advocated by 'the arbitrator' in *Somnium Vigilantis* was not fully implemented. To do so, however, would have sparked countless local rebellions, and Henry knew he lacked the military means and the leadership qualities required to impose it.

The same consideration explains why Stanley got a pass for his treachery during the Blore Heath campaign. He was so greatly the dominant lord in southern Lancashire that only military force could evict him. He was also lord of the Isle of Man, and with York himself now in Ireland the prospect of the island becoming a Yorkist base was unthinkable. All Henry could do was to prevent Parliament from including Stanley in the Acts of Attainder, and (vainly) hope he would be grateful.

The favour shown to the two Lords Grey fits the pattern of Marguerite's strategy of trying to weaken York's hold on central and north Wales. It worked with Powys, who was made steward of Montgomery, later raised troops for the crown in Shropshire, and remained loyal for as long as it was practicable. Ruthyn was a much higher risk gamble. It was worth trying to detach him from his alliance with York in Denbigh, but it was deeply unwise to trust him. He was at daggers drawn with the Duke of Exeter over Ampthill, and he was also responsible for the murder of Speaker Tresham in 1450. Possibly the court's judgement was influenced by his Lancastrian ancestry: he was a great-grandson of John of Gaunt.

A third view of the aftermath of Ludford Bridge is that the settlement, as pursued, was the only viable option. The attainted estates were kept intact as an incentive for the exiled lords to submit, and resume their titles and their essential local functions without presuming to dictate to the king how he should govern. There was little chance they would, but in the meantime, the revenues from the forfeited lands could begin to pay off the crown's debts. The alternative would have been to award the estates to today's loyal lords, who would in all probability prove to be tomorrow's over-mighty subjects.

Although almost every lord spiritual and temporal apart from those in exile swore an oath of loyalty to Henry and his son during the Coventry Parliament, Marguerite's triumph was more apparent than real. Every legal right was on her side, but in the end the case for the defence, rejected in *Somnium Vigilantis*, proved prophetic. The rebel lords were not received into mercy, and subsequently did not seek it. The author of the document should have remembered the Latin aphorism *inter arma enim silent leges*: laws are silent in matters of arms.

XX

WARWICK'S APOTHEOSIS

THE YORKISTS SPLIT UP WHEN THEY FLED LUDLOW. Warwick, his father, York's eldest son Edward, Wenlock, Colt and Pickering made their way to south Wales, sailed across the Bristol Channel to Devon, and travelled overland to the Channel coast. They were assisted by John Dynham of Nutwell, a manor on the bank of the River Exe, for which he later joined them in attainder. He provided them with a balinger, a single-masted vessel similar to a Viking longship, and sailed them to Jersey in the Channel Islands, where they were warmly received by Warwick's governor, John Nanfan. Presumably they then boarded one of Warwick's own, more substantial ships.

They sailed into Calais harbour on 2 November, only days before the arrival of about 1,000 men including Anthony Trollope and others who deserted at Ludlow. This expedition was led by 23-year-old Henry Beaufort, Duke of Somerset, appointed governor of Calais by the Coventry Parliament, with Lords Roos and Audley and Humphrey Stafford of Hooke. While he was away in England Warwick had left his uncle, Lord Fauconberg, and Countess Anne in charge, but with no news of him in the twenty days since the Ludford debacle, they would have had difficulty persuading the garrison to hold out if he had not arrived opportunely.

As it was, Thomas Findern and John Marney, Beaufort loyalists from Somerset's father's time as governor of Calais in the early 1450s, opened the gates of the castle at Guînes and the fort at Hammes to him (see Map 11). Findern and Marney were no more motivated by loyalty to the son of their old commander or to the House of Lancaster than Trollope and Clifton had been at Ludford. They simply placed the wrong bet on the eventual outcome, having failed to appreciate that the Company of the Staple would go the other way after the king pronounced an embargo on all trade with Calais.

Bearing in mind that by this time customs officers in every port except Southampton were Warwick's nominees, the embargo may have been the most counter-productive of all the exercises of the royal prerogative during Henry's reign. Trade with Calais was not affected and, far from cowing the Staplers, it resolved any remaining doubts they may have entertained. Somerset arrived with a war chest of 200 marks [£85,000], all Wiltshire had been able to scrape together in addition to the first payment of Somerset's indentures for troops. In contrast the Staplers made Warwick a personal loan of £3,850 [£2.45 million] and became his financial partners in the military exploits that followed.

Almost as tellingly, the Duke of Burgundy also backed Warwick. He renewed the truce negotiated at Marck in 1457, and ignored a delegation sent by King Henry. At the same time his heir Charles, Count of Charolais, became fascinated by Somerset's bold playing of a very weak hand. One gets the impression that, for the Burgundian court, reports from their agents about the doings of the English at Calais became something like a soap opera, or at least a large-scale chivalric tournament with wonderfully entertaining characters.

Warwick's quid pro quo for the truce had been to desist from attacking Burgundian shipping, while continuing his naval war against France, and the English court could offer nothing of comparable value. In addition he now provided political cover for Burgundian raids into north-eastern France by claiming them as his own, burnishing his credentials as the champion of England against the hated French, at no expense to himself.

The asking price of a warlord in contemporary Italy reflected his cunning (*furbizia*) more than his military prowess. Thus also Warwick. The key to understanding his international stature is that he embodied the paradigm shift which took place during the Renaissance, from lip service to Christian values to the unashamed exaltation of Classical manliness – bravery, strength, pride and ruthlessness (Niccolò Machiavelli's amoral *virtù*). Pope Pius II lamented the change in his autobiographical *Commentaries* (my italics): 'While men live they take pleasure in the glory of the present, which they hope will continue after death. It is this which sustains the most brilliant intellects, *and even more than the hope of a celestial life*, which once begun shall never end, cheers and refreshes the heart of man.'

Adding to Warwick's already extravagant *fortuna*, Charles VII of France was by now very ill with what sounds like diabetes, and beset by other problems. Chief among them was that the Dauphin Louis had sought asylum with the Duke of Burgundy in 1456, and furiously rejected all his father's attempts at reconciliation. Louis of Luxembourg, Count of Saint-Pol, Jacquetta's brother and Marguerite's brother-in-law, was also involved in a military-diplomatic rats' nest too off-topic to unravel here. Suffice it to say that the chronic problems England had with Scotland were fully replicated in France's north-eastern March.

Charles also had to deal with Jean V, Count of Armagnac, one of the more outrageous French nobles. Jean embarked on a relationship with his sister Isabelle, who bore him three children, and they were excommunicated after Jean forged a Papal Bull to permit them to marry. When he also rejected the candidate for Bishop of Auch agreed between the king and the pope, and installed his own bastard half-brother, Charles VII had no option but to invade Armagnac once more.

Somerset's campaign must have been covertly subsidized by Charles VII because Warwick, decisively assisted by his Kentish supporters, prevented any significant support reaching him from England. Some of Warwick's most important warships had been impounded at Sandwich, where a second expedition of 1,000 men was being assembled by Richard Woodville, Baron Rivers, and Gervase Clifton, the previous Calais treasurer and another Ludford defector to the royalists. Rivers had replaced Buckingham as Warden of the Cinque Ports, and was accompanied by Jacquetta and 19-year-old Anthony, their eldest son.

Warwick gambled by sending his remaining ships and his most trustworthy troops under Dynham and Wenlock to make a combined assault on Sandwich. Wenlock landed nearby during the night of 14/15 January and in the morning, when Dynham sailed into harbour firing his guns, achieved tactical surprise by attacking from the landward side. Clifton got away, but Rivers, Jacquetta and Anthony were captured. Warwick's men sailed back to Calais with them, and with the ships, money, equipment and no few of the troops so painfully assembled. The exploit marked the apotheosis of Warwick among the Kentish men, and they were to remain his most devoted followers in the years to come.

Among the men captured at Sandwich were men who had deserted Warwick at Ludford, and they were brought to Calais for execution in a barbaric night-time ritual that included parading Rivers and his son through the streets by torchlight. They were spared, but brought before Warwick, Salisbury and March, sitting on a dais in the central square, who berated and humiliated them as parvenus while boasting of their own royal blood and ancient lineages.

Warwick now had his fleet back and put it to good use. Piracy resumed, the good times rolled once more in Calais, and defections to Somerset ceased. The traffic in fact reversed. In one of Somerset's frequent attacks on the Calais perimeter, Lord Audley and Humphrey Stafford of Hooke were captured. Honourably treated by Edward, they became two of his most devoted followers. Warwick felt so secure that in late February he set out to meet York in Ireland, leaving his father and March behind and seizing prizes indiscriminately as he went, to arrive magnificently on 16 March. As York's biographer acutely comments:

It must have been evident, as Warwick's twenty-six ships sailed into Waterford harbour, that the earl was not only a very able commander, but that whole companies of men and ships were defecting from the Lancastrian regime to serve him. Such defections had been singularly absent from York's career hitherto. The duke may have had the blood of kings in his veins, but it was Warwick who knew his way to his potential subjects' hearts.

Warwick's mother, Countess Alice, was among those who welcomed him. It is not recorded how she made her way from Middleham to Ireland, but reasonable to assume, since she had to pass through Lancashire, that Lord Stanley had much to do with it. Unlike 'proud Cis' in the less than tender care of her sister, Alice bore her husband no ill will, so it is also reasonable to assume she and Salisbury had prepared an escape plan before he set out for the ill-fated rendezvous at Ludlow. Of course it helped that Alice had no minor children, although 17-year-old Margaret, her unmarried youngest, probably accompanied her.

York, Warwick and the fleet soon transferred to Dublin, where the Irish Parliament was in session from 7 March to 5 May. The concrete evidence in the harbour of the strength of the Yorkist cause must have influenced the proceedings, which were entirely favourable to York's cause. As Earl of Ulster he was already strong, and even before Warwick's arrival the Parliament had ratified his appointment as lieutenant, and declared that in the absence of the king himself, York was due all the rights and privileges of royalty.

This was heady stuff both for York and the Anglo-Irish under the leadership of York's deputy, Thomas Fitzgerald, Earl of Kildare, who emerged with a far greater degree of self-government than they had previously enjoyed. It may have been at the suggestion of Warwick, applying the lessons learned from his control of the money supply in Calais, that York also created an autonomous Irish currency to halt the outflow of silver to England. The effect of this and other measures designed to boost Irish trade, however, did little to address

York's immediate need of money and men with which to return to England.

The Irish economy was mainly subsistence-agrarian, and Parliament struggled even to collect the annual subsidy of £360 [£230,000] voted in 1458. Given that Ireland was in a perpetual state of war, and the local lords needed their armed retinues to defend their own lands, the best they could do was grant York a mounted archer for every twenty freeholders – while he was in Ireland. York raised some money from the English merchants of Dublin by the sale of a royal charter to form a guild, and some Anglo-Irish families did contribute men-at-arms to his eventual return to England – but the initiative plainly lay with Warwick.

Before Warwick departed in early May the two men agreed a manifesto listing twelve grievances. The first concerned the abuse of the church, the significance of which is explained below. The second and fourth concerned the crown's abuse of purveyance, the right of the sovereign to fix the price of provisions and transport below market price in time of war. Indeed, much of the manifesto dwelt on the increasingly arbitrary expedients to which the court had been driven by its rejection of resumption, including repeated accusations that the dreaded French *taille* (land tax) was being introduced by the back door.

Taken together the charges had the propaganda virtues of being reasonably close to the truth, and also harking back to the arguments used by Henry IV to justify overthrowing Richard II. They also fastened culpability around the neck of Marguerite, doubly guilty of being both French and a 'designing woman'. She and Beaumont, Shrewsbury and Wiltshire were alleged to have enriched themselves at public expense, and to be seeking to abolish ancient English liberties.*

After Warwick sailed back to Calais, driving a fleet hastily assembled by the Duke of Exeter back to port, the papacy provided the

---

* Anyone who thinks there is anything modern about artfully spinning naked self-interest as a boon to humankind would be well advised to study this document.

cherry on the top of his brimming sundae of *fortuna*. As in everything to do with the medieval Church, the backstory is wonderfully intricate; but as it affects our narrative the key component is that Pius II had become obsessed with launching a crusade against the Ottoman Empire. In 1459 he appointed Francesco Coppini, made Bishop of Terni in 1458 at the instigation of Duke Francesco Sforza of Milan, as his legate to England, charged with obtaining King Henry's support for the crusade.

Pius was deeply misogynist, probably from self-disgust over his sexual incontinence as a young man. In the course of political missions to Scotland, England and Strasbourg in the 1430s, he had sired two bastard children. During 1459–61 the pope's opinion of events in England, as recorded in his *Commentaries*, seems to have been based on Coppini's reports. These, in turn, reflected Coppini's ambition to win an English bishopric and/or a cardinalate, in which he was encouraged by Warwick after they met in Calais in May 1460.

Pius would not have promoted Coppini to legate *a latere* (plenipotentiary) in England and its dominions without the consent of Archbishop Bourchier, who had his own axe to grind with the Lancastrian regime. In February 1460 the pope granted Coppini the right to 'compel the disobedient by ecclesiastical censure and deprivation and to appoint preachers' to proselytize the crusade, and to offer indulgences for all their sins to those who made even modest financial contributions.

Yet, a month later, Coppini wrote to Sforza from Bruges, alleging he had left England on the advice of Warwick – who was at the time embarked on his expedition to Ireland. So, Coppini lied to his patron but not to his employer, as the pope continued to show confidence in his ability to raise funds in England for the crusade, something he would not have done if Coppini's departure had been unauthorized.

What was it Coppini could not tell Sforza, but had no need to explain to Pius II? The most likely answer is that he was acting on the advice of Archbishop Bourchier, who had convinced the pope that Marguerite was the greatest obstacle to England contributing to the crusade.

Forensic analysis of correspondence between Canterbury and Rome may reveal secret writing (commonly used by Renaissance princes when plotting nefarious deeds) in which the archbishop committed secular treason, and which influenced the pope to support the Yorkist cause. Using the vainglorious Coppini as their cat's-paw gave pope and archbishop deniability, while the ambitious legate, frantic for advancement, had every reason to conceal the source of his instructions. It was no less significant that wealthy Bishop William Grey of Ely, a papal appointee and previously neutral, came out for the Yorkists at this time.

Archbishop Bourchier's full siblings were committed Yorkists, and he was also acutely aware that the sympathy of his dangerously volatile Kentish flock was overwhelmingly favourable to Warwick. Thus it came about that when Warwick invaded England in June 1460, Bourchier had summoned a convocation in London to vote the ecclesiastical tenth requested by the pope for his crusade. Presumably it went to Warwick instead, as Pius never saw a penny of it.

Whether or not the hypothetical backstory can be established, when Coppini and Warwick met in May the legate became an active partisan of the Yorkist cause, without rebuke from the pope at the time, or subsequently in the *Commentaries*. On 24 June Fauconberg and Dynham launched another pre-emptive raid on Sandwich, where Osbert Mountfort, previously in command of Rysbank and dismissed by Warwick in 1456, was gathering reinforcements for Somerset. This time there was no surprise and Dynham was seriously wounded in the fighting, but Fauconberg prevailed. Mountfort was sent back to Calais and beheaded.

Two days later Warwick, Salisbury and March arrived at Sandwich and set out on a triumphal progression to London. Kentish men flocked to their banners, and two lords sent to oppose them defected. They were the perennial Yorkist Cobham, who had gained some measure of Lancastrian trust by not joining the Ludlow rebellion, and Bergavenny, the uncle whom Warwick had dispossessed. An explanation why Buckingham had been replaced by Rivers as Warden of the Cinque Ports emerges from the modifications made to the Yorkist manifesto as they marched towards London: the Kentish men demanded Buckingham be added to the short list of evil councillors to be done away with, for being 'fat of grease' from profiteering.

If it were not that Warwick had given himself so little time to prepare it since returning from Ireland, one would be tempted to believe the unbridled popular joy at his return reported by Wavrin had been carefully orchestrated. The Yorkist lords swept into London, where a popular uprising forced Lord Scales and several other Lancastrian lords to retreat to the Tower. The Yorkists were welcomed by the mayor and aldermen, the Bishop of Ely and Warwick's brother, the Bishop of Exeter. They then went to St Paul's, where the Canterbury Convocation was in session, and renewed their oath of allegiance to the king, swearing they had come to rescue him from his wicked entourage.

As though the loss of Kent and London was not enough, Coppini now made public the text of a long letter from him to the king, copies of which had been sent to the pope and to Marguerite. It portrayed the Yorkist lords and their motives in the best possible light, and called on Henry to accept Coppini's mediation, or else bear full responsibility for the consequences: 'You can prevent this if you will, and if you do not you will be guilty in the sight of God in that awful day of judgement in which I shall also stand and require of your hand the English blood, if it be spilt.' In his covering letter to Pius II, Coppini waxed eloquent about his own skills as a conciliator:

> Since fate and necessity had caused me to be as it were an angel of peace and a mediator, [the people] looked upon me also with incredible applause, with reverence and tears, welcomed me,

honoured me, praising the Lord and giving thanks with clasped hands to Your Holiness because you had sent back and restored to them your legate, whose departure with his work undone they had lately mourned.

Self-seeking charlatan he may have been, but Coppini's authority as papal legate *a latere* was unquestionable. The effect of his letter on the deeply pious Henry – if he were permitted to read and respond to it – would almost certainly have been capitulation. It follows that either it was kept from him, or else he was no longer a free agent. Either way, it helps to explain what happened in one of the most enigmatic battles of the Wars of the Roses.

XXI

BETRAYAL

FOLLOWING THEIR TUMULTUOUS WELCOME IN KENT and unopposed admission to London, Warwick, Salisbury, Fauconberg and Edward of March were joined by John Mowbray, Duke of Norfolk and Henry, Viscount Bourchier. The bigger turn-out, however, was by the lords spiritual conveniently convoked by Henry's brother Thomas, Archbishop of Canterbury. Along with Coppini, they were to play a uniquely public role in the following campaign.

Within a few days, on 4 July, Fauconberg set out for the Midlands along Watling Street with a Van of mounted archers and hobilars. Word had come that the king's army was trundling south from the queen's triangle of Kenilworth, Tutbury and Leicester with about 80 guns previously taken from the Tower and used to equip her castles. Fauconberg's task was to cause the royal army to halt well short of London, to give time for Warwick to recruit more troops and to gather guns. We know Warwick set out from London with perhaps thirty guns, and with the Tower armoury still in enemy hands he probably got them from his fleet.

Humphrey Stafford, Duke of Buckingham, commanded the royal army, which, by the time it halted just south of Northampton, included John Talbot, Earl of Shrewsbury, John, Viscount Beaumont, Thomas Percy, Baron Egremont, and Edmund, Baron Grey of Ruthyn. It was probably not Fauconberg who caused them to halt where they did. Northampton was 67 miles from London and roughly equidistant from Kenilworth and Leicester. It was close to some of Buckingham's larger manors, notably Oakham, and to Beaumont's estates in Lincolnshire and Leicestershire. Fatefully, however, it was also very close to the Bedfordshire lands of the recently pardoned Grey of Ruthyn, which explains his presence in an army otherwise composed of unswervingly loyal Lancastrians.

We have no idea how many men each side brought to the field. Since Buckingham adopted a static defensive position he must have been outnumbered, and an educated guess is that he had 10,000 or less against the rebels' 15,000 or more. Much of the Shrewsbury affinity would have been on guard to prevent York landing in north Wales while Jasper Tudor guarded the south, and Egremont had no significant following. He was there in representation of the Percys while the northern lords rallied to his brother Northumberland at York. Possibly the idea was to hold off the rebels until the northerners could join the royal army.

Warwick, Fauconberg, March and Viscount Bourchier left Salisbury and the other Yorkist lords to besiege the Lancastrian lords in the Tower and to secure London. The rebel army was not only more numerous but also had a high proportion of volunteers, including many veterans of the fall of Normandy. They caught up with Fauconberg at Dunstable and then marched together on Northampton, accompanied by Archbishop Bourchier, Papal Legate Coppini and several bishops. The rebel army camped for the night of 9/10 July at a 'mountain', possibly Hunsbury Hill, 2 miles south-east of Northampton.

In terms of eyewitness or at least close contemporary testimony, on a scale of one to ten among the battles of the Wars of the Roses, Northampton is the ten.* Since the combat was almost perfunctory, the principal interest lies in locating exactly where it took place. I beg the reader's indulgence while I illustrate the difficulty medieval

---

* Mortimer's Cross, as we shall see, is the zero.

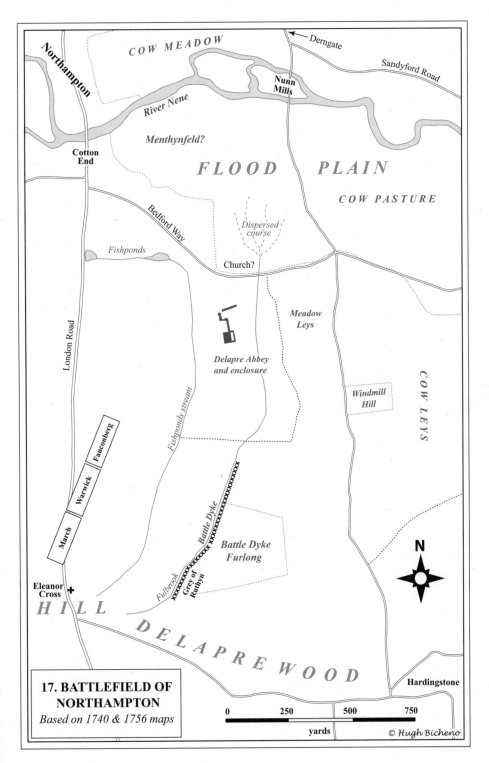

Northampton

COW MEADOW

Derngate

Sandyford Road

River Nene

Nunn
Mills

Menthynfeld?

Cotton
End

FLOOD   PLAIN

COW PASTURE

Bedford Way

Dispersed
course

Fishponds

Church?

Meadow
Leys

London Road

Delapre Abbey
and enclosure

Windmill
Hill

COW LEYS

Fishponds stream

Fauconberg

Warwick

Battle Dyke

Battle Dyke
Furlong

March

N

Eleanor
Cross

Fulbrook

Grey of
Ruthyn

HILL

DELAPRE   WOOD

Hardingstone

**17. BATTLEFIELD OF
NORTHAMPTON**
Based on 1740 & 1756 maps

0   250   500   750

yards

© Hugh Bicheno

historians encounter even when dealing with apparently well-documented events.

According to *An English Chronicle of the reigns of Richard II, Henry IV, Henry V and Henry VI*, written by a Yorkist Londoner: 'The king at Northampton lay at Friars, and had ordained there a strong and mighty field, in the meadows beside the Nunnery, armed and arrayed with guns, having the river at his back.' Warwick's Burgundian hagiographer Jehan de Wavrin locates it 'in a park outside the town beside a little stream'. Dating from 1471, *An English Chronicle* states it took place 'beside Northampton in the Newfield between Hardingstone and Sandyford'.

Written between 1462 and 1471, *Benet's Chronicle* says Henry had 20,000 men in a fortified camp between Hardingstone and Delapre Abbey, but Benet's figures are always exaggerated. Finally, and possibly reflecting comments by Archbishop Bourchier, who viewed the battle from the top of the hill crowned by the Eleanor Cross (erected by Edward I in 1292 and still there, albeit headless, today), the Canterbury monk John Stone wrote: 'And for the field's name on the one part on the north-east side is called Cowemedewe. And that other part is called Menthynfeld. And for the other part is called Sandyngford bridge next to the towne. On the east side there is a water mill called Sandford mill.'

This is not helpful. As Map 17 shows, Cow Meadow was north of the River Nene outside the town walls, bounded by the Sandyford Road, which entered Northampton through the south-western Derngate. Possibly Stone confused it with Cow Pasture, the name given to the flood plain south of the river in a 1740 map. This map also identifies a 'Moorfield', which might have been 'Menthynfeld' 280 years earlier. The only water mills were on an island in the river, with bridges to both banks. The fundamental problem with Stone's description is that he seems to locate the battlefield between the abbey and the river, which would not have been observable from the Eleanor Cross.

A 1756 map identifies a 'Battle Dyke' on the west side and the adjacent 'Battle Furlong' on the east side of the Fulbrook, a stream born of a spring on Hardingstone Hill, on top of which the Eleanor Cross is located. Over time the brook may have altered its course to follow the line of excavation behind the rampart once built along its eastern bank – in fact it may have begun to do so during the battle, as one account says the rain was so heavy 'the guns lay deep in the water', which would be consistent with the stream overflowing.*

The hypothesis portrayed in Map 17 accepts that Benet's description of the location is correct and that Wavrin was right about the topographical details. Thus the Fulbrook was the 'little stream', and the abbey farmlands, which might be described as a 'park', stretched to the woods running from the Eleanor Cross towards the township of Hardingstone. Another source states that Bishop Wainflete resigned as Lord Chancellor and returned the Great Seal to the king three days before the battle in 'Hardingstone Field', next to Delapre Abbey.

The artillery fortification along the Fulbrook commanded the London Road, with the woods covering the left flank and the abbey enclosure the right. Another stream, feeding two fish ponds, presented a further obstacle to a frontal assault, while any attempt to outflank the position along the Hardingstone Road would have been vulnerable to ambush from Delapre Wood. It was a strong position, akin to the one at Castillon on which Talbot's last charge broke in 1453.

The fullest account of the battle is in *An English Chronicle*, which also illuminates the role played by Archbishop Bourchier:

> The earls... sent certain bishops to the king beseeching him that to avoid the effusion of Christian blood he should admit and suffer the earls to come to his presence to declare themselves as they were. The Duke of Buckingham that stood beside the

---

* My reconstruction draws heavily on Northampton Council's online *Site of the Battle of Northampton 1460: Conservation Management Plan*, and on 'War in Writing' in *Medieval Warfare* (June 2015) by battle of Northampton guru Mike Ingram.

king said to them, 'You come not as bishops to treat for peace but as men of arms', because they brought with them a notable company of men of arms. They answered and said, 'We come thus for the security of our persons, for those that be about the king are not our friends'. 'Forsooth', said the duke, 'the Earl of Warwick shall not come to the king's presence, and if he comes he shall die'.

The *Registra* of Abbot Whethamstede of St Albans identifies Richard Beauchamp, Bishop of Salisbury, as the leader of this episcopal delegation. The other bishops were probably Grey of Ely and Neville of Exeter. However, *An English Chronicle* adds that the archbishop then sent Bishop Stanberry of Hereford, the king's confessor, who instead of appealing for the king to accept mediation, 'exhorted and encouraged the king's party to fight'. Stanberry did not return from a second visit 'but privily departed away'. As a result, 'after the battle he was committed to the castle of Warwick, where he was long in prison'.

In his *Commentaries* Pope Pius II states that Coppini was with Warwick's army and 'raised the standard of the Church of Rome, and on the ground that they were to do battle against the enemies of the Faith, he granted plenary remission of sins to those who were to fight on the side of the Earl of Warwick'. He also 'pronounced anathema on their enemies, exhibiting before the camp an Apostolic letter which was believed to contain this formulation, though in reality its contents were quite different'.

Six months later, when the tide of war seemed to have turned against the Yorkists, Coppini sent an indirect message to Marguerite frantically denying he had excommunicated the king's army. But why would Pius II have lied in his private journal? He did dismiss Coppini from his bishopric in 1462, but for other reasons. Unless we are to believe the pope was attempting to deceive himself, there can be no doubt Coppini acted in an outrageously partisan manner, and that Pius II approved.

Apoplectic fury that the Church had come out for the Yorkists would, of course, explain why Buckingham refused the bishops access to the king, and Stanberry would have warned the duke and Beaumont of their likely fate if Henry accepted Coppini's mediation. Buckingham's baffled rage was further inflamed by seeing his Bourchier half-brothers openly among the enemies in arms against him, many of them Kentish men who would kill him on sight.

The Yorkists formed the usual three battles parallel to the earthworks along the London Road, and Wavrin says the attack was led by the 'advance guard, commanded by Lord Fauconberg'. Warwick's battle arrived at the Fulbrook a little later, and March's later still. If accurately described, this was an oblique attack of the kind later made famous by Frederick the Great. It works by drawing the enemy's attention and reserves to the first flank attacked and then to the centre, leaving the remaining flank vulnerable to the knockout blow. In this case, the last flank attacked, on the Lancastrian left, was held by Grey of Ruthyn.

Grey was probably a Yorkist Trojan Horse from the start, and must also have insisted that his submission should be made to March as his father's representative; such a vital role would not otherwise have been entrusted to an 18-year-old who was leading men into battle for the first time. While the rain had silenced the royal artillery, it also made the earth rampart impossibly slippery, and Grey's men had to help March's troops climb over it.* The royalist position collapsed immediately and the levies fled towards the bridges over the Nene, where the crush pushed hundreds to drown in the river.

As their army collapsed the Lancastrian lords made a last stand around the king's tent and were slaughtered. Apart from them, however, there were remarkably few combat casualties – one source estimates as few as fifty-eight. This would be consistent with a battle in which the rain not only silenced the guns but also wet the archers' bowstrings, so they could only loose a shaft or two with the

---

* His reward for this well-designed act of cold-blooded treachery was the definitive award of Ampthill and, eventually, the earldom of Kent.

spare strings they kept in their hats. If the earthworks were too slick to climb, then Fauconberg's and Warwick's battles may not have come to hand strokes at all, but rather milled around in the mud on the other side, making a lot of noise. As at St Albans, the battle was decided by a distraction followed by an abrupt dislocation of expectations.

The defeat was an unqualified disaster for the Lancastrian cause. The king was now in their enemies' possession and they had also lost three of their greatest magnates. Buckingham was succeeded by his 5-year-old grandson and Shrewsbury by his 12-year-old son, leaving two of the largest Lancastrian affinities leaderless. Only Beaumont's affinity still had a leader in his 22-year-old son, who was with his father at Northampton. He was wounded but survived to join the other lords bent on avenging the deaths of their sires.

Of the named 'evil councillors' only Wiltshire had escaped the net. Following the failure of the Duke of Exeter to intercept Warwick on his return voyage from Ireland to Calais, Wiltshire had been entrusted with raising a fleet to guard the Irish Sea and to rouse the Butler affinity against York's authority in Ireland, meeting with success in neither endeavour. Not long after Northampton he sailed to Brittany on instructions from Marguerite to ask the new Duke Frañsez II to back the Lancastrian cause. The death of Arzhur III, his immediate predecessor, was a heavy blow to Marguerite as he was none other than the Count de Richemont, erstwhile Constable of France and a loyal supporter of the House of Anjou.

Two weeks after Northampton the Lancastrian lords holding the Tower of London capitulated. Although their leader, Lord Scales, was granted a safe conduct, it was not respected by the watermen supposed to row him to safety. They murdered him and dumped his body in the grounds of a riverbank priory. He was 63 years old, a distinguished Normandy veteran who had led an army for York in the later stages of the Hundred Years War, and godfather to Edward of March.

Warwick and March attended his funeral and deeply regretted

the murder; but they also executed – for treason – six of the Duke of Exeter's retainers who had fought their way into the Tower. They had acted in the service of their legitimate sovereign, which clearly could not be treason, but the Yorkist lords needed to throw the mob a bone. They could only hope to channel popular fury – they could no more control it than a surfer controls a wave.

The other lords who had held the Tower with Scales were more fortunate. Henry Bromflete, Baron Vescy, had not previously participated, and after this wisely retired from the conflict. Richard West, Baron de la Warr, temporarily defected to the Yorkist cause. John, Baron Lovell, held multiple titles of nobility and had landholdings in the Midlands an earl might envy. He continued to fight for Lancaster. Robert, Baron Hungerford, had only recently returned from French captivity after payment of a ruinous ransom. He was released to go on a pilgrimage.

Northampton also destroyed any hope Somerset retained of capturing Calais. Warwick returned and on 8 August met Somerset to agree terms of capitulation for Guînes and Hammes. As the alternative was that Somerset might sell them to France, the terms were generous. Somerset, Roos, Trollope and their men were paid to march unhindered to France with their equipment, and Rivers and his son were released to join them.* They were welcomed by Charles VII, who gave them more money and lent them ships and an escort to take them back to England. Somerset had sworn not to bear arms against Warwick in the future, but saw no reason to keep his word to an oath-breaker.

Following the battle Marguerite and her son fled from Kenilworth with what remained of the royal plate and jewellery, and a small escort. According to William Gregory she was robbed near Malpas in Cheshire by a member of her entourage whom she had raised from nothing to the status of gentleman, and completed the journey to Harlech Castle riding pillion behind a young squire. The people

---

* Jacquetta would have been sent back to England soon after capture.

of north Wales received their prince and his mother warmly, but she could not remain once the Yorkist lords learned where she was:

> And from there she moved in secret to Lord Jasper, Lord and Earl of Pembroke, for she dared abide in no place openly. The cause was that counterfeit tokens were sent to her as though they had come from [her husband]... but she gave them no credence; for at the king's departing from Coventry toward the field of Northampton, he kissed her and blessed the prince, and commanded that she should not come to him until he sent her a special token that no man knew but the king and she. For the [Yorkist] lords greatly wished to bring her to London, as they knew full well that all the workings that were done were her doing, for she was much more clever than the king...

Some spirit remained in the defeated and captive king, it seems. Despite his many failings, one cannot withhold sympathy for him, miserably aware his life hung by a thread and humiliatingly paraded through London in a cynical mockery of a triumphal procession. Most devastating of all would have been to discover that not only his bishops but even the pope had turned against him. The following passage in the *Commentaries*, although its words are attributed to Warwick by Pius II, reflects the pontiff's own opinion and crusading hopes:

> Our king is a dolt and a fool who is ruled instead of ruling. The royal power is in the hands of his wife and those who defile the King's chamber... Many feel as I do, among them the Duke of York, who would now be on the throne if there were any regard for justice... If God gives us victory, we shall drive our foes from the King's side and ourselves govern the Kingdom. The King will retain only the bare name of sovereign... before long, when the Kingdom is again at peace, we will equip a fleet in defence of religion.

Images illustrating the fall of Normandy as depicted in the fifteenth-century manuscript *Vigiles du Roi Charles VII.*

Top The mercenary François de Surienne takes the Breton border fortress of Fougères for the English.

Centre Modern French artillery batters the English fortress of Château Gaillard.

Below Crude stone-firing bombards at the siege of Caen.

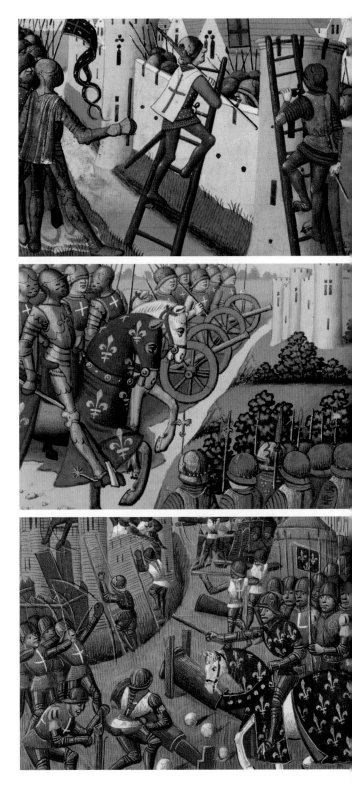

Details from panels of the St Ursula Shrine (1489) by Hans Memling.
Left, a fifteenth-century soldier wearing partial plate armour; *right*, another
wears the reinforced canvas garment known as a brigandine.

The tomb effigy of Sir Ralph Fitzherbert in the Church of St Mary and St Barlok, Norbury, Derbyshire, *left,* is a fine example of a late fifteenth-century suit of armour, and has been used as the basis for a modern replica, *right.*

A modern replica of a poleaxe, the principal weapon of the late-medieval man-at-arms.

An accurate re-enactment of a Wars of the Roses battle in which billmen
try to hook each other's legs.

The key element of the English way of war: direct shooting by massed longbowmen.
By kind permission of Perry Miniatures (www.perry-miniatures.com).

An illustration by the battle artist Richard Caton Woodville (1856–1927) of the
slaughter at the Cock Beck following the Battle of Towton in 1461.

Middleham Castle, North Yorkshire, was a stronghold of the Neville family from the late thirteenth century.

Warwick Castle fell into the hands of Richard Neville when his wife Anne Beauchamp became 16th countess of Warwick in 1449.

Kenilworth Castle, Warwickshire, a key fortress in Marguerite d'Anjou's Midlands power base.

Ludlow Castle, Shropshire: the administrative centre of Richard of York's holdings in Wales and the Marches.

The Micklegate Bar, York, was adorned with the heads of fallen Yorkist lords after their defeat at the Battle of Wakefield in 1460.

If Pius believed the already bankrupt English crown would be able to contribute to his crusade after a further round of civil war, he had parted company with reality. It is a sobering thought that the papacy's decisive intervention in the internal affairs of the kingdom was based on a delusion as profound as any of poor Henry's wishful thinking.

XXII

MARGUERITE
AND SON

A FTER NORTHAMPTON MARGUERITE'S SITUATION WAS desperate. Her husband was now a prisoner and, although this freed her to take personal command of the defence of her son's right, it permitted her enemies to issue orders in the king's name. Financially, the loss of London and the South East, and the defection of the Canterbury Convocation, were body blows. Strategically, the battle had nullified the power base she had built up since 1455: her Midlands domain around the fortress-triangle of Kenilworth, Tutbury and Leicester was lost, as were her castles at Wallingford and Berkhamsted.

Any chance of limiting Stanley's influence in Cheshire had gone with the death of Shrewsbury and the ensuing defection of the previously dog-loyal Dudley. Her attempt to undermine York's influence in the Marches was also undone, but in Wales itself loyalists held a crescent from recently taken Denbigh Castle around the coast to Carmarthen. Grey of Powys held Montgomery for her, and Buckingham's affinity was still strong in Brecknock, but the only really safe area was Jasper Tudor's isolated Pembroke.

Possession of the Welsh coast would have been more useful if there had been any hope of supplanting York in Ireland, but that was a pipe dream. Wiltshire had neglected his earldom of Ormonde, and leadership of the Anglo-Irish was now exercised by the firmly Yorkist Earl of Kildare. Money might persuade the Gaelic lords to provide troops, but they were mainly concerned with fighting among themselves. The ports on the Pembroke peninsula were, nonetheless, among the few geostrategic assets remaining to the Lancastrian cause.

With the return of Somerset to Corfe the situation in the West Country was more promising. Henry Beaufort was a vigorous and now militarily experienced 24-year-old, and loyal to the House of Lancaster in a way his father had never been. Marguerite also had the unqualified support of 28-year-old Thomas Courtenay, who was married to her niece and had succeeded his namesake father as Earl of Devon two years previously. A Yorkist triumph would see his efforts to drive Bonville out of Devon reversed. Lastly, she could count on Alexander Hody, a major landowner around Yorkist Bridgwater in north-central Somerset and, for what he was worth, the Duke of Exeter, who had lands in Somerset and Dorset.

Wales and the West Country aside, the principal hope of the Lancastrian cause now lay in the North. With Stanberry imprisoned, apart from her confessor Walter Lyhert at Norwich and Thomas Bird at St Asaph, she could no longer count on the support of any of the bishops in the archdiocese of Canterbury. In contrast, with the Booth brothers at York and Durham, and William Percy at Carlisle, the archdiocese of York was solidly hers. While far poorer than Canterbury, in the absence of any other major source of revenue it can be assumed the church in the North subsidized the Lancastrian cause in 1460–1.

Added to which Yorkist influence in the North had been curtailed to the benefit of the Percys and their allies. However, the degree to which Neville influence had been supplanted in the region should not be overestimated. Before he set out from Middleham Castle in 1459, Salisbury appears to have secretly agreed that Ralph, Baron Greystoke, would act as his Trojan Horse within the Lancastrian ranks should the rebellion not prosper. It is probable that Salisbury had also made a similar arrangement with his son-in-law Lord FitzHugh, but it seems FitzHugh's head may have been turned when he benefited so greatly from Salisbury's attainder.*

With the king now the hostage of their enemies, Northumberland and the other northern lords needed no urging from Marguerite to cast off the restraint he had imposed on them, and they raided Yorkist manors across the North. The raids were not destructive and were more akin to peremptory tax collections. Although the Parliament summoned by Warwick had repealed the 1459 attainders, the letter of the law was now irrelevant in the North.

What Marguerite could and did do, using dispatch boats out of Tenby, was to coordinate the mobilization of her own West Country followers and officials. She begged Somerset, Devon and Hody to gather their followers and march north to meet her at the port of Hull, on the River Humber in the East Riding of Yorkshire. To 'all those servants that loved her or wished to keep and enjoy her office', she wrote, 'all excuses ceasing and other occupations left, you shape yourselves to be with us [at Hull] in all haste possible, for certain causes that move us, which shall be declared to you at your coming'. This they did, marching up the Fosse Way past Bath, through Cirencester and past Coventry to join the northern lords.

The Lancastrians quickly agreed they would all wear the Prince of Wales's livery, and one of the very few surviving Lancastrian proclamations from this time took the form of a letter from Prince Edward to the inhabitants of London. It was written after York dropped the pretence of being a loyal subject and tried to claim the throne for himself (see following chapter). In it the prince denounced 'that horrible and falsely forsworn traitor calling himself duke of York, mortal enemy unto my lord, to my lady and to us, [who] has blinded my lord's subjects and, to [the end of] obtaining his subtly contrived treason, by untrue means often times provoked them to commotions, stirrings and unlawful assembly against his royal estate'.

Aware that Warwick's propaganda machine was already cranking

---

* Greystoke did well out of it, but several years passed before Warwick forgave FitzHugh.

up atavistic fear of 'the Northmen' among the southern English, Marguerite herself wrote a rebuttal addressed to the council of the City of London, in which she announced her intention to rescue her husband:

> We will have you know for certain that at such time as we and our son shall be disposed to see my lord, as our duty is and so binds us to do, that none of you shall be robbed, despoiled or wronged by any person that at that time we or our son shall be accompanied with, or any other sent in our or his name, praying to you in most hearty and desirous wise that you will diligently extend all earthly means to the security of my lord's royal person in the meantime.

The designation of Hull as the rendezvous point suggests Marguerite had already received a favourable response to a request for a meeting with Mary of Guelders, queen mother and regent for 8-year-old King James III of Scotland. If the aim was only to join the northern lords, she could have sailed to Cumberland, bypassing Stanley in Lancashire, even though that would have put her on the wrong side of the Pennines in mid-winter. The choice of Hull indicates Marguerite already knew she would sail to south-eastern Scotland, then cross to the North Sea and take another ship down the coast.

It was politically impossible for Marguerite to accept open support from her uncle Charles VII of France. With Yorkist propaganda branding her a French whore, her Valois parentage was something she needed to downplay in the competition for hearts and minds. As for the allegations of infidelity, such evidence as we have supports the view that it was not believed. She continued to enjoy considerable popular sympathy as the wife of the man all regarded as the legitimate king, and the mother of a no less legitimate Prince of Wales. Sympathy would evaporate, however, if she made any overt alliance with England's foreign enemies.

Wiltshire/Ormonde had her authority to treat with the Duke of Brittany and to recruit foreign mercenaries, but that was at suitably arm's length and, anyway, she had nothing to offer Brittany in exchange for more substantial support. She did, however, have something to offer Scotland, but could entrust no one else with the task. Having first obtained a private letter from her uncle Charles VII supporting her mission, and leaving Jasper Tudor to await the arrival of Wiltshire and whatever forces he had gathered, she sailed with her son from Tenby to Kirkcudbright, then travelled to Lincluden Abbey, near Dumfries.

· ℰ૭ ·

The Scottish backstory is in many respects a mirror image of events in England. It will be recalled that the first (of six successive) King James fell in love with and married Joan Beaufort when he was a hostage in England. James was murdered in February 1437 by assassins sent by the Earl of Athol, his uncle and nearest adult relative. Joan was wounded but escaped with her 6-year-old son to the protection of Alexander Livingston, warden of Stirling Castle. The *coup d'état* failed and Athol and his co-conspirators were executed.

The chronic threat came from the over-mighty Black Douglas dynasty. The 5th Earl of Douglas acted as regent until he died in 1439, but a year later his 16-year-old heir and his next eldest son were invited to the infamous 'Black Dinner' by James II and murdered by his Lord Chancellor, whom the king promptly ennobled.* Twelve years later James II himself murdered the 8th earl at Stirling Castle. James Douglas, the 9th earl, was attainted for rebellion and for conspiring with the English in 1455. After his brothers were killed in battle by the Red Douglas Earl of Angus, James Douglas took refuge in England. Angus was awarded the Douglas title and core domain, but James II prudently retained the wider Black Douglas estates.

* The inspiration for the 'Red Wedding' in George R. R. Martin's *A Storm of Swords*.

Also in 1455, as we have seen, James II proposed a joint war against England to Charles VII of France to take advantage of the Yorkist rebellion, and tried to stir the pot by falsely alleging that York had been in treasonous correspondence with him. Charles refused the invitation but James followed up the defeat of the Black Douglases by leading a raid into England. He withdrew when York was made Protector and marched north, only to launch a six-day *chevauchée* into Northumberland the following year, after York's protectorship was ended. James agreed to a one-year truce in July 1457 mainly because he needed to assert royal authority in the Highlands and to initiate far-ranging institutional reforms.

Although the 2nd Duke of Somerset, his maternal uncle, had been killed at St Albans, sentiment played no part in James II's calculations. War with England was one of the few policies capable of uniting his unruly nobles, and in conjunction with his reforms rallied the common people behind him. He was also a pioneer in the use of siege artillery, the bane of the castle-based feudal order, and had used it to complete the destruction of the Black Douglases and their allies.

In July 1460, following the Battle of Northampton, James set out to remove the irritant of Roxburgh, an English stronghold on the north bank of the upper River Tweed, which was regarded by the Scots as their natural frontier. The Anglo-Scottish border shown on the maps in this book is today's; in the fifteenth century it was more like a wide ribbon of no man's land running on either side of a line from Berwick to Carlisle, populated by infamous border 'reivers' and studded with fortified houses and Pele towers.

Roxburgh town fell quickly, but James had to bring up his guns to reduce the castle. In early August, while supervising the bombardment, he was killed by a fragment when one of the guns exploded. He was only 29 years old, and the timing of his death could not have been more fortunate for the Lancastrians.

• ℰℐ •

Marguerite sailed to Scotland in December 1460 to win peace on the border so her supporters could concentrate against the Yorkists. Like Marguerite with Henry, Mary of Guelders had been 15 years old when she was betrothed to James II in 1449. Unlike Marguerite, however, she came with a magnificent dowry of 60,000 crowns [£9.54 million] provided by her cousin Duke Philippe of Burgundy, in whose household she had grown up. The Scots regarded her as such a splendid asset that the palace of Holyrood House was built to receive her, and her dowry underpinned her husband's consolidation of royal power.

Mary was well regarded by all strata of Scots society, especially after producing the required heir in 1452. When she learned of her husband's death she took her son, now King James III, to Roxburgh, arriving five days later to direct the successful conclusion of the siege and the demolition of the hated castle. Having thus established her credentials as a leader, she had no difficulty in assuming the role of regent to the infant king and quickly appointed her own men as keepers of the most strategically located royal fortresses.

The only significant opposition she had to deal with for the remaining three years of her life came from her principal minister, Bishop James Kennedy of St Andrews. Superficially their differences concerned the correct manner to exploit the situation south of the border, with Mary to some extent swayed by the Yorkist sympathy of her surrogate father the Duke of Burgundy, and Kennedy fiercely advocating the 'auld alliance' with France. The real problem was that Kennedy was another episcopal misogynist who tried to smear Mary with the usual allegations of promiscuity, for no better reason than his own psychology and the Church's hostility towards women it judged insufficiently submissive.

Understandably, given that their countries were at war, the December meeting at Lincluden Abbey was conducted in the strictest secrecy, between the two queens alone. They had much in common. Marguerite was still only 30 years old, Mary four years her junior, and their sons were respectively 10 and 8 years old. The

Auchinleck Chronicle, the sole source for what was discussed, states they tentatively agreed a marriage alliance between the Prince of Wales and one of Mary's daughters. We can deduce from subsequent events that they also discussed the cession of the fortress at Berwick if Mary helped the Lancastrians to defeat the Yorkists, but all we can be sure of is that Mary agreed to an immediate truce.

While they were still at Lincluden, electrifying news arrived from south of the border – news that made it imperative for Marguerite and her son to join the army raised in his name as soon as possible. An agreement, presumably relating to the marriage, was signed by the two queens on 5 January, after which Mary arranged for Marguerite and Edward to be rushed across Scotland to the port of Leith. Here they boarded a royal ship provided by Mary and accompanied by an escort, and sailed south – for Yorkshire.

XXIII

RICHARD'S HUMILIATION

WARWICK ACTED AS THE KING'S CHIEF MINISTER following Northampton and, using Henry as a rubber stamp, summoned Parliament to revoke the Acts of Attainder passed nine months previously. Salisbury was obsessively concerned with recovering and adding to his vast estate, and content to leave the politics to his son. Nor is there any evidence that Edward of March acted as his absent father's deputy; to the contrary, both before and after York's belated return from Ireland, Edward plainly acted as Warwick's apprentice.

Warwick petitioned the pope to appoint Coppini cardinal, and for permission to award him an English bishopric, but neither was forthcoming. Archbishop Bourchier remained benevolent and Viscount Bourchier replaced Wiltshire/Ormonde as Lord Treasurer. The office of Lord Chancellor, resigned by Bishop Wainflete three days before Northampton, went to Bishop George Neville of Exeter, and Bishop John Stillington of Bath and Wells replaced Bishop Laurence Booth of Durham as Lord Privy Seal.

Any pretence that the king could command even his own household was swept away, a situation also facilitated by so many of the household having joined the queen. The only survivor was the neutral figure of Lord Beauchamp of Powick, who remained as steward because his expertise was irreplaceable. Warwick's brother John became the king's chamberlain and other Warwick appointees filled the lesser household offices. Warwick also made himself and his father joint chief stewards of the king's duchy of Lancaster estates.

Warwick recovered the governorship of the Channel Islands and had himself appointed Warden of the Cinque Ports. He got Parliament to renew his commission as Keeper of the Seas, now supported by the customs revenues of Sandwich and Southampton as well as all other ports. The Staplers were delighted to surrender their nominal right to the receipts from the two great wool ports in return for the resumption of uninterrupted trade. The City of London Corporation and the individual livery companies were likewise grateful, and lent Warwick large sums in the months ahead. He also collected £7,000 [£4.45 million] in a forced levy from all crown servants who wished to retain their offices.

Warwick was a whirlwind on a tightrope, with every move designed to maintain the momentum won at Northampton, and he expended no political, still less financial capital to address the chronic problems that had brought successive kings' governments into disrepute. The Commons were not required to vote any new taxation, which would have opened the door for a reiteration of demands for radical resumption to put royal finances on a sustainable basis.

One unpostponable reckoning was the issue of legitimacy. Marguerite may have been the first to see that a puppet king could not long survive, but now the Yorkist lords ran into the contradiction at the heart of their rebellion. If, as they had repeatedly sworn by the most sacred oaths, they were the loyal liegemen of the anointed sovereign, then by what authority did they presume to dictate to him how he should rule? A present-day historian of the period offers a perfect summary of the issue:

> The real problem of Henry's reign was that an authority which should have been whole and located in one man, was actually fragmented and dispersed: royal blood, personal lordship, executive power and the capacity to represent the public were

scattered among a host of magnates, clerks and gentlemen of the household. The tragedy is that the efforts to restore this authority involved the great in conflicts among themselves, conflicts which were actually between the constituent parts of the monarchy. From these conflicts, unmodified by the saving power of genuine royal grace, there was no escape.*

Every argument the Yorkist lords had used to justify their defiance now backfired. As they had at all times acquitted the king of personal responsibility for the chronic ills besetting the nation, they found themselves promoted to the role of the 'evil councillors' who must, perforce, be to blame for everything. Added to which, the avidity with which the Nevilles awarded themselves lucrative offices made it clear they were just Suffolks writ large, and that their claim to uphold the greater good had always been a cynical pretence.

York did not return to England from Ireland until 9 September 1460 when, his lordship of Denbigh still held against him, he stepped ashore at the Wirral, Stanley's manor on the peninsula between the Mersey and Dee rivers. Like Grey of Ruthyn, Stanley had not yet received any significant reward for his treachery, and he made a further effort to curry favour from York by organizing a civic reception for him at Chester, the administrative capital of the Prince of Wales's county palatinate of Cheshire. Blore Heath cast a long shadow.

From the time of his arrival York assumed the full arms of England and omitted Henry VI's regnal year in the dating of his correspondence. He had come to claim the throne, and Warwick's later protestations that it had come as a complete surprise were false. The two men had probably agreed he must do so when they met in Dublin, and York delayed his arrival for a triumphal progress to London to be organized. In mid-September Warwick travelled to meet him in Shrewsbury, where they spent four days together

---

* From John Watts' brilliant essay in Kekewich et al., *The Politics of Fifteenth-Century England*.

before he returned to London. He did not, however, prepare the ground along the route later followed by York.

If York hoped to replicate Warwick's triumphal procession through Kent he was soon disappointed. He had gone to the well too many times. The loyalty he once commanded had been eroded by his failure to protect his supporters over the preceding decade, and only his retainers turned out to greet him at Ludlow. Although Cecily and, presumably, his younger children joined him at Hereford, Edward of March pointedly did not come to replace his younger brother Rutland at their father's side.

Whether or not York perceived it, there was a fundamental weakness at the heart of his relationship with the Nevilles. What would Warwick have gained if York became king? He stood only to lose if his rubber-stamp king was replaced by a man he could not control. York's ambition was to establish strong, orderly government, whereas Warwick and his father had done very well indeed out of weakness at the centre. It did not require a crystal ball to see that the alliance the Nevilles had made with York would survive only as long as they faced a common enemy.

Conversely York knew that the only alternative to claiming the throne was to become, once more, the Protector of a king he did not control and a government differing only in personnel from those against which he had rebelled. It is irrelevant whether he was coldly calculating or deluded by arrogance of ancestry and the urgings of his Irish and Marcher entourage, or to what degree he was encouraged – or not – by Warwick. What followed is best seen as a power play within the Yorkist alliance.

When York entered London, his sword held before him point upward in royal style, he was not greeted by the popular enthusiasm Warwick could have organized had he wished to do so. Even though things were clearly not proceeding to plan, York still went ahead as though his acclamation as king was a foregone conclusion, which strongly suggests Warwick misled him about the reception he could expect from the handful of lords assembled in Westminster Hall.

On 10 October York entered the Hall, walked to the throne and laid his hand on it. There was a deafening silence until Archbishop Bourchier spoke, to ask him if he sought an audience with the king. York blustered 'I know of no person in this realm whom it does not behove to come to me and see my person rather than that I should go and visit him', but his humiliation was as complete as it was, to him, unexpected. He had been hung out to dry.

After the debacle a furious altercation took place in private between York and the Nevilles. Edward of March was present and did not support his father, but it was probably Salisbury who prevailed on the duke to accept the logic of 'hang together or all hang separately', and that they must make way for younger blood. Salisbury was 60 years old, but York was not yet 50 and it was a bitter pill to swallow, made worse by the galling knowledge that March's young blood was not his. We can readily imagine his rage.

A charade of parliamentary consultation ensued before Warwick proposed a compromise the bishops could accept. Very few secular lords had responded to the summons, and the Act of Accord agreed on 31 October was probably a deal worked out with Archbishop Bourchier. Even though York's attempt to supplant Henry was ruled out for several reasons, not least the many oaths of allegiance he had sworn, it was judged expedient to accept the validity of his claim to a superior hereditary right, as the matrilineal descendant of Edward III's second son. Henry was eleven years younger than York, so the most likely heir would be March, who carried none of his father's baggage of sacred undertakings.

Modelled on the 1420 Treaty of Troyes, the Act required the king to recognize York and his issue as his heirs. Pope Pius II recorded that it was the egregious Coppini who prevailed on Henry to accept it, arguing it was his Christian duty to do so in order to avoid further bloodshed. Fear for his own life may have influenced Henry less than is commonly supposed. Without even his confessor to advise him, he may have reasoned that no agreement reached under duress was binding, and that he should buy time for his beloved son to grow up and for York and the Nevilles to turn on each other, as they inevitably must.

Sugaring the pill for York, the Act also appointed him Protector for life, with an annual salary of 10,000 marks [£4.24 million], of which 3,500 was for March and 1,500 for Rutland, to be drawn from disinherited Prince Edward's lands in Wales, Cornwall and Chester. In point of legal fact the accord was never formally enacted – it was not even submitted to the Commons, which underlined that it was no more than a face-saving expedient. Underlining it further was that Warwick, not York, carried the king's sword before him in the procession to St Paul's to celebrate the Accord, while March carried his train.

York's claim and the Act of Accord caused widespread outrage. York and the Nevilles seriously underestimated the extent of the opposition they had aroused, and the only explanation for the carelessness that characterized the next act in the drama is if they were seriously misinformed about the situation developing in the North. All they had to work with were reports – which would have lost nothing in the telling – of raids, mainly against Salisbury's estates, which seemed to follow the pattern of defiance last seen in 1454.

As Protector York had to move quickly to suppress the disorder and Salisbury, as the person most directly affected, accompanied him. The crucial factor in the conduct of the ensuing campaign in the north was probably York's state of mind. He behaved in a lackadaisical and rash manner; if depression is anger turned inward, he was probably deeply depressed. Also, his relations with Salisbury, brother and father of the woman and the man who had first intimately and now publicly humiliated him, may have been barely civil.

The composition of their army suggests that York was not pleased to be leading an expedition whose main purpose was to re-establish Salisbury's authority in Yorkshire. Apart from the duke, his son Rutland and Edward Bourchier, the youngest son of York's brother-in-law Viscount Bourchier, the notables who marched north with him were members of Salisbury's affinity, including his son-in-law William Bonville, Baron Harington.

When they set out from London on 9 December they may have had a siege train, intending to recover Pontefract Castle, but at some point they abandoned the guns and decided to march instead to Sandal Castle, in York's south Yorkshire manor of Wakefield. Why they went there rather than to his larger castle at Conisbrough, less than a day's march to the south-east, is a mystery. Along the Great North Road they passed through or close to several of York's boroughs in Hertfordshire and Lincolnshire, but he made no great effort to summon his affinity. Nor did he ensure that Sandal was adequately provisioned, so when they arrived on 24 December 1460 there was little in the way of Christmas cheer.

Sandal was a compact fortification that could only accommodate a few hundred men within its walls. The adjacent village of Sandal Magna was also small, so the bulk of the Yorkist forces must have camped in the open, probably clustered around the entrance to the castle, overlooking the plain leading to the River Calder, with Wakefield on the other side across a narrow bridge. There was a 40-acre, wooded and fenced deer park close to the castle, but the earliest land use maps show no evidence of woods anywhere on the plain.

York and Salisbury were unaware that there was a large Lancastrian force at Pontefract, where the West Country lords had met up with Northumberland, Clifford, Roos and Lord John Neville, acting for his demented brother the Earl of Westmorland. There also cannot have been outposts stationed in every direction to give early warning of an enemy approach. The omission of such an elementary precaution strongly suggests the weather was appalling. Bad visibility would also have discouraged the lookouts atop the castle keep.

So, we have perhaps 5,000–6,000 men, cold, wet and ill fed, huddled around a castle where their leaders had brought them for no discernible purpose. Meanwhile, 9 miles away at Pontefract, at least twice and perhaps three times as many Lancastrians were gathered under leaders who knew exactly what they wanted to do. Somerset,

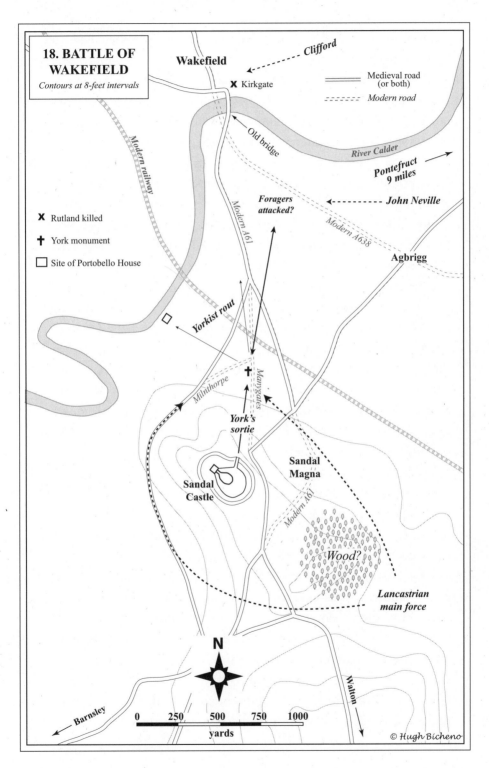

18. BATTLE OF WAKEFIELD

Contours at 8-feet intervals

Wakefield

✗ Kirkgate

Clifford

Medieval road (or both)

Modern road

Old bridge

River Calder

Modern railway

Pontefract 9 miles

Foragers attacked?

John Neville

Modern A638

✗ Rutland killed

✝ York monument

☐ Site of Portobello House

Agbrigg

Modern A61

Yorkist rout

☐

✝

Milnthorpe

Manygates

York's sortie

Sandal Magna

Sandal Castle

Modern A61

Wood?

Lancastrian main force

N

Walton

Barnsley

0   250   500   750   1000

yards

© Hugh Bicheno

Northumberland and Clifford could scarcely believe their luck to find two of the three men responsible for the deaths of their fathers on their doorstep, and were determined they should not get away.

The hatred between the Nevilles of Raby and of Middleham ran deep, and Lord John Neville had also deeply offended York by obtaining a commission of array from him to raise troops and then joining the enemy camp. It may well have been he who proposed using himself as bait in a trap. By this time his men had teamed up with Clifford's elite force of mounted archers and hobilars, known as the 'Flower of Craven' from the district around Skipton. It was probably they who scouted Wakefield and Sandal, and reported that the enemy was sending foraging parties north of the river.

Clifford and Neville proposed to make a rapid advance north and south of the river to trap the enemy foragers and, if that failed, Neville would make a provocative display in front of the castle to lure the Yorkists out. The main Lancastrian force, having set out during the night, would march well to the south to approach from the direction of Walton, halting out of sight below the (possibly wooded) southern end of the ridge on which Sandal Castle stood. Once the Yorkists sortied they would charge around both sides of the ridge to cut off their retreat.

On 30 December, whether because one of their foraging parties was cut up in full view of the castle, or in response to jeers and taunts from Neville's men – or both – York led a mounted charge out of the castle and chased the coat-trailing enemy force. When the trap was sprung York and his men tried to fight their way back to safety, but were slaughtered. Some made a last stand on the riverbank, where centuries later excavations for Portobello House (see Map 18) found a great deal of battle debris. Seventeen-year-old Rutland managed to flee across Wakefield Bridge, but not far beyond it he was killed after surrendering by Clifford.

Shakespeare made the event one of the most dramatic scenes in Part III of *Henry the Sixth*. Despite the pleas of Rutland's tutor to spare 'this innocent child', the fictional Clifford overflows with a hate that was probably not far from the historical truth:

> Had thy brethren here, their lives and thine
> Were not revenge sufficient for me;
> No, if I digg'd up thy forefathers' graves
> And hung their rotten coffins up in chains,
> It could not slake mine ire, nor ease my heart.
> The sight of any of the house of York
> Is as a fury to torment my soul;
> And till I root out their accursed line
> And leave not one alive, I live in hell.

York might have made a good king, or even a good 'Hand of the King' if Henry VI had emerged from catatonia with sufficient wit to continue the work of conciliation begun by Marguerite. As it was, the traditional mnemonic for the sequence of colours in a rainbow provides a sadly accurate epitaph: Richard of York gave battle in vain.

Salisbury, his son Thomas, his Harington son-in-law and some of their retainers survived the battle and surrendered on terms. It is possible they never left the castle, which would indicate a last, fatal disagreement with York. They were taken to Pontefract, but their captors did not protect them from a mob that dragged them out and beheaded them. Salisbury's death was dishonourable, but then so was his life: there was no shortage of people who passionately wanted him dead.

The heads of the fallen lords were taken to York and mounted on spikes on the Micklegate Bar. Richard of York's head was adorned with a paper crown and mocking placards were hung below the grisly trophies. We should not make too much of this. It was traditional for traitors' heads to be displayed on Tower Bridge, but since it was in the possession of Warwick, Micklegate would have to do for the time being.

When Marguerite and young Edward arrived at York, it must have been exhilarating to have hundreds of fierce warriors wearing the Prince of Wales's livery kneel before them, with their enemies' heads grimacing down on them. Free at last from the constraint of trying to work through her dithering husband, Marguerite could work with men as determined as she was herself. The northern lords were delighted by the truce she had obtained at Lincluden, which permitted them to summon their whole strength.

All the Lancastrian lords wrote a joint letter to Charles VII endorsing the agreement. They would not have done so had it contained any suggestion that Berwick, the gateway to the North, might be ceded to the Scots. There is also no evidence there were any Scots in their army. It was never likely that English Marchers would put aside a hatred nurtured by centuries of raid and counter-raid to conduct a joint *chevauchée* deep into England with their ancestral enemies. Yet both of these allegations were made in Yorkist pronouncements.

The primary sources for the climax of the first phase of the Wars of the Roses must be treated with caution. All of them were written under Edward IV, when to record anything other than the 'party line' might have had severe consequences for the author. If we add that the most generally trusted source for the period 1459–61 is the *Registra* of John Whethamstede, Abbot of St Albans, a subtle apologia for the Duke of York written to curry favour with his son, it is not at all remarkable that the black legend of Marguerite put down deep roots.

The Lancastrians' strategic objective was to recover the king, and the operational design was a fluid concept, regularly reviewed by assemblies of the most experienced officers. Prince Edward was the nominal commander-in-chief, which finessed any issue of precedence that might have caused friction between the Dukes of Exeter and Somerset. And if the prince was present at the councils of war, then so was Marguerite. Her mother, who herself once led an army in an attempt to liberate her own ineffectual husband, would have been proud of her.

EDWARD OF MARCH

WHILE YORK, RUTLAND AND SALISBURY MADE FOR the North, 18-year-old Edward, Earl of March set out, separately, to affirm the new regime's authority in the South West and to counter the threat posed by Lancastrian Wales under the leadership of Jasper Tudor. With him went the Marcher retainers who had accompanied York to London, at whose urging he had tried to claim the throne even though the popular acclaim promised by Warwick had failed to materialize. Thus during Edward's first independent command he was surrounded by men who would have been outspokenly scornful of Warwick's duplicity.

Edward was seen as 'one of their own' by the Marcher retainers in a way his father had never been. We know nothing of his childhood and very little about his adolescence – apart from the very salient fact that he spent his teens at Ludlow and the other Yorkist Marcher manors. From a joint letter sent by Edward and his brother Edmund to their father complaining about being bullied by the somewhat older Croft brothers, it is clear they were brought up with the sons of York's retainers rather than, as customary, in a noble house. The reason is evident: by the time they were old enough to leave their mother's household their father was locked in a power struggle with the court, and there was no senior peer to whom he could entrust them.

The result was more practical training in military matters than

Edward would have received in a court-oriented household, where the emphasis would have been on tournament skills. As the acting lord of Ludlow Edward would have received guidance from York's steward, the elder Walter Devereux, and would certainly have spent time at York's other manors in the March. He could not have prayed for a better place to exercise his first independent command, or for more militarily experienced and dependable advisers and nominal subordinates.

The principal Yorkist Marchers were Herbert of Raglan, steward of York's manors of Caerleon and Usk (also Warwick's Sheriff of Glamorgan), the younger Walter Devereux (*de jure* Lord Ferrers) of Weobley, who had succeeded his father at Ludlow, and Roger Vaughan of Tretower and Crickhowell in the Usk valley. Other Vaughans were Thomas of Bredwardine in the Wye valley and his uncle Thomas of Hergest and Kington in the Arrow valley. The older Thomas and Philip Vaughan were also stewards of the Buckingham manors of Huntington (between Hergest and Kington) and Hay, respectively. With them was Reginald, Lord Grey of Wilton in south Herefordshire.

Making his first appearance in our narrative is William Hastings, who had been at Ludford Bridge and was among those who stayed and obtained a royal pardon. Like his father, he was a Yorkist retainer with lands in Leicestershire and Warwickshire, who became involved in the Marches as ranger of York's vast Wyre forest and chase in Shropshire. As such he would have played host to young Edward on several occasions. Hastings was twelve years older, but the cascade of honours bestowed on him as soon as Edward became king argues that they had formed a very close friendship before the events of 1461.

As they had during the Ludlow campaign, Warwick's Abergavenny and Glamorgan retainers stayed at home to guard his estates. The only notables with Edward who were not his father's retainers were Lord Audley and Humphrey Stafford of Hooke, who had defected to him in Calais, and John Wenlock, whose loyalty Warwick had

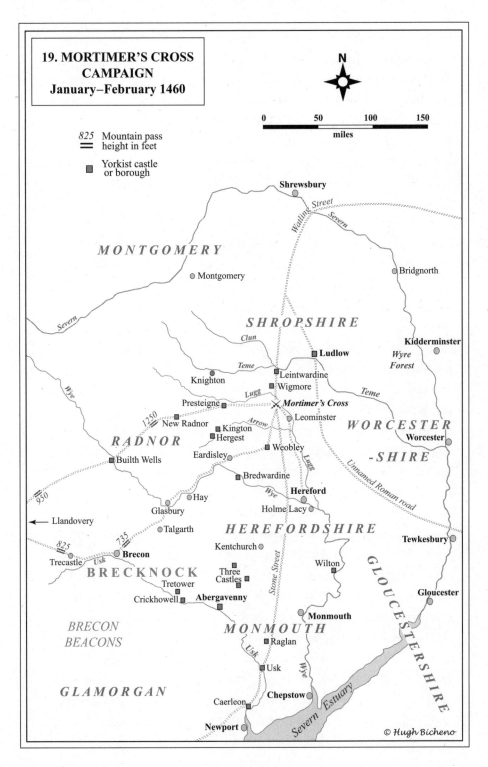

19. MORTIMER'S CROSS CAMPAIGN
January–February 1460

N

0   50   100   150
miles

825 Mountain pass
     height in feet

☐ Yorkist castle
   or borough

Shrewsbury

Watling Street
Severn

MONTGOMERY

● Montgomery

Bridgnorth ●

SHROPSHIRE

Clun

Ludlow ■

Teme

Kidderminster ●

Wyre
Forest

Knighton ●

Leintwardine ■
Wigmore ■

Teme

Severn

Presteigne ■

Lugg

✕ *Mortimer's Cross*

Leominster ●

WORCESTER

Wye

1250
New Radnor ■

Arrow

Kington ■
Hergest ■

Worcester ●

RADNOR

Eardisley ●

Weobley ■

-SHIRE

● Builth Wells

Bredwardine ■

Lugg

950

● Hay

Wye

Hereford ●

Unnamed Roman road

Glasbury ●

Holme Lacy ●

← Llandovery

735

● Talgarth

HEREFORDSHIRE

Tewkesbury ●

825

Kentchurch ●

Trecastle
Usk
● Brecon

Wilton ●

GLOUCESTERSHIRE

BRECKNOCK

Tretower ●

Three
Castles ■

Crickhowell ■

● Abergavenny

Stone Street

Gloucester ●

BRECON
BEACONS

MONMOUTH

● Monmouth

GLAMORGAN

Usk

■ Raglan

■ Usk

Wye

Caerleon ■

Chepstow ●

Severn Estuary

Newport ●

© *Hugh Bicheno*

bought in 1459. Wenlock may have acted as Warwick's eyes and ears, but it is remarkable he did not also send a member of his own Marcher affinity to represent his considerable interest in the area.

Edward moved first to Gloucester, to control the Severn valley and to discourage the West Country from sending any more support to the queen's army, although most would already have joined the march north by Somerset, Devon and Exeter. The town was in the midst of many Buckingham, Wiltshire and Talbot manors, but with their lords either recently killed or absent, they would have been easily overawed. Gloucester was also a good base from which to counter an advance through south Wales by Jasper Tudor, on whose doings the Yorkists were kept informed by the Dwnns of Kidwelly.

Thanks to Jasper's good lordship and close alliance with Thomas and Owain, the heirs of Gruffudd ap Nicholas and stewards of the absentee Bishop of St David's, he had a firm hold on south-west Wales. Before departing for Scotland Marguerite had also made him her son's deputy for the Principality, but required him to wait for the arrival of Wiltshire/Ormonde, who was supposed to be recruiting an army with funds provided by the Duke of Brittany. If instead she had authorized him to march north at the same time as Somerset, Exeter and Devon, Jasper would have been able to fall on York's Marcher domain while he and his principal retainers were away in London.

Now, his situation was unenviable. The Skydmores of Holme Lacy and Kentchurch in Herefordshire should have been able to keep him informed about Edward's strength and movements, but do not appear to have done so. Perhaps, menaced by their Yorkist neighbours, they had already fled to join Jasper in Pembroke. It was mid-winter, so although there were more men available for war, provisioning was meagre everywhere in Wales, and any march through the barren interior was out of the question. Jasper's options, once Wiltshire arrived, were either to march up the coast through the miserably poor Principality into Cheshire, or along the south coast into the rich heart of the Yorkist Marches.

Time was not on his side, but Wiltshire was delayed. When he finally arrived, late in January 1461, he brought with him a force of Irish mercenaries and, perhaps, some Breton men-at-arms as well. These were troops who had to be employed as soon as possible, before supplies ran out and they began to plunder indiscriminately. The Roman road from Carmarthen through south Wales offered the fastest route, but Glamorgan and southern Monmouth were solidly Yorkist, and the Lancastrians would have had to fight their way through, dissipating their strength before they encountered Edward's main force.

Accordingly they had to march north of the Brecon Beacons through Llandovery, after which they could either continue north through Builth Wells, or east through Brecon. There really was no choice. The Builth route would take them through two high mountain passes that might be choked with snow, along a route studded with Yorkist manors. At Brecon they could obtain supplies and possibly also recruits from Buckingham's bereft retainers, after which the first Yorkist manor they would encounter was Weobley. Both routes met at the bridge over the River Lugg at Mortimer's Cross where, unless they could achieve operational surprise, they were certain to encounter Edward's army.

The element of surprise was denied to them. Jasper ranked the Dwnns among his most damaging enemies, acknowledging the crucial role played by the information they provided on his movements. By this time both sides had learned of York's defeat and death at Wakefield, and Jasper may have believed that Herbert and the other Yorkist Marchers had gone north with him to destruction. He may also have discounted Edward's ability to rally and lead what he hoped was the remnant of the Yorkist affinity, as otherwise he would not have attacked a larger army, deployed in an immensely strong position.

In fact, nothing could have united the Marchers more than an incursion by 'deep' Welshmen, and Edward's appeal to turn out against the men of Pembroke coming to ravage the Yorkist estates ensured that every able-bodied flocked to his banner. At dawn on the bitter cold battle day a phenomenon occurred that Edward made his own. Three suns appeared to be rising together, the effect of light refraction through atmospheric ice crystals known as a parhelion, or 'sundogs'. Although he does not even mention the ensuing battle, Shakespeare described the apparition superbly in Part III of *Henry the Sixth*:

> Three glorious suns, each one a perfect sun;
> Not separated with the racking clouds,
> But sever'd in a pale clear-shining sky.
> See, see! they join, embrace, and seem to kiss,
> As if they vow'd some league inviolable:
> Now are they but one lamp, one light, one sun.
> In this the heaven figures some event.*

Noting uneasiness among his men, Edward rode among them to pronounce it a favourable omen, claiming that the phenomenon was symbolic of his rise to glory, flanked by his two younger brothers. Another account has him saying it was a divine blessing and symbolized the Trinity, but the first version must get the nod, as Edward thereafter adopted a sunburst as his personal badge. It was his command moment, and he seized it with both hands.

It is fortunate the terrain at Mortimer's Cross is so eloquent, because our only source of tactical information is two stanzas from Michael Drayton's epic poem *The Miseries of Queen Margaret*, published in 1627, which is scraping the bottom of the military-historical barrel. For dramatic effect Drayton described Jasper as 'young Tudor', although he was 30 years old. Wiltshire was ten years older and Jasper's father Owen, commanding the third Lancastrian battle, was at least 60.

---

* Shakespeare puts these words in the mouth of the future Richard III. The real Richard was 8 years old at the time, and in Burgundy.

20. BATTLE OF MORTIMER'S CROSS 2 February 1461

Contours at 5-feet intervals

The Earl of Ormond, an associate then
With this young Tudor, for the king that stood,
Came in the vanguard with his Irish men,
With darts and skains; those of the British [Welsh] blood
With shafts and gleaves them seconding again,
And as they fall, still make their places good:
That it amaz'd the Marchers, to behold
Men so ill-armed upon their bows so bold.

Now the Welch and the Irish so their weapons wield,
As tho' themselves the conq'rors meant to call;

Then are the Marchers masters of the field,
With their brown bills the Welchmen so they maul;
Now th' one, now th'other, likely were to yield;
These like to fly, then those were like to fall:
Until at length (as Fortune pleas'd to guide)
The conquest turned upon the Yorkists' side.

The 'darts' were throwing spears and the 'skains' (actually *scians*) were long dirks, the characteristic secondary armament of the Irish gallowglasses (*gallóglaigh*). They were mercenary heavy infantry who wore mail coats over padded jackets and fought with two-handed axes or the huge swords known as claymores. Although they also used bows, they were not longbows. Each of them had a boy to carry whatever weapons they were not using at a given moment and their battle tactic was to fire their arrows first, then close in to hurl their spears before charging to close quarters, where they were terrifyingly effective. The *scians* were for use in the crush, when there was no room to swing the heavier weapons.

If Drayton's description is accurate, Ormonde's gallowglasses were the Lancastrian shock troops, backed by Pembroke's Welsh billmen, none of them wearing adequate harness. They would have been hopelessly outranged and decimated by the Marcher bowmen, and any who managed to come through the arrow storm would have been rapidly dispatched. It is possible Herbert positioned a group of mounted men in a re-entrant on the wooded hill crowned by Mortimer's Rock, to charge into the rear of the Lancastrian left wing once it approached the Yorkist line. If so, it was the icing on the cake of an already lopsided battle.

If even the Welsh bards barely refer to it, we may be sure the battle saw no feats of derring-do. No notable Yorkist was killed, as there certainly would have been if the gallowglasses had managed to get to hand strokes. Battlefield archaeology may eventually reveal more, but it seems likely the Lancastrian left wing crumbled first, possibly precipitated by the flight of Wiltshire/Ormonde. If the monument at the entrance to Kingsland along the modern A4110 does indeed mark a place of special interest, it may be where the right-hand battle commanded by Owen Tudor made a last stand, covering the retreat of his son's battle along the Leominster road.

In the pursuit following the battle no mercy was shown to the defeated Lancastrians, in revenge for the slaughter at Wakefield and Pontefract. Owen Tudor and other captured Lancastrian knights were summarily beheaded in Hereford marketplace. The lists of men killed in the battle or executed are undependable, but the definitely dead included Marguerite's steward of Harlech, two of John Skydmore's sons and his brother William of Kentchurch, and Thomas ap Gruffudd ap Nicholas.

Edward's forces did not, however, pursue Jasper Tudor and his Pembrokemen, who retreated in good order. Most of them made it home and were to turn out for their lord again and again in the years to come. Instead, the victorious army returned to Gloucester, and stayed there while events in England unfolded. It is not clear whether Wenlock was at Mortimer's Cross, and it could be he is first recorded with Edward now, at Gloucester, because Warwick sent him. The message he brought was that Marguerite and the main Lancastrian army was marching south, and that Edward should join him as soon as possible. Warwick may have worded his request as an order to a man who was now a duke and outranked him.

Edward had left London with commissions of array for Somerset and Gloucestershire as well as Hereford and Shropshire, but with a war chest of only 650 marks [£275,600]. This was enough to keep his modest army of volunteers supplied for about a month, but a larger force for a longer period required more. The attraction of Gloucester was that all five of the major monastic orders had large abbeys there, making it a pot of gold for anyone who held the city. No threats were necessary, because the oppressively taxed people of Gloucester were violently Lollard and the abbots, who never ventured out without a strong bodyguard, were highly motivated to ingratiate themselves with the civil power.

It was not, therefore, lack of men or money that kept Edward from marching to join his mentor. He bided his time, and in the end Warwick was forced to come to him. It must have come as a nasty shock to discover that the young man was coldly willing to put the entire Yorkist enterprise at risk in order to assert his own leadership so soon after the death of his father.

Edward's rise in the English political firmament was as sudden as a shooting star. There had been no previous indication that he was anything other than a loyal lieutenant to Warwick, even siding with him against his own father. But therein, I believe, lies the key. York quite clearly favoured his second son Edmund over Edward. Even if Salisbury and Warwick did not know that Edward was the product of their, respectively, sister and aunt's adultery, he was of their blood and they gave him the adult male approval denied him by his coldly distant father.

More than his victory at Mortimer's Cross, therefore, the death at Wakefield of his father and his favoured younger sibling would have had a galvanically liberating effect on Edward. There is little indication he mourned their loss. He perfunctorily reunited their heads with their bodies at Pontefract, but did not rebury them in the family vault at Fotheringhay until 1476, and even then the leading role was played by Richard, his youngest brother, who also commissioned the construction of their tomb monuments. In an era when the aristocracy practised thinly disguised ancestor worship, Edward could not have made it plainer that he felt no debt of filial gratitude to the man who was not, in fact, his blood father.

If this interpretation is correct, Edward would have been transformed to learn of York's death, to win his first independent battle, and to see his surrogate father Warwick come to him with his tail between his legs, all in a period of little more than a month. In a wider sense, despite his youth Edward now assumed the stature of the king English society needed to enforce the law, without which there could be, in Thomas Hobbes's famous phrase, 'no arts; no letters; no society; and which is worst of all, continual fear and danger of violent death; and the life of man, solitary, poor, nasty, brutish, and short'.

Although modern research indicates that the Wars of the Roses impacted less than one would expect on the general population, Hobbes' aphorism sounds like a pretty good description of what England had become by 1461. What we are looking at, therefore, is the coincidence of Edward's emancipation from a father who did not love him with the final breakdown of the limited amount of order the Lancastrian regime had been able to provide.

Henry, the anointed father of the nation, had utterly failed to enforce the law and so permit his people to prosper. Looming chaos made it imperative to anoint another, and suddenly to hand there was a victorious, noble, physically imposing and sexually potent candidate. In the absence of Sigmund Freud to explain how it was all a function of their libidos, many – not least Edward himself – saw it as proof that the forefinger of God had reached down to designate him.

XXV

THE BUBBLE
REPUTATION

THE PARADOX OF RICHARD 'THE KINGMAKER' NEVILLE'S epic life is that his brilliance as a politician was not matched by similar skill as a general. At St Albans in 1455 he was a subordinate, and Northampton, his one great victory, had been won by intrigue before the armies ever came into contact. Subsequently, he seems to have been guided by the maxim (devoutly practised by contemporary Italian *condottieri*, who were above all businessmen) that battle should be the last resort.

This was the principle the French finally adopted to win the Hundred Years War; but it was completely at variance with the English way of war. The English were renowned for their ferocity and were not temperamentally suited to positional warfare, which may explain why castles played such a peripheral role in the conflict. It is hard to think of any other reason why siege artillery, so crucial in the fall of English Normandy, had to be deployed against only two English castles between 1455 and 1485.

The strategic value of castles was that a few men could tie down a large force for months, dissipating the besieger's resources and exposing his troops to attrition through camp diseases. An example of what might have been achieved was set by Lord Lovell's castle at Thorpe Waterville in Northamptonshire, the only significant Lancastrian hold-out south of the River Trent in early 1461. Edward had to send John Wenlock with three bombards and commissions of array for five counties to deal with it, but he cannot have used the guns because the castle was undamaged when it was surrendered two months later. Just a few more like that and Edward would not have been able to march north with sufficient strength.

Isolated Harlech, supplied by sea, held out for Lancaster from 1461 to 1468, and the only other castles held for any considerable time were also coastal. Inland, we simply do not know why Pontefract, ferociously Lancastrian at the time of Wakefield, was not held against the Yorkists only three months later. It was folly not to use castles to slow down opposing armies as they marched the length of the country, yet neither side appears to have believed it worth attempting. The only obvious explanation is that, apart from Calais, none had a permanent, professional garrison, which in turn reflected the English fixation on the quick campaign and climactic battle as the be-all and end-all of warfare.

A climactic battle was what Marguerite's army of allegedly ravening 'Northmen' marched south to seek in January 1461, supposedly wreaking havoc as it went. Contrary to Yorkist propaganda, there were no Scots or French contingents in Marguerite's army: her supporters came from all over England. There is also no evidence whatever to support the over-the-top tales of Lancastrian atrocities recorded in the rolls of Edward IV's first Parliament.[*]

Considering the treasonous support given to the Yorkists by the Canterbury Convocation, systematic looting of the wealthy abbeys and churches along the line of march might have been an understandable act of vengeance – but it would not have been queenly. Marguerite's behaviour was governed by the need not to burn any bridges of allegiance over which today's Yorkist supporters might cross back to her husband once she recovered him, or, if he were killed, to her son. Likewise, it made no sense to sack the previously Yorkist boroughs and manors through which her army passed because, following the 1459 attainders, they were legally crown estates.

---

[*] Bonita Cron took a well-researched war-hammer to that interpretation in the December 1999 issue of *The Ricardian*.

This is not to say that her army did not take what it needed in the way of food and other supplies against an uncertain promise of reimbursement, or that looting did not take place; but it was no *chevauchée*. Several edicts issued by Warwick at this time clearly point to the Lancastrians receiving significant voluntary support in Leicestershire, Lincolnshire and Cambridgeshire. A general order was issued to all sheriffs to raise the shires to repress 'the malice of riotous people', which may have been a precaution against a general breakdown of law and order, but could have been aimed at suppressing Lancastrian supporters.

Warwick was acutely aware how thin popular support for the Yorkist cause was outside Kent and London. Having the church on his side was financially beneficial, but in strongly Lollard areas like Sussex, East Anglia and the South West it was probably harmful. Edward's primary mission had been to shore up support for the regime in the South West as well as the Marches, assisted by the fact that the more determined Lancastrians had already marched north; but his assignment was only one of Warwick's initiatives.

Warwick's most notable coup was to bring about Yorkist near-hegemony in traditionally fractured East Anglia. The cornerstone was to entice John Mowbray, Duke of Norfolk, out of political hibernation, and to reconcile him with 19-year-old John de la Pole, Earl of Suffolk, who had married York's daughter Elizabeth in early 1458, but who only now became an active Yorkist. Added to the other Yorkist lords' affinities in the region, this alliance persuaded the Lancastrian Earl of Oxford to keep his head down.

For Sussex, Warwick persuaded William FitzAlan, Earl of Arundel, to come off the fence, joined by Richard Fiennes, Baron Dacre of the South. Warwick also convoked the Order of the Garter and had himself elected, along with three others: John Wenlock and Thomas Kyriell for services rendered, and William, Lord Bonville, mortal enemy of the Courtenay Earls of Devon, whose heir, Lord Harington, had died with York at Wakefield.

The picture that emerges is not one of the Yorkist south united against the Lancastrian north, but of frantic coalition building by Warwick – which is what one would expect after a *coup d'état*. The peers who took sides after the coup were evenly divided, but all the Lancastrians fought at the climactic Battle of Towton except for Oxford, Pembroke cut off in Wales and Wiltshire who was in transit. In contrast many Yorkist peers did not, even though all had burned their bridges with Lancaster. Warwick probably judged it more important for them to stay in their shires to control the populace, a further indication that he was far from confident of having won southern hearts and minds.

During the Lancastrians' march south they were accurately informed about enemy numbers and movements, and the Yorkists were not. There is no way this could have happened if the Yorkists had enjoyed the southern support against the northern bogeymen that their propaganda sought to generate. For example, although Grantham and Stamford had been York's boroughs, the affinities of Lords Beaumont, Roos, Welles and Willoughby made Lincolnshire, through which Marguerite's army marched south from York, a strongly Lancastrian county. Furthermore, if the people had indeed fled before the Lancastrian advance, refugees would have kept Warwick fully informed about their movements.

This quite evidently did not happen. Consequently, instead of marching north from London to meet Marguerite's army head-on, Warwick reacted uncertainly and tentatively. He sent the Van under his younger brother John to St Albans with most of the guns. The Main, with Warwick himself, his 55-year-old uncle Lord Fauconberg and the king, marched through Waltham Cross to Ware. Thereabouts they rendezvoused with the Duke of Norfolk, whose East Anglian contingent constituted the third battle of an army 10,000–15,000 strong.*

At Ware, Warwick learned that Marguerite's army had left the

---

* The Earl of Arundel, Earl of Suffolk and Viscount Bourchier took part in this campaign, probably joining forces with Norfolk. The recently turned Baron de la Warr also participated, after which he went home and stayed there.

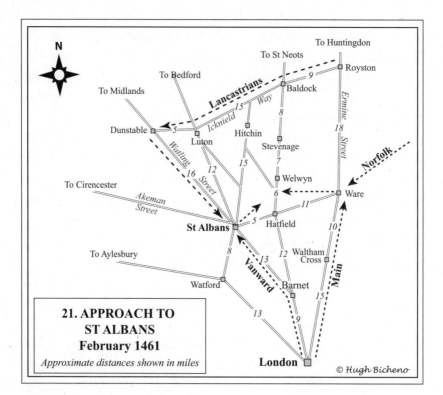

**21. APPROACH TO
ST ALBANS
February 1461**

Approximate distances shown in miles

© Hugh Bicheno

Great North Road at Royston, turning west along the Icknield
Way. Convinced she would turn south again between Baldock and
Luton, he set out his battles accordingly. John Neville left most of
his archers in St Albans and marched about a mile north-east to a
massive Iron Age earthwork known as Beech Bottom Dyke, with
a commanding view of the surrounding area. There, he set up an
artillery fort seemingly modelled on the one that gave victory to the
French at Castillon. Warwick's battle was at Sandridge, a mile further to the north-east, and Norfolk's another mile along the same
road, covering roads from Hitchin and Welwyn/Baldock.

It was not necessarily a bad idea to cover a wide front while
keeping the three battles within supporting distance of each other
– if adequate advance notice of an impending enemy attack could
be obtained. Although a mile is no great distance, it takes time to
create a column of march at one end and to deploy at the other. It
appears Warwick was failed by his scouts, as they clearly did not

maintain a close watch on the enemy. As a back-up he would have had outposts covering all the roads running south from the Icknield Way. No doubt he had them on the Baldock, Hitchin and Luton roads, and believed Watling Street was well covered by several hundred local levies at Dunstable.

Fortuna notoriously favours the bold. Moving fast, the Lancastrian Van – probably Lords Clifford and Neville again, accompanied by Andrew Trollope, the most experienced officer in the Lancastrian army – surrounded and annihilated the Dunstable levies. Their unfortunate commander, a local butcher, survived but later hanged himself for shame. Watling Street was a well-defined thoroughfare

and the Lancastrians then did something unheard of in medieval warfare: they marched by night to St Albans, arriving at dawn.

Crossing the River Ver at St Michael's Mill, they first attempted to rush the town by charging along Fishpool Street, but were stopped by an arrow storm as they tried to debouch into the marketplace. Dead and dying men and horses soon blocked the street and they fell back. However, another force raced along Folly and Catherine Lanes to cut off the defenders' retreat. Attacked from two sides, the Yorkist archers were doomed. Some got away to warn a shocked John Neville, but Clifford's 'Flower of Craven' would not have been far behind.

The second battle of St Albans enjoys the distinction of having left us not one but two accounts written by men who were there. The first witness was, as before, the Abbot of St Albans, whose ornate Latin is sometimes enlightening. The second was the anonymous and regrettably laconic continuator of *Gregory's Chronicle*, who may have served in Warwick's army. His explanation for the operational surprise achieved by the Lancastrians is a priceless variant on the infantryman's eternal grumble about the cavalry: 'As for spearmen [lancers], they are good for riding before the footmen and to eat and drink up their victuals, and many more such pretty things they do, [but] hold me excused though I say the best, for in the footmen is all the trust.'

Neville did not have time to reposition his artillery and could only turn his battle through almost 90 degrees to take up a new position on a broad stretch of flat ground known as Bernard's Heath. He had with him a great novelty in English warfare: after Wakefield, Warwick had appealed for help to the Duke of Burgundy, who sent him a contingent of hand-gunners. *Gregory's Chronicle* gives a detailed description of these professional soldiers:

> For the Burgundians had such instruments that would shoot both pellets of lead and arrows of an ell [45 inches] of length with 6 feathers, 3 in the middle and 3 at the other end, with a

great mighty head of iron at the other end [he then asserts that these 'instruments' exploded in the gunners' hands if loaded in haste]. Also they had nets of great cords of 4 fathoms of length and 4 foot broad… and at every second knot there was a nail standing upright such that no man could pass over it without the likelihood of hurt. Also they had pavises, like doors with a folding strut that they could set down where they wished, and loop-holes with shutting windows to shoot out of [and bristling with] three penny nails. When their shot was spent and done, they cast down the pavises in front of them [so that] no man could come at them over the pavises for the nails that stood upright, without mischief to himself.

The weapons described are hook guns [Dutch *hakebusse*, hence 'arquebus'], man-portable cannon with a brutal recoil, which had to be fired hooked over a solid support, in this case the traditional crossbowman's propped *pavise* or heavy wooden shield. Gregory adds that the Burgundians also set out ground nets to tangle horses' hooves, and scattered caltrops – four spikes welded together, such that one always stood upright.

Neville expected his Burgundians to halt the Lancastrian attack, but they failed to do so. Gregory snorts that all this new-fangled defensive array had to be abandoned, and the matter was decided by 'mauls of lead, bows, swords, glaives [pole arms topped with single-edged blades] and axes'. Reading between the lines, his message is clear – Neville tried to fight the battle according to the best practice developed on the European mainland, and was overcome by good old English speed and ferocity.

The battle on Bernard's Heath was over so quickly that Warwick, whilst marching to support his brother, encountered only the fleeing remnants of Neville's command. At which point many of the levies in his own battle recalled an urgent appointment elsewhere, and he was left to fight a desperate rearguard action back through Sandridge. He was not able to make a stand until later on

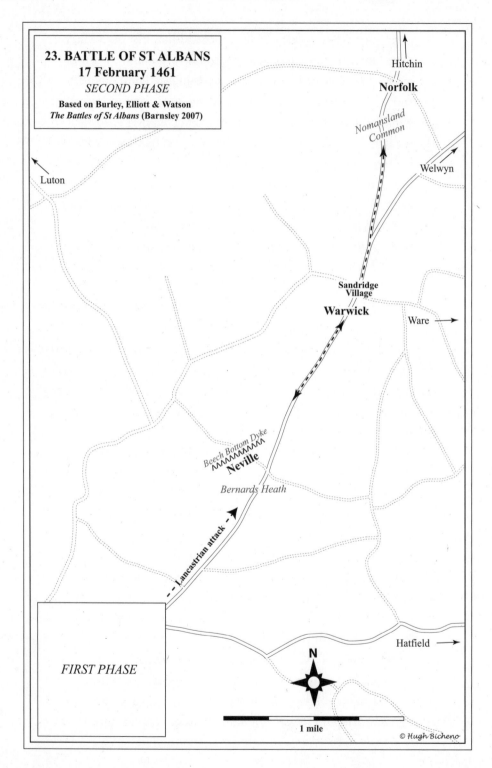

**23. BATTLE OF ST ALBANS
17 February 1461**
SECOND PHASE

Based on Burley, Elliott & Watson
The Battles of St Albans **(Barnsley 2007)**

Hitchin

Norfolk

Nomansland Common

Luton

Welwyn

**Sandridge
Village**

Warwick

Ware

Beech Bottom Dyke
Neville

Bernards Heath

- - Lancastrian attack - -

Hatfield

FIRST PHASE

N

1 mile

© Hugh Bicheno

when he reached Norfolk's intact battle on Nomansland Common.

By this time, the epic Lancastrian attack had run out of momentum. They had been marching and fighting hard for twenty-four hours or more, and were exhausted. A strong counter-thrust would now have inflicted a severe reverse on them, but the Yorkists' will was broken. Warwick later tried to blame the defeat on treachery by a Kentish captain called Lovelace, but it was glaringly evident to all that he had been comprehensively out-generalled and out-fought. Shakespeare called it 'the bubble reputation', and Warwick's had burst.

Either at Bernard's Heath or during the retreat, Thomas Kyriell was killed and John Neville, Lord Berners (John Bourchier) and Lord Bonville were captured. The greatest prize, however, was the king. The most plausible explanation for how Henry was recovered safely is that his guards abandoned him in the chaos of the Yorkist retreat through Sandridge. Clifford's outriders found him sitting alone under a tree, singing to keep his spirits up, and brought him back to their lord's tent, where he was reunited with Marguerite and his son. According to Gregory:

> The night after the battle the king blessed his son the Prince, and Doctor Morton brought forth a book that was full of prayers, and there the book was opened and blessed that young child and made him knight... And the Prince made many knights. The first that he made was Andrew Trollope, for he was hurt and might not go for a caltrop in his foot; and he said 'My lord, I have not deserved it for I slew but fifteen men, for I stood still in one place and they came unto me, but they abode still with me.' And then came Whittingham, Tresham and many more others, and were made knights that same time.

The precedence granted to Robert Whittingham is suggestive: he was from Salden in Buckinghamshire, only a few miles north-east of Dunstable, and may have been instrumental in sealing off the town so that none should get away to give warning. Thomas Tresham of Rushden in Northamptonshire was the son of the Speaker murdered by Grey of Ruthyn's men in 1450, and had himself been the Speaker of the 1459 'Parliament of Devils' at Coventry.

There was also justice of another kind to be dispensed. The Earl of Devon demanded Bonville's head, and Marguerite could not afford to deny him. Henry might have done so, but after agreeing to the Act of Accord his personal authority was nil. Marguerite made sure it was, instead, 7-year-old Prince Edward who pronounced sentence. Neville and Berners were spared because Warwick retained hostages, including Edmund, the second of the Beaufort brothers, captured trying to holding the Isle of Wight for his brother.

Yorkist propaganda made much of the execution of Bonville, claiming Kyriell was beheaded as well. It was alleged that he and Bonville had remained behind to guard the king, and Henry's promise that they would be held harmless was overridden by Marguerite. One can forgive Shakespeare for typecasting Marguerite for reasons of dramatic licence, but there is no reason to believe she would have undermined her husband's authority. The anecdote is of a piece with Yorkist accounts of Marguerite's supposedly undisciplined, looting and pillaging army, which somehow became a tightly organized and fast-moving fighting force for long enough to win at St Albans and Bernard's Heath, before reverting to rabbledom once more.

Warwick's army was scattered and his reputation for invincibility destroyed. The East Anglian lords' levies having returned to their homes, he cannot have had more than 4,000 men under command when he marched west to meet Edward near Chipping Norton in Oxfordshire, 35 miles from Gloucester but 70 miles from the scene of his defeat. Edward by now commanded a Marcher army perhaps twice as large, and had money to pay his troops independently. Furthermore the men around him had seen Warwick humiliate York, and were coldly determined that history should not repeat itself with his son.

XXVI

TWO KINGS

ARGUERITE'S PURPOSE HAD BEEN TO RECOVER THE king, and with him the legal authority of the state. This had been achieved at relatively little cost. Only one Lancastrian of rank was killed at second St Albans: John Grey, heir to the barony of Ferrers of Groby and husband to Elizabeth Woodville, eldest daughter of Lord Rivers and Jacquetta. However, since setting out from Pontefract the Lancastrian army had marched 180 miles in mid-winter. The levies were at the end of their enlistment period and many of them had gone home before the battle, which Gregory affirmed was won by no more than 5,000 'household men and feed men'.

Supplies were scarce, money to pay the troops even more so, and there is no evidence to indicate the Lancastrians could have continued the march south to London even if they had wished to. Although Marguerite had written the capital off as a political dead loss since 1457, there is a near-unanimous consensus among historians that she committed a strategic blunder in not marching her army into London, there to await the arrival of the combined forces of Edward and Warwick. In effect, she stands accused of failing to put her head into a noose.

She was certainly guilty of not committing that stupidity. Her army never moved from St Albans, where it blocked the fastest route – Roman Akeman Street – by which Edward could reach London from the west. He notably did not accept the challenge, which is only remarkable if we accept the view that a Lancastrian occupation of London would have been devastating to his cause. Clearly he did not think so, and his veteran Marcher councillors probably persuaded him to mark time in Oxfordshire, hoping Marguerite would march into London so they could cut off her retreat.

Understandably, the mayor and aldermen of London did not share Edward's relaxed view of the situation. Warwick's propaganda had generated a healthy fear of the northern army, and the mayor sent a delegation to St Albans led by the two most senior ladies in the land after Marguerite: the dowager Duchesses of Bedford (Jacquetta, Lady Rivers) and Buckingham. Their Lancastrian loyalty was unquestionable, and their warning about the temper of the people of London would have confirmed there was no hope of conducting the king on a procession through the city.

It is not clear whether the first Lancastrian emissaries were sent after the duchesses arrived at St Albans, or crossed paths with them. Either way, the Lancastrians brought only a request for supplies, which the mayor made haste to provide. A convoy of wagons set out from Cripplegate (today's Barbican), but was set upon by a mob and looted. It would be unwise to read any political intent into the violent behaviour of the London underclass at a time of political instability. The mob is a wild beast, and any excuse to commit mayhem will do.

What happened next, however, was definitely partisan. A party of Lancastrians carrying a warrant from the king declaring Edward a traitor was assaulted, resulting in a street battle with many casualties, after which the mayor announced a curfew 'in order that the king and his forces might enter and behave peacefully'. This provoked a riot, at which point the authorities unleashed the city guard and the rioters were violently dispersed. Meanwhile, a second Lancastrian delegation skirmished with an advance party of Yorkists outside the city gates, now closed against them both.

The king's warrant, dated 'at Westminster', never achieved the form and the signet of law and so did not have to be officially recognized as valid by the London authorities. It was, instead, published as a proclamation on 26 February, the same day a demand for admittance arrived from Edward and Warwick, now close to London after taking the cross-country route from Chipping Norton through Oxford and High Wycombe. The mayor replied that the Yorkist lords might enter the city, but not their troops.

On the same day the Lancastrian army departed St Albans, heading for York. Although they did not expect the Yorkists to be able to trump their possession of the king, in purely military terms it was essential to fall back on their area of greatest popular support. It was also a strategic retreat. Hoping to recreate the circumstances that gave them victory at Wakefield, their aim was to oblige the Yorkists to pursue them through a countryside emerging from winter, which could offer little in the way of supplies. It would have worked better if they could have conducted a scorched-earth campaign, but that was politically unthinkable.

With the loss of the king's person the Yorkist regime could make no claim to the obedience of royal officials and the general populace. With remarkable aplomb, Edward now styled himself 'by the grace of God of England, France and Ireland the true and just heir'. He based his claim not on the unratified Act of Accord, but on his superior right of descent from Lionel of Clarence over the usurping House of Lancaster. The claim, seen as patently contrived when made by York after all his sacred oaths of fealty, had far greater credibility coming from his heir, who had made no such solemn undertakings.

Edward and his captains took up residence at Baynard's Castle, the York family's grand Thames-side palace, but the Nevilles handled the stage-managing of his accession. On 1 March the Chancellor, Bishop George Neville, addressed a large crowd, composed mainly if not exclusively of Yorkist troops, outside London at St George's Fields (today's Bayswater), and set out Edward's claim. Popular acclamation was an important prerequisite for claiming the throne, and the partisan crowd duly cheered when required.

Next day the articles of Edward's title were published and announced throughout London, and on the following day a hastily convened 'Great Council' consisting of Archbishop Bourchier, Bishops Beauchamp of Salisbury and Neville of Exeter, Norfolk, Warwick and the most prominent of Edward's Marchers met at Baynard's Castle and formally begged Edward to assume the throne. Henry IV had based his claim on conquest, and Henry VII was to do the same. Edward claimed the throne by hereditary right.

On 4 March Edward rode the short distance to St Paul's Cathedral to hear a *Te Deum*, then rode in a magnificent procession to the Palace of Westminster. In the Great Hall he swore to uphold the laws and customs of England, after which, duly robed, he took his seat on the king's bench and personally proclaimed his title to the throne. After the sparse assembly acclaimed him, he formally 'took possession of the realm of England'. He then walked to Westminster Abbey, where he sat on the throne and received St Edward's sceptre, and again declared his title.

The ceremonies served the purpose of absolving the assembled lords from their previous oaths of allegiance. This was particularly important to the bishops, who had previously found them an insuperable obstacle to York's claim. A proper coronation would have to wait until Edward had made good his claim against Henry VI, now recast as a usurper after nearly forty years during which his right to reign had never been impugned.

However contrived the formula to justify his usurpation, the young and virile Edward was a dream come true for those yearning for the glory days of Henry V, and from this time forward Warwick could only hope to be the first among equals, all illuminated by the rising sun of York. The abrupt reversal of roles could be finessed while they had a common cause, but in the end Warwick was sure to find it intolerable to be subordinate to his younger cousin and one-time apprentice.

For the time being, however, they had to win the war they had begun together. With the loss of Bonville at St Albans, preceded by his heir, killed at Wakefield, they no longer had a local counterweight to Lancastrian sympathizers in the West Country. Also, despite Mortimer's Cross, much of Wales remained loyal to the Prince of Wales and Jasper Tudor. There were also the Beaumont and Oxford affinities in East Anglia to be considered. All might erupt behind them when they marched north, and several important Yorkist lords remained behind to prevent this.

On 6 March proclamations in Edward's name were sent to the sheriffs of all the counties south of the River Trent, ordering them to prevent any support to pass over the river 'towards our adversary'. Any follower of Henry VI who submitted within ten days was to have 'grace and pardon of his life and goods', except for those with an annual income of more than 100 marks [£42,000] – which was to say all peers and greater gentry – and twenty-two named individuals. Finally, a bounty of £100 [£63,600] was offered for each of the heads of eight individuals.

The named men were not particularly prominent, but all had given personal offence to one or other of the Yorkist leaders. But then, the whole conflict was highly personal in nature. It is as well to recall how much it was a Neville family matter. Warwick was brother-in-law to Arundel, Worcester, FitzHugh, Stanley and Bonville, while the Dukes of Norfolk, Buckingham and York were or had been his uncles by marriage. Ranged against him, the entire Percy clan, the Nevilles of Brancepeth, Clifford, Dacre of the North and Beaumont were all cousins of one degree or other.

Nor should we forget the Beaufort connection. Somerset and his two brothers were the only descendants in the male line, but one great-aunt had been the matriarch of the Nevilles of Middleham and guardian of Richard of York, and another the mother of the Earl of Devon. Through the marriages of their father and uncle, and the subsequent marriages of their widows, they were related to Roos, Welles and to the Talbots and Lisles, all of them Warwick's mortal enemies from the Beauchamp inheritance feud.

PARTISAN PEERS IN 1461

k. = killed; x. = executed; * = peers not present at Towton

Lancaster			York		
Title	Age	Main estates	Title	Age	Main estates
Dukes					
Exeter	31	Southwest	York	19	Many counties
Somerset	25	Southwest	Norfolk	46	Most counties
Earls					
Devon (x.)	29	West Country	Warwick & Salisbury	32	North; Glamorgan; Southwest; Bucks
Northumberland (k.)	40	North; Sussex			
Shrewsbury	13	Shropshire; Derby	Suffolk	19	East Anglia; Oxford
* Oxford [1]	53	East Anglia; Oxford	* Arundel	44	Sussex; Dorset
* Pembroke	30	Wales			
* Wiltshire (x.)	41	Southwest; Cambridge			
Viscounts					
Beaumont	23	Lincoln; Norfolk	* Bourchier [2]	56	East Anglia
Barons (excluding de jure)					
Clifford (k.)	26	Yorks; Westmorland	Clinton	30	Northants
Dacre North (k.)	49	Cumberland	Dacre South	46	Sussex; Dorset
FitzHugh	32	Yorkshire	Dudley	60	Cheshire
Grey of Codnor	26	Midlands	Fauconberg	56	Yorkshire
Lovell	28	Midlands	Grey of Ruthyn	45	Denbigh; Bedford
Neville (k.) [3]	41	Durham	Scrope of Bolton	24	Yorkshire
Rivers (Woodville)	56	Kent; Northants	Scrope of Masham	33	Yorkshire
Roos	34	Midlands; Yorkshire	* Audley	41	Shropshire; Midlands
Rougemont Grey (x.)	43	West Country	* Bergavenny	49	Monmouth
Scales (Woodville)	21	Norfolk	* Bonville (x.)	68	West Country
Welles (k.)	55	Lincolnshire	* Cobham	50	Somerset
Willoughby [4]	33	Lincolnshire	* Grey of Wilton	40	Herefordshire
			* Saye and Sele	33	Kent
			* Stanley [5]	26	Cheshire; Lancashire

1. Contained; only his third son, George Vere, fought for Lancaster at Towton.
2. Brother John, Baron Berners, was a POW. Sons William and Humphrey fought for York.
3. Led the affinity of the Earl of Westmorland, his demented brother.
4. Richard Welles, also heir to his namesake barony.
5. Brother William fought for York.

There was no such complexity in the York family. Edward had only one aunt, married to Viscount Bourchier. Other than that, he was brother-in-law to Suffolk, now an ally, and to Exeter, who could not have been a more furious enemy. His desire to create a substantial extended family to rival Warwick's was to define his subsequent reign.

Although the Lancastrian army that retreated from St Albans to York was relatively small, Edward and Warwick knew it would swell rapidly once back in the North. They could not ignore the challenge, but once they, too, crossed the Trent, they knew the northerners would see them as an invading army and react accordingly. There was, therefore, a premium on acting as fast as possible.

Warwick departed immediately after the coronation to raise troops in the Midlands. Less than a week later, on 11 March, the Van, mainly consisting of the mounted men who had ridden to London in late February, set off up the Great North Road under Fauconberg. Meanwhile, Norfolk summoned his own and allied East Anglian lords' followers to rejoin him in London or on his way north.

Edward also remained in London, to raise a further loan of £4,000 [£2.54 million] from the City, plus contributions from individual merchant houses. Money worked its usual magic and volunteers flocked to London from all over the Home Counties. They were equipped from the royal armouries, and an enormous wagon train assembled to supply the army on its way north.

The contemporary poem 'The Rose of Rouen' is virtually the only source for who actually fought on the Yorkist side at the Battle of Towton, identified by their heraldic banners. Edward's retainers fought under Lionel of Clarence's Black Bull, Edmund of Langley's Falcon and Fetterlock, and the White Lion of the Mortimer Earls of March. The Duke of Burgundy sent a contingent led by a representative of the French Dauphin Louis, under the dolphin banner of the Dauphiné. In addition to the banners of the nobles listed in the 'Partisan Peers' box, the poem describes the banners of Bristol, Canterbury, Coventry, Gloucester, Leicester, Northampton,

Nottingham, Richmond, Salisbury, Windsor and Worcester.

We have no way of knowing how the different contingents were distributed among the battles, but Edward led the Reserve, Fauconberg the Van, Warwick the Main and Norfolk the Rear. Fauconberg, with the majority of the mounted archers and hobilars, did not need to recruit. He raced ahead to clear the way along the Great North Road, springing Lancastrian ambushes as he went. Warwick went to draw on his own and other Yorkist lords' extensive holdings in the Midlands. Edward and Norfolk set out along the Great North Road on 13 March, guarding the main wagon train and recruiting from their own and other Yorkist lords' manors along the way.

The core of the Reserve would have been the army recruited by Edward before and after Mortimer's Cross, with the addition of an unknown number of Burgundians. Those who marched with Warwick to the Midlands would have been the Calais veterans, the Londoners and Kentish men who had stuck with him despite St Albans. Norfolk was in bad health – he died eight months later – but his own and associated affinities turned out in sufficient strength under his cousin, the Essex squire John Howard, to form a fourth battle.

Sadly there are no records on the composition of the Lancastrian army or how it was organized. A reasonable assumption is that Somerset, ably advised by Trollope, was in overall command and would have led the tactical reserve under the banners of King Henry. Exeter must have been with him, as his ego would not have tolerated being under the Earls of Northumberland and Devon, who perforce commanded the other two battles.

Devon fell ill and could not lead his battle to Towton, so the army fought broadly divided into two groups, with Northumberland and the northerners forming on the right, and Somerset, Exeter and the southerners on the left. As before, the mounted archers and hobilars under Clifford and Neville had a roving commission to keep the Yorkists under observation, and to attack any enemy scouting or foraging groups that ventured too far away from their army.

Warwick's battle joined Edward's and Norfolk's before Doncaster and they arrived together at Pontefract on 27 March. There were too many alternative crossings to make the Don a defensible line, but the next place where the Great North Road crossed a river, the Aire at Ferrybridge, a little over 2 miles from Pontefract Castle, was another matter altogether. The Romans never bridged it because the river meanders through a broad flood plain, and there was a serviceable alternative crossing where it ran wide and shallow at Castleford. The Normans replaced the ferry with a bridge in 1198, but it was not until the end of the fourteenth century that it was rebuilt with seven piers, a chapel, and a causeway over marshy ground to Brotherton, on a peninsula of firm ground north of the river, with flood plain on either side.

It was an ideal chokepoint, yet Fauconberg found it undefended. The wooden upper works of the bridge had been demolished, but as long as the piers are still standing any bridge can be easily repaired. With no evidence that the Lancastrians intended to contest the crossing, Fauconberg must have assumed they intended to make their stand at the Wharfe, a bigger river and the last before York, 12 miles further north. He had no engineers or building materials, so rode on to establish whether the crossing at Castleford was passable. Finding it was, he sent squadrons of fore-riders across to reconnoitre north of the river.

The Van, therefore, was astride the Aire at Castleford before the other battles arrived at Pontefract. Edward occupied the castle, while Warwick camped at Ferrybridge and sent workmen and materials to repair the bridge. The workmen set up their camp at the southern end of the bridge, guarded by a small force commanded by a Norfolk lord, John Radcliffe, *de jure* Baron FitzWalter, accompanied by Richard Jenny, one of Warwick's illegitimate brothers. By the evening of Saturday 28 March the engineers had repaired the bridge and returned to camp for the night. They were not destined to enjoy their rest.

XXVII

KNIGHT'S GAMBIT

B EFORE THE DAWN OF PALM SUNDAY, CLIFFORD'S AND Lord John Neville's men crept along the causeway from Brotherton and silently disposed of any sleepy sentries there may have been at the southern end of the repaired bridge over the Aire. Once the rest of the raiders had crossed, they attacked the engineers' camp. According to *Hall's Chronicle*: 'The Lord Fitzwalter hearing the noise, suddenly arose out of his bed and unarmoured, with a poleaxe in his hand, thinking that it had been an affray among his men, came down to appease the same, but before he could say a word, or knew what the matter was, he was slain, and with him the bastard of Salisbury, brother to the Earl of Warwick.'

The survivors fled towards Warwick's camp at Ferrybridge, pursued by Clifford's men. Panic is particularly contagious in low-light conditions, and with arrows raining down on them from an unseen enemy, several thousand men milled around, some probably fighting each other. Gregory says that Warwick, who cannot have had time to don harness, was wounded in the leg by an arrow, but whether he was or not, he did not stay to steady his men. Hall again:

> He like a man desperate, mounted on his hackney and came blowing to King Edward saying, 'Sir I pray God have mercy on their souls, which in the beginning of your enterprise hath lost their lives, and because I see no success of the world, I remit the

vengeance and punishment to God our creator and redeemer'
and with that he alighted down and slew his horse with his
sword, saying 'Let him fly that will, for surely I will tarry with
him that will tarry with me' and he kissed the cross hilt of his
sword.

Although obviously embellished – Hall was much given to putting
words in his subjects' mouths for dramatic emphasis – if any part of
this account is true it reflects appallingly badly on Warwick, com-
pounding his panic and desertion of his men with an histrionic act
that would have made any fighting man's lip curl.

Having created chaos and inflicted a gratifying number of casualties, the raiders retreated once Warwick's battle recovered from its
initial disorder and began to fight back. They would have been too
closely pursued to tarry on the bridge long enough to damage it
again, but would have taken up positions on the other bank to cover
the bridge, slowly falling back towards Brotherton and shooting at
the Yorkists as they advanced along the causeway.

Although most histories assume Clifford retreated on learning
that Fauconberg's men were approaching from Castleford, there is
no reason to doubt the passage along the causeway to Brotherton
was forced by Edward's men-at-arms, led by hand-gunners and
crossbowmen protected by their pavises. Clifford's men would then
have mounted up and ridden off along the Great North Road, well
satisfied with as neat a delaying action as anyone could wish to have
carried out.

Several hundred crack archers would have done terrible execution among crowds of sleepy and unharnessed men spilling from
their tents, and casualties must have been heavy. This would
explain why Yorkist-inspired accounts gloss over the battle at
Ferrybridge. Clifford would have sent messengers back to Somerset
and Northumberland in York with an account that would have lost
nothing in the telling, and they set their army in motion.

Two things spoiled the party for them. First, Edward was no

Warwick. Knowing the enemy would expect him to pause to lick his wounds, he ordered an immediate general advance. He sent Warwick's shaken battle to Castleford, to advance along the Roman Ridge Road screened by Fauconberg's Van, while he led his battle from Pontefract across the bridge and north along the Great North Road, leaving Norfolk to follow with the wagons.

Secondly, Lady Luck did not smile on the Lancastrians. It seems Clifford had not sent scouts to check the crossing at Castleford, perhaps assuming it was not viable because the river was in spate. Therefore, unaware that Fauconberg had sent squadrons of fore-riders across the Aire the day before, he conducted a leisurely retreat

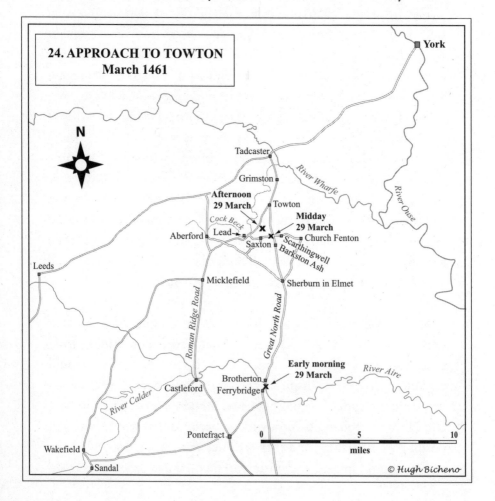

24. APPROACH TO TOWTON
March 1461

York

Tadcaster

Grimston

River Wharfe

River Ouse

**Afternoon
29 March**

Towton

**Midday
29 March**

Cock Beck

Aberford

Lead

Church Fenton

Saxton

Scarthingwell

Barkston Ash

Leeds

Micklefield

Sherburn in Elmet

Roman Ridge Road

Great North Road

**Early morning
29 March**

River Aire

Brotherton

River Calder

Castleford

Ferrybridge

Pontefract

0   5   10

miles

Wakefield

Sandal

© Hugh Bicheno

along the Great North Road, dropping off pairs of riders to watch for pursuit.

As the miles passed without any of them riding back to him, the pace would have dropped to a comfortable walk, and his tired men would have relaxed in their saddles. It is probable Clifford had received confirmation that the main Lancastrian army was on its way and would rendezvous with him at the hill overlooking the village of Saxton. Turning west at the crossroads of the Great North Road and the lane leading to Saxton, he led his command into an ambush in the little valley called Dinting Dale.

Leadman, the best of the Victorian historians of the battle,

25. ROAD DISTANCES & MARCHING TIMES
At 3 mph

N

York

9 miles
3 hrs

Tadcaster

River Wharfe

River Ouse

3 miles
1 hr

Towton

Cock Beck

Saxton

10 miles
3:20 hrs

9 miles
3 hrs

River Aire

River Aire

3.7 miles
1:15 hrs

Castleford

Ferrybridge

River Calder

3.5 miles
1:10 hrs

2 miles
40 mins

Pontefract
Castle

© Hugh Bicheno

says 'they met with some that they had not looked for, and were attrapped', in a context which suggests the trap was set by men sent racing up the Roman Ridge Road by Fauconberg after the battle at Ferrybridge. Alternatively they may have been fore-riders who had narrowly missed encountering Clifford's men on their way south, and had plenty of time to prepare an annihilating ambush for them when they returned. Clifford, Neville and most of their men were killed.

Not only was this a severe loss of inspiring leaders and elite troops, it also caused Somerset and Northumberland to slow their advance after the survivors reached them. As a result, Fauconberg's Van was the first substantial body of troops to arrive at Saxton. His scouts would have fanned out towards Tadcaster and kept him informed about the progress of the Lancastrian army, while preventing theirs from providing the same service.

The most recent research argues persuasively that Ferrybridge, Dintingdale and Towton all took place on the same day, it being understood that a medieval 'day' was calculated very differently from the way it is today.* The proper anniversary of the battle is 6 April, which was 29 March in the Julian calendar then in use, and the day when the moveable feast of Palm Sunday was celebrated.

As to timings, the medieval day began 6 a.m. with the liturgical Prime (first hour), a fixed time of prayer of the traditional Divine Office. Lauds marked actual daybreak, and so varied in time from place to place and season to season. Prime was timekeeping, as were the daytime offices of Terce, Sext, None and Vespers at three-hourly intervals, and Matins punctuated the night hours. Variable Compline marked actual nightfall.

The chart shows the timings of dawn and nightfall in Yorkshire on 6 April 2014. I have no idea what, if any, variation there may have been in the rotational axis of the Earth in the intervening 553

---

* See Tim Sutherland's brilliant online article 'Killing time: challenging the common perceptions of three medieval conflicts – Ferrybridge, Dintingdale and Towton', *Journal of Conflict Archaeology*.

24 hour	By the clock	Liturgical	Julian calendar
0600	6 a.m.	Prime	**Start 29 March 1461**
0625	**Variable**	**Lauds**	**Dawn**
0900	9 a.m.	Terce	
1200	Midday	Sext	
1500	3 p.m.	None	
1800	6 p.m.	Vespers	
1950	**Variable**	**Compline**	**Nightfall**
2100	9 p.m.	Matins	
2400	Midnight	Matins	
0300	3 a.m.	Matins	
0600	6 a.m.	Prime	**Start 30 March 1461**

years, but it will not have made more than a few minutes of difference. The point is there would have been nearly fourteen hours of sufficient light for fighting, and that the medieval Palm Sunday ran on to what we would consider 0600 the following Monday.

In a letter to Papal Legate Coppini, his physician wrote: 'the battle was begun on Palm Sunday, at the hour of prime, at Pontefract'. The Lord Chancellor, Bishop George Neville, wrote the earliest account, also to Coppini, in which he stated: 'on Palm Sunday, near a town called Feurbirga… there was a great conflict, which began with the rising of the sun, and lasted until the tenth hour of the night'. 'The Rose of Rouen' also contains a highly significant timing. The stanza goes as follows (my italics):

> The northern party made them strong with spear and shield,
> On Palm Sunday, *after the none*, they met us in the field
> Within an hour they were right fayne to flee, and eke to yield.

The highlighted phrase has generally been misunderstood as 'afternoon', whereas it means very specifically 'after 3 p.m.' If the battle that took place between Saxton and Towton began between 3 and 4 p.m., then 9–10 hours had already elapsed since the battle of

Palm Sunday began. That was more than double the time the two armies required to march to the battlefield from, respectively, York and Pontefract, without guns or wagons to slow them down. It is not only entirely possible but highly likely that fighting began at Ferrybridge at 0600–0630, and continued until 0600 the next day by modern reckoning.*

Coppini had fled to Flanders after Wakefield, but those who wrote to him knew he would share the information they sent with the pope and the Duke of Burgundy. Accordingly Bishop Neville's letter was what we now call 'informal communication', which also explains why he ridiculously alleged that 28,000 had died in the battle. He wanted to reassure Pius II and Duke Philippe that they had backed the right horse, and sought to evoke Pharsalus, Julius Caesar's crushing victory over Pompey in 48 BC, which brought their civil war to an end.

· ❧ ·

A death toll 28,000 would have been not only vastly more than for any other battle of the Wars of the Roses, but also 40 per cent more than the British Army suffered on the first day on the Somme, 455 years later. Furthermore, if 28,000 were killed, at least as many suffered survivable wounds, for a minimum total of 56,000 combat casualties. Just to account for these, each side would have had to field an army more than twice as large as any other in the Wars of the Roses.

A combined total of 56,000 men would also have been nearly twice as many as Charles VII of France assembled for the reconquest of Normandy, after years of preparation, drawing on a larger population, possessed of superior organization and enjoying greater resources. Since a minimum casualty rate of 100 per cent is an

---

John Benet's Chronicle does state that it was a battle in three phases, all on Palm Sunday, but his account contains too many serious errors about the numbers and commanders involved to be accepted as corroboration.

evident absurdity, the actual number of combatants would have had to be greater even than the hallucinatory 100,000 claimed in Edward Hall's *Chronicle*, allegedly based on the original muster rolls.

The largest army assembled during the Wars of the Roses was probably Henry's during the Ludford Bridge campaign, in which he was supported by three dukes, six earls, a viscount and at least eleven barons, all of whom had been issued commissions of array. Even though there appears to have been a bigger turn-out of the gentry for the Towton campaign, there is no way they could have compensated for the notably lower number of peers. The city of Coventry only sent forty men initially and sixty more later, and the average knight or squire would have brought far fewer.

If each army at Towton, including non-combatant personnel, numbered between fifteen and twenty thousand, it would have been pushing the upper limit of what the country could provide and sustain. As to the number killed, the estimate of 9,000 in William Worcester's 'Annales Rerum Anglicarum' is at least possible – if it includes all those killed in the three separate battles that day.

With regard to the battle itself, everything written about it before 2000 (and some since) must be revised in the light of the findings of the Towton Battlefield Archaeological Survey (TBAS). For the purposes of establishing how the battle was fought, the principal value of the TBAS has been the belated recognition it brought to the outstanding private enterprise of Simon Richardson, who since 1985 has scrupulously plotted many hundreds of metal detector hits over the entire area where fighting may have taken place.

In the following chapter I propose a battle development to match the areas where Richardson found dense concentrations of hits. Some will be metallic debris from later dates, but not many: there were no hits at all in areas where we know no fighting took place. That he found so few near the Cock Beck in Towton Dale and Bloody Meadow is probably attributable to the unsystematic work of metal detector hobbyists, who will have concentrated their efforts in these areas on the basis of the canonical account of the battle. Other artefacts in this area will have washed into the Cock Beck, which I have shown in Map 27 (next chapter) swollen by spring run-off, with pools in the two places where modern contours suggest it could have been backed up on Palm Sunday 1461.

Richardson also found no hits in the area where the lane now called the Old London Road once crossed the Cock Beck, supposedly the site of the 'bridge of bodies' massacre. This is another legacy of Victorian historiography, which had the Great North Road dog-legging at Towton to cross the stream west of the town, before turning sharp right to Tadcaster and York. The lane does not appear in the earliest road maps, which all show the Great North Road following the line of the modern A162, bridging the Cock Beck not far from where it runs into the River Wharfe, close to Tadcaster.*

For several reasons we can dismiss the tale told in Hall's *Chronicle*, in which Fauconberg provoked the Lancastrians out of their defensive posture by sending his archers forward, with the wind and snow at their backs, to fire a long-range volley:

> The northern men feeling the shoot, but by reason of the snow not knowing the distance between them and their enemy, like hardy men shot their sheaves of arrows as fast as they might, but all their shot was lost and their labour was in vain. When their shot was almost spent, the Lord Fauconberg marched forward with his archers, which not only shot their own full sheaves, but also gathered the arrows of their enemies and let a great part of them fly against their own masters.

Archers would not have wasted their arrows in blind, parabolic flight: they would have saved them for use in the accurate killing range of 50 yards or less, and few arrows driven deep into the ground would have been immediately reusable. As to the snow, spring was well under way, hence the streams and rivers in spate.

* See John Davey's online article 'The Battle of Towton 1461 – A Re-Assessment'.

Temperatures were declining from the Medieval Warm Period, but the Little Ice Age, from which we are still emerging, only really got going in the sixteenth and seventeenth centuries. If any snow did fall, it was a light, unseasonal flurry. Since Hall's account depends on the Lancastrian archers being blinded by the snow, he may have invented it as the necessary *deus ex machina*.

Furthermore, if the Lancastrians had arrived first with the intention of taking up a strong defensive position, they would have formed up on the hill overlooking the village of Saxton. The position is so strong, facing south, that two late Victorian historians argued it *must* have been held by the Lancastrians. Archaeology, however, has confirmed the Lancastrian start line was indeed on the next hill to the north, on the other side of Towton Dale, between the two roads that converge on the village of Towton.

Indisputable truth is not something to look for in any military-historical reconstruction. What follows is a hypothesis that accepts some of the more general parts of contemporary reports, but which is shaped above all by the testimony of the only reliable witnesses: geography, topography and archaeology.

XXVIII

ENDGAME

FAUCONBERG WOULD HAVE QUICKLY APPRECIATED THAT the Great North Road and the offshoot of the Roman Ridge Road along which he had advanced were both dominated by the hill north of Saxton. He would have occupied its eastern end, with Warwick's battle pounding up the road behind him to form up on his left. Believing the Lancastrians intended to make a stand at the Wharfe, Edward would have had no reason to hurry his advance along the Great North Road until he was made aware of the developing situation, and so his battle arrived last.

Long before then, messengers would have galloped frantically back down the Great North Road to tell Norfolk at Brotherton to abandon the wagons and close up as fast as his East Anglians could foot it. If not previously, Norfolk's battle now came under the operational command of John Howard, the duke's cousin. Without the hand-over of command to the more vigorous Howard, the East Anglians would not have arrived in time.

The view across Towton Dale was alarming. As Northumberland's men peeled off to form opposite Warwick, followed by the southerners under Somerset and Trollope, with Rivers coming up with the reserve, the Yorkist commanders would have seen that they were badly outnumbered. As more and more Lancastrians poured down the Great North Road, they extended their left wing well beyond Fauconberg's battle.

This was the moment when Fauconberg would have sent his archers forward to disrupt the orderly deployment of the Lancastrian left. Fortuitously, Warwick's battle, the least steady of the Yorkist formations, was separated from Northumberland's men by the deepest section of Towton Dale. The hill also fell off quite steeply to the right of Fauconberg's position, but the ground between the centres of the two armies was almost flat. Edward would have positioned his reserve there, behind Warwick's right flank and Fauconberg's left. According to Wavrin:

> [Edward] jumped from his horse and told them, sword in hand, that on this day he would live or die with them in order to give them courage. Then he came in front of his banners [that is, in full view of the whole army] and waited for the enemy which was marching forward with great noise.

Somerset attacked as soon as his army had formed for battle, the outflanked and outnumbered Yorkist right wing falling back before him. Richardson's metal detecting hits indicate that the fighting on the eastern end and the centre of the hill was ferocious, much less so on the Yorkist left. This may help to extract some value from what is otherwise one of Wavrin's wilder embellishments:

> When Lord Rivers, his son and six or seven thousand Welshmen [?] led by Andrew Trollope, following the Duke of Somerset himself with seven thousand men, charged [Edward's] cavalry who fled and were chased for about eleven miles. It seemed that Lord Rivers' troops had won a great battle, because they thought that the Earl of Northumberland had charged on the other side, unfortunately he had not done so and this became his tragic day for he died that day. During this debacle many of [Edward's] soldiers died and when he learned the truth of what had happened to his cavalry he was very sad as well as very annoyed.

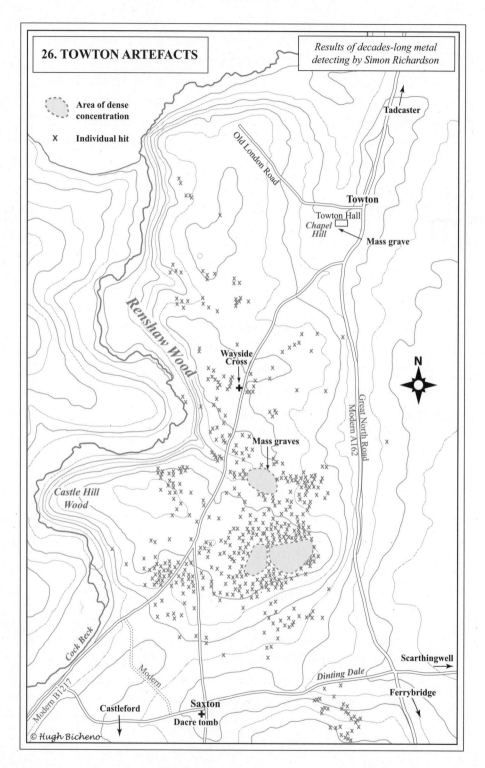

26. TOWTON ARTEFACTS

Results of decades-long metal detecting by Simon Richardson

Area of dense concentration

x Individual hit

Tadcaster

Old London Road

Towton

Towton Hall

Chapel Hill

Mass grave

Renshaw Wood

Wayside Cross

N

Mass graves

Castle Hill Wood

Great North Road
Modern A162

Cock Beck

Modern

Dinting Dale

Scarthingwell

Ferrybridge

Modern B1217

Castleford

Saxton
Dacre tomb

© *Hugh Bicheno*

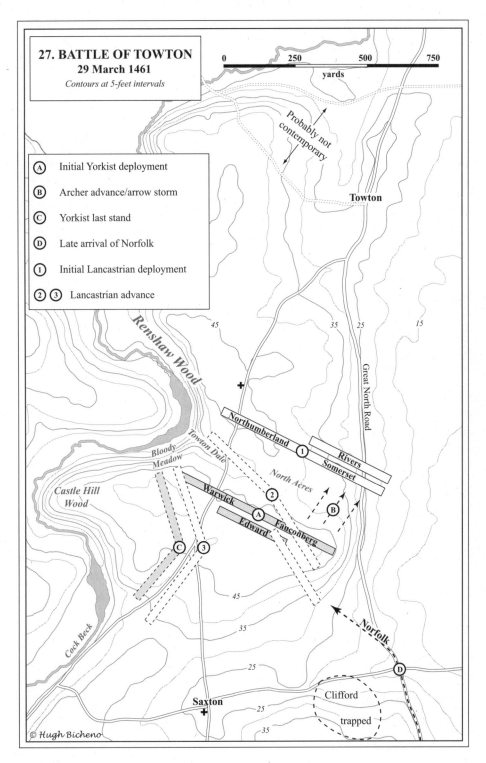

27. BATTLE OF TOWTON
29 March 1461
Contours at 5-feet intervals

0   250   500   750
yards

Probably not contemporary

Towton

Ⓐ   Initial Yorkist deployment

Ⓑ   Archer advance/arrow storm

Ⓒ   Yorkist last stand

Ⓓ   Late arrival of Norfolk

①   Initial Lancastrian deployment

② ③   Lancastrian advance

Renshaw Wood

45

35   25

15

Great North Road

Northumberland

①

Rivers

Somerset

Bloody Meadow

Towton Dale

North Acres

②

Castle Hill Wood

Warwick

Ⓐ **Fauconberg**

Ⓑ

Edward

Ⓒ ③

45

Cock Beck

Norfolk

35

Ⓓ

25

Saxton

Clifford

25

trapped

35

© *Hugh Bicheno*

Indeed he would have been, if his cavalry had ended up back at Pontefract! Let us assume Wavrin collected threads of the truth, but without a map to hand failed to understand them and so was unable to weave them into a coherent narrative. If for 'Welshmen' we read 'West Countrymen' and if for 'Edward's cavalry' we understand Fauconberg's battle, which had most of the Yorkist light horse, the opening sentence makes sense. Roughly three-fifths of the Lancastrian army under Somerset and Rivers crunched into Fauconberg's men, who were driven back hundreds of yards to the line of the modern B1217.

On the other flank, the northerners made less progress against Warwick's men, in part because of Towton Dale but also because of the early loss of Northumberland, who was mortally wounded, and Dacre, who was killed by a crossbow bolt in the throat when he lifted his bevor to take a drink. The earlier loss of Clifford was now felt strongly, as the senior remaining northern peer was the semi-Trojan Horse FitzHugh, who could not compensate for the disheartening loss of Percy and Dacre, even if he tried. FitzHugh quite possibly did not – he would have had no stomach for a fight with Warwick, his brother-in-law.

In this scenario, the Yorkist army was kept from defeat by Edward's battle, which held the centre and drew the greater Lancastrian effort, permitting the other two battles to fall back in an orderly manner. There is not much doubt that Edward himself, towering over his men and dealing out death under his family's ancestral banners, was the glue that kept his army together. This all happened very quickly. Not many Yorkists of note fell, however, which must mean their billmen held together, leaving few of the men-at-arms exposed.

Men with nowhere to run will fight to the bitter end, whereas those who see open country behind them are more tempted to flee. The rapid retreat of Fauconberg's battle meant that the Yorkist army soon found itself backed up into a large bend in the Cock Beck and fighting for their lives. It was at this moment that Lady Luck dealt them the ace of trumps with the belated arrival of Norfolk's battle along the Great North Road, behind the Lancastrian left.

There is no possibility this was planned. Edward did not expect to fight another battle this day, otherwise he would not have divided his army in the advance from the Aire. It was a battle in which expectations were dislocated three times. Edward's rapid advance dislocated the Lancastrians' assumption that the battle at Ferrybridge would delay him, and permitted the Yorkists to occupy the hill where the Lancastrians had intended to form up. Edward's assumption the Lancastrians would wait for him behind the Wharfe put him at a grave disadvantage when they advanced to meet him instead. The final, devastating dislocation was Norfolk's arrival behind the Lancastrians when they thought victory was in their grasp.

One minute the exultant Lancastrians were pressing forward to deliver the *coup de grâce*, and the next they had to extricate themselves from a trap. Some would have panicked, but others closed up on their banners and made a fighting retreat across the fields where so many of their comrades already lay dead and wounded. These twice fought-over areas are where Richardson found the densest concentration of hits. The formed units making their way to the Great North Road would have been left alone by the now feral Yorkist foot soldiers, who would have pursued disorganized prey fleeing from the battlefield.

As the door swung back, it would have been the northerners on the far right of the Lancastrian line who were the last to realize that their army was collapsing. Some, trapped against the Cock Beck, gave Bloody Meadow its name. Others on this wing, cut off from the Great North Road, would have been the ones who left the pathetic trail of debris extending north past Renshaw Wood.

Excavation of a mass grave under Towton Hall by the TBAS has added grim detail to what took place during the pursuit phase. It is a product of the hunting instinct provoked by a fleeing enemy and the explosive release of the pent-up rage required for hand-to-hand combat. The skeletons show evidence of frenzied hacking and stabbing, and the injuries to the skulls suggest the butchered men had thrown away their helmets as well as their arms to speed their flight. Not enough to outpace their over-adrenalized pursuers, however, as many of the injuries were inflicted by poleaxes, the preferred weapon of men-at-arms fighting on foot.

Once the horses were brought up a more systematic pursuit ensued. There was no baggage train to distract their pursuers, so the men retreating along the Great North Road were harried through the night. No major fighting could take place in the darkness, but with riders snapping at their heels the pace of the retreat would have been unsustainable for many exhausted men, and their screams out of the murk would have caused the others to hurry even more. Cohesion would have been impossible to maintain, leading to mass panic and the final disaster following the collapse of the bridge over the Cock Beck near Tadcaster.

Most of the lords, including the dying Northumberland, got away. Apart from Dacre, only Welles was killed on the field, while Rougemont Grey and (possibly) Beaumont were captured. Otherwise this was a battle in which, for once, the knights did not ride away, leaving the foot soldiers to be massacred. Trollope and some others were killed during the fighting, but a large number of gentry from all over England fell during the pursuit. Many of them were later attainted and their families ruined.

Henry, Marguerite and Prince Edward fled to Scotland accompanied by Somerset, Exeter, Roos (who had remained with the royal family in York) and Ralph Percy, Northumberland's remaining brother. Devon was captured in York, too ill to travel. He had to pay for Bonville and was executed on 3 April in Edward's presence. So was Rougemont Grey, brother of the turncoat Grey of Ruthyn, for what particular offence is not recorded. Young Viscount Beaumont was spared, perhaps because Edward was ashamed at the manner in which his father had been killed at Northampton.

Elsewhere, the flying Earl of Wiltshire's luck finally ran out. Following defeat at Mortimer's Cross he had made his way back to Pembroke, then took ship to join the northern army. He was not with it at Towton, however, and was trying to board a ship again when he was captured at Cockermouth. Edward saw him beheaded at Newcastle on 1 May.

Captured along with Wiltshire were Marguerite's clerks, Doctors John Morton and Ralph Mackerell. Morton was one of the men specifically excluded from pardon in the proclamation of 6 March, so it was his great good fortune to be brought before Edward a month after Towton, when his thirst for vengeance had been assuaged by the execution of Wiltshire. He ordered Morton and Mackerell imprisoned in the Tower while a commission investigated their treasons, from which they escaped to rejoin Marguerite in France a year later.

While Edward was replacing the Yorkist heads on the Micklegate Bar with Lancastrians, Lords Montagu and Berners, captured at second St Albans, were found alive and well. Possibly because their lives had been saved by the city authorities, they interceded with Edward not to exact collective punishment, and a pattern was set for the generous treatment of all boroughs and individuals who submitted to his grace.

On past and future form we may be sure that Warwick was not so magnanimous. The Trojan Horse Lord Greystoke, who had stayed clear of the final battle, now dropped his Lancastrian mask and advised Warwick which of the Neville tenants had been disloyal. If Lord FitzHugh did betray the Lancastrian cause at Towton, he gained nothing from it except immunity for having too willingly taken possession of Neville lands during the 1459–60 attainder.

Edward rode on to Durham, where he made Bishop Lawrence Booth, previously Lord Privy Seal and Marguerite's chancellor, his confessor. He even promised 'good lordship' to the Prior of Durham, who had lent the queen 400 marks [£170,000] and now had the chutzpah to ask the new king to reimburse him. Thirteen years later he was still trying to collect. Edward rode no further north than Newcastle, where he remained only to see Wiltshire executed, then rode back to Durham.

He then embarked on a progress through Lancashire, Cheshire and Staffordshire. Continuing south-east, at Stony Stratford he received the submission of Lord Rivers, who came from his nearby manor of Grafton. Rivers and his son Anthony, Lord Scales, had been imprisoned in the Tower after Towton but were released in July, probably through the intercession of Jacquetta. Edward sent a letter to Bishop Neville, the Lord Chancellor, stating he had 'of our grace especial pardoned and remitted and forgiven unto Richard Woodville, knight, Lord Rivers, all manner of offences and trespasses of him done against us'.

Among those trespasses was breaking his parole, given to Warwick when he was released from captivity in Calais. Edward may have taken a liking to Rivers during his Calais captivity, as he certainly behaved with remarkable generosity towards a man who had come close to killing him at Towton – although this was not a demerit in knightly terms. Three years later he married Rivers' and Jacquetta's stunningly beautiful eldest daughter Elizabeth, and ushered in a whole new round of woe.

From Stony Stratford Edward rode to Sheen, where he was immediately beset by the host of problems that Henry had never addressed, and which the last two years of war had greatly exacerbated. Parliament was summoned for 6 July and Edward's formal coronation was scheduled to take place six days later. What seemed to be a perfect storm of combined threats from France and Scotland, detailed in the next chapter, caused him to postpone the summons until 4 November, and to bring forward the coronation to 28 June.

Edward made his state entry into London on 26 June and was escorted to the Tower by the mayor, aldermen and 400 leading citizens. That evening and the next morning he created thirty-two new knights. They included Norfolk's cousin John Howard, Norfolk's 17-year-old heir John Mowbray and the late Duke of Buckingham's son John, Lord Stafford. Others honoured were the Treasurer of Calais Walter Blount and Lord Stanley's brother William. Edward also knighted his younger brothers, 11-year-old George and

8-year-old Richard, newly returned from the Burgundian court, where their mother had sent them after Wakefield.

The following day, Sunday 28 June, was fully taken up by a magnificent ceremony in which Archbishops Bourchier of Canterbury and Booth of York anointed and crowned him, and by a sumptuous banquet. No expense was spared, but as the crown's secular revenue stream had dried up completely, it was all with money borrowed against the security of a further tenth voted by the Canterbury Convocation. We may be sure the new king also received gifts in cash and kind from those anxious to win or keep his favour.

On Monday, Edward created his brother George Duke of Clarence, and four months later he made Richard Duke of Gloucester. A month later Norfolk died, his heir still a minor. With the dukedom of York now merged with the crown, the heir to the dukedom of Buckingham also a minor, and Exeter and Somerset attainted, no adult dukes remained. Despite this, Edward did not make Warwick a duke, either now or later, on the face of it an outstandingly ungrateful act of omission. Perhaps he felt that Warwick's behaviour at second St Albans and Ferrybridge had cancelled out his previous achievements – or maybe he just wanted to show Warwick who was the boss. Whatever his reasons, it was a slap in the face.

On Tuesday 30 June he made Viscount Bourchier Earl of Essex, and Lord Fauconberg Earl of Kent. By summons to Parliament Edward created six new barons in their own names: William, Baron Hastings, William, Baron Herbert, Thomas, Baron Lumley, Robert, Baron Ogle, Humphrey, Baron Stafford of Southwick (previously known as 'of Hooke') and John, Baron Wenlock, and confirmed Walter Devereux as Baron Ferrers of Chartley by marriage.

All the new creations had distinguished themselves in the recent battles, most of them at Mortimer's Cross. Edward's intention was plain – he wished to refresh the nobility with men of proven courage and loyalty. Apart from Ogle, Lumley and Wenlock, they were unequivocally his men, not Warwick's. Some were to become Edward's closest councillors and even companions in debauchery.

Acts of Attainder in late 1461 deprived Northumberland, Devon, Wiltshire, Pembroke, Clifford, Dacre of the North, Neville, Rougemont Grey and Welles, the majority killed on Palm Sunday or executed shortly afterwards. Of the living peers attainted, Somerset, Exeter and Roos were still in rebellion, but Beaumont was not, and was probably attainted because Hastings wanted his lands. Thirty-nine of the seventy-one attainted knights, squires, gentlemen, yeomen, clerks and two tradesmen had also been killed. Most attainders of the nobility were later reversed, but Edward had less compunction in permanently depriving commoners.

Edward did not become personally involved in the suppression of continuing Lancastrian resistance. This showed a precocious understanding that kings should lend their presence only to great enterprises, and that a war of sieges and skirmishes offered no prospect of gain commensurate with the risk of death or disgrace. It was a surprisingly mature appreciation for a man who had only just, on 28 April, celebrated his twentieth birthday.*

---

* For a fuller account of the beginning and the rest of Edward IV's reign see *Blood Royal*, the second volume of this two-part history of the Wars of the Roses.

CHECKMATE

OBJECTIVELY **HENRY VI'S REIGN ENDED ON PALM** Sunday 1461, but he lived on for a further ten miserable years. It would have been infinitely better for the Lancastrian cause if he had been killed at the second battle of St Albans, leaving his son as king. After Marguerite recovered him she had to step back from the leading role she and her son had been playing. The dithering at St Albans during February 1461 seems more typical of Henry than of his consort, as does the fact that no progress was made to conclude a Scottish alliance on the foundations laid at Lincluden Abbey.

Now, too late, Marguerite finally stopped trying to make her husband behave like a king, and resumed acting as though she were queen in her own right. Behind the scenes she had not ceased to do so: after St Albans she sent Morice Doulcereau to France to conduct clandestine negotiations with her uncle Charles VII through Pierre de Brézé, Grand Seneschal of Normandy and Charles's foremost military commander. Brézé owed his eminence to Agnès Sorel, placed in the king's bed by Isabelle of Lorraine. He was to prove a devoted friend to Isabelle's daughter, whom he had known since childhood.

Doulcereau was a Brézé retainer and had been with Henry VI at Northampton. Given that Brézé had played such a prominent role in the fall of Normandy, and had led the attack on Sandwich in 1457, the appearance of his personal emissary among the Lancastrian courtiers suggests he was there at Marguerite's invitation. What passed between them before 1461 we do not know, but in February 1461 Doulcereau brought secret offers to Brézé which, had they become known in England, would have destroyed Marguerite's credibility.

In a letter to his king dated 24 February, Brézé warned Charles not to send letters to Marguerite 'by any hands except Doulcereau's, because, if his letters were captured and the queen's intentions discovered, her friends would unite with her enemies, and kill her'. There is no reason to doubt that the secret offers Doulcereau brought were an outright gift of the Channel Islands to Brézé if he could conquer them, and to sell Calais to Charles in return for his financial support against the Yorkists.

By a Dominican friar sent directly to Charles VII, she requested 80,000 crowns [£12.72 million], and that he should mobilize a fleet to wrest control of the Channel from Warwick. Another Dominican went to Rome to denounce Coppini. Charles agreed to Brézé recruiting an army and a fleet to seize the Channel Islands, but told Marguerite he was not in a position to send the money she needed, and that the matter of Calais must await a successful suppression of the Yorkist insurgency.

Brézé sent his son-in-law to conquer the islands, Warwick's through the right of his wife, Anne Beauchamp. John Nanfan, the warden who had welcomed Warwick and his party after their flight from Ludlow, was taken by surprise and surrendered Mont Orgueil Castle, a fortress on the eastern coast of Jersey. Although a simultaneous attack on Guernsey failed, Brézé proclaimed himself Lord of the Isles of Jersey, Guernsey, Alderney and Sark. In fact his rule did not even extend to the whole of Jersey; the Lord of St Ouen in the north-west of the island never bent the knee to him.

Marguerite's luck continued to be unfailingly bad. Whatever Charles VII might have done to help her after Towton became moot when he succumbed to the illness that had been crippling him for years. He became delirious, an abscess in his mouth prevented him from eating, and he died on 22 July. His son, who refused to be reconciled with him even on his deathbed, became Louis XI, and among his first acts was to strip Pierre de Brézé of his offices.

Before that blow landed, Marguerite had been tending another iron in the fire. As soon as the royal party fled to Scotland after Towton, she renewed her friendship with Mary of Guelders. Henry was sent out to Linlithgow Palace, 18 miles west of Edinburgh, while Marguerite and her son were made welcome by Mary 50 miles away at Falkland Palace in Fife, with Bishop Kennedy also excluded from the proceedings. There, the two queens made a deal they may have discussed at Lincluden Abbey, but which could not have been concluded while Marguerite's Marcher lords lived.

Trusting to the truce previously agreed, Northumberland had drawn his retainers from the border and left Berwick with a skeleton garrison. Now that he was dead and his 12-year-old heir was in Yorkist custody, Ralph Percy, as the senior member of the family, consented to the hand-over of Berwick on 25 April. Nothing could better illustrate the depth of northern bitterness after Towton than that a Percy should have remained loyal to the Lancastrian dynasty despite the surrender of Northumberland's border fortress.

In addition, Marguerite's remaining supporters not only agreed Scotland should have Carlisle, gateway to the western March as Berwick was to the eastern, but also to march with Scots troops to capture it. Along with Brézé's assault on Jersey, this constituted the 'perfect storm' referred to in the last chapter, which caused Edward IV to postpone the summoning of Parliament and to bring forward the date of his coronation.

Although the Scots border levies cannot have been happy to find themselves under the command of such as Dacre's brother Humphrey and other English knights, they cheerfully laid waste the countryside around Carlisle. With remarkable stupidity (if, that is, they ever intended to mount a siege) they then burned the town, simplifying the castle garrison's task while depriving themselves of shelter. The raiding force retreated back over the border at the approach of Montagu with a locally raised army.

There, in a nutshell, was the conundrum posed by Marguerite's Scottish alliance. The Marcher commons may have hated the Yorkists, but they hated the Scots even more. Regional identities were very strong, but an emerging national identity trumped them in any confrontation with foreigners. Although there were strong local dialects, almost all who lived within the kingdom of England spoke the same language, unlike France with its four major and several minor language groups.

Yorkist propaganda insisted that Marguerite was not English, and that support for her was not only treason to the new king but also treason to England. Having spent her entire adult life in England without once returning to France, Marguerite was a thoroughly naturalized Englishwoman, and in many ways an exemplar of the profound English belief expressed in the clichéd phrase 'I know my rights'. The Yorkist portrayal of Marguerite gained little traction until she was compelled to ally with England's foreign foes. Even then, awareness of the great wrong done to her may have inclined many to forgiveness.

She remained the guiding light to the small band of Lancastrians who continued to fight for her in a right-angle triangle of land north of Hadrian's Wall and south of the border. At the western tip of the triangle, in Cumberland, Humphrey Dacre forted up in the family castle at Naworth. East of Naworth, the lord of the large but sparsely populated Harbottle and Redesdale estates in north-central Northumberland was none other than William Tailboys, whose ceaseless troublemaking in the 1440s and 1450s had done so much to undermine Henry VI's authority. The main body of the triangle, however, consisted of Percy lands.

The main focus of the war shifted to the royal castles of Bamburgh and Dunstanburgh, each on a headland jutting into the North Sea, and the great Percy castle at Alnwick. Alnwick was on the Great North Road, but the other two were in such remote locations that the only strategic threat they posed was as staging posts for seaborne invasion. They had harbours, plentiful water from wells dug deep into the rock on which they stand, and the walls of Dunstanburgh enclose one of the largest spaces of any castle ever built in England.

Bamburgh had been the capital of the Anglo-Saxon kingdom of Bernicia and of the preceding British kingdom, and is only a few miles from the Holy Island, Lindisfarne, from which the north of England was evangelized at the invitation of Oswald, king and saint. Today we live detached from our history, and 'folk tale' is a term of derision. Not so in the fifteenth century, and Bamburgh's talismanic quality may account in some measure for the tenacity with which it held out against the Yorkist tide.*

Alnwick, Bamburgh and Dunstanburgh all initially capitulated to Warwick in the summer of 1461 on the easiest of terms. Ralph Percy was left in command of all three, in the hope of reconciling the Percy affinity. He did not, however, regard an oath of loyalty extracted under duress as binding, and when a Lancastrian force under Tailboys marched south in October, he opened the gates. The castles now fulfilled their purpose by obliging the new regime to expend treasure and political credit, while buying time for Marguerite to raise an army.

Her problem, underlined by the ignominious performance of the Scots at Carlisle, was that her hosts could not, even if they wished to do so, field an army capable of defeating the English, or even march far beyond the border. The Lancastrians could mount troublesome raids, one of which got as far as the Clifford manor of Skipton in the West Riding of Yorkshire before turning back; but without the credibility needed to rouse popular support, they were just pinpricks. With Duke Philippe of Burgundy fully committed to the Yorkists, there was only one place where she could hope to obtain the resources to recover the kingdom.

She sent her first formal embassy to France before news of Charles VII's death arrived. She probably knew he was dying, as she also sent Somerset to the Burgundian court to make contact with

---

* Bamburgh's significance as the very heart of historic Northumbrian identity is made clear in Max Adams' brilliant *The King in the North*.

Duke Philippe's heir Charles, Count of Charolais, with whom he had formed a warm friendship during his attempt to seize Calais. To Paris she sent Lord Hungerford, recently returned from his pilgrimage and a rare example of a rat boarding a sinking ship, and Robert Whittingham. They had safe conducts from Charles VII, but Somerset did not.

When they disembarked at Le Tréport in the County of Eu, at the border of French and Burgundian territory, they were arrested and their papers seized by men sent by Louis XI, who was on his way to Reims for his coronation. Somerset was taken inland to the castle at Arques, outside Saint-Omer in Artois, whence he could as easily be handed over to Warwick's men at Calais as to Duke Philippe. Hungerford and Whittingham were moved to Dieppe, from where they sent desperate letters to Marguerite warning her not to come to France herself, still less with the king and the prince, as Louis had disbanded the fleet his late father had assembled to wrest control of the Channel from Warwick.

Marguerite was now trapped in the web of intrigue Louis XI began to spin across Europe from the moment his father died, which was to earn him the well-deserved nickname 'the Universal Spider'. Although there is hot competition for the title of the most devious prince of the Renaissance, Louis probably edges out the likes of the della Rovere Pope Sixtus IV and the Borgia Pope Alexander VI, who would otherwise have little secular competition. Warwick was a babe in arms by comparison with any of them.

Marguerite's last opportunity to act as a free agent came in 1462, when Louis' machinations very nearly provoked the hostile Anglo-Burgundian alliance he most feared. She travelled to France and her cousin agreed to prepare a fleet and an army for an invasion of England, to be led by Brézé, now conditionally back in favour. The moment passed, and she and Brézé set out with only 800 men, in an expedition Brézé had to finance himself. Their arrival at Bamburgh in October finally persuaded Edward he must lead an army himself to suppress the northern rebellion and to intimidate Scotland.

Marguerite and Brézé re-embarked with most of their men but their ships were overwhelmed by a storm. The surviving soldiers came ashore on Lindisfarne, but Marguerite and her champion made it to Berwick in an open boat. In the spring of 1463, along with her son, she took part in a raid across the border which ended with them in flight and at the mercy of strangers. A romantic legend has it that they owed their survival to the compassion of one of a band of brigands, but sadly it has no basis in fact.

Finally, leaving Henry behind at Bamburgh, in July 1463 she sailed with her son and courtiers to Flanders, where her precarious situation was described by Georges Chastellain: 'destitute of all goods and all desolate [with] neither credence, nor money, nor goods, nor jewels to pledge... and finally she had no other provision, not even bread to eat, except from the purse of her knight Sir Pierre de la Brézé... It was a thing piteous to see, truly, this high princess so cast down and laid low in such great danger.'

Charles, Count of Charolais, took pity on her and gave her the means to travel to her father René d'Anjou's county of Bar. With little support from René she formed a court in exile at Saint-Mihiel, now a suburb of Bar-le-Duc, and tried without success to prevent Edward agreeing treaties with France in October and, following the death of Mary of Guelders, with Scotland in December, in which they agreed to lend no assistance to each others' enemies.

The apparently total extinction of her hopes came with the death of Brézé on 16 July 1465, while fighting for Louis XI against Burgundy. Three days earlier Henry VI had been captured in Lancashire; he was to be subjected to a humiliating parade through the streets of London with his feet tied under his horse before being imprisoned in the Tower. Of Marguerite's pathetic court in Saint-Mihiel, John Fortescue wrote, 'We be all in great poverty, but yet the queen sustaineth us in meat and drink. Her highness may do no more than she doth.'

No one could have done more than she did, at any time since she first stepped into the void created by her husband's abdication of responsibility in 1450. No one could have animated him more and sustained his cause longer, but he was too great a burden to carry. It is hard to identify any moment in her life when she was blessed with unalloyed good fortune, but like all the great women of history she scorned self-pity and never saw herself as a victim. Her indomitability should be a source of inspiration to men and women alike.

APPENDICES

ENGLISH PEERAGE 1440–62

By date of creation

KG = Knight of the Garter   k. = killed in battle

DUKES

Date created	Name	Dates	Comments
York (1385)	Richard Plantagenet, KG, 3rd duke	1426–60	k. Wakefield
	Edward, Earl of March	1460–1	Merged with Crown
Norfolk (1397)[1]	John Mowbray, KG, 3rd duke	1432–61	
	John Mowbray, 4th duke	1461–76	
Gloucester (1414)	Humphrey of Lancaster, KG	1414–47	Extinct
Exeter (1416)	John Holland, KG, 2nd duke	1439–47	
	Henry Holland, 3rd duke	1447–61	Attainted
Somerset (1443)	John Beaufort, KG	1443–4	Extinct
Buckingham (1444)	Humphrey Stafford, KG	1444–60	k. Northampton
	Henry Stafford, 2nd duke	1460–83	
Warwick (1445)	Henry Beauchamp	1445–6	Extinct
Somerset (1448)	Edmund Beaufort, KG	1448–55	k. St Albans
	Henry Beaufort, 2nd duke	1455–61	Attainted
Suffolk (1448)	William de la Pole, KG	1448–50	Murdered, forfeit
Clarence (1461)	George Plantagenet	1461–78	
Gloucester (1461)	Richard Plantagenet	1461–83	

1. Also Earl of Nottingham, Baron Mowbray and Baron Segrave.

MARCHER LORDSHIP

Glamorgan (1439)	Henry Beauchamp	1439–46	*See Duke of Warwick*
Glamorgan (1449)	Richard Neville, KG	1449–71	*See Earl of Warwick*

MARQUESSES

Dorset (1442)	Edmund Beaufort, KG	1442–55	*See Duke of Somerset*
Suffolk (1444)	William de la Pole, KG	1444–50	*See Duke of Suffolk*

EARLS

	Richard Beauchamp, 13th earl	1401–39	
	Henry Beauchamp, 14th earl	1439–46	*See Duke of Warwick*
Warwick (1088)	Anne Beauchamp, 15th countess	1446–8	Daughter of duke
	Anne Beauchamp, 16th countess	1448–92	Sister of duke
	Richard Neville (son), KG, 16th earl	1449–71	
Arundel (1138)	William FitzAlan, 16th earl	1438–87	
Oxford (1142)	John Vere, 12th earl	1417–62	Executed
March (1328)	Richard Plantagenet, KG, 6th earl	1425–45	*See Duke of York*
	Edward Plantagenet, 7th earl	1445–61	Merged with Crown
Devon (1335)	Thomas Courtenay, 5th earl	1422–58	
	Thomas Courtenay, 6th earl	1458–61	Executed, attainted
Salisbury (1337)	Alice Montacute, 5th countess	1428–62	
	Richard Neville (father), KG, 5th earl	1442–60	k. Wakefield
	Richard Neville, KG, 6th earl	1461–71	
Stafford (1351)	Humphrey Stafford, KG, 6th earl	1403–44	*Eldest sons of the dukes of Buckingham*
	Humphrey Stafford, 7th earl	1444–58	
	Henry Stafford, 8th earl	1458–83	
Suffolk (1385)	William de la Pole, KG, 4th earl	1415–50	*See Duke of Suffolk*
	John de la Pole, KG, 5th earl	1450–92	
Rutland (1385)	Richard Plantagenet, KG, 2nd earl	1415–45	*See Duke of York*
	Edmund Pantagenet, 3rd earl	1445–60	k. Wakefield, extinct
Huntington (1387)	John Holland, 3rd earl	1417–47	*See Duke of Exeter*
	Henry Holland, 4th earl	1447–61	Attainted
Somerset (1387)	John Beaufort, KG, 3rd earl	1418–44	*See Duke of Somerset*

Westmorland (1397)	Ralph Neville, 1st earl	1397–1425	
	Ralph Neville, 2nd earl	1425–84	Dementia from *c.*1459
Pembroke (1414)	Humphrey, Duke of Gloucester	1414–47	Extinct
Northumberland (1416)	Henry Percy	1416–55	k. St Albans
	Henry Percy, 2nd earl	1455–61	k. Towton, attainted
Cambridge (1426)	Richard Plantagenet, KG, 2nd earl	1426–45	*See Duke of York*
	Edward Plantagenet, 3rd earl	1445–61	Merged with Crown
Dorset (1441)	Edmund Beaufort, KG	1442–55	*See Duke of Somerset*
	Henry Beaufort	1455–61	Attainted
Shrewsbury (1442)	John Talbot, KG	1442–53	k. Castillon
	John Talbot, KG, 2nd earl	1453–60	k. Northampton
	John Talbot, 3rd earl	1460–73	
Kendal (1443)	John Beaufort, KG	1443–4	*See Duke of Somerset*
Somerset (1444)	Edmund Beaufort	1444–55	*See Duke of Somerset*
Kendal (1446)	Jean de Foix, KG, Captal de Buch	1446–62	Resigned
Pembroke (1447)	William de la Pole, KG	1447–50	*See Duke of Suffolk*
Gloucester (1448)	William de la Pole, KG	1448–50	*See Duke of Suffolk*
Wiltshire (1449)	James Butler, KG, Earl of Ormonde	1446–61	Executed, attainted
Worcester (1449)	John Tiptoft, KG	1449–70	
Surrey (1451)	John Mowbray	1451–76	*See Duke of Norfolk*
Richmond (1452)	Edmund Tudor	1452–6	
	Henry Tudor, 2nd earl	1456–61	Forfeit
Pembroke (1452)	Jasper Tudor, KG	1452–61	Attainted
Essex (1461)	Henry Bourchier, KG	1461–83	
Kent (1461)	William Neville, KG	1461–3	
Pembroke (1461)	William Herbert, KG	1461–9	

VISCOUNTS

Beaumont (1440)	John Beaumont, KG	1440–60	k. Northampton
	William Beaumont, 2nd viscount	1460–1	Attainted

Bourchier (1446)	Henry Bourchier, KG	1446–72	*See Earl of Essex*
Lisle (1451)	John Talbot, KG	1451–3	k. Castillon
	Thomas Talbot, 2nd viscount	1453–70	

BARONS

Roos (1264)	Thomas Roos, 9th baron	1421–61	Attainted, executed 1464
Fauconberg (1295)	Joan Fauconberg, 6th baroness	1429–90	
	William Neville, KG, 6th baron	1421–63	*See Earl of Kent*
FitzWalter (1295)	Elizabeth FitzWalter, 8th baroness	1431–85	
	John Radcliffe, 8th baron (de jure)	1431–61	k. Ferrybridge
FitzWarine (1295)	Thomasine Hankeford, 9th baroness	1433–53	
	William Bourchier, 9th baron	1433–70	*See Viscount Bourchier*
Furnivall (1295)	Maud Neville, 6th baroness	1407–22	
	John Talbot, KG, 6th baron, et seq.	1407–53	*See Earl of Shrewsbury*
Grey of Wilton (1295)	Richard Grey, 6th baron	1396–1442	
	Reginald Grey, 7th baron	1442–93	
Morley (1295)	Robert Morley, 6th baron	1435–42	
	Alianore Morley, 7th baroness	1442–76	
	William Lovel, 7th baron	1442–76	By marriage
Neville of Raby (1295)	Ralph Neville, 5th baron	1425–84	*See Earl of Westmorland*
Clinton (1298)	John Clinton, 5th baron	1431–64	
Bardolf (1299)	Elizabeth Phelip, 6th baroness	1408–41	
	William Beaumont, 7th baron	1436–61	*See Viscount Beaumont*
Clifford (1299)	Thomas Clifford, 8th baron	1422–55	k. St Albans
	John Clifford, 9th baron	1455–61	k. Towton, attainted

Ferrers of Chartley (1299)	William Ferrers, 6th baron	1435–50	
	Anne Ferrers, 7th baroness	1450–68	
	Walter Devereux, 7th baron	1461–85	*De jure* from 1450
Ferrers of Groby (1299)	William Ferrers, 5th baron	1388–1445	
	Elizabeth Ferrers, 6th baroness	1445–83	
	Edward Grey, 6th baron [2]	1445–57	
	John Bourchier, 6th baron	1462–83	
Lovell (1299)[3]	William Lovell, 7th baron	1414–55	
	John Lovell, 8th baron	1455–65	
Scales (1299)	Thomas Scales, 7th baron	1419–60	Murdered
	Elizabeth Scales, 8th baroness	1460–73	
	Anthony Woodville, KG, 8th baron	1460–83	By marriage
Strange of Knockyn (1299)	Richard Strange, 7th baron	1397–1449	
	John Strange, 8th baron	1449–77	
de la Warr (1299)	Reginald West, 6th baron	1427–51	
	Richard West, 7th baron	1451–76	
Welles (1299)	Lionel Welles, KG, 6th baron	1421–61	k. Towton, attainted
Zouche (1308)	William Zouche, 5th baron	1415–63	
Beaumont (1309)	John Beaumont, KG, 6th baron	1417–60	*See Viscount Beaumont*
Audley (1313) *Also Tuchet*	James Tuchet, 5th baron	1408–59	k. Blore Heath
	John Tuchet, 6th baron	1459–90	
Cobham (1313)	Joan Brooke, 5th baroness	1434–42	
	Edward Brooke, 6th baron	1442–64	
Willoughby (1313)	Robert Willoughby, KG, 6th baron	1409–52	
	Joan Willoughby, 7th baroness	1452–62	
	Richard Welles, 7th baron	1452–70	
Dacre of Gilsland (1321)	Thomas Dacre, 6th baron	1398–1458	
	Joan Dacre, 7th baroness	1458–86	Granddaughter of Thomas
	Richard Fiennes, 7th baron	1458– 83	By marriage

2. First father-in-law of Elizabeth Woodville, who married Edward IV in 1464.
3. Also Baron Holland, Deincort, Bedale and Grey of Rotherfield.

FitzHugh (1321)	William FitzHugh, 4th baron	1425–52	
	Henry FitzHugh, 5th baron	1452–72	
Greystoke (1321)	Ralph Greystoke, 5th baron	1436–87	
Grey of Ruthyn (1325)	Reginald Grey, 3rd baron	1388–1441	
	Edmund Grey, 4th baron	1441–90	
Harington (1326)	William Harington, 5th baron	1418–58	
	William Bonville, KG, 6th baron	1458–60	k. Wakefield
	Cecily Bonville, 7th baroness	1460–1530	*Combined with Bonville*
Burghersh (1330)	Henry Beauchamp, KG, 6th baron	1439–45	*See Duke of Warwick*
	Anne Beauchamp, 7th baroness	1445–9	Abeyant
Maltravers (1330)	William FitzAlan	1438–83	*See Earl of Arundel*
Talbot (1331)	John Talbot, KG, 7th baron	1421–53	*See Earl of Shrewsbury*
	John Talbot, KG, 8th baron	1453–60	
	John Talbot, 9th baron	1460–73	
Poynings (1337)[4]	Robert Poynings, 5th baron	1387–1446	
	Eleanor Poynings, 6th baroness	1446–82	
	Henry Percy, 6th baron by marriage	1446–61	*Earl of Northumberland*
Bourchier (1342)	Henry Bourchier, KG, 5th baron	1433–83	*See Earl of Essex*
Scrope of Masham (1350)	John Scrope, 4th baron	1426–55	
	Thomas Scrope, 5th baron	1455–75	
Botreaux (1368)	William Botreaux, 3rd baron	1392–1462	
	Margaret Botreaux, 4th baroness	1462–77	
Scrope of Bolton (1371)	Henry Scrope, 4th baron	1420–59	
	John Scrope, KG, 5th baron	1459–98	
Cromwell (1375)	Ralph Cromwell, 3rd baron	1417–55	Abeyant
Beauchamp of Bletsoe (1379)	Margaret Beauchamp, 4th baroness	1429–82	
	John Beaufort, KG, 4th baron	1441–4	*See Duke of Somerset*
	Lionel Welles, KG, 4th baron	1447–61	*See Welles*

4. Also baronies of FitzPayne and Brian.

Bergavenny (1392) *Dispute with 1450 creation*	Elizabeth Beauchamp, 3rd baroness	1421—47	
	Anne Beauchamp, 4th baroness	1447—92	Countess of Warwick
Grey of Codnor (1397)	Henry Grey, 3rd baron	1431—44	
	Henry Grey, 4th baron	1444—96	
Tuchet (1403) *Also Audley*	James Tuchet, 2nd baron	1408—59	k. Blore Heath
	John Tuchet, 6th baron	1459—90	
Berkeley (1421)	James Berkeley	1421—63	
Hungerford (1426)	Walter Hungerford, KG	1426—49	
	Robert Hungerford, 2nd baron	1449—59	
	Robert Hungerford, 3rd baron	1459—62	Attainted, executed 1464
Tiptoft (1426)	John Tiptoft	1426—43	
	John Tiptoft, KG, 2nd baron[5]	1443—70	*See Earl of Worcester*
Latimer (1432)	George Neville (disputed)	1425—69	Ruled incompetent 1447
	Richard Neville (custodian)	1447—69	*See Earl of Warwick*
Fanhope (1433)	John Cornwall, KG	1433—43	Also Milbroke, extinct
Dudley (1440)	John Sutton, KG	1440—87	
Sudeley (1299/1441)	Ralph Boteler, KG, 6th/1st baron	1441—73	
Milbroke (1442)	John Cornwall, KG	1442—3	Also Fanhope, extinct
Lisle (1444)	John Talbot, KG	1444—53	*See Viscount Lisle*
	Thomas Talbot, 2nd baron	1453—70	
Moleyns (1445)	Alianore Moleyns, 2nd baroness	1428—76	*See Hungerford*
	Robert Hungerford, 2nd baron	1449—64	
Beauchamp of Powick (1447)	John Beauchamp, KG	1447—75	
Hoo and Hastings (1447)	Thomas Hoo, KG	1447—55	Extinct
Saye and Sele (1447)	James Fiennes	1447—50	Murdered
	William Fiennes, 2nd baron	1450—71	
Rivers (1448)	Richard Woodville, KG	1448—69	

5. Shared the lordship and castle of Powys with Henry, de jure Baron Grey of Powys.

Stourton (1448)	John Stourton	1448–62	
	William Stourton, 2nd baron	1462–79	
Bonville (1449)	William Bonville, KG	1449–61	Executed St Albans
	Cecily Bonville, 2nd baroness	1461–1530	*Combined with Harington*
Egremont (1449)	Thomas Percy	1449–60	k. Northampton, extinct
Vescy (1449)	Henry Bromflete	1449–69	
Bergavenny (1450)	Edward Neville, 1st/3rd baron	1450–76	*Dispute with 1392 creation*
Rougement Grey (1450)	Thomas Grey	1450–61	Executed, extinct
Berners (1455)	John Bourchier, KG	1455–74	
Stanley (1456)	Thomas Stanley, KG	1456–9	
	Thomas Stanley, 2nd baron	1459–1504	
Dacre of the North (1459)	Randolph Dacre	1459–61	k. Towton, attainted
Montagu (1461)	John Neville, KG	1461–71	
Cromwell (1461)	Humphrey Bourchier	1461–71	
Hastings (1461)	William Hastings, KG	1461–83	
Lumley (1461)	Thomas Lumley	1461–85	
Herbert of Raglan (1461)	William Herbert, KG	1461–69	
Ogle (1461)	Robert Ogle	1461–69	
Wenlock (1461)	John Wenlock, KG	1461–71	

ENGLISH PEERAGE
1440–62
Alphabetical

KG = Knight of the Garter   k. = killed in battle

DUKES

Date created	Name	Dates	Comments
Buckingham (1444)	Humphrey Stafford, KG	1444–60	k. Northampton
	Henry Stafford, 2nd duke	1460–83	
Clarence (1461)	George Plantagenet	1461–78	
Exeter (1416)	John Holland, KG, 2nd duke	1439–47	
	Henry Holland, 3rd duke	1447–61	Attainted
Gloucester (1414)	Humphrey of Lancaster, KG	1414–47	Extinct
Gloucester (1461)	Richard Plantagenet	1461–83	
Norfolk (1397)[1]	John Mowbray, KG, 3rd duke	1432–61	
	John Mowbray, 4th duke	1461–76	
Somerset (1443)	John Beaufort, KG	1443–4	Extinct
Somerset (1448)	Edmund Beaufort, KG	1448–55	k. St Albans
	Henry Beaufort, 2nd duke	1455–61	Attainted
Suffolk (1448)	William de la Pole, KG	1448–50	Murdered, forfeit
Warwick (1445)	Henry Beauchamp	1445–6	Extinct
York (1385)	Richard Plantagenet, KG, 3rd duke	1426–60	k. Wakefield
	Edward, Earl of March	1460–1	Merged with crown

1. Also Earl of Nottingham, Baron Mowbray and Baron Segrave.

MARCHER LORDSHIP

Glamorgan (1439)	Henry Beauchamp	1439–46	*See Duke of Warwick*
Glamorgan (1449)	Richard Neville, KG	1449–71	*See Earl of Warwick*

MARQUESSES

Dorset (1442)	Edmund Beaufort, KG	1442–55	*See Duke of Somerset*
Suffolk (1444)	William de la Pole, KG	1444–50	*See Duke of Suffolk*

EARLS

Arundel (1138)	William FitzAlan, 16th earl	1438–87	
Cambridge (1426)	Richard Plantagenet, KG, 2nd earl	1426–45	*See Duke of York*
	Edward Plantagenet, 3rd earl	1445–61	Merged with crown
Devon (1335)	Thomas Courtenay, 13th earl	1422–58	
	Thomas Courtenay, 14th earl	1458–61	Executed, attainted
Dorset (1441)	Edmund Beaufort, KG	1442–55	*See Duke of Somerset*
	Henry Beaufort	1455–61	Attainted
Essex (1461)	Henry Bourchier, KG	1461–83	
Gloucester (1448)	William de la Pole, KG	1448–50	*See Duke of Suffolk*
Huntington (1387)	John Holland, 3rd earl	1417–47	*See Duke of Exeter*
	Henry Holland, 4th earl	1447–61	Attainted
Kendal (1443)	John Beaufort, KG	1443–4	*See Duke of Somerset*
Kendal (1446)	Jean de Foix, KG, Captal de Buch	1446–62	Resigned
Kent (1461)	William Neville, KG	1461–3	
March (1328)	Richard Plantagenet, KG, 6th earl	1425–45	See Duke of York
	Edward Plantagenet, 7th earl	1445–61	Merged with crown
Northumberland (1416)	Henry Percy	1416–55	k. St Albans
	Henry Percy, 2nd earl	1455–61	k. Towton, attainted
Oxford (1142)	John Vere, 12th earl	1417–62	
Pembroke (1414)	Humphrey, Duke of Gloucester	1414–47	Extinct

Pembroke (1447)	William de la Pole, KG	1447–50	*See Duke of Suffolk*
Pembroke (1452)	Jasper Tudor, KG	1452–61	Attainted
Pembroke (1461)	William Herbert, KG	1461–9	
Salisbury (1337)	Alice Montacute, 5th countess	1428–62	
	Richard Neville (father), KG, 5th earl	1442–60	k. Wakefield
	Richard Neville, KG, 6th earl	1461–71	
Stafford (1351)	Humphrey Stafford, KG, 6th earl	1403–44	*Eldest sons of the dukes of Buckingham*
	Humphrey Stafford, 7th earl	1444–58	
	Henry Stafford, 8th earl	1458–83	
Suffolk (1385)	William de la Pole, KG, 4th earl	1415–50	*See Duke of Suffolk*
	John de la Pole, KG, 5th earl	1450–92	
Richmond (1452)	Edmund Tudor	1452–6	
	Henry Tudor, 2nd earl	1456–61	Forfeit
Rutland (1385)	Richard Plantagenet, KG, 2nd earl	1415–45	*See Duke of York*
	Edmund Pantagenet, 3rd earl	1445–60	k. Wakefield, extinct
Shrewsbury (1442)	John Talbot, KG	1442–53	k. Castillon
	John Talbot, KG, 2nd earl	1453–60	k. Northampton
	John Talbot, 3rd earl	1460–73	
Somerset (1387)	John Beaufort, KG, 3rd earl	1418–44	*See Duke of Somerset*
Somerset (1444)	Edmund Beaufort	1444–55	*See Duke of Somerset*
Surrey (1451)	John Mowbray	1451–76	*See Duke of Norfolk*
Warwick (1088)	Richard Beauchamp, 13th earl	1401–39	
	Henry Beauchamp, 14th earl	1439–46	*See Duke of Warwick*
	Anne Beauchamp, 15th countess	1446–8	Daughter of duke
	Anne Beauchamp, 16th countess	1448–92	Sister of duke
	Richard Neville (son), KG, 16th earl	1449–71	
Westmorland (1397)	Ralph Neville, 1st earl	1397–1425	
	Ralph Neville, 2nd earl	1425–84	Dementia from *c*.1459
Wiltshire (1449)	James Butler, KG, Earl of Ormonde	1446–61	Executed, attainted
Worcester (1449)	John Tiptoft, KG	1449–70	

VISCOUNTS

Beaumont (1440)	John Beaumont, KG	1440–60	k. Northampton
	William Beaumont, 2nd viscount	1460–1	Attainted
Bourchier (1446)	Henry Bourchier, KG	1446–72	*See Earl of Essex*
Lisle (1451)	John Talbot, KG	1451–53	k. Castillon
	Thomas Talbot, 2nd viscount	1453–70	

BARONS

Audley (1313) *Also Tuchet*	James Tuchet, 5th baron	1408–59	k. Blore Heath
	John Tuchet, 6th baron	1459–90	
Bardolf (1299)	Elizabeth Phelip, 6th baroness	1408–41	
	William Beaumont, 7th baron	1436–61	*See Viscount Beaumont*
Beauchamp of Bletsoe (1379)	Margaret Beauchamp, 4th baroness	1429–82	
	John Beaufort, KG, 4th baron	1441–4	*See Duke of Somerset*
	Lionel Welles, KG, 4th baron	1447–61	*See Welles*
Beauchamp of Powick (1447)	John Beauchamp, KG	1447–75	
Beaumont (1309)	John Beaumont, KG, 6th baron	1417–60	*See Viscount Beaumont*
Bergavenny (1392) *Dispute with 1450 creation*	Elizabeth Beauchamp, 3rd baroness	1421–47	
	Anne Beauchamp, 4th baroness	1447–92	Countess of Warwick
Bergavenny (1450)	Edward Neville, 1st/ 3rd baron	1450–76	
Berkeley (1421)	James Berkeley	1421–63	
Berners (1455)	John Bourchier, KG	1455–74	
Bonville (1449)	William Bonville, KG	1449–61	Executed St Albans
	Cecily Bonville, 2nd baroness	1461–1530	Combined with Harington
Botreaux (1368)	William Botreaux, 3rd baron	1392–1462	
	Margaret Botreaux, 4th baroness	1462–77	
Bourchier (1342)	Henry Bourchier, KG, 5th baron	1433–83	*See Earl of Essex*

Burghersh (1330)	Henry Beauchamp, KG, 6th baron	1439–45	*See Duke of Warwick*
	Anne Beauchamp, 7th baroness	1445–9	Abeyant
Clifford (1299)	Thomas Clifford, 8th baron	1422–55	k. St Albans
	John Clifford, 9th baron	1455–61	k. Towton, attainted
Clinton (1298)	John Clinton, 5th baron	1431–64	
Cobham (1313)	Joan Brooke, 5th baroness	1434–42	
	Edward Brooke, 6th baron	1442–64	
Cromwell (1375)	Ralph Cromwell, 3rd baron	1417–55	Abeyant
Cromwell (1461)	Humphrey Bourchier	1461–71	
Dacre of Gilsland (1321)	Thomas Dacre, 6th baron	1398–1458	
	Joan Dacre, 7th baroness	1458–86	Granddaughter of Thomas
	Richard Fiennes, 7th baron	1458–83	By marriage
Dacre of the North (1459)	Randolph Dacre	1459–61	k. Towton, attainted
Dudley (1440)	John Sutton, KG	1440–87	
Egremont (1449)	Thomas Percy	1449–60	k. Northampton, extinct
Fanhope (1433)	John Cornwall, KG	1433–43	*Also Milbroke* Extinct
Fauconberg (1295)	Joan Fauconberg, 6th baroness	1429–90	
	William Neville, KG, 6th baron	1421–63	See Earl of Kent
Ferrers of Chartley (1299)	William Ferrers, 6th baron	1435–50	
	Anne Ferrers, 7th baroness	1450–68	
	Walter Devereux, 7th baron	1461–85	*De jure* from 1450
Ferrers of Groby (1299)	William Ferrers, 5th baron	1388–1445	
	Elizabeth Ferrers, 6th baroness	1445–83	
	Edward Grey, 6th baron[2]	1445–57	
	John Bourchier, 6th baron	1462–83	
FitzHugh (1321)	William FitzHugh, 4th baron	1425–52	
	Henry FitzHugh, 5th baron	1452–72	
FitzWalter (1295)	Elizabeth FitzWalter, 8th baroness	1431–85	
	John Radcliffe, 8th baron (de jure)	1431–61	k. Ferrybridge

2. First father-in-law of Elizabeth Woodville, who married Edward IV in 1464.

FitzWarine (1295)	Thomasine Hankeford, 9th baroness	1433–53	
	William Bourchier, 9th baron	1433–70	*See Viscount Bourchier*
Furnivall	Maud Neville, 6th baroness	1407–22	
	John Talbot, KG, 6th baron, et seq.	1407–53	*See Earl of Shrewsbury*
Grey of Codnor (1397)	Henry Grey, 3rd baron	1431–44	
	Henry Grey, 4th baron	1444–96	
Grey of Ruthyn (1325)	Reginald Grey, 3rd baron	1388–1441	
	Edmund Grey, 4th baron	1441–90	
Grey of Wilton (1295)	Richard Grey, 6th baron	1396–1442	
	Reginald Grey, 7th baron	1442–93	
Greystoke (1321)	Ralph Greystoke, 5th baron	1436–87	
Harington (1326)	William Harington, 5th baron	1418–58	
	William Bonville, KG, 6th baron	1458–60	k. Wakefield
	Cecily Bonville, 7th baroness	1460–1530	*Combined with Bonville*
Hastings (1461)	William Hastings, KG	1461–83	
Herbert of Raglan (1461)	William Herbert, KG	1461–9	
Hoo and Hastings (1447)	Thomas Hoo, KG	1447–55	Extinct
Hungerford (1426)	Walter Hungerford, KG	1426–49	
	Robert Hungerford, 2nd baron	1449–59	
	Robert Hungerford, 3rd baron	1459–61	Attainted, executed 1464
Latimer (1432)	George Neville (disputed)	1425–69	Ruled incompetent 1447
	Richard Neville (custodian)	c.1447–69	*See Earl of Warwick*
Lisle (1444)	John Talbot, KG	1444–53	*See Viscount Lisle*
	Thomas Talbot, 2nd baron	1453–70	
Lovell (1299)[3]	William Lovell, 7th baron	1414–55	
	John Lovell, 8th baron	1455–65	

3. Also Baron Holland, Deincort, Bedale and Grey of Rotherfield.

Lumley (1461)	Thomas Lumley	1461–85	
Maltravers (1330)	William FitzAlan	1438–83	*See Earl of Arundel*
Milbroke (1442)	John Cornwall, KG	1442–43	*Also Fanhope* Extinct
Moleyns (1445)	Alianore Moleyns, 2nd baroness	1428–76	
	Robert Hungerford, 2nd baron	1449–64	*See Hungerford*
Montagu (1461)	John Neville, KG	1461–71	
Morley (1295)	Robert Morley, 6th baron	1435–42	
	Alianore Morley, 7th baroness	1442–76	
	William Lovel, 7th baron	1442–76	By marriage
Neville of Raby (1295)	Ralph Neville, 5th baron	1425–84	*See Earl of Westmorland*
Ogle (1461)	Robert Ogle	1461–69	
Poynings (1337)[4]	Robert Poynings, 5th baron	1387–1446	
	Eleanor Poynings, 6th baroness	1446–82	
	Henry Percy, 6th baron by marriage	1446–61	*See Earl of Northumberland*
Rivers (1448)	Richard Woodville, KG	1448–69	
Roos (1264)	Thomas Roos, 9th baron	1421–61	Attainted, executed 1464
Rougement Grey (1450)	Thomas Grey	1450–61	Executed, extinct
Saye and Sele (1447)	James Fiennes	1447–50	Murdered
	William Fiennes, 2nd baron	1450–71	
Scales (1299)	Thomas Scales, 7th baron	1419–60	Murdered
	Elizabeth Scales, 8th baroness	1460–73	
	Anthony Woodville, KG, 8th baron	1460–83	By marriage
Scrope of Bolton (1371)	Henry Scrope, 4th baron	1420–59	
	John Scrope, KG, 5th baron	1459–98	
Scrope of Masham (1350)	John Scrope, 4th baron	1426–55	
	Thomas Scrope, 5th baron	1455–75	
Stanley (1456)	Thomas Stanley, KG	1456–9	
	Thomas Stanley, 2nd baron	1459–1504	

4. Also baronies of Fitzpayne and Brian.

Stourton (1448)	John Stourton	1448–62	
	William Stourton, 2nd baron	1462–79	
Strange of Knockyn (1299)	Richard Strange, 7th baron	1397–1449	
	John Strange, 8th baron	1449–77	
Sudeley (1299/1441)	Ralph Boteler, KG, 6th/1st baron	1441–73	
Talbot (1331)	John Talbot, KG, 7th baron	1421–53	*See Earl of Shrewsbury*
	John Talbot, KG, 8th baron	1453–60	
	John Talbot, 9th baron	1460–73	
Tiptoft (1426)	John Tiptoft	1426–43	
	John Tiptoft, KG, 2nd baron[5]	1443–70	*See Earl of Worcester*
Tuchet (1403) *Also Audley*	James Tuchet, 2nd baron	1408–59	k. Blore Heath
	John Tuchet, 6th baron	1459–90	
Vescy (1449)	Henry Bromflete	1449–69	
de la Warr (1299)	Reginald West, 6th baron	1427–51	
	Richard West, 7th baron	1451–76	
Welles (1299)	Lionel Welles, KG, 6th baron	1421–61	k. Towton, attainted
Wenlock (1461)	John Wenlock, KG	1461–71	
Willoughby (1313)	Robert Willoughby, KG, 6th baron	1409–52	
	Joan Willoughby, 7th baroness	1452–62	
	Richard Welles, 7th baron	1452–70	
Zouche (1308)	William Zouche, 5th baron	1415–63	

5. Shared the lordship and castle of Powys with Henry, de jure Baron Grey of Powys.

ARCHBISHOPS AND BISHOPS 1440–62

Diocese	Incumbent	Dates	Offices
CANTERBURY	John Stafford	1443–52	Lord Chancellor 1432–50
	Cardinal John Kemp	1452–4	Lord Chancellor 1426–32, 1450–4
	Cardinal Thomas Bourchier	1454–86	Lord Chancellor 1555–6
Bath and Wells	John Stafford	1424–43	Lord Treasurer 1422–6. *To Canterbury*
	Thomas Beckington	1443–65	Lord Privy Seal 1443–4
	Robert Stillington	1465–91	Lord Privy Seal 1460–67
Chichester	Richard Praty	1438–45	
	Adam Moleyns	1445–50	Lord Privy Seal 1444–50. Murdered
	Reginald Pecock	1450–59	*Deprived for heresy*
	John Arundel	1459–77	
Exeter	John Lacey	1420–55	
	George Neville	1455–65	Lord Chancellor 1460–7
Ely	Thomas Bourchier	1444–54	*To Canterbury*
	William Grey	1454–78	Papal Notary
Hereford	Thomas Spofford	1421–48	
	Richard Beauchamp	1448–50	To Salisbury
	Reginald Boulers	1450–53	King's secretary. *To Lichfield/Coventry*
	John Stanberry	1453–74	King's confessor. Carmelite monk
Lichfield/Coventry	William Heyworth	1420–47	
	William Booth	1447–52	Queen's Chancellor 1445–51. *To York*
	Reginald Boulers	1453–9	
	John Hales/Halse	1459–90	
Lincoln/Dorchester	William Alnwick	1436–50	
	Marmaduke Lumley	1450	
	John Chedworth	1452–71	
London	Robert Gilbert	1436–48	

	Thomas Kemp	1448–89	*Nephew of Archbishop John Kemp*
Norwich	Thomas Brunce	1436–45	
	Walter Lyhert	1446–72	Queen's Confessor
Rochester	William Wells	1437–44	
	John Lowe	1444–67	
Salisbury	William Ayscough	1438–50	King's Confessor. *Murdered*
	Richard Beauchamp	1450–81	
Winchester	Cardinal Henry Beaufort	1404–47	Lord Chancellor 1413–17, 1424–6
	William Wainflete	1447–86	Lord Chancellor 1456–60
Worcester	Thomas Bourchier	1434–43	To Ely
	John Carpenter	1443–76	
Bangor (Wales)	Thomas Cheriton	1436–48	Dominican monk
	John Stanberry	1448–53	Carmelite monk. *To Hereford*
	James Blakedon	1453–64	Dominican monk
Llandaff (Wales)	Nicholas Ashby	1440–58	
	John Hunden	1458–76	Resigned
St Asaph (Wales)	John Low	1433–44	Friar Eremite. *To Rochester*
	Reginald Pecock	1444–9	To Chichester
	Thomas Bird	1450–63	*Deprived for rebellion*
St David's (Wales)	Thomas Rodburn	1433–42	
	William Lyndwood	1442–6	Lord Privy Seal 1432–43
	John de la Bere	1447–60	*Absentee.** Resigned.
	Robert Tully	1460–81	Benedictine monk
YORK	John Kemp	1425–52	*To Canterbury*
	William Booth	1452–64	*Brother of Laurence*
Carlisle	Marmaduke Lumley	1429–49	Lord Treasurer 1446–9. *To Lincoln*
	Nicholas Close	1450–52	To Lichfield/Coventry
	William Percy	1452–62	*Brother of the Earl of Northumberland*
Durham	Robert Neville	1437–57	*Brother of the Earl of Salisbury*
	Laurence Booth	1457–76	Queen's Chancellor 1451–6, Lord Privy Seal 1456–60

* The temporalities were administered by Gruffudd ap Nicholas. The future Henry VII was conceived at the bishop's palace at Lamphey, outside Pembroke.

THE BEAUCHAMP INHERITANCE

k. = killed in battle   x. = executed

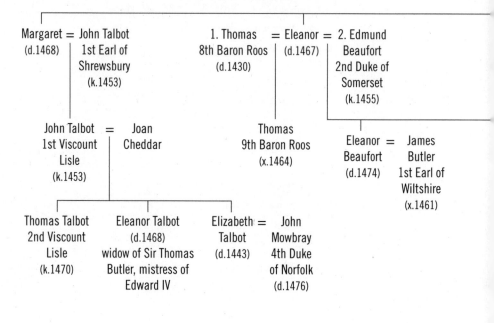

Margaret = John Talbot
(d.1468)   1st Earl of
Shrewsbury
(k.1453)

1. Thomas = Eleanor = 2. Edmund
8th Baron Roos   (d.1467)   Beaufort
(d.1430)   2nd Duke of
Somerset
(k.1455)

John Talbot = Joan
1st Viscount   Cheddar
Lisle
(k.1453)

Thomas
9th Baron Roos
(x.1464)

Eleanor = James
Beaufort   Butler
(d.1474)   1st Earl of
Wiltshire
(x.1461)

Thomas Talbot
2nd Viscount
Lisle
(k.1470)

Eleanor Talbot
(d.1468)
widow of Sir Thomas
Butler, mistress of
Edward IV

Elizabeth = John
Talbot   Mowbray
(d.1443)   4th Duke
of Norfolk
(d.1476)

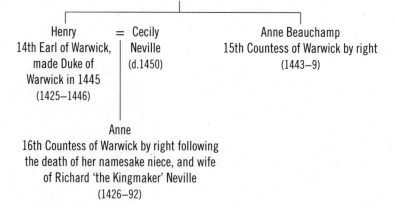

= 2. Isabel Despenser
(d.1439)
*Beauchamp entailed most of his own and part of the Berkeley
and Lisle inheritances to his children from this marriage.*

Henry = Cecily
14th Earl of Warwick,   Neville
made Duke of   (d.1450)
Warwick in 1445
(1425–1446)

Anne Beauchamp
15th Countess of Warwick by right
(1443–9)

Anne
16th Countess of Warwick by right following
the death of her namesake niece, and wife
of Richard 'the Kingmaker' Neville
(1426–92)

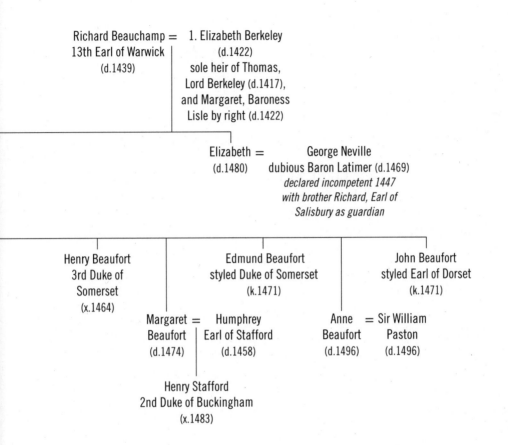

Richard Beauchamp = 1. Elizabeth Berkeley
13th Earl of Warwick   (d.1422)
(d.1439)   sole heir of Thomas,
                        Lord Berkeley (d.1417),
                        and Margaret, Baroness
                        Lisle by right (d.1422)

Elizabeth = George Neville
(d.1480)   dubious Baron Latimer (d.1469)
            declared incompetent 1447
            with brother Richard, Earl of
            Salisbury as guardian

Henry Beaufort   Edmund Beaufort   John Beaufort
3rd Duke of   styled Duke of Somerset   styled Earl of Dorset
Somerset   (k.1471)   (k.1471)
(x.1464)

Margaret = Humphrey   Anne = Sir William
Beaufort | Earl of Stafford Beaufort   Paston
(d.1474) | (d.1458)   (d.1496)   (d.1496)

Henry Stafford
2nd Duke of Buckingham
(x.1483)

——— OTHER INHERITANCES ———

Isabel Despenser, Richard Beauchamp's second wife, was the sole heir of Thomas (k.1399), Earl of Gloucester, who was attainted for conspiring against Henry IV. Her mother was Constance of York, whose role in the 1415 conspiracy against Henry V is mentioned in Chapter 4. Isabel was also the sole heir of her older brother Richard, Baron Burghersh (d.1414). The only child of Isabel's first marriage to Richard's cousin (also Richard Beauchamp), 1st Earl of Worcester, was Elizabeth, Baroness Bergavenny by right (d.1448), who married Edward Neville (d.1476), uncle of the Kingmaker.

The Kingmaker claimed all the Beauchamp, Bergavenny, Burghersh and Despenser estates in the name of his wife. Various parts of this were strongly contested by the older two daughters of Richard Beauchamp's first marriage, supported by their husbands, John Talbot, Earl of Shrewsbury and Edmund Beaufort, Duke of Somerset.

There was a separate, deadly sub-dispute known as:

THE BERKELEY–LISLE FEUD

James Berkeley (d.1463) was heir to the title and property entailed in the male line of his uncle Thomas, 5th Baron Berkeley (see above). This was disputed by Thomas's daughter and named heir Elizabeth Berkeley, Richard Beauchamp's first wife. To finesse the dispute, in 1421 James was summoned to Parliament as the 1st, not the 6th Baron Berkeley.

Elizabeth held Berkeley Castle until her death in 1422, when James recovered it. In 1451 Elizabeth's grandson John Talbot, later Viscount Lisle, took it back. James retaliated by sacking the manor house at Wotton-under-Edge owned by Lisle's mother Margaret, wife of John Talbot, Earl of Shrewsbury. Lisle then kidnapped Isabel Mowbray, James's third wife, whom Margaret imprisoned in Gloucester Castle, where she died in 1452.

Following the deaths at Castillon of Margaret's husband and son, James Berkeley married Joan Talbot, Margaret's stepdaughter from her husband's first marriage, whom she had raised from infancy.* This achieved a cessation of hostilities – until the next generation. Isabel's and James's son William, 2nd Baron Berkeley, was the victor of the last private battle in English history at Nibley Green in 1470, where Thomas, 2nd Viscount Lisle was killed.

The lawsuit, one of the most protracted in English legal history, dragged on until 1609.

---

* John Talbot married first Maud Neville, Baroness Furnivall by right and sister of Ralph, Earl of Westmorland, who died in 1422 giving birth to Joan. Their son John (k.1460) became 2nd Earl of Shrewsbury.

WORKS CONSULTED

Place of Publication London unless otherwise stated.

If you read only one other book, make it *The Politics of Fifteenth-Century England: John Vale's Book* (Stroud, 1995) by Margaret Kekewich, Colin Richmond, Anne Sutton, Livia Visser-Fuchs and John Watts. It is an exemplary presentation of selections from a unique treasure trove of primary sources, accompanied by brilliant analytical essays. See also Simon Payling's invaluable articles listed separately at the end of this bibliography.

Most of the printed works listed are only available in research libraries. However, anyone can access the first section below by searching for the titles online. There may well be more, but these are the ones I consulted. Also, the learned articles I consulted are listed separately and by journal for the benefit of those with access to JSTOR.

ONLINE SOURCES (PRIMARY AND SECONDARY)

Anon., *The Edward IV Roll* (1461?).

Anon., *The Talbot Shrewsbury Book* (1445).

Anon., *A Chronicle of London from 1089 to 1483* (1828).

Bain, John (ed.), *Calendar of Documents Relating to Scotland 1357–1509* (1988).

Brooke, Richard, *Visits to the Fields of Battle in England of the Fifteenth Century* (1857).

Brown, Horatio (ed.), *Calendar of state papers and manuscripts relating to English affairs, existing in the archives and collections of Venice, and in other libraries of northern Italy* (1864).

Burley, Peter, Michael Elliott and Harvey Watson, *The Battles of St Albans* (Barnsley, 2007).

Carpenter, Christine, *Locality and polity: a study of Warwickshire landed society, 1401–1499* (1992).

Castor, Helen, *The King, the Crown and the Duchy of Lancaster* (Oxford, 2000).

Commynes, Philippe de (trans. Michael Jones), *Memoirs: the reign of Louis XI, 1461–83* (1972).

Coward, Barry, *The Stanleys, Lords Stanley and Earls of Derby* (Manchester, 1983).

Curry, Anne, *The Hundred Years' War* (2003).

Davey, John, 'The Battle of Towton 1461 – A Re-Assessment' (2003).

Davies, John (ed.), *An English Chronicle of the reigns of Richard II, Henry IV, Henry V, and Henry VI written before the year 1471* (1856).

Dictionary of National Biography (Oxford, 2004–).

Dillon, Viscount and W. Hope (eds.), *Pageant of the birth, life and death of Richard Beauchamp, Earl of Warwick* (1914).

Dockray, Keith, 'The Battle of Wakefield and the Wars of the Roses', *The Ricardian* (June 1992).

Du Boulay, Francis (ed.), *Documents Illustrative of Medieval Kentish Society* (Ashford, 1964).

Ellis, Henry, *Hall's Chronicle* (1809, reprinted 1965).

English Heritage, *Battlefield Reports: Blore Heath, Northampton, Towton* (1995).

Flenley, Ralph (ed.), *Six Town Chronicles of England* (1911).

Fortescue, Sir John (ed. Shelley Lockwood), *On the Laws and Governance of England* (1997).

Gairdner, James (ed.), *The Historical Collections of a Citizen of London* (1876) (mainly a history of London from 1189 to 1469 known as *Gregory's Chronicle*).

Gairdner, James (ed.), *Three Fifteenth-Century Chronicles* (1880).

Gairdner, James (ed.), *The Paston Letters, 1422–1509* (1904).

Giles, John (ed.), *The Chronicles of the White Rose of York* (1845) (includes 'Hearne's Fragment', the 'Warkworth Chronicle' (q.v.) and the 'Historie of the Arrivall' (*q.v.*).

Given-Wilson, Chris (ed.), *Parliament Rolls of Medieval England 1275–1504*, vols. 10–16 (Woodbridge, 2005).

'Gregory's Chronicle' – see Gairdner, James (ed.), *The Historical Collections of a Citizen of London*.

Haliwell, James (ed.), *Warkworth's Chronicle* (1839).

'Hearne's Fragment' – see Giles, John (ed.), *The Chronicles of the White Rose of York*.

Hinds, Allen (ed.), *Calendar of State Papers and Manuscripts in the Archives and Collections of Milan – 1385–1618* (1912).

'Historie of the Arrivall' – see Giles, John (ed.), *The Chronicles of the White Rose of York*.

Kingsford, Charles (ed.), *Chronicles of London* (Oxford, 1905).

Knowles, R., 'The Battle of Wakefield: the Topography', *The Ricardian* (June 1992).

Michael Drayton, 'The Miseries of Queen Margaret' in Samuel Johnson (ed. Alexander Chalmers) *The works of the English poets, from Chaucer to Cowper* (1810).

New Advent, *The Catholic Encyclopedia* (1917).

Nichols, John (ed.), *Chronicle of the Rebellion of Lincolnshire 1470* (1847).

Oxford Dictionary of National Biography (2004–).

Pollard, A., 'Percies, Nevilles and the Wars of the Roses', *History Today* (1993).

Power, Eileen, *The Wool Trade in English Medieval History* (1941).

Richmond, C., 'Propaganda in the Wars of the Roses', *History Today* (1992).

Riley, Henry (ed.), *Registra quorundam abbatum monasterii S. Albani*, 2 vols. (1872–3).

Rosenthal, Joel, 'Other victims: peeresses as war widows, 1450–1500', *History*, 72 (1987).

Rous, John, *The Warwick Roll* (1483).

Site of the Battle of Northampton, 1460: Conservation Management Plan (Northampton, 2013).

Stevenson, Joseph (ed.), *Letters and Papers Illustrative of the Wars of the English in France during the reign of Henry the Sixth* (1861) (contains William Worcester's 'Annales Rerum Anglicarum').

Sutherland, Tim, 'Killing time: challenging the common perceptions of three medieval conflicts – Ferrybridge, Dintingdale and Towton', *Journal of Conflict Archaeology*, 5:1 (2010).

Thomson, Thomas (ed.), *The Auchinleck Chronicle: Ane Schort Memoriale of the Scottis Corniklis for Addicioun* (1819).

The Towton Battlefield Archaeological Survey Project, *Unknown soldiers: the discovery of war graves from the battle of Towton.*

UK Battlefields Resource Centre.

Vergil, Polydore (ed. Dana Sutton), *Anglica Historia* (1555) (critical edition, 2005).

Vigiles du roi Charles VII (1487) – illustrations only.

Walker, John, *Fourmilab Calendar Converter* (2009).

'Warkworth Chronicle' – see Giles, John (ed.), *The Chronicles of the White Rose of York.*

Wavrin, Jehan de (trans. William and Edward Hardy), *Collection of the chronicles and ancient histories of Great Britain* (1864).

Worcester, William, 'Annales Rerum Anglicarum' – see Stevenson, Joseph
(ed.), *Letters and Papers Illustrative of the Wars of the English in France
during the reign of Henry the Sixth*.

PRINTED PRIMARY SOURCES

'Benet's Chronicle' – see Harriss, G. and M. (eds.), *John Benet's Chronicle for
the Years 1400 to 1462*.
'Crowland Chronicle Continuations' – see Pronay, Nicholas and John Cox
(eds.), *The Crowland Chronicle Continuations, 1459–86*.
Dockray, Keith, *Henry VI, Margaret of Anjou and the Wars of the Roses: a
Source Book* (Stroud, 2000).
Fiorato, Veronica, Anthea Boylston and Christopher Knüsel (eds.), *Blood
Red Roses: The Archaeology of a Mass Grave from the Battle of Towton*
(Oxford, 2000).
Hallam, Elizabeth (ed.), *The Wars of the Roses: From Richard II to Bosworth
Field as seen through the eyes of contemporaries* (1998).
Harriss, G. and M. (eds.), *John Benet's Chronicle for the Years 1400 to 1462*,
Camden Miscellany, Vol. XXIV, 4:9 (1972).
Myers, Alec (ed.), *English Historical Documents: Volume 4, 1327–1485* (1995).
Pisan, Christine de (trans. Sarah Lawson), *The Treasure of the City of Ladies,
or, The Book of the Three Virtues* (2003).
Pius II, Pope (ed. and trans. Margaret Meserve and Macello Simonetta),
Commentaries (2003).
Pronay, Nicholas and John Cox (eds.), *The Crowland Chronicle
Continuations, 1459–86* (1986) (though there is a nineteenth-century
version online, this one is superior).
'Somnium Vigilantis' – see article in *Historical Research* by Margaret
Kekewich.
'The Stow Relation' – see Kekewich et al., *John Vale's Book*.
Sutherland, Tim and Simon Richardson, 'Arrows point to mass graves:
finding the dead from the Battle of Towton', in Scott, Babits and
Haeker (eds.), *Fields of Conflict: Battlefield Archaeology from the Roman
Empire to the Korean War* (2007).

SECONDARY SOURCES

BOOKS

Adams, Max, *The King in the North* (2013).

Allmand, Christopher, *Lancastrian Normandy, 1415–1450* (Oxford, 1983).

Ambühl, Rémy, *Prisoners of War in the Hundred Years War: Ransom Culture in the Late Middle Ages* (Cambridge, 2013).

Archer, Rowena and Simon Walker (eds.), *Rulers and ruled in late medieval England* (1995).

Baldwin, David, *Elizabeth Woodville* (Stroud, 2012).

Barber, Richard (ed.), *The Pastons: A Family in the Wars of the Roses* (Woodbridge, 1993).

Barker, Juliet, *Conquest: The English Kingdom of France in the Hundred Years War* (2009).

Bean, John, *The Estates of the Percy Family* (Oxford, 1958).

Bell, Adrian, Anne Curry, Andy King and David Simpkin (eds.), *The Soldier in Later Medieval England* (Oxford, 2013).

Bicheno, Hugh, *Vendetta: High Art and Low Cunning at the Birth of the Renaissance* (2007).

Boardman, Andrew, *The Medieval Soldier in the Wars of the Roses* (Stroud, 1998).

Boardman, Andrew, *The Battle of Towton* (Stroud, 2000).

Boardman, Andrew, *The First Battle of St Albans* (Stroud, 2006).

Bramley, Peter, *A Companion & Guide to the Wars of the Roses* (Stroud, 2011).

Brenan, Gerald, *A History of the House of Percy*, Vol. I (1902).

Carpenter, Christine, *The Wars of the Roses: Politics and the Constitution of England, 1437–1509* (Cambridge, 1997).

Cheetham, Anthony, *The Wars of the Roses* (2000).

Chrimes, Stanley, Charles Ross and Ralph Griffiths (eds.), *Fifteenth-century England, 1399–1509: Studies in Politics and Society* (Manchester, 1972).

Clark, Linda and Christine Carpenter (eds.), *Political Culture in Late Medieval Britain* (Woodbridge, 2004).

Contamine, Philippe (trans. Michael Jones), *War in the Middle Ages* (1984).

Cox, Helen, *The Battle of Wakefield Revisited* (York, 2010).

Dockray, Keith, *William Shakespeare: The Wars of the Roses and the Historians* (Stroud, 2002).

Duggan, Anne (ed.), *Queens and Queenship in Medieval Europe* (Woodbridge, 1997).

Evans, Howell, *Wales and the Wars of the Roses* (1995).

Goodman, Anthony, *The Wars of the Roses: Military Activity and English Society* (Stroud, 2004).

Goodman, Anthony, *The Wars of the Roses: the Soldiers' Experience* (Stroud, 2005).

Goodwin, George, *Fatal Colours: Towton 1461* (2011).

Gregory, Philippa, David Baldwin and Michael Jones, *The Women of the Cousins' War* (2013).

Griffith, Paddy (ed.), *The Battle of Blore Heath, 1459* (Nuneaton, 1995).

Griffiths, Ralph (ed.), *Patronage, the Crown and the Provinces* (Gloucester, 1981).

Griffiths, Ralph, *King and Country: England and Wales in the Fifteenth Century* (1991).

Griffiths, Ralph, *The Reign of King Henry VI* (Stroud, 1998).

Haigh, Philip, *The Battle of Wakefield* (Stroud, 1996).

Harriss, Gerald, *Cardinal Beaufort* (Oxford, 1988).

Harriss, Gerald, *Shaping the Nation: England 1360–1461* (Oxford, 2005).

Harvey, Isobel, *Jack Cade's rebellion of 1450* (Oxford, 1991).

Hicks, Michael, *Warwick the Kingmaker* (Oxford, 1998).

Hicks, Michael, *The Wars of the Roses* (2010).

Hilton, Lisa, *Queen's Consort: England's Medieval Queens* (2008).

Hodges, Geoffrey, *Ludford Bridge & Mortimer's Cross: the Wars of the Roses in Herefordshire and the Welsh Marches* (Little Logaston, 2001).

Johnson, P. A., *Duke Richard of York, 1411–1460* (1988).

Karsten, Peter, *The Military-State-Society Symbiosis* (1999).

Kendall, Paul, *Warwick the Kingmaker* (2002).

Lander, Jack, *Conflict and Stability in Fifteenth-Century England* (1969).

Lander, Jack, *Crown and Nobility 1450–1509* (Montreal, 1976).

Lander, Jack, *The Limitations of English Monarchy in the Later Middle Ages* (Toronto, 1989).

Laslett, Peter, Karla Oosterveen and Richard Smith (eds.), *Bastardy and its Comparative History* (1980).

Loades, Mike, *The Longbow* (Oxford, 2013).

MacFarlane, Alan, *The Origins of English Individualism* (Oxford, 1978).

McFarlane, Kenneth, *England in the Fifteenth Century* (1981).

Maurer, Helen, *Margaret of Anjou* (Woodbridge, 2003).

Nicholson, Ranald, *Scotland: the Later Middle Ages* (Edinburgh, 1974).

Payling, Simon, *Political Society in Lancastrian England: The Greater Gentry of Nottinghamshire* (Oxford, 1991) – see list of articles by author.

Pollard, Anthony, *North-eastern England during the Wars of the Roses* (Oxford, 1990).

Pollard, Anthony (ed.), *The Wars of the Roses* (Basingstoke, 1995).

Pollard, Anthony, *Warwick the Kingmaker* (2007).

Rawcliffe, Carol, *The Staffords, 1394–1512* (Cambridge, 1978).

Reid, Peter, *A Brief History of Medieval Warfare: The Rise and Fall of English Supremacy at Arms: 1344–1485* (2008).

Rodger, Nicholas, *The Safeguard of the Sea: A Naval History of Britain, 660–1640* (1997).

Rose, Susan, *Calais: An English Town in France, 1347–1558* (Woodbridge, 2008).

Rosenthal, Joel and Colin Richmond (eds.), *People, Politics and Community in the Later Middle Ages* (Gloucester, 1987).

Ross, Charles, *The Wars of the Roses* (1976).

Ross, Charles (ed.), *Patronage, Pedigree and Power in Later Medieval* England (Gloucester, 1979).

Sadler, John, *Towton: the Battle of Palm Sunday Field 1461* (Barnsley, 2011).

Santiuste, David, *Edward IV and the Wars of the Roses* (Barnsley, 2013).

Scofield, Cora, *The Life and Reign of Edward the Fourth*, Vol. I (New York, 1967).

Starkey, David, *Crown and Country: a History of England through the Monarchy* (2011).

Storey, R. L., *The End of the House of Lancaster* (Gloucester, 1999).

Spufford, Peter and Wendy Wilkinson, *Handbook of Medieval Exchange* (1986).

Tuck, Anthony, *Crown and Nobility: England 1272–1461* (Oxford, 1999).

Vale, Malcolm, *Charles VII* (1974).

Vale, Malcolm, *War and Chivalry: Warfare and Aristocratic Culture in England, France and Burgundy at the End of the Middle Ages* (1981).

Wagner, John, *Encyclopedia of the Wars of the Roses* (Santa Barbara, 2011).

Watts, John, *Henry VI and the Politics of Kingship* (Cambridge, 1996).

Weir, Alison, *Lancaster and York* (1995).

Wolffe, Bertram, *Henry VI* (Yale, 2001).

ARTICLES

(alphabetical by journal and chronological)

Archaeologia

Madden, F., 'Political poems of the reigns of Henry VI and Edward IV', 29 (1842).

Archivum Historiae Pontificiae

Head, C., 'Pius II and the Wars of the Roses', 8 (1970).

Bulletin of the Institute of Historical Research
> McFarlane, K., 'Bastard feudalism', 20 (1943–45).
> Armstrong, C., 'Politics and the Battle of St Albans, 1455', 33 (1960).
> Hicks, M., 'Descent, partition and extinction: the Warwick inheritance', 52 (1979)
> Hicks, M., 'The Beauchamp Trust, 1439–87', 54 (1981).
> Kekewich, M., 'The attainder of the Yorkists in 1459: two contemporary accounts', 55 (1982).

Bulletin of the John Rylands Library
> Myers, A. (ed.), 'The household of Queen Margaret of Anjou, 1452–3', 50 (1957–8).
> Virgoe, R., 'The death of William de la Pole, duke of Suffolk', 47 (1964–5).
> Virgoe, R., 'William Tailboys and Lord Cromwell: crime and politics in Lancastrian England', 55 (1972–3).

English Historical Review
> Ransome, C., 'The Battle of Towton', 4 (1889).
> Gilson, J., 'A Defence of the proscription of the Yorkists in 1459', 26 (1911).
> Baskerville, G., 'A London chronicle of 1460', 28 (1913).
> Kingsford, C., 'An historical collection of the fifteenth century', 29 (1914).
> Kingsford, C., 'The Earl of Warwick at Calais in 1460', 37 (1922).
> Gray, H., 'Incomes from land in England in 1436', 49 (1934).
> Storey, R., 'The wardens of the marches of England towards Scotland 1377–1489', 72 (1957).
> Harriss, G., 'The struggle for Calais: an aspect of the rivalry between Lancaster and York', 75 (1960).
> Jones, M., 'Somerset, York and the Wars of the Roses', 104 (1989).

Historical Research
> Kekewich, M. 'The Attainder of the Yorkists in 1459: Two Contemporary Accounts', 55 (1982) – contains text of *Somnium Vigilantis*.
> Rawcliffe, C., 'Richard, Duke of York, the king's "Obesiant Leigeman": a new source for the protectorates of 1454 and 1455', 60 (1987).
> Pugh, T., 'Richard, Duke of York, and the rebellion of Henry Holland, Duke of Exeter, in May 1454', 63 (1990).

Journal of Medieval History
> Cron, B., 'The Duke of Suffolk, the Angevin marriage, and the ceding of Maine, 1445', 20 (1994).

Medieval History
> Hicks, M., 'Warwick: the reluctant Kingmaker', 1:2 (1991).

Medieval Warfare
> Ingram, M., 'War in Writing', 5:3 (June 2015).

Northern History
> Hicks, M., 'The Duke of Somerset and Lancastrian localism in the North', 20 (1986).

Nottingham Medieval Studies
> Richmond, C., 'The nobility and the Wars of the Roses 1459–61', 21 (1977).

Royal Historical Society Studies in History
> Pollard, A., 'John Talbot and the War in France, 1427–1453', 35 (1983).

Speculum
> Bennett, J., 'The Medieval Loveday', 33 (1958).
> Griffiths, R., 'Local rivalries and national politics: the Percies, the Nevilles, and the Duke of Exeter', 43 (1968).

The Ricardian (not all are online)
> Cron, B., 'Margaret of Anjou and the Lancastrian march on London'(December 1999).

Transactions of the Royal Historical Society
> Armstrong, C., 'The inauguration ceremonies of the Yorkist kings, and their title to the throne', 4:30 (1948).

University of Birmingham Historical Journal
> Kenecht, R., 'The Episcopate and the Wars of the Roses', 6 (1957).

Yorkshire Archaeological Society
> Leadman, A., 'The Battle of Towton', 10 (1889).
> Markham, C., 'The Battle of Towton', 10 (1889).

ARTICLES BY SIMON PAYLING

'The Ampthill dispute: a study in aristocratic lawlesness and the breakdown of Lancastrian Government', *English Historical Review*, 104 (1989).

'Social mobility, demographic change, and landed society in late-medieval England', *Economic History Review*, 45 (1992).

'A Disputed Mortgage: Ralph, Lord Cromwell, Sir John Gra. and the Manor of Multon Hall', in R. Archer and S. Walker (eds.), *Rulers and Ruled in late Medieval England: Essays Presented to Gerald Harriss* (1995).

'The Politics of Family: Late Medieval Marriage Contracts', in R.H. Britnell and A.J. Pollard (eds.), *The McFarlane Legacy* (Stroud, 1995).

'The Later Middle Ages', in R. Smith and J.S. Moore (eds.), *The House of Commons* (1996).

'Murder, motive and punishment in fifteenth-century England: two gentry case-studies', *English Historical Review*, 113 (1998).

'County parliamentary elections in fifteenth-century England', *Parliamentary History*, 17 (1999).

'The economics of marriage in late medieval England: The marriage of heiresses', *Economic History Review*, 54 (2001).

'The Rise of Lawyers in the Lower House, 1395–1536', in L. Clark (ed.), *Parchment and People: Parliament in the Middle Ages* (Edinburgh, 2004).

'Identifiable Motives for Election to Parliament in the Reign of Henry VI: the Operation of Public and Private Factors', in L. Clark (ed.), *The Fifteenth Century, VI: Identity and Insurgency in the Late Middle Ages* (Woodbridge, 2006).

'War and Peace: Military and Administrative Service amongst the English Gentry in the Reign of Henry VI', in P. Coss and C. Tyerman (eds.), *Soldiers, Nobles and Gentlemen: Essays in Honour of Maurice Keen* (Woodbridge, 2009).

'The House of Commons, 1307–1529', in C. Jones (ed.), *A Short History of Parliament* (Woodbridge, 2009).

ACKNOWLEDGEMENTS

To George R. R. Martin for the inspiration and for creating a compelling parallel world.

In particular I want to thank:
Ian Drury, agent extraordinaire, who encouraged me to develop the idea of writing 'The Real Game of Thrones';
Dr Tobias Capwell FSA, Curator of Arms and Armour at the Wallace Collection, for sharing his unique expertise on medieval warfare;
My sister Lyn McMeekin for patiently beta-reading the manuscript;
Richard Milbank, non-fiction publisher at Head of Zeus, for comprehensive editing;
Annabel Warren of Whitefox, only the second copy editor ever to add value to my books.

Many others – you know who you are – have helped me in many ways and I thank you all.

IMAGE CREDITS

FIRST PLATE SECTION

Catherine de Valois (© Dean and Chapter of Westminster)

Henry VI (© National Portrait Gallery, London, UK)

Henry VIII (© The Berger Collection at the Denver Art Museum, USA / Bridgeman Images)

Humphrey, Duke of Gloucester (Bibliothèque Municipale, Arras, France / Bridgeman Images)

Cardinal Henry Beaufort (Kunsthistorisches Museum, Vienna, Austria / Bridgeman Images)

Isabelle, Duchess of Lorraine (Wikimedia Commons)

René, Duke of Anjou (The Art Archive / Musée du Louvre, Paris / Gianni Dagli Orti)

John Talbot's wedding gift (Topfoto / British Library Board)

Medal of Marguerite of Anjou (© Victoria and Albert Museum, London, UK)

Philippe of Burgundy (The Art Archive / Kharbine-Tapabor / Cheuva)

Charles VII of France (The Art Archive / Musée du Louvre, Paris, France / A. Dagli Orti)

Isabella of Portugal (Fine Art Images / HIP / Topfoto)

Illuminated image of court dress from the *Très Riches Heures* (World History Archive / Topfoto)

Images of Richard Beauchamp, Earl of Warwick's tomb (courtesy of the Collegiate Church of St Mary's, Warwick)

SECOND PLATE SECTION

Images from *Les Vigiles du Roi Charles VII* (Bibliothèque nationale de France)

Images from the St Ursula Shrine (Universal History Archive / Getty Images)

Tomb of Sir Ralph Fitzherbert and modern replica of armour (courtesy of William West of Englyshe Plate Armourie)

Modern replica of a poleaxe (iStockphoto.com)

Battle re-enactment (Wikimedia Commons)

Longbowmen (Perry Miniatures / www.perry-miniatures.com)
Illustration of Cock Beck (Wikimedia Commons)
Middleham Castle (Shutterstock)
Warwick Castle (Wikimedia Commons)
Kenilworth Castle (Wikimedia Commons)
Ludlow Castle (Wikimedia Commons)
Micklegate Bar, York (Shutterstock)

INDEX